"As a practicing psychoanalyst, the author of this book opens the rigorously social work of trauma psychoanalysis up to the realm of fiction, so often wrongly dismissed as escapist, and makes the relationship between the two domains mutual, in a most productive way. She demonstrates the *point*—for social reality—of literature, as she had already done in her two volumes edition of the seminars of Jean-Max Gaudillière. In this book on Sterne's masterpiece, laughter is as important as grief, pursuits of love as weighty as slavery and other forms of violence, and above all, the past, she demonstrates, incisively intervenes in the present. No other author that I know of is so skilled and refined in reading—both the literary text and the psyche of traumatized people. This book enriches the life of its readers on many levels".

Mieke Bal, *Cultural Analyst and video artist*

"The literary wit of Sterne and the unique analytic wit of Davoine go head-to-head in this remarkable book, which teaches us to read in Sterne's humor and style the workings of 'Shandean psychoanalysis', a singular treatment of historical trauma and a 'mad' challenge to the totalitarian politics of all centuries. Sterne takes his place, in Davoine's surprising reading, within a dazzling array of literary, philosophical and psychoanalytic writers who 'don the fool's cap' to offer new resources for reinscribing the lost catastrophes of history and for resisting varying forms of political perversion. Davoine weaves into her reading of the book her own personal history growing up in war as well as her innovative development of a psychoanalysis of madness, one that draws on and illuminates the literary therapeutics of Sterne's writing. Tristram Shandy ultimately provides for her, in its profound insight into history and madness, a 'memory of the future' that anticipates the traumas—and the treatments—of the 20th and 21st centuries, challenging our doctrinal approaches to the understanding of catastrophic history and the treatment of historically and politically produced trauma. In Davoine's extraordinary reading, Tristram Shandy finally speaks to our contemporary 21st century crises while offering unexpected resources, in its rich 'art of storytelling', for responding to the powers of erasure and denial and for enabling the emergence of a new kind of political subject".

Cathy Caruth, *Professor of English, Cornell University*

"Francoise Davoine is a highly respected expert in the clinical psychoanalysis of madness; she is also a respected authority in regard to the application of psychoanalytic theory to world literature, and the corollary illumination of trauma within fiction (*Don Quixote*, and now, *Tristram Shandy)*. Davoine's coverage of her subject is exhaustive and wide-ranging, drawing upon a multitude of philosophic and literary sources. Her approach is highly creative, engaging, and high-spirited—filled with surprising insights and associations. *Shandean Psychoanalysis* is a revelatory reinterpretation of Sterne's novelistic masterpiece, with profound implications for the theory and treatment of trauma and other extreme states".

James E. Gorney, *PhD*

"Françoise Davoine, is a highly regarded and respected psychoanalyst and author who has written at the forefront of psychoanalysis involving extreme states and literature. She is the author of numerous books in this field which are much quoted and used in both areas of expertise. In a previous book on Don Quixote, she rattled the cage of psychoanalysis, to use a description from Bion, allowing us to see through literary fiction how we can understand psychological trauma. This book takes Lawrence Sterne's *Tristram Shandy* and further rattles the cage, introducing through the rhythm of her writing more psychoanalytic animals, allowing them to appear from her own history and Sterne's history/fiction, teaching us about forgotten wars, trauma and what it is to be a therapist/therapon and stand with those who have suffered from madness".

Alfred Gillham, *MSc Consultant Clinical Psychologist*

Shandean Psychoanalysis

This unique book examines the psychoanalysis of madness and trauma through an extended discussion of *The Life and Opinions of Tristram Shandy, Gentleman*, the provocative eighteenth-century novel by Laurence Sterne.

Françoise Davoine explores the entire novel—each of her chapters corresponding to a volume of the novel—viewing it through a psychoanalytic lens: the monologue by Tristram's embryo in the opening chapter, the war traumas of Captain Toby and Corporal Trim and several key themes, including confinement, love and history. In parallel to her own analytic comments on these inventions, Françoise Davoine follows the writing of the novel itself, keeping the reader constantly aware that Sterne's endeavour is a race against death—his own. Davoine points out that time acts as a major character in the novel, constantly upsetting chronology, and bringing about the same impasses as the psychoanalysis of madness and trauma does.

The book presents Shandean wit as a valuable tool in therapeutic work. *Shandean Psychoanalysis* will be of great interest to psychoanalysts and to academics and students engaged in psychoanalytic studies, literary studies and trauma-related studies.

Françoise Davoine is a Psychoanalyst based in France. She is former Professor at the Centre for the Study of Social Movements, École des Hautes Études en Sciences Sociales (EHESS) in Paris, where she and Jean-Max Gaudillière conducted a weekly seminar on "Madness and the Social Link" for 40 years. She presents internationally and is the author of many books and articles.

Shandean Psychoanalysis

Tristram Shandy, Madness and Trauma

Françoise Davoine
Translated by Agnès Jacob

Routledge
Taylor & Francis Group

LONDON AND NEW YORK

Designed cover image: duncan1890 / Getty Images

First published in English 2023
by Routledge
4 Park Square, Milton Park, Abingdon, Oxon OX14 4RN

and by Routledge
605 Third Avenue, New York, NY 10158

Routledge is an imprint of the Taylor & Francis Group, an informa business

Comme des fous. Folie et trauma dans Tristram Shandy,
Françoise Davoine © Éditions Gallimard, Paris, 2017.

British Library Cataloguing-in-Publication Data
A catalogue record for this book is available from the British Library

ISBN: 9781032125091 (hbk)
ISBN: 9781032125121 (pbk)
ISBN: 9781003224907 (ebk)

DOI: 10.4324/9781003224907

Typeset in Times New Roman
by codeMantra

Contents

The embryo's "I wish"

Preamble

Lawrence Sterne wrote a *Don Quixote* in the 18th century "to fence against the infirmities of ill health, and other evils of life, by mirth". *Tristram Shandy*[1] opens with "I wish". Tristram's embryo wishes "his parents had minded what they were about when they begot" him. This initial desire is also that of Sterne, who decided to "turn author" in his mid-forties, when Captain Toby appeared to him, just as Don Quixote had appeared in Cervantes's Seville prison cell, at a catastrophic moment when time stopped. Setting time in motion again was the subject of seminars I gave with Jean-Max Gaudillière for over thirty years at the École des Hautes Études en Sciences Sociales (EHESS), under the title "Madness and the Social Link", until his death in 2015. This book continues our dialogue with Sterne, who never ceases to address the reader directly.

Like Tristram, I would have liked my parents to think twice when they went about conceiving me in a meadow, not long before my mother got caught crossing the demarcation line covertly, so that we spent several months of her pregnancy and my gestation in prison.

How do you know it happened in a meadow?

My father told me recently, when he was over a hundred. You can see the place on Google Maps—a map plays a major role in Sterne's book. In fact, his biographer, Ian Campbell Ross,[2] insists on his "radically democratic writing style which underlines the unique value of personal experiences". Sterne gives examples, like Jonathan Swift does in his "Digression on Madness",[3] of the importance of "something individual in human Minds, that easily kindles at the accidental Approach and Collision of certain Circumstances, which [...] often flame out into the greatest Emergencies of Life".

It was the subject of our seminar.

Swift dreamt of an Academy of Modern Bedlam, a School of Advanced Studies in Mad Sciences, where research would focus on attaining "the

DOI: 10.4324/9781003224907-1

Serene peaceful State of being a Fool among Knaves". He defines a knave as follows:

> When a Man's Fancy gets astride on his Reason, when Imagination is at Cuffs with the Senses, and common Understanding, as well as common Sense, is Kicked out of Doors, the first Proselyte he makes is Himself, and when that is once compass'd, the Difficulty is not so great in bringing over others.

But entrance to Swift's academy is not granted to everyone. The admission exam, which he himself takes, consists of analysing the occasions when our "imaginations are hard-mouthed, and exceedingly disposed to run away with [...] a very light rider's reason, and [he is] easily shook off".

On such occasions, the psychoanalyst thinks, like Little Gibus in The War of the Buttons[4]: *"If I had known, I wouldn't have come"!*
Sterne's war, when he was a child, was first that which his father fought against the armies of Louis XIV in Flanders. His mission, according to his biographer, was "to mend his father's injuries", like Don Quixote mended Cervantes's war traumas, who calls him "his son" in his Preface to Book I.[5]
If you have time, I would like to tell you a little about Sterne's life.

At this point, I can take my time.
Laurence Sterne, the son of Roger Sterne, was born in 1713, after an older sister, in Tipperary, Ireland, where his father's regiment was stationed. Do not forget that date, the year of the Treaty of Utrecht which ended the War of the Spanish Succession. As a result, Roger Sterne's regiment was disbanded. When he took up active service again the following year, to prevent the restoration of the Stuarts, he went to Plymouth, where a squadron was to land, led by the duke of Ormonde—James Butler, supporter of the Catholic pretender to the throne, opposing the reigning Hanover dynasty. In the novel, James Butler is the birth name of Trim, the counterpart, for Captain Toby, of Cervantes's Sancho Panza. Laurence became accustomed to garrison life, "from one barrack to the other", between Ireland and England.
Roger Sterne was the youngest son of a youngest son, in a family of gentlemen—a status announced in the title of the novel. Laurence's great-grandfather was Richard Sterne, a learned cleric and a contemporary of Don Quixote. Imprisoned at the Tower of London under Cromwell, he was made Archbishop of York after the Stuart Restoration.
In the meantime, Richard Sterne was Master of Jesus College in Cambridge, where he founded scholarships for poor students, which his great grandson Laurence was to receive seventy years later. At Cambridge, Laurence developed a passion for Cervantes, Rabelais and 16th-century French literature. Yet, when he left, the only path open to him was the church. He became a clergyman in two rural Yorkshire parishes, with no hope of

preferment, just like his father, who remained an ensign until he was promoted to lieutenant *in extremis*, four months before his death. In addition,
the rule of primogeniture, which granted inheritance to the firstborn, had
benefitted Roger's elder brother Richard, while Roger married a suttler's
daughter, an officer's widow, and remained penniless all his life.

It is not known why Roger Sterne stagnated at the rank of ensign, why
his family—whose prestige had been improved by his mother, an heiress of
ennobled merchants—did nothing for his advancement. When he died of
fever in Jamaica in 1731, at forty-eight, Laurence was seventeen. He had not
seen his father since he was eleven, when Roger took him from Ireland to
Halifax in Yorkshire, home of the Sterne family, to entrust him to the care
of the boy's wealthy Uncle Richard, governor of the school Laurence was to
attend.

Another military man who ruled his son with an iron hand.

On the contrary. In 1758, Sterne wrote a Memoir for his only daughter
Lydia, who was then ten, about the age he had been when he saw his father
for the last time. The Memoir speaks tenderly of:

> a little smart man — active to the last degree in all exercises—most
> patient of fatigue and disappointments, of which it pleased God to give
> him full measure; he was in his temper somewhat rapid and hasty, but of
> a kindly, sweet disposition, void of all design, and so innocent in his own
> intentions, that he suspected no one; so that you might have cheated him
> ten times a day, if nine had not been sufficient for your purpose.

You don't think he's idealising?

Roger Sterne exemplifies "the errant knight", for whom arms and letters
go together. He has a quixotic soul—"generous, imprudent, he doesn't hold
his tongue" and "brings on himself, unsuspectingly, all manner of hate".

When he was demobilised and placed on half-pay in 1713, he waited until
Laurence was six months old before going back to his family in Yorkshire,
hoping to receive some help, without any success. However, the worst misfortune "it pleased God to give him" was the loss of his children. Four of
them died at an early age while Laurence was still in Ireland.

*Some learned minds state as a fact that in those days of high infant mortality
parents were not particularly heartbroken.*

Laurence Sterne was not as insensitive as your learned minds. Like his
father, he himself lost several small children. A servant recounted that after
the death of his first little Lydia he was unable to leave his bed for a week.

He was six years old when the series of deaths started: his four-year-old
brother Joram died of smallpox in 1719, while their father was fighting in
Spain. Then "all unhinged again". In 1721, three-year-old Anne, their
"pretty blossom" was killed by a fall in the barracks of Dublin.

The family enjoyed a period of serenity when a distant relative on the Irish side, Robert Stearne—brigadier-general in the Royal Irish Regiment—invited them to stay in his castle near Dublin for a year. The generosity of this military man foreshadows that of Captain Toby Shandy, Tristram's uncle. Like him, Robert Stearne must have prided himself on his participation in seven campaigns, for having survived seven battles, fifteen sieges, seven major attacks, and especially the 1695 siege of Namur, where Uncle Toby "had the honour to receive his wound".

The following year, in 1723, three-year-old Devicher died while in the care of a wet nurse. "Another child [was] sent to fill his place, Susan. This babe too left us behind in this weary journey". At the age of ten, Laurence and his elder sister Mary were the only two of six children to have survived. After Laurence left for Yorkshire, another child, Catherine, was born. The music left in the wake of the departed children is heard throughout the novel.

The Kindertotenlieder *(Songs on the Death of Children), Gustav Mahler.*
Sterne died on March 18, 1768. In the last months of his life he too suffered from fever. His diary records his delusions about Eliza, a young woman he met in London and called his "sister", whom he imagines at his side during his solitary walks through the parish cemetery.

That year, while he was devastated by Eliza's return to India to join her husband, he finished writing *A Sentimental Journey through France and Italy,*[6] which takes place partly in Paris. The contrast between the wacky style of his diary and that of his novel has given rise to much speculation. Yet there is no mystery there: writing kept him alive: "Living and writing are all one to me". He invented a new term for the therapeutic action of this regeneration: "shandy", "to shandy"—noun and verb—meaning "to mix together". In his book, Sterne tells the reader: "I shandy more than ever".

Andante! After having quixotised, let's shandy!
"Tristram Shandy, Gentleman" is an oxymoron, since Tristram is a barefoot gentleman. His first name is that of a 15th-century life-size wooden statue of a beggar named "Ole Tristram", standing before the church in Halifax, next to the school where Laurence found himself at the age of eleven, "naked, penniless, with no friends or protectors, except a cousin", Richard, the eldest son of Uncle Richard. The statue of the beggar embodies the boy's abandonment. It is a "surviving image, *nachleben*", of the agony of a child, in the sense given to this term by Aby Warburg, who nearly died as a child, along with his mother, just after the war of 1870.

But Warburg really went mad when traumatic revivals resurfaced during the First World War.
It's true that Sterne escaped madness, although, in his novel, he dons a fool's cap more than once and identifies, through the name Tristram, with the tramp on the road.

In Yiddish, it would be "schlemihl", the word Hannah Arendt uses in the first
chapter of Rahel Varnhagen,[7] "a Jewess and a Schlemihl", to describe Rahel's
uprootedness, cut off as she is from her ancestors' history.

Laurence discovered early that he was excluded from his lineage history.
Uncle Richard not only discarded him, but even asked him to reimburse the
cost of his upkeep and education. He would only be able to buy books after
the success of *Tristram Shandy*. In Halifax, an adult seemed to have paid
attention to him. The classroom had been repainted; Laurence climbed up
on the ladder left in the room and, with a brush, wrote LAU STERNE on
the ceiling. He was whipped by the usher, but the Master of the school sent
for him and said, much to his surprise: "that name should never be effaced,
for [he] was a boy of genius".

But the reader knows nothing of all this.

First Cry

You will soon learn, through the protest "I wish", made by Tristram while
still in an embryonic state, and given voice by the author—"Believe me,
good folks"—that this tiny character called HOMUNCULUS, in capital
letters, has barely escaped a *coitus interruptus*. Later, we learn that his unno-
ticed disappearance was planned by his mother's vengeful design directed
against his father.

A call for witnesses, Dori Laub[8] would say, for an event without a witness,
impossible to put into words, even for oneself.

The witness called to the defence of the egg fecundated *in extremis* is the
reader. As an adult, Tristram speaks to the endangered embryo, whom he
affectionately calls "my little gentleman", and who instantly inherits the
traumas of his lineage: an indifferent mother who never speaks to him
throughout the novel, a father who loves theories more than being with his
child, an uncle wounded in the war and a castrating great-grandmother.

To break through the gloom, the subject of desire makes a tumultuous
entrance in the very first sentence, which I quote now in full: "I wish either
my father or my mother, or indeed both of them, as they were in duty both
equally bound to it, had minded what they were about when they begot
me".

That's nothing new. Sterne is describing the famous primal scene.

Which he asks you to witness in the parent's bedroom. There you discover that sexual desire is programmed on the first Saturday and Sunday of
every month. On that day, Walter, the father, winds up the large house clock
and performs his conjugal duty, "to get them [both] out of the way at one
time". And you hear the embryo remind them of their responsibility in the
catastrophes awaiting him. The list is long enough to constitute a file in an

institution for disturbed children: Tristram will be born blue in the face, his nose broken by the forceps, his first name deformed, "his muscular strength and virility worn down to a thread; — his own animal spirits ruffled beyond description", yet he claims the title of Gentleman, just as Don Quixote did that of Hidalgo—of *la Mancha*, meaning "the stain".

It's time to quote your dear Wittgenstein[9]: "*It is indeed important that I must also make my own the contempt that anyone may have for me, as an essential and significant part of the world as seen by me*".

A Half-Bungled Conception

Having made his own the contempt that anyone may have for him, Sterne is now able to refine the deadly question Mrs. Shandy asked her husband Walter, at a most climatic moment, in three-quarter time: "Pray, my dear / have you not forgot / to wind up the clock"?

The suspected forgetting of the clockworks puts an abrupt end to:

> the animal spirits [...] cluttering like hey-go-mad [...]; when they are once set a-going [...], by treading the same steps over and over again, they presently make a road of it, [...] which [...], the Devil himself sometimes should not be able to drive them off it.

But we are forced to face the fact: Mrs. Shandy's incantatory phrase is more powerful than the Devil in person.

I can just imagine the onslaught of comments about castration.

Soon, the phrase spread through London, where the word "clock" could not be pronounced without provoking a little shiver, which prompted ladies of the night to ask gentlemen: "Pray, my dear, would you like me to wind up your clock".

Walter was not amused. He exclaimed, between two explosive hyphens: "—*Good G*—*!* cried my father [...] —Did ever woman, since the creation of the world, interrupt a man with such a silly question"?[10]

What do you expect, when she is wound up by her husband on the first Sunday of every month?

She nurtures a grudge that goes back to the time when her husband forced her to live in the country against her will. But for the moment, Sterne asks us to concentrate on the point of view of the future Tristram.

Once disaster has been narrowly avoided, the bed changes into a battle field where the unborn child emerges, determined—"I wish"—not to let himself be wiped out so easily. The *Homunculus* claims the right to exist and protests against his parent's carelessness in "the production of a rational being, [...] the happy formation [...] of his body, perhaps his genius and the very cast of his mind".

You can already glimpse his talent as a future analyst: "Had they duly weighed and considered all this, and proceeded accordingly, — I am very persuaded I should have made a quite different figure in the world from that in which the reader is likely to see me".

"What was your original face, before you were born"? Lin-Chi,[11] *the Chan master, was already asking in 9th-century China.*

The *Homunculus* solves this riddle easily. After drawing attention to his parents' thoughtlessness, he points out the consequences of their desire:

> Well, you may take my word that nine parts in ten of a man's sense or his nonsense, his successes and miscarriages in this world depend upon the motions and activity, and the different tracks and trains you put them into.

And what is the reader supposed to do all this time? Be a third wheel?

You must help Sterne save his embryonic book from early sabotage. But be careful not to preach about the Third party's speech. When the reader intercedes timidly: "Pray, what was your father saying"?, his terse answer is: "— Nothing". The novel could have stopped there if the initial "wish" had not suddenly changed from regret to insurrection. The outraged *Homunculus* is now demanding redress.

The Revolutions of the future: human rights, civil rights, are marching on.

Homunculus's Rights

The Habeas Corpus of the homunculus is based on the writ issued by Cromwell's Parliament in 1679. His first right is the freedom of speech: "Let me tell you".

Sterne hands the microphone to the fertilised ovule at the moment of the critical encounter.

In its speech, it describes the shipwreck it barely escaped, his animal spirits all "scattered and dispersed [...]" when his mother's should have "escorted and gone hand in hand with him", looking out for his safety.

Is that safety where Winnicott got his famous "holding"?

I am sure he knew *Tristram* inside out. To convince the reader of the reality of intrauterine trauma, the *homunculus* addresses him very politely, calling him Sir, and analyses what happened to him personally while his parents left him all alone in the womb.

His definition of trauma—the betrayal by one's own people—is that of Jonathan Shay, a psychiatrist at the Boston Veterans' Hospital, who treated Vietnam war veterans. In his book Achilles in Vietnam,[12] *Shay points out that their post-traumatic symptoms were the same as those of Achilles, enraged at the beginning of the* Iliad *by the betrayal of his commander Agamemnon, who stole his share of the war-booty, the captive Briseis.*

This is why we are asked, you, "sir", and me, "madam", to support the betrayed *homunculus*"in however low and ludicrous a light he may appear, in this age of levity, to the eye of folly or prejudice; — to the eye of reason in scientific research".

Imagine biologists campaigning for the rights of mitochondria!

Tristram's embryo sticks to his opinion that he is "guarded and circumscribed with rights, [...] — as much and as truly our fellow creature as my Lord Chancellor of England. — He may be benefited, he may be injured".

I can hear our respective homunculi reproach our parents for having conceived us at the worst possible time, in 1942, after our fathers escaped from their prison camps.

Sterne is certain that they "may obtain redress", that they have "all the claims and rights of humanity".

A Slippery slope...

The parents don't quarrel about abortion, if that's what you're hinting at, but about a clause in their marriage contract, which will come up again later.

For now, listen to what my homunculus could have said *in utero*, in the Châlons, Autun and Compiègne prisons, where she nearly met her end, together with her mother:

> Now, dear sir, what if an accident had befallen [her] in [her] way alone? — or that, thro' terror of it, natural to so young a traveller, my little [gentlewoman] had got to [her] journey's end miserably spent; — [her] muscular strength and [feminity] worn down to a thread; — her own animal spirits ruffled beyond description, — [...] a prey to sudden starts and melancholy dreams ...

Are you referring to your insomnias?

Wait a minute, and listen to the rest: "In this sad disorder'd state of nerves", she would have to spend "nine long, long months together. I tremble to think what a foundation has been laid for a thousand weaknesses both of body and mind, which no skill of the physician or the philosopher—nor of the psychoanalyst, I should add—"could ever afterwards have set thoroughly to rights". I also tremble to think that some quack Diafoirus could have given me a prognosis of psychic illness—according to statistics—and very likely prescribed one of those "ever so harmless treatments ..."

Never mind the statistics. They were invented in Sterne's era in England to assess the risk of maritime transport and trade.

Precisely! Trade was Walter's occupation and he used statistics to diagnose his baby. Before he retired to Shandy Hall, which he inherited, he was a "Turkey merchant" in London, doing import-export business with the Middle-East. Hence his obsession with calculating probabilities which prompted him to predict that the odds were ten, twenty or ninety to a hundred that his son would be born with a defect of the brain.

Sterne seems to adhere to the dogma which holds that neither the doctor nor the philosopher can help.

The word "dogma" is a *faux ami* that means "opinion" in the Epictetus quote placed at the beginning of Sterne's book: "It is not events themselves, *ta pragmata*, that trouble people, but their opinions *dogmata* about those events". In the novel, the only person who allows Tristram to form his own opinions is Captain Toby, his father's younger brother, who rights the wrongs in the child's life.

A military man turned child analyst?

Uncle Toby Makes His Appearance

Uncle Toby is also Sterne's analyst. When he appears on March 26th, 1759, Sterne's decision to write his novel is confirmed. He is just as enthralled to see "this most whimsical character" as Cervantes was when Don Quixote appeared in his Seville prison, where he thought, once again, that he was done for. Likewise, Toby came to the rescue when domestic, social and political catastrophes were at their worst. That year, Sterne declared: "I turn author".

His wife was raving mad, taking herself for the Queen of Bohemia. His uncle Jaques—Roger's younger brother, Archdeacon of Cleveland and a staunch supporter of the Whigs—pursued him with his hatred ever since he had escaped his influence and had decided "not to employ his brain for other's people advantage". Through him, Laurence had been involved in the civil war between the Jacobites and the House of Hanover. In fact, Laurence's involvement almost landed him in prison.

"Speed bonnie boat..." I know the tune of The Skye Boat Song.

The expedition had none of the romance of a Scottish ballad. The duke of Cumberland, nicknamed by the Jacobites "Stinking Billy" and by Haendel at the Hanover Court, the "Darling of the People", massacred the Highlanders in 1746 on Culloden Moor.

Uncle Jaques was a fanatic, determined that the papist troops retreating towards York should be hanged. He mercilessly persecuted the nuns in a convent, sickening his nephew. From 1742 on, Sterne refused to produce any more "party writing" on behalf of his uncle, and retired to his parish, hoping to develop his little domain, thereby forfeiting any advancement. But his physiocratic project failed owing to epidemics that struck both humans and animals. Thinking that writing could save him from disaster, he published— as was done at the time—the sermons he preached at the York Cathedral. In 1759, the year when he started to write his novel, his first book, entitled *A Political Romance*, satirising the clergy, was condemned to be burnt.

Yes... Literature in the Ashes of History.[13] I had time to read Cathy Caruth's last book, where she asserts "the need for a new kind of writing, when History seems constantly on the verge of disappearing".

This same need impelled Sterne to write *A Fragment in the Manner of Rabelais*, which he sent to the famous London publisher Robert Dodsley. Once again, his manuscript was rejected, yet with the advice that he remove all references to local politics. After that, events speeded up. In 1760, the first two volumes of *Tristram Shandy* were published anonymously, at the author's expense, in York, and then by Dodsley in London, under Sterne's name.

During the dark spring of the previous year, Sterne had no inkling that his "turning author" would lead to stunning success; that Toby would chase away our blues wherever we might be, as Don Quixote had helped Cervantes "to combat melancholy".

The knight is Uncle Toby's role model. Captain Toby Shandy, wounded in the battle of Namur in 1695, when the English troops took back the fortress from the French, sixteen years before Tristram's birth, spends his time, with his footman Corporal Trim, building and attacking scale models of sieges carried out during the war raging in Europe—on the bowling green of his little house close to Shandy Hall, his brother's mansion.

An engineer of lost time, as Marcel Duchamp calls himself.

And a second in combat for his nephew, as both of them had come face to face with death. So he owes Tristram the truth. "To my uncle Mr Toby Shandy I do stand indebted for the preceding anecdote [about my careless conception]".

Is he a substitute father?

Walter doesn't neglect his son, but his interest in him is filtered through his theories. In fact, he is writing an educational manual, the "Tristra-paedia". But his scientific observations are always behind the boy's actual development. He was so very slow and the boy was beginning to live and grow at such a rate that his work "was rendered entirely useless".

Famous analysts like Melanie Klein also put their own children through the mill of their concepts.

In the same spirit of objectivity, Walter discloses his diagnosis to his brother: "from a thousand [...] observations he had made upon me", pointing out "a most unaccountable obliquity [...] in my manner of setting up my top". In "a tone more expressive [...] of sorrow than reproach", he concludes that his son would "neither think nor act like any other man's child". This is when he reveals to Toby the ill-fated origin of Tristram's psychological structure: "*But alas!* continued he, shaking his head a second time and wiping away a tear which was trickling down his cheeks, My Tristram's misfortunes began nine months before ever he came into the world". The boy's obliquity is not due to a brain defect, but to his disorderly conception. And to intergenerational transmission as well. You will learn[14] that Tristram's misfortunes go back as far as his great-grandmother, who demanded from her husband and the following generations an annual jointure to compensate for his small nose.

A case of foreclosure of the nose of the father?

And of silence on the part of the mother. During the exchange between the two brothers about her son's ill fate: "My mother, who was sitting by, look'd up, — but she knew no more than her backside what my father meant. Mr. Toby Shandy who had been often informed of the affair, understood him very well". And he immediately gave his nephew access to the traces of his origin. Thus, Chapter IV can start with "I know", after the "I wish" which introduced the book.

Reverend Sterne pays attention to his opening lines.

I Know

This knowledge has three components: (1) *In principio erat trauma*, in the beginning there was trauma. (2) *In principio erat sermo*, in the beginning there was dialogue—here, Sterne quotes Erasmus's translation of the Genesis, in which *verbum* is replaced by *sermo*, dialogue. (3) When "the tool with the name is broken", as Wittgenstein says, one can show with gestures and through jest matters silenced as early as one's conception, and even earlier. That's Shandean psychoanalysis.

Indeed, but honestly, what psychoanalyst will be interested in a British novel written over two centuries ago, and hardly quoted by Lacan?

I just wanted to point out that Tristram's desire, "I wish", is grounded in his veteran uncle's search for the truth. And the author's too. He is their *therapon*, their second in combat, offering both of them the safe space of his bowling green, to perform the psychotherapy of their respective traumas.

The novel is also Sterne's bowling green. He becomes one with his heroes and practices, like they do, a martial art against stupidity and perversity, on a transitional space between "I wish" and "I know", where he defends the novelty of his analysis: "I [...] go on tracing everything *ab ovo*, and not, as that gentleman Horace recommends in his Poetic Art, *in medias res*".

Translated into our jargon, he starts his therapy with the preverbal and the pre-oedipal.

And this beginning will "likely make some noise in the world, [and will] be no less read than the *Pilgrim's Progress* or the works of Montaigne and Cervantes". "From a backwardness of my nature, I have been so very particular already that... in writing what I have set about, I shall confine myself neither to [Horace's] rules, nor to any man's rules that ever lived".

This does not tell us when the egg will be hatched.

Hush! "Shut the door". First, Sterne has to tell us "curious readers" that he was conceived on March 25th and was born in early November.

A rather short timespan.

In order to remove all doubt, Sterne presents us with the official announcement of his birth, which he has drawn up himself:

> On the fifth day of November 1718, which to the era fixed on was as near nine calendar months as any husband could in reason have expected — was I Tristram Shandy, Gentleman, brought forth into this scurvy and disastrous world of ours.

It brings to mind Cervantes's "depraved era".

The Earth, at that time, was not in any better shape than it is today:

> I wish I had been born in the Moon, or in any of the planets (except Jupiter or Saturn, because I never could bear cold weather), [...] [rather than] in this vile, dirty planet of ours, — which o' my conscience, with reverence be it spoken, I take to be made up of the shreds and clippings

of the rest [...]; [unless] a man could be born [...] to a great title or to a great estate; or could anyhow contrive to be called up to public charges and employments of dignity or power; — but that is not my case; [...]; I have been the continual sport of what the world calls Fortune; [...] yet with all the good temper in the world, I affirm it of her that in every stage of my life, and at every turn and corner where she could get fairly at me, the ungracious Duchess has pelted me with a set of as pitiful misadventures and cross accidents as ever small HERO sustained.

Sterne speaks of his life like your patient philosopher whose delusions, he said, emerged "at the crossroads of his personal history and world History".

He does, in fact, add: "let me go on and tell my story my own way", even if "I sometimes put on a fool's cap with a bell to it. [...] But 'don't fly off'", he begs us, since to continue his analysis, he relies on us.

After stating his "I wish" and his "I know", which reveals the moment "when" he was conceived and when he was born, the question the reader still wants answered is "how" his life unfolded. So, the stages of the transference to the reader are carefully outlined. "At the beginning, Sir, you and I are in a manner, perfect strangers to each other... You must have a little patience". An intimacy has to be established little by little. "[...] the slight acquaintance which is now beginning betwixt us will grow into familiarity; and that [...] will terminate in friendship, — *O diem praeclarum!* — then nothing which has touched me will be thought trifling in its nature or tedious in its telling".

Here we have the Proximity principle required by Thomas Salmon in the analysis of traumas.

And the Immediacy principle as well:

> As you proceed further with me, [...] if I should seem now and then to trifle upon the road, [...] and as we jog on, either laugh with me or at me, or in short do anything, — only keep your temper.

Once Sterne tells us to stay calm and collected, the parson—a friend of the family—can be brought onto the stage to set the transference in motion.

Still, there is one more question: "where?" Where is his analysis taking place?

Liberty, Equality, Dada![15]

Sterne lived in a village, at a time when rural society was limited to a circle "of four English miles' diameter or thereabouts". The reader is introduced into the Shandys' parish through the midwife, an honourable, unschooled widow who has, nevertheless, sound obstetrical knowledge. Thanks to the "female part of the parish", she was given a title to practice, paid for by the parson and amended by Didius the lawyer, whose whim-wham was the "taking to pieces and new fragmenting" of the law.

The lawyer's whim-wham opens the way for the HOBBY HORSE—the carrier of transference—to make a grand entrance, justified by the Latin formula introducing Chapter 8: *De gustibus non est disputandum.*

There is no arguing about tastes.
The Shandean translation would be:

> There is no arguing about hobby-horses... Have not, Sir, the wisest men in all ages, their running horses, —their coins and their cockle shells, their drums and their trumpets, their fiddles, their pallets, —their maggots and their butterflies? —So long as a man rides his HOBBY-HORSE peaceably and quietly along the King's highway and neither compels you or me to get up behind him, —pray, sir, what have either you or I to do with it?

Sterne claims the human right to have a hobby horse of one's own, without feeling obliged to ride someone else's. In the same way every child has his own teddy bear, doll, blanket or wooden horse, without giving in to global marketing. Personally, I have nothing against those who are addicted to social networks as long as they don't force them on me.

And yet, you ride behind Sterne on his hobby horse....
When the fancy struck him, Sterne played Scarlatti on his bass viola de gamba and painted at certain "changes of the moon". But his favourite way to fend off adversity was his *Tristram Shandy*, born the year everything went wrong, when he good humouredly set aside all pretence:

> But the truth is, —I am [...] a mortal of so little consequence in the world, it is no much matter what I do, so I seldom fret or fume at all about it: nor does it much disturb my rest when I see such great Lords and tall Personages [...] all of a row, mounted upon their several horses, Some with large stirrups, others tuck'd on their very chins.

He parades them before us like a frieze of riders: "God speed them.—for were their worships unhorsed this very night, —'tis ten to one but that many of them would be worse mounted tomorrow morning".

The circus is still going on.
Any resemblance to you-know-who is purely coincidental.

Stern's satire spares one person, the one to whom his novel is dedicated, before whom he lets down his guard:

> [...] when I see one born for great actions and, [...] whose nature ever inclines him to good ones;—when I behold such a one, my Lord, like yourself [...];—when I see such a one, my Lord, mounted, though it is but for a minute beyond the time which my love to my country has prescribed to him [...], —then, my Lord, I cease to be a philosopher and in the first transport of an honest impatience I wish the HOBBY-HORSE, with all his fraternity, at the devil.

His declaration of the unalienable right to a hobby horse doesn't stop him from licking the boots... of whom, by the way?

Sterne has no clue; the name of the Right Honourable William Pitt, the Minister of Foreign Affairs, will appear only in the second edition of the book. But no matter, for lack of a great personage, he addresses the Dedication itself, by personifying it.

In the tradition of medieval theatre.

A constant source of inspiration for him. So be it. He praises his Dedication for having no protector whatsoever. She is "honestly, a true virgin dedication untried on upon any living soul". Therefore, he can offer it up with a sales pitch specifying that it was made:

> for no one prince, prelate, [...] duke, marquis, [...] of this or any other realm in Christendom;—nor has it yet been hawk'd about or offered publicly or privately, directly or indirectly, to any person or personage, great or small.

Like a true pimp, he praises its virginity to better sell it for fifty guineas, without "chaffering and higgling for a few guineas in a dark entry". No, the deal shall be made openly, as long as the little darling perfectly suits the needs of a dirty old man, to whom he promises a considerable discount. Sterne has a talent for marketing. He is credited with having promoted the entry of 18th-century literature into the business era.

He should be taught in business schools.

At that level, his talent does not quite equal Voltaire's. Still, as he foresees feminist criticism, he finally decides to dedicate his book to the moon, the divinity of childbirth: "*Bright Goddess*, if thou art not too busy with CANDID and Miss CUNEGUND's affairs, — take Tristram Shandy under thy protection also".

Candide *was indeed published in 1759, and translated into English the same year.*

The knight of the space in-between two deaths

Diana or Artemis answered his prayer by offering him the chance to deal with the beyond. Left behind in Chapter VII, in which he bought the mid-wife's licence, the parson will soon die, in Chapter XII, as a result of a "villain affair" during a fatal dinner with his hierarchy, recounted in Chapter XXVII of Volume 4, where the question of the "debaptisation" of Tristram was raised. Since we are now close to the imminent death of the parson. Chronology does not hold, for Tristram will be born in Volume 3 and his baptism will take place in Volume 4. We have been warned.

Indeed, I have trouble following.

You have to get used to the reversibility of the arrow of f Time, as Erwin Schroedinger says when he explains quantic physics to dummies like us. In an analysis too, time has its whims: it stops, starts again, changes direction, goes backwards, mixes the present with the future and the past. But don't worry: Sterne foresaw your crestfallen look and advised that you put the book down for at least half a day, to consider the grounds for the entanglement that he will outline patiently for you.

It all started five years before the parson bought the midwife's qualifications. At that time, he had made himself the talk of the county "by a breach of all decorum", when he was seen, a sorry figure, mounted "upon a lean, jackass of a horse, [...] full brother to Rocinante". Broken-winded and as chaste as his model, the nag resembled a ghostly apparition from the Beyond which only "HUMILITY herself could have bestrided".

It reminds me of a cowboy song, "Ghost Riders in the Sky"—do you remember?—which revives, in a Far West setting, the medieval theme of the Wild Hunt led by the king of the dead *Herla, Erlköning*, or *Harlequin.*

But the parson's gaunt appearance is not at all frightening.

Yet he is not exactly this-worldly either:

> [...] it was greatly in the parson's power to have helped the figure of this horse of his, —for he was master of a very handsome demi-peak'd saddle, [...] garnished with [...] a noble pair of shining brass stirrups, [...] purchased in the pride and prime of his life [...] But not caring to banter his beast, he had hung all these up behind his study door.

Of course, since he dwells in a sphere outside time.

How do you know that Roger Sterne's ghost is about to appear? The atmosphere is made ghostly by recourse to slow motion. "In the several sallies about his parish [...]—, you will easily comprehend that the parson, so appointed, would both hear and see enough to keep his philosophy from rusting". Movement stops, people are frozen in place and objects are personified:

"Labour stood still as he pass'd, —the bucket hung suspended in the middle of the well, — the spinning wheel forgot its round, —even chuck-farthing and shuffle-cap themselves stood gaping till he had got out of sight". Uncanny! In this eerie suspense, "he had generally time enough [...] to hear the groans of the serious, —and the laughter of the light-hearted;—all which he bore with excellent tranquility".

It allows him to mask his own the contempt the world had for him, as Wittgenstein put it.

Like Sterne, he "loved a jest in his heart—and as he saw himself in the true point of ridicule, he would say he could not be angry with others for seeing him in a light in which he so strongly saw himself". Another fool among knaves, "his foible was not the love of money".

Lin Tsi speaks of the "True man with no rank", whom his French translator Paul Demiéville compares to Robert Musil's Man without Qualities.[16]

Like Ulrich, the parson in fact has many qualities. As he rides along, he meditates on the vanity of the world, *de vanitate mundi*, and the swift passing of time, *de fuga saecul.* "Centaur like", taking his time, " he could compose his cough, he could compose his sermon, [...] draw up an argument or a hole in his breeches, [...] for brisk trotting and slow argumentation, like wit and judgement, [are] two incompatible movements".

A portrait of Reverend Sterne on horseback?

Who is conducting his self-analysis from a vantage point of derision he alone is aware of: But he did not give others the true cause "out of nicety of temper, because he thought it did honour to him".

The word is out of fashion

Honour was already out of date at the time of Don Quixote, Sterne's role model. To understand the parson, you have to know his other quality: a total lack of *philautia*, self-love. "In the first years of this gentleman's life, [...] he was said to have loved a good horse, and generally had one of the best in the whole parish standing in his stable always ready for saddling". But the midwife lived far from the village, and "he had not the heart" to refuse lending his horse. The upshot was generally this: the horse came back in bad shape so that, every nine or ten months he had to purchase a good one.

For the parson, the "true cause" of his "point of ridicule" springs from a dilemma similar to the aporia your Zen master presents to his disciples. He either flatters his parishioners by maintaining a good horse and stops lending it, which he could not bear to do, or he disappoints them by ruining his decorum. Finally, he decides:

> that with half the sum thus galloped away, he could do ten times as much good, [...] and chose to bear the contempt of his enemies and his friends' laughter rather than suffer the pain of telling a story which might seem a tribute to himself.

Much "to his honour", Sterne adds.

The parson pays no more attention to what people say than his author. Quickly worn out by the critics, Sterne kept his head high thanks to "the honest refinements of the peerless knight of La Mancha, whom, by the by, with all his follies, I love more and would actually have gone further to have paid a visit to than the greatest hero of antiquity".

In The Zen Teachings of Lin-Chi,[17] *this type of aporia is called a "kôan". It is formulated in the course of "dialogues between host and visitor". The master challenged him to solve an enigma. If the latter could not answer, he received a thrashing. If he succeeded, the master was pulled out of his chair.*
One day, a follower of Zen brought me such a riddle.

And you fell out of your chair?

Kôan

Almost. This visitor came from a distant land to train as a psychoanalyst. I gave him the names of various training institutes, but he insisted on staying. He had read *Wittgenstein's Folly*,[18] in which the philosopher vehemently argues with me and my patients; and wanted to join the fight.

After a number of trips back and forth to his faraway country, he brought me a letter I can quote by heart for it has remained etched in my memory. He wrote:

> The enigma I brought you can be presented as follows: A bird was placed in a bottle and left there as he grew. After a time, it had grown too much to be able to leave the bottle. How can he be brought out of the bottle without being injured?

You then asked me: "How can you put a child out of your heart without hurting him"?

You immediately thought of Sterne's brothers and sisters.
I had not read *Tristram Shandy* yet at the time, and I thought I had committed a blunder, when I read the next sentence: "Your question shocked

me. I wrote a letter to a friend right away, telling him about this great shock that left me speechless". And he continued:

> This child in my heart was already outside, since it is my brother and sister abandoned by my father when he fled his country for political reasons. When he wanted to come back for them and their mother, the border was closed. I was born from my father's second marriage with another refugee.

The resolution of this kôan can be stated as follows:

> So, these children entered my heart since my father was searching, in me, for traces of the lost ones. We never found out if they were alive or dead. There is no need to bring them out, since they are already out. Until now, I could not find the answer because I was keeping them inside me like a burden I was taking care of to heal my father. My heart was heavy with the weight of this child-burden. Now I realise that I cannot carry them as if they were real children, but I can look after them by honouring their memory. The meaning of the verb "to heal" and of the noun "therapy" reflects the ethics of psychoanalysis: we have to take care of lost souls.

And that's not all. He had decided to become an analyst in his country:

> Buddhist legacy tells us that the one who has achieved enlightenment comes down from the mountain of his own free will to care for the people with great pleasure. I do too. So far, I achieved "my" analysis; from now on, I have a different goal. As soon as I became aware of this, just outside your door after I left your office, I wanted to ring the bell again to tell you all this. For I felt a great joy. I had told you that everything was mixed up in my consciousness.

Shandied, as Sterne would say.

> But now, everything acquires shape, as if a drop of reagent added to mirky water had made the liquid clear and transparent. I wanted to share this joy with you. As you know, many Chan monks have experienced awakening after a dialogue between guest and host, on the doorstep of their master's chamber. I believed this experience to be very different from mine. But yesterday, when I left your office, on the landing in front of your door, a sudden awakening struck me. Back at the residence where I live, I was seized with a fit of laughter so wild that everyone thought I was a madman. But I don't know which one of us was mad. Everyone is mad in his own way.

In Chan Buddhism, it is the tradition to sing an *odo song*, or Song of Awakening, after enlightenment. I didn't quite understand this tradition and I was asking myself: "Why an *odo song*?" I thought that awakening always came in silence, and I saw singing as a sign of pride. But now I understand completely. It is not man's will, but the great power of I-know-not-what which impels me to sing this *odo song* that this letter is for me. Yesterday was the Lunar New Year. You gave me the gift of a great teaching.

When I finished reading the letter, I thought: *Sunt jocundae rerum...* there is laughter in the world, and not only tears, as in Virgil's verse of the *Aeneid*: *Sunt lacrimae rerum.*

Sterne, Zen Buddhism and Virgil—what a mixture!
Let me shandy as I see fit, and listen now to the story of the parson, a mix of laughter and tears.

"Yorick was this parson's name"

When the name is revealed at last, it takes the form of a solemn announcement: "Yorick was this parson's name".

"To be or not to be"? Hamlet asks Yorick's skull in the famous graveyard scene. It is also Tristram's question at the moment of his conception.
Yorick embodies the spirit of Roger Sterne, described in the *Memoir* written for his daughter, which I mentioned earlier. Laurence would have liked to tell her more about her ancestors, but the Sterne's ancestry did not go very far back—except for the famous archbishop Richard Sterne—so that "in a course of years, the story will so blend and confound us [...] that no one shall be able to stand up and swear that his own great-grandfather was the man who did either this or that". Hence his decision to join a lineage of fools.

A footnote specifies that Yorick's family name was attested since the 13th century in Saxo-Grammaticus's Danish history, which served as a reference to Shakespeare's play. Yorick's ancestors were among the chief jesters at the court of the King of Denmark during the reign of Horwendillus, king of Jutland, whose son Amleth pretended to be mad to avoid being killed by his uncle, who had already slain his father.

At that time, Yorkshire, the cradle of the Sterne and Shandy families, belonged to the Viking kingdom of East Anglia and was under "Dane Law"; York had been its capital since 876. Through his kinship to the Yorick dynasty, Laurence can lay claim to the bauble and the fool's cap passed down by his father's jest.

A little far-fetched.

At the psychiatric hospital, I indeed met Sisi, Empress of Austria-Hungary. Elizabeth Sterne took herself for the Queen of Bohemia for a time. So why couldn't Sterne be Yorick, if he liked? In fact, he published his sermons under that name, "The Sermons of Parson Yorick", and gave the same name to the hero of *A Sentimental Journey*.

Another reason for this identification is to be found in the whims of the English climate, which has made the British lose the Danes' equanimity long ago. "We are all ups and downs", Sterne tells the reader:

> Either you are a great genius;—or 'tis fifty to one, sir, you are a great dunce and a blockhead, [...] but the two extremes are more common [...] in this unsettled island, where nature [...] is most whimsical and capricious.

What about British phlegm and Anglo-Saxon pragmatism?

Fiddlesticks! Sterne would say. Parson Yorick has no more phlegm or pragmatism than his own father. Like him, he is "mercurial, with much life and whim and *gaîté de coeur*",[19] without:

> one ounce of ballast. [...], so that upon his first setting out, the brisk gale of his spirits [...] ran him foul ten times in a day of somebody's tackling; and as the grave and more slow-paced were oftenest in his way [...], t'was with such he had generally the ill luck to get the most entangled.

Freud's unconscious play with the *Witz* is at work:

> For, to speak the truth, Yorick had an invincible dislike and opposition in his nature to gravity; — not to gravity as such [...];—but he was an enemy to the affectation of it, and declared open war against it, (...) — and then, whenever it fell in his way [...], he seldom gave it much quarter.

Here, the fool is all ready to fight knaves.

Yorick is an offspring of Mother Folly, the main character of *Sotties*, a 15th century form of political theatre in France, after the Great Plague and the Hundred Years' War. Sterne is very familiar with this theatre of fools which staged mock trials. At the end of the play, the fools used to drag an important personage on stage and, after attacking his abuses with verbal virtuosity, they jumped on him to tear off his cloak of smugness, revealing publically the fool's costume hidden under his double talk.

What this striptease reveals is not "the state of serenity of a fool among knaves" Swift dreamed of.

Not exactly. In Yorick, it triggers a kind of exaltation. When he encountered that sort of person wearing a mask of gravity and respectability, he calls him:

> an errant scoundrel, and of the most dangerous kind too, — because a sly one; and that, he verily believed, more honest, well-meaning people were bubbled out of their goods and money by it in one month than by pocket-picking and shoplifting in seven.

On such occasions, Yorick went berzerk with words, saying what came to his mind without much ceremony. He was to pay a high price for it.

The murderous uncle unmasked by Hamlet's folly thinks only of killing him. Sterne uses Shakespearian adjectives to describe Yorick:

> He was a man unhackneyed and unpractised in the world. [...] 'twas a taught trick to gain credit in the world for more sense and knowledge than a man was worth; and that, with all its pretentions ... A French wit [La Rochefoucauld], had long ago defined I that trick as [a] *mysterious carriage of the body to cover the defects of the mind*; —which definition [...] with great imprudence, [Yorick] would say deserved to be wrote in letters of gold.

The parson's fate is sealed. Surrepticiously, a war is being waged against him, in which he will be killed.

I thought we were in for some laughs...

Eavesdropping on the Mind

In Rabelais's era, jesters were sometimes hanged. Until the start of the 19th century, theatre was prohibited in New England. In Paris a few years ago, cartoonists, music lovers and people sitting in cafés paid for their *gaîté de coeur* with their lives, when they fell victim to murderous attacks. The parson was all the more exposed to such danger since he could not resist a *bon mot*.[20] He spoke in "plain English without any periphrasis, —and too oft without much distinction of either personage, time or place;—so that when mention was made of [...] a dirty action, —without more ado, —the man was a dirty fellow".

Likewise, Sterne's vocabulary, borrowed from the neoliberalism of his time, describes perversion as the capitalisation of hate. On the contrary, Yorick "had but too many temptations in life of scattering his wit and his humour, his quips and his jests. They were not lost for want of gathering".

Thus, a relentless mechanism is set in motion. The jester "raises a laugh" at the expense of the jestee—"his creditor" who will one day be "demanding principal upon the spot, together with full interest". The place from which the jester's wit springs is transformed into a financial market where dividends payable to the goddesses of vengeance are calculated in secret: when the one who was mocked demands the interest due, murder is set in motion.

"La vendetta!" Bartolo sings in The Marriage of Figaro.
For once, Sterne adopts a tragic tone:

> To speak the truth, [Yorick] had wantonly involved himself in a multitude of small book-debts of this stamp, which, [...] he disregarded, thinking that as not one of them was contracted thro' any malignancy; — but [...] from an honesty of mind and a mere jocundity of humour, — they would all of them be cross'd out in course.

Yorick's friend Eugenius—a fellow student from Cambridge, alias John Hall-Stevenson, master of "Crazy Castle" near Sterne's parsonage, where he hosted his friends in the spirit of Rabelais's Abbey of Thelema—tried to warn him of the danger hanging over his head. He predicted that "one day or other [Yorick] would certainly be reckoned with [...] to the uttermost mite". Yorick took no notice "with his usual carelessness of heart", and fell prey to an extravagant arithmetic: "[...] for every ten jokes". Eugenius insists: "... thou hast got an hundred enemies; [...] a swarm of wasps about thy ears". To which Yorick merely opposed a scornful "pshaw"!
Massen psychology!
Like Freud in his prophetic text, Eugenius proffers a warning:

> [...] they will carry on the war in such a manner against thee, my dear friend, as to make thee heartily sick of it, and of thy life too. REVENGE [...] shall level a tale of dishonour at thee [...]. The fortunes of thy house shall totter [...], —thy character shall bleed on every side of it, —thy faith questioned, —thy work belied, —thy wit forgotten, —thy learning trampled on. To wind up the last scene of the tragedy, CRUELTY and COWARDICE, twin ruffians, hired and set on by MALICE in the dark, shall strike together at all thy infirmities and mistakes.

Sterne knows what he is talking about. When his work *A Political Romance* was condemned to the stack, the spectre of terror appeared. Eugenius continues:

> my dear lad, [...] trust me, [...] when to gratify a private appetite it is once resolved upon that an innocent and an helpless creature shall be sacrificed, 'tis an easy matter to pick up sticks enew from any thicket [...], to make a fire to offer it up with.

The prophecy comes to pass, as we shall learn in Volume 4: " a grand confederacy, with ***** and *****at the head of it, was form'd [...] with so little mercy", while he expected a preferment. Yorick:

> fought it out with all imaginable gallantry for some time; till, overpower'd by numbers and worn out at length by the calamities of the war, — but more so by the ungenerous manner in which it was carried on, —he threw down the sword; and though he kept up his spirits in appearance to the last, —he died [...] quite broken-hearted.

Does this sound familiar?

I did not die of a broken heart.

Yorick's Death

Sterne did not die of a broken heart either. The critics who attacked him when they learned that the author of *Tristram* was a man of the cloth were unable to quell the wit of his humour or silence the words he did not have a chance to tell his father.

From the start of his novel, without further ado, he offers him an epitaph. Yorick's death in the first volume of *Tristram Shandy* follows upon Don Quixote's at the end of the second novel where Cervantes brings about his hero's death on purpose. After the international success of the first novel, envious authors, including the great Lope de Vega—who proclaimed: "No [...] poet is as bad as Cervantes, none so foolish as to praise Don Quixote"—had paid a forger, Avellaneda de Tordessillas, whose true identity is still unknown, to write a sequel of "The Adventures", debasing its heroes. Don Quixote's death, Cervantes asserted, would prevent such a fraud.

So Cervantes becomes Sterne's therapon, *his second in combat against malevolent reviewers.*

And his ritual double, who helps him accomplish his funeral duties. The reader is also invited to witness Yorick's last breath and the farewell Laurence could not bid his father. The ritual will be repeated in Volume 4, where we will witness the demise of Lieutenant Le Fever, in the presence of his eleven-year-old son; and later, in Volume 7, when we attend Uncle Toby's anticipated funeral.

Yorick thanks Eugenius for the many tokens of his friendship: "[...] if it was their fate to meet hereafter—he would thank him again and again—he told him he was within a few hours of giving his enemies the slip for ever". His friend bursts into tears: "I hope not—[...], Yorick replied with a look up and a gentle squeeze of Eugenius's hand, and that was all". The latter pleads: "Come, —come, [...]—my dear lad, be comforted, —let not all thy spirits and fortitude forsake thee at this crisis when thou most wants them". Yorick laid his hand on his heart and shook his head gently. Eugenius was crying bitter tears: "I know not, Yorick, how to part with thee", and added, cheering up his voice: "there is still enough left of thee to make a bishop, —and that I may live to see it".

The last gesture of the jester reveals what he left unspoken until then. Making one last effort, the dying man "[took] off his nightcap as well as he could [...] —I beseech thee to take a view of my head". But Eugenius sees nothing since psychological torture leaves no visible scars:

> Then, alas! my friend, said Yorick, let me tell you that 'tis so bruised and misshapen'd with the blows which***** and ***** and some others have so unhandsomely given me in the dark that I might say with Sancho Panza that [...] 'mitres thereupon be suffer'd to rain down from heaven as thick as hail, not one of 'em would fit it'.

In these situations, Hannah Arendt speaks of "a secret society in daylight".[21] We are reminded of Sancho's thrashing by the Duke and Duchess' henchmen, and of the beating Don Quixote and Doña Rodriguez suffered after the session in which she revealed the perversion of the ducal castle.

The reference to Don Quixote is clear. Yorick speaks his last words in "a Cervantic tone", with his last breath "hanging upon his trembling lips", and as he spoke:

> Eugenius could perceive a stream of lambent fire lighted up for a moment in his eyes;—faint picture of those flashes of his spirit which (as Shakespeare said of his ancestor) were wont to set the table in a roar!

We are watching the look in Roger Sterne's eyes as he sees his son off without knowing if he will ever see him again.

And the look I watched in yours. The moment that follows the farewell is concretely marked in the book by a black page, an obituary notice and gravestone combined, bearing as an epitaph the words spoken by Hamlet as he stood on the edge of the fool's grave who was for him a father: "Alas, poor Yorick"! And Sterne adds: "Ten times in a day has Yorick's ghost the consolation to hear his monumental inscription read over with such a variety of plaintive tones as denote a general pity and esteem for him".

Now we're really engaged in a Dialogue of the Dead.

Sterne's ghost was also likely to roam the countryside, for he was buried hastily, like Mozart, and his corpse was stolen to be used for dissection at a

London hospital. A century later, a commemorative slab bearing the same epitaph "Alas, Poor Yorick!" was erected near his presbytery.

Your eyes are bright.

Sterne's explicit wish, made on the threshold of death, was to escape being the subject of weeping and lament. The reader will find his final wishes in Chapter XII of Volume 7.

Then why all the tears shed upon Yorick's demise?

A Shakespearian Hero

They are the tears the child was never able to cry. Listen to Shakespeare's version of the "banalisation of evil", in the words the Queen of Denmark addresses to her son in a maternal tone, as early as the second scene of Act I:

> Do not for ever with thy vailed lids
> Seek for thy noble father in the dust:
> Thou know'st 'tis common; all that lives must die,
> Passing through nature to eternity.
> Ay, madam, it is common.
> If it be,
> Why seems it so particular with thee?
> Seems, madam! nay it is; I know not 'seems'.

We can imagine the same indifference displayed by Agnes Sterne, who landed on her son's doorstep seventeen years after he left Ireland, to lay claim to her daughter-in-law's dowry, which she believed to be substantial. "She wanted me to remember that I was her son, when she had forgotten to be a mother", Sterne said. She joined her brother-in-law, uncle Jaques, in spreading slanderous rumours about him, which persisted into the next century.

Hamlet's uncle and stepfather is of the same ilk; he lectures his nephew about mourning, calling his bereavement "obstinate", his sorrow "obsequious" and "stubborn", his grief "unmanly", his will "incorrect", his heart "unfortified", his mind "impatient" and "unschool'd". Modern diagnoses are no better when they take someone like him for a depressive or a melancholic who insists on making a fuss when his uncle says: "Think of us as a father".

Laurence's uncles probably spoke these words at the death of their brother, paying lip service, as people do. But I remember that Hamlet's definition of a fool is far from Swift's.

You are referring to Act I, Scene 4, when Hamlet asks the ghost: "What may this mean/ that, [...] we fools of nature/ So horribly to shake our disposition/ With thoughts beyond the reaches of our souls"? In Sterne's novel, the black page appearing before our eyes also represents the darkness the parson had to confront. Tristram's birth emerges from this black page, "beyond the reaches of our souls".

Fortunately, the midwife mentioned in Chapter VI arrives on the scene just in time, to be included in Sterne's "rhapsodical" work—a rhapsody is made up of songs patched together and jumbled—"shandied". Then she disappears again and will come back to deliver the baby in Volume 3.

In the meantime, the black page is imprinted on our retina.

This typographical invention—among many others, like the famous "Shandean dashes", the words in capital letters or in Gothic script, the hand with the pointing index to draw the reader's attention—brings to mind his poem "The Unknown" composed as he listened to the "pass-bells" in 1742,[22] as he was freeing himself from the grip of Uncle Jaques.

And for whom did the bells toll?

For all the spirits behind "[a] dark impenetrable screen/All behind which is yet unseen"!," Laurence's departed siblings are perhaps "watching him though unseen" from behind the black page, waiting for the right moment to jump into his book with their model building blocks, their tin soldiers and their rocking horses. From time to time, Sterne mentions "my dear, dear Jenny! [who] may be my child, my sister, may be my friend".

Mon enfant, ma soeur, songe à la douceur d'aller là-bas vivre ensemble.

Sterne has no time to think of Baudelaire's "Invitation to the voyage". He has a multitude of things to attend to, all methodically listed in Chapter 14: "Accounts to reconcile; Anecdotes to pick up; Inscriptions to make out; Stories to weave in; Tradition to sift; Personages to call upon; Panegyrics to paste up at this door; Pasquinades at that". As a result, although he has been writing for six weeks, Tristram is still not born, and Sterne concludes that it is best "not to be in a hurry;—but to go on leisurely writing [...] which [...] I shall continue to do as long as I live".

He doesn't feel guilty about procrastinating?

On the contrary, since the Unknown required that Yorick die before Tristram is born, chronological order reverses itself. You will read in the next volumes that the child will have ample time to get to know him.

This is how the inscription of the cut-out unconscious of trauma takes place, when time is out of joint.

Sterne juggles constantly with the different levels of memory—traumatic or not, suppressed or repressed, warning us of the "unforeseen stoppages, which I own I had no conception of when I first set out". He straddles his story, like a muleteer his mule, without foreseeing his journey's end, since "the thing is, morally speaking, impossible: for [...] he will have fifty deviations from a straight line [...], which he can no way avoid".

My mule has gotten into the habit of crossing the pass back and forth between the unknown and the world here below.

Feminism

So much the better, for now we will discover that Tristram's troubles started before his conception, when his mother refused to be shut away in a remote rural hamlet.

Like your mother when she couldn't wait to leave the valley where you were born in the Alps, as soon as the war was over.
Leave my private life alone, and besides, I was two years old by then.
Still, Mrs. Shandy was smarter, and made her arrangements before she married. If her husband forced her to stay in the country against her will, she would make him pay for it. Their marriage contract, drawn up in Gothic script, specified that in case Mr. Shandy left his business in London to return to the country, and Mrs. Shandy became pregnant:

> Walter Shandy shall pay ... within six weeks of her [...] supposed and computed delivery, for the hiring of one coach [...] to carry [her] unto the city of London [...] to live and reside [...] within the said city of London [...] as if she was a *femme seule* and unmarried.

It is further specified that she may "reside in such family or families, and with such relations, friends and other persons [...] as she [...] shall think fit".

And escape boredom...
The only one who understands what is happening is Toby. Well versed in military tactics, he grasps his sister-in-law's strategy long before his brother does, and suggests adding an article to the contract, to protect Walter's rights in case a trip to London is undertaken based on a false claim of pregnancy. And indeed, such a situation does occur, when Mrs. Shandy pretends to be pregnant in order to enjoy the capital.

You blame her for her feminism?
Tristram is the one who blames her, for "the whole weight of the article [fell] entirely upon myself. [...] I was doom'd by marriage articles..."

The dispute between the spouses is recounted in Chapter 15, after Mrs. Shandy's journey to London—for peanuts—a year before he was born. The French expression *pour des prunes*, "for plums", is perfectly suited here, since Walter promptly took her back to Shandy Hall, where the ripe Greengage plums waited on their espalier trees to be harvested. On the trip back, in the coach, Walter was "pshawing and pishing" more and more emphatically at each stage of the journey, until, in Chapter 17, he took "the resolution of doing himself justice" by invoking uncle Toby's article. He therefore left his wife no choice but to "lye-in of her next child in the country".

A great subject for Gender Studies.
Especially as Walter waited thirteen months before announcing his decision, and in the meanwhile, he nurtured a grudge against her: "…he had a strong spice of that in his temper which [is] known by the name of perseverance in a good cause—and of obstinacy in a bad one". The punishment is delivered on the famous night which introduces the narrative, while the spouses are lying in bed chatting—"She would lye-in of her next child in the country, to balance the last year's journey".
Knowing that it was no good arguing, she instantly brandished the unbeatable argument of the midwife, a choice of which her husband disapproved, favouring instead the brand new discovery of the forceps, which the local physician happened to possess. This is when, running out of options, she tried to make the clock perform a contraceptive function, cutting off "the animal spirits [that] go cluttering like hey-go-mad", in a race to reach the ovule—like in a Woody Allen movie whose title I forgot.

"Everything you always wanted to know about sex but were afraid to ask".
Mrs. Shandy never makes a scene. Her weapon is silence: she waits for the right moment in a state of apparent submission to do just what her husband doesn't want—call in the midwife he detests, although in the course of twenty years of practice, she has done her work "without any one slip or accident".
The disagreement is amplified in the court of public opinion. Mrs. Shandy spreads the rumour that her husband's miserliness is what prompts him to endanger the life of mother and child by entrusting them to this woman, instead of acquiring the services of a reputable London doctor.

Some analysts may diagnose a hysterical structure, no doubt about it.
Sterne would agree. This is what he likes about women, the all or nothing character of their desire. His "dear, dear Jenny" displays "the same greatness of soul".

I don't disagree.

France suffers from state-apoplexy

No personal innuendos, please, about our past squabbles. Walter's viewpoint is "political": "My father had extensive views of things, —and stood, moreover, [...] deeply concern'd [...] for the public good, from the dread he entertained of the bad uses an ill-fated instance might be put to". His theory was based on a single principle: "*distemper* was identically the same in the body national as in the body natural", and some countries, like France, suffered from "state-apoplexy".

We are regularly told there is to be a remedy.

Walter displays his "remedy" through gestures more eloquent than any dissertation. "Was I an absolute prince", he would say, pulling up his breeches with both hands as he rose from his armchair, "I would appoint able judges at every avenue of my metropolis who should take cognizance of every fool's business who came there". Walter considers that his wife's preference for London contributes to the rural exodus turning the countryside into a wasteland. He wants to bring back the idyllic time of the pastoral, when "meadows and cornfields [...] laugh and sing"; he wants, above all, to give back their influence to country squires, whom Louis XIV had turned into courtiers.

Why is this Englishman meddling in our business?

Walter wants to teach us a lesson, while he walks across the room as "throughout so many delicious provinces in *France*", asking with emotion:

> Why is it that the few remaining *chateaux* [...] are so dismantled [...]? —Because, sir, in that kingdom no man has any country interest to support;—the little interest [...] is concentrated in the court and the looks of the Grand Monarch; by the sunshine of whose countenance, or the clouds which pass across it, every French man lives or dies.

When applied to the domestic sphere, Mrs. Shandy's absolutist stand "would in the end prove fatal to the monarchical system of domestic government established in the first creation of things by God".

The French Revolution would soon solve Walter's problem.

For the moment, they continue to quarrel. He wants the obstetrician "by all means, and she by no means". He begs:

> she insists upon her privilege, in that matter, to choose for herself. — What can my father do? He was almost at wit's end, [...] argued with her the matter like a Christian, like a heathen, like a husband, like a patriot, like a man. [...] My mother answered everything only like a woman. [...] —'twas no fair match.—'twas seven to one.

But she regained the advantage by suffering in silence until the affair was settled, so that "both sides sung the *Te Deum*".

The peace process has redefined the borders as follows:

> In a word, my mother was to have the old woman, —and the operator
> was to have licence to drink a bottle of wine with my father and my
> uncle Toby in the back parlor, for which he would be paid five guineas.

One can tell that the author is an expert in domestic disputes.
Sterne sweeps away your insinuation in a single sentence:

> I must beg leave, before I finish this chapter, to enter a caveat in the
> breast of my fair reader;— and it is this:—not to take it absolutely for
> granted from an unguarded word or two which I have dropp'd in it, —
> that I am a married man.

So, you see, you were wrong, the novel is not an autobiography.

The Signifier

It doesn't much matter, since the word "autobiography" only appeared
early in the 19th century. In any case, Sterne is in bad faith as regards references to his own life. As I already said, the name Tristram, which Walter
loathes, is certified by his biographer to be that of the statue of a tramp—
Ole Tristram—in front of the church near Laurence's school. Hence Walter's premonitory interest in signifiers: "good or bad names [...] irresistibly
impress upon our characters and conduct". The name Tristram, "melancholy dissyllable of sound", struck his ear in unison with "Nincompoop".

It does not strike mine. Perhaps we need the Yorkshire accent.
Sterne foresaw your objection:

> I would sooner undertake to explain the hardest problem [...] than pre-
> tend to account for it that a gentleman of my father's good sense [...],
> — could be capable of entertaining a notion in his head so out of the
> common track.

Walter would have loved Lacan.
Sterne is even afraid that the reader, "if he is the least of choleric temper,
will immediately throw the book by; if mercurial, he will laugh most heartily at it;—and if he is of a grave and saturnine cast, he will [...] absolutely
condemn [it]". As a result, he hesitates to present you with an idea so clearly
ahead of its time.

*Ahead... well... Don Quixote baptised himself and his horse with care, and
chose harmonious phonemes for Dulcinea.*
Sterne also quotes Cervantes to justify Walter's obsession, but admits that
his passion for signifiers is so extravagant that instead of making him merry

in the spirit of *vive la bagatelle*,[23] "he would move both heaven and earth, and twist and torture everything in nature to support his hypothesis".

He is not the only one to trip over linguistic theories.

Sterne explains how this happens even to the most enlightened analysts. At first, "odd opinions" enter into our brains and work there as gentle passions. But at length they become established and ferment like yeast, giving birth to dogmatic sentences, so that "what began in jest ends in downright earnest". This is how "[my father's] judgement, at length, became the dupe of his wit". He was convinced that the influence of a bad name was irreversible; about this, he was not only serious, "he was systematical. [...] But of all the names in the universe, he had the most unconquerable aversion for TRIS-TRAM", so that at the mere mention of it, he would raise his voice "a full fifth above the key of the discourse", demanding whether "a man call'd Tristram" had ever performed "anything great or worth recording? —No, — TRISTRAM!—The thing is impossible". Yet it happened.

"*C'est la Fatalité*" la Belle Hélène would sing in Offenbach's comic opera, a century later. Walter's misfortune is akin to that of Menelaus:

> When this story is compared with the title page, —will not the gentle reader pity my father from his soul?—to see an orderly and well-disposed gentleman who, tho' singular, —yet inoffensive in his notions, —so played upon [...] by cross purposes.

Sterne invites us:

> to look down upon the stage and see him baffled and overthrown in all his little systems and wishes [...]. In a word, to behold such a one, in his old age, ill-fitted for troubles [...]—ten times in a day calling the child of his prayers TRISTRAM!

Here, the hero would love to comment on "the malignant spirit who took pleasure in traversing the purpose of a mortal man", except he cannot yet since "it is necessary I should be born before I am christened".

When will it happen at last?

My Fair Lady

Not yet, much later, but I have no time to explain since right now Sterne puts me on the spot: "—How could you, madam, be so inattentive...? I told you [...] *that my mother was not a papist*". He urges me to go back to the previous chapter, and "make wise reflections to draw curious conclusions". I do so and return, still puzzled, to be greeted with "...here comes my fair Lady".

My Fair Lady, *the musical based on Bernard Shaw's* Pygmalion?

Like you, I am lost in anachronisms. Mercifully, he gives me the answer: papists can baptise their children before birth, while still in the womb, so that in case of premature death, those souls would not be lost to the Church. Does it mean that such a procedure performed on Mrs. Shandy could have conjured fate? We will never know since we are now lectured on papist baptism.

Sterne found proof for his far-fetched theory in a "Memoire presented in 1733 to the doctors at the Sorbonne", which recommends the baptism of children *in utero* "using a little cannula, without any harm to the mother, despite St. Thomas' opinion that unborn children cannot be counted among human beings".

Hence, Sterne's Modest Proposal, in the spirit of Swift, to increase Catholic capital, is "the baptizing of all HOMUNCULI at once, slapdash, by injection", on condition "that if the HOMUNCULI do well and come safe into the world after this, that each and every one of them shall be baptized again".

It's not such a wacky idea. Today, so-called schizophrenics are baptized, slapdash, in the genes of their parents, before being conceived.

From Tristram's "I wish" to uncle Toby's "I think"

The only one who counters this scholastic banter is uncle Toby, on the long-awaited day of the delivery.

Better late than never.

At last, the famous November 5th, 1718, announced in Chapter 5, actually arrives. When Toby hears Walter ask: "I wonder what's all that noise and running backwards and forwards for, above stairs", he takes his pipe from his mouth, strikes the head of it two or three times upon the nail of his left thumb and says, "I think..." This gesture will set the rhythm throughout Sterne's novel.

The scene takes place in the back parlour downstairs, where, as had been agreed between the parents, the obstetrician was to sit with them when he arrived. The two brothers had been sitting in silence before the fire, on either side of the hearth, for an hour and a half. Toby goes back to the contemplation of a new pair of black-plush breeches he has on, until Walter cuts into his thoughts: "What can they be doing brother? [...]—we can scarce hear ourselves talk". Toby repeats his "I think", and will say it again for a third time thirty pages later, in Chapter VI of Volume 2, without giving us any hint of what he might be thinking.

Though the "cogito" was promoted in 1637, by another veteran, who fought in the Thirty Years' War, it's not Descartes's fault that Cartesians ignore his war traumas and reduce him to dualism.

Sterne wants to protect uncle Toby from such a fate and takes advantage of the interval afforded by the period of silence before the brothers resume their conversation to depict his character in an original way.

On the day Sterne is writing this, the 26th of March 1759, there is heavy rain between the hours of nine and ten in the morning. Sterne declares that this climate is responsible for the advancement of knowledge in England, in every field: physics, metaphysics, physiology, polemics, and the list goes on... all the way to obstetrics. Thanks to this awful weather, English comedies outwit French ones, "giving us something to make us merry when we cannot go outdoors". What do you think of that?

Without being a chauvinist, I find his enumeration to be a copy-and-paste of Rabelais.
And also of our *Encyclopedia*. Sterne says that if he is to judge by the advances of the past seven years, the knowledge brought by the Enlightenment would soon reach its "acme".

Indeed, thanks to cognitivism, behaviourism, systemism and genetics, all the secrets of the human mind will soon be revealed.
Sterne estimated that this *acme* would arrive thirty years later, in 1789, if my calculations are correct. According to him, this apogee would put an end to all writing and reading, and "we shall [...] be exactly where we started".

Well, Sterne was wrong. The end of reading and writing is happening now. Seriously, do you think he had foreseen the French and American revolutions?
I can't answer you now because I'm rushing to keep up with Sterne, who's making a U-turn back to the past: "But I forget my uncle Toby, whom all this while we have left knocking the ashes out of his tobacco pipe". It's time to depict his character, not in general terms, but by focusing on a particular trait, "his humour [...] which does honour to our atmosphere", in which there were "many strong lines [...] of a family likeness".

Does this have anything to do with Wittgenstein's[24] family resemblances?
Perhaps. Wittgenstein was very fond of Tristram Shandy and especially of Corporal Trim. Probably at ease in the Shandy family, in which "they were of an original character throughout; —[...] the males, —the females had no character at all, —except, indeed, my great-aunt DINAH" who, sixty years earlier, had married the coachman. This event still disturbed the cordial relation between the two brothers. "But nothing ever wrought with our family after the ordinary way".

Your Shandean analysis practices anamnesis, back to family history.

Captain Toby's post-traumatic stress disorder

As I told you, Shandean analysis starts with transference to the readers, but not to all of us: "...to [the inquisitive] I write, —and by them I shall be read, —if any such reading as this could be supposed to hold out [...] to the very end of the world".

This is why he speaks directly to me again: "My uncle TOBY SHANDY, madam, was a gentleman who, with the virtues which usually constitute the character of a man of honour and rectitude, —possessed [...] a most extreme and unparallel'd modesty of nature".

What does nature have to do here?

Sterne asks himself the same question, and erases the word since he can't decide what to do with it. But Toby's modesty was "not in regard to words, for he was so unhappy as to have very little choice in them, —but to things". It resembled the modesty of a woman, an "inward cleanliness of mind and fancy".... Please don't laugh! According to Sterne, "it makes our sex the awe of yours".

For once, he lacks foresight.

No matter, now he's speaking to me:

> You will imagine, madam, that my uncle Toby had contracted all this from this very source;—that he had spent a great part of his time in converse with your sex [...]. I wish I could say so, —for unless it was with his sister-in-law [...], my uncle Toby scarce exchanged three words with the sex in as many years.

Freud thought that life in the army promotes same-sex relationships.

On this point, Sterne departs from classical ùùùùùù interpretations and returns to Freud's original interest in trauma. Toby acquired this turn of mind as a result of a blow. "A blow"! he supposes I will exclaim. "—Yes, madam, it was owing to a blow from a stone" which almost killed him at the Siege of Namur in 1695—"a stone broke off by a ball from a parapet of horn-work, [and] struck full upon my uncle Toby's groin". The English editor, who takes me for a dunce, pointed out the sexual innuendo in "horn work".

He thought it clever to point out the repressed sexual signifier.

We'd better go over our history lessons. Namur had been in French hands since the victory in 1692, celebrated by Racine and Boileau. Three years later, the English reconquered the city with their Dutch and German allies. This is when the stone "struck full upon by uncle Toby", hitting his modesty as well, through the shame of having been left helplessly exposed, body and soul, to any curious gaze. Sterne says no more. "The story of that, madam, is long and interesting;—but it would be running my history all upon heaps to give it you here.—'Tis for an episode hereafter".

The victim doesn't give us his version of the story?

Sterne is not a fan of quick debriefing. The story of Toby's trauma will have to wait to be told in the context of his psychotherapy, described in the first chapter of Volume 2. For the moment, Sterne only gives us an illustration of the captain's modesty, "subtilized and rarified by the constant heat of a little family pride".

The captain can't bear to hear any mention of aunt Dinah's affair:

> The least hint of it was enough to make the blood fly into his face;—but when my father enlarged upon the story in mixed companies, which the illustration of his hypothesis frequently obliged him to do, —[this] would set my uncle Toby's honour and modesty o'bleeding; and he would often take my father aside [...] telling him he would give him anything in the world only to let the story rest. [...]

Of course, his brother insists.

There was a bit of sadism mixed with "the truest love and tenderness [...] that ever one brother bore towards another". Walter couldn't help it: aunt Dinah's affair excited him as much as "the retrogradation of the planets [excited] Copernicus". When he quoted the adage: *"Amicus Plato, sed magis amica veritas, Dinah was my aunt; but TRUTH is my sister"*, Toby would beg him to let her ashes sleep in peace. But his brother would scarce let a day pass without some hint at the affair: "—What is the character of a family to a hypothesis?" was Walter's reply.

Rather inhibited, our military man.

On the contrary, as you will see by his reaction, when Walter asserted coldly that "many thousands of [families] [...] every year are cast away"—as almost happened to Sterne's family, in his childhood, between the Isle of Skye and Ireland. On these occasions, "Toby would say, throwing himself back in his armchair and lifting up his hands, his eyes and one leg [...]— every such instance is downright MURDER". Then Walter would reply: "—'tis only DEATH, brother.—My uncle Toby would never [...] answer this by any other kind of argument than that of whistling [...] *Lillibullero*".

An Italian tune?

Lillibullero

You don't know this Irish ballad, set to music by Henry Purcell? I didn't know it either, until I met uncle Toby. In England, it spread throughout the country, becoming a popular song among city dwellers and country folk—"never did such a small thing have such a great effect", for it "sung a monarch out of three kingdoms". In 1641, the Irish Catholics adopted it as a war song during the massacre of Irish Protestants, who used it as a rallying cry to force James II into exile in France. Finally, the ballad was made into a hymn when stadholder William of Orange was enthroned.

For uncle Toby, this melody "was the usual channel thro' which his passions got vent", especially when he was shocked by the absurdity of "logical thinkers", like his brother. He would whistle *Lillibullero* when he had no other argument to offer.

We're back to Wittgenstein: "When the tool with the name is broken, a language-game has to be invented".[25]
This musical language-game allows the captain to counter his brother's intellectual onslaught with a new form of logic. Sterne suggests that to arguments *ex absurdo* and so on should be added the *argumentum fistulatorium* invented by Toby.

Children's songs have long made use of this type of argument. In 1712, at the Battle of Denain, Marshal de Villars's troops sang Auprès de ma blonde*; in 1754, during the Battle of Fontenoy, where the French invited the English to fire first, they sang* Trois jeunes tambours *and also* Malbrough's enva-t-en-guerre *to mock the Duke of Marlborough, the Commander of uncle Toby's army.*
You've brought back voices from long ago. I was ten and I can still hear my grandfather whistle an air just for me, with the virtuosity of men from the era before recordings. He had been in the Great War as a stretcher-bearer, "because I was in the music", he used to say. A few days before his death he asked for his trumpet, but had to do without it when he saw, as I did, the looks exchanged around him. So he whistled his *Lillibullero*, forever etched in my memory.

During the Falklands War, an Irish military surgeon Morgan O' Connell said that he used the musicians for their therapeutic talent during the long sea voyage and as stretcher-bearers during combat.
Why didn't I think of it sooner? I became a psychoanalyst to the tune of a *Lillibullero*. It was only sixty years later that I read the story of my grandfather's regiment in a book published in 1919, *La Division Barbot*, dedicated to the survivors. They were on every front. One of his favourite songs was *Le Régiment de Sambre et Meuse*—the confluence of the two rivers where uncle Toby received his wound. Speak of a Memoir of the Future!—the title of British psychoanalyst Wilfred Bion's book, written fifty years after his war experience.
Sterne does not want Tristram to come into the world before the novel tells the story of his father's war campaigns, a task he assigns to uncle Toby. The novel was to be the favourite book of the "glorious Viscount Ligonier", an officer who had taken part in the Vigo expedition, with Roger Sterne. When his friend's son visited him in June 1764, the eighty-four-year-old veteran told him that in his old age *Tristram Shandy* was the only book he enjoyed.
Sterne is proud of his *argumentum fistulatorium*, which allows him to lead us out of this impasse. "... it may be said by my children's children, when my head is laid to rest, —that their learned grandfather's head had been busied to as much purpose once as other people's:—that he had invented a name".

"There is an air for which I would give all Rossini, all Mozart, and all Weber...", *writes Gérard de Nerval, son of a surgeon in Napoleon's Army, whose wife followed him, leaving her baby behind. She died when Gérard was two, somewhere in Poland, where she was buried. I've lost the thread...*

Digressions

Don't worry if you feel lost as Sterne displays his mastery at digression. Right now, he explains his situation as follows:

> I was just going [...] to have given you the great outlines of my uncle Toby's most whimsical character, —when my aunt Dinah and the coachman came across us and led us a vagary some millions of miles into the very heart of the planetary system.

Specifically to "the backsliding of Venus in her orbit [...] and the backsliding of my aunt Dinah in her orbit", causing her to find herself with child and to marry the coachman.

What of it? We're in the 18th century, aren't we?
   More precisely in the 17th century, since aunt Dina lived sixty years earlier. Speaking of planets, Sterne might have presented uncle Toby's character from the perspective of Sirius, as Voltaire did in *Micromégas*—but he preferred to draw his portrait in small strokes, rendering him familiar to us little by little, so that "we are much better acquainted with him than we were before".

A forerunner of the Impressionists.
   Rather a proponent of the theory of chaos, when he asserts: "I believe the greatest of our boasted improvements and discoveries have come from some [...] trifling hints". Moreover, "the machinery of his work" is opposed to that of classical mechanics: "My work is digressive and it is progressive too, —and at the same time. This, sir, is a very different story from that of the earth's moving round her axis".
   This is why digressions are:

> the sunshine [...], the life, the soul of reading;—take them out of this book for instance, —you might as well take the book along with them;— one cold eternal winter would reign in every page of it; restore them to the writer;—he steps forth like a bridegroom, —bids 'All hail', brings in a variety and forbids the appetite to fail.

Still, this art requires great skill. "If [the author] begins a digression, [...] his whole work stands stock still—and if he goes on with his main work, — then there is an end of his digression".

Another kôan. What's the solution?

Hard labour which Sterne performs through two opposite motions: "the digressive and progressive, one wheel within the other, so that the whole machine [...] has been kept a-going"—the machine of body and spirit, his fountain of health which should provide him with forty more years in which to finish his work.

In 1799 he would have been eighty-six years old.

The Hobby Horse

This prospect lightens his mood. He starts the next chapter with "the wish to write nonsensically", and invokes the God of laughter, Momus, who, according to Lucian of Samosata, criticised Hephaestus for not placing a window in man's breast through which to see his thoughts.

Today, this is possible thanks to brain imaging. Through a confocal micro-scope, I saw with my own eyes synapses stretching their claws towards some protein. But I could not detect the psyche yet.

Sterne imagines the soul to be like a beehive that we could observe, thanks to "one fine transparent body of clear glass". But in the end, he forgoes all "mechanical help" in drawing uncle Toby's portrait and nor does he rely on a "camera": the word is actually written in Chapter 23.

A positron camera?

It doesn't matter, since he won't use one. He prefers his own device: "in a word, I will draw my uncle Toby's character from his HOBBY-HORSE". I surmise that the nephew's life and opinions are grounded in his uncle's tool for survival.

You mean, in the intergenerational transmission of trauma.

Not so fast! Let us follow Sterne's user guide. "If I was not morally sure that the reader must be out of all patience [...], —I would here previously have convinced him that there is no instrument so fit to draw my uncle Toby's character".

Instructions for use: the hobby horse acts like an electrified body:

> by means of the heated parts of the rider, which come immediately into contact with the back of the HOBBY-HORSE [...], the body of the rider is at length fill'd as full of HOBBY-HORSICAL matter as it can hold. [...] Now, the HOBBY-HORSE which my uncle Toby always rode upon was, in my opinion, a HOBBY-HORSE well worth giving a description of, if it was only upon the score of his great singularity.

But first, we should learn how it was acquired.

Its origin is revealed during Toby's psychotherapy for physical and psy-chic trauma. Let me remind you of the circumstances. He was wounded in the groin at the Siege of Namur in 1695 and was sent back to London, where he was bedridden in his brother's house for four years, "suffering unspeakable miseries owing to a succession of exfoliations from the *os pubis* and [...] the *os ileum*, —both which bones were dismally crush'd as much by the irregularity of the stone [...] as by its size". Note the clinical precision.

Sterne probably saw wounded soldiers in his childhood, as you may have in the first two years of your life, which you spent in a combat zone.

I have no memory of it, although I recently learned that the hospital where I was born was full of wounded and dead people. Toby had the good fortune of being welcomed into his brother's home in London, where Walter was setting up his business. He gave him the best room, had him treated by a doctor and provided moral support:

> he would never suffer a friend or an acquaintance to step into the house on any occasion but he would take him by the hand and lead him upstairs to see his brother Toby and chat an hour by his bedside.

Walter knew that "[the] history of a soldier's wound beguiles the pain of it". The visitors thought so too.

This is the passage where you found the principles of war psychiatry, long before they were formulated by Thomas Salmon in 1917.

Not quite, since things did not go as expected. At first, the patient felt great relief, but little by little these conversations brought him "some unforeseen perplexities which [...] retarded his cure greatly". The more Toby told his story, the worse his wound got.

Talking is helpful, but sometimes the symptoms worsen; we learned about these negative therapeutic reactions in our own practice.

Toby was plagued by such reactions. "These conversations were infinitely kind; [but] if he had not hit upon an expedient to extricate himself out of them, I verily believe they would have laid him in his grave". Sterne challenges you to discover what this expedient might be.

Let us begin with the word "expedient", which translates the Greek word Poros used by Socrates when quoting Diotima's discourse in the Symposium. Poros is Eros's father; his mother is Penia, poverty. In fact, Poros means "passage". Thus, Toby found a passage to extricate himself from the impasse of traumatic revivals. I would like to know more about it.

Sterne, who has read the *Symposium*, sees this as the key to Toby's psychotherapy, presented in the second volume. But he leaves us in suspense:

If you could [guess], —I should blush; not as a relation, —not as a man, —not even as a woman, —but I should blush as an author [...]. And in this, sir, I am of so nice and singular humour that if I thought you was able to form the least judgement or probable conjecture to yourself of what was to come in the next page, —I would tear it out of my book.

Shall we stop here for now? Thanks to our dialogue, I'll be able to continue on my own.

Notes

1 Sterne, L., *The Life and Opinions of Tristram Shandy, Gentleman,* New York, London: Norton, 1980.
2 Ross, I. C., *Laurence Sterne: A Life,* Oxford University Press, 2001.
3 Swift, J., *A Tale of a Tub and Other Works,* Section IX, Oxford University Press, 2008.
4 Pergaud, L., *The War of the Buttons,* New York: Walker and Co., 1968.
5 De Cervantes, M., *Don Quixote,* Ormsby, J. (Trans.). San Diego: Canterbury Classics/Baker & Taylor, 2013.
6 Sterne, L., *A Sentimental Journey through France and Italy,* London: Penguin Classics, 1967.
7 Arendt, H., *Rahel Varnhagen: The Life of a Jewess,* Baltimore: Johns Hopkins University Press, 2000.
8 Felman, S. and Laub, D., *Testimony. Crisis of Witnessing in Literature, Psychoanalysis and History, New York and London:* Routledge, 1992.
9 Wittgenstein, L. *Remarks on Frazer's Golden Bough,* in Wittgenstein, *Sources and Perspectives,* Ithaca, NY: Cornell University Press, 1987, p. 71.
10 In *Tristram Shandy,* Sterne introduced typographical novelties such as hyphens of variable lengths or black pages and marbled pages, which were part of his exploration of the limits of the novelistic genre, and would later inspire James Joyce and Georges Perec, among many others.
11 Lin-Chi . *The Zen Teachings of Master Lin-Chi,* Watson, R. (Trans.), New York: Columbia University Press, 1999.
12 Shay, J. *Achilles in Vietnam,* New York: Touchstone, 1995.
13 Caruth, C. *Literature in the Ashes of History,* Baltimore: Johns Hopkins University Press, 2015.
14 In Volume 3 of *Tristram Shandy.*
15 French term for hobby horse.
16 Musil, R. *The Man Without Qualities,* New York: Alfred A. Knopf, 1995.
17 Lin-Chi, *The Zen Teachings of Master Lin-Chi,* op. cit.
18 Davoine, F. *Wittgenstein's Folly,* Hurst, W. J. (Trans.), New York: YBK Publishers, 2012.
19 In French in the original.
20 In French in the original.
21 Arendt, H. Totalitarianism. In: *The Origins of Totalitarianism,* Cleveland: The World Publishing Company, 1951.
22 Ross, I. C., *Laurence Sterne: A Life,* op. cit., p. 110.
23 In French in the original.
24 Wittgenstein, L. *Philosophical Investigations,* London: Wiley-Blackwell, 1978.
25 Wittgenstein, L., *Philosophical Investigations,* op. cit.

2

Psychotherapy of Uncle Toby's war traumas and the reading of a sermon on perversion

Did you ever read such a book as *Tristram Shandy*? "Don't answer me rashly—because many, I know, quote the book, who have not read it—and many have read it who understand it not".[1] Sterne's question about John Locke's *Essay upon the Human Understanding* applies to his own book, which I view through the prism of Shandean psychoanalysis of madness and trauma. I read it after having written two books in which I presented *Don Quixote*[1] as the best textbook on the analysis of madness and after I learned that it had been Sterne's wish to write a *Don Quixote* of the 18th century. I did not yet know about Sterne's huge success in Paris in the middle of that century. In fact, he inspired Diderot to write *Jacques the Fatalist and His Master.*

Shandean psychoanalysis lives up to Sterne's master, Cervantes. It displays an art of transference specific to the sphere of war traumas, in which 20th-century analysts of madness received their training, at a time when transference in a context of psychosis was considered impossible. To show the extent to which Sterne paved the way, I quote him abundantly, and I refer to Cervantes each time Sterne gives me the chance, throughout the nine volumes of the novel.

While Shandean analysis started in Volume 1 with Tristram's prenatal analysis described in that volume, Volume 2 starts with Toby's psychotherapy after he is wounded in battle. The captain's psychotherapy relies on his Sancho Panza, "his man", corporal Trim; it involves the use of a map, has recourse to war games that might have inspired Winnicott, presents a sermon on perversion—Wittgenstein's favourite passage—and ends with a discussion on the possible location of the psyche in the brain.

Reading Sterne's novel is not so easy, since we often lose the thread of the narrative. I am reminded of my own way of working when time is suspended, remaining locked in traumatic revivals that create an eternal present, making classical psychoanalysis fail. Indeed, at critical moments in an analysis when we are back to square one, we are faced with a lawless agency for whom the other does not exist. The assurance of truth collapses, as does the symbolic order; time stops because its flow cannot be marked. What is

DOI: 10.4324/9781003224907-2

required then is a new bond of trust created through a chance encounter with elements of the analyst's history, since causality, which needs the past of the cause and the future of the effect, does not function without the flow of time.

Such interference gives rise to criticism in mainstream institutions, as Sterne found out when he defied established practice, interrupting his narrative whenever he saw fit, to inform the reader of his blunders and his writer's block and to ask for his help. I was willing to offer mine so that I might have his at critical moments in my work with madness and trauma, when the unconscious is not repressed in the past, but manifests in the present. Freud himself described this in his commentary of Wilhelm Jensen's *Gradiva*,[2] the story of the healing of a delusional young man fascinated by the catastrophe of Pompeii with its arrested time.

Analytic psychotherapy of an 18th-century war trauma

A Shandean Psychoanalysis is an account of my conversation with Laurence Sterne, undertaken in response to his invitation[3]:

> Writing, when properly managed [...], is but a different name for conversation: as no one who knows what he is about in good company would venture to talk all [...]: the truest respect which you can pay to the reader's understanding is to halve this matter amicably and leave him something to imagine in his turn, as well as yourself.

My imagination is set in motion by Sterne's art of transference displayed in different therapeutic situations. First is in his relation to the reader, whom he constantly addresses directly. In Volume 1, I felt directly concerned by the prenatal psychoanalysis of Tristram's "homunculus", who speaks in the very first sentence: "I wish my father or my mother [...] had minded what they were about when they begot me".

Tristram heard the story of his conception from a traumatised war veteran, his uncle Toby. This story brought to mind the time when my mother, pregnant with me, spent a period of her pregnancy at the end of 1942 and the beginning of 1943 imprisoned by the Nazis. Like Tristram, I wish that my parents had paid more attention to the timing of my conception.

And I am not the only one to speak from the viewpoint of the embryo. Carlos Fuentes lets Cristobal's embryo speak in his novel *Christopher Unborn*.[4] Psychoanalyst Wilfred Bion also invites his germ cells called "Somites" to speak in *A Memoir of the Future*,[5] written during his exile in Los Angeles when he was over 70. These Somites engage in a dialogue with versions of himself at other ages of his life, especially with *Captain* Bion, his army rank at the age of twenty in World War I. Bion defines as "psychotic transference" the moment when sensorial survival reactions are able to connect to language, thought and time.

Thus, Tristram's prenatal analysis could not have taken place without the transference tying him to his uncle *Captain* Shandy, the only person who really takes care of him throughout the novel. The captain felt he owed him the truth not only about his conception—which he learned from his brother Walter, Tristram's father—but also about his birth, recounted in Volume 3—both rendered near-failures by the conflict between his parents.

The value placed on truth allows Toby to escape certain death after being severely injured at the 1665 Siege of Namur—where the English, led by the Duke of Marlborough, triumphed over Louis XIV's troops in the War of the Spanish Succession. The captain recovers, thanks to a psychotherapy which reveals the truth about the battle.

Failure of mainstream psychoanalysis[6]

"Go and speak to someone", victims of trauma are told. But retelling what happened in psychotherapy or in debriefing sessions often provokes traumatic revivals in the present, since time has stopped at the instant of the trauma. This is what happened to the captain.

Injured in the groin, Toby was taken from Namur to his brother's home in London, for he "could nowhere be so well nursed and taken care of as in [Walter's] house". He spent four years there, the first without being able to move. Walter encouraged him to speak:

> And what was a much more sincere mark of his affection still, he would never suffer a friend or an acquaintance to step into the house on any occasion but he would [...] lead him upstairs to see his brother Toby and chat an hour by his bedside. The history of a soldier's wound beguiles the pain of it;—my uncle's visitors at least thought so [...]. These conversations were infinitely kind; and my uncle Toby received great relief from them.[7]

The virtues of the talking cure have been known since antiquity as have its paradoxical effects. Although Toby received great relief from talking with his visitors, their compassion put him "out of his wits" and his wound worsened. This wound, the only witness to the battle while he lay unconscious, bleeds and becomes infected when he is once again exposed, defenceless, to the scrutiny of others. This unconscious memory of the body—which "keeps the score", as Bessel Van der Kolke[8] says—wreaks havoc with his mind, which tries to remember in the past, while his body reacts in the present to a threat to his life. "... the many perplexities he was in arose out of the almost insurmountable difficulties he found in telling his story intelligibly".

This is what even the best-intentioned psychotherapists find discouraging. Lying on his bed, as he had lain on the stretcher when he was evacuated, Toby cannot see the enemy and loses all notion of time. Words become hollow, since his visitors are completely unfamiliar with terms like scarp and counterscarp, glacis, covered way and ravelin. So, "my uncle Toby did oft times puzzle his visitors; and sometimes himself too". Is army jargon to be blamed for these perplexities? Sterne rejects this explanation. The difficulty does not lie in a lack of education or unsuitable terminology, but in the visitors' well-meaning but dispassionate interest.

Having fought in World War I, Wittgenstein was of the same opinion during the decade he spent in Vienna, where he abandoned philosophy after returning in a post-traumatic state from the Austrian front and from his year-long captivity in Monte Cassino. Back in Cambridge in 1929, he took up philosophy again "as a therapy", to ask what must be done "when the tools with the names are broken".[9] The tool with the name breaks in a situation of extreme danger when the other disappears. Yet, Toby's visitors are present. Today, psychoanalysts say: "I am listening", and listen for what has been repressed, without paying attention to suppressed traumatic memory coming back through images of things or to words left out of a spoken exchange.

Another captain, William Rivers[10]—a neurologist and anthropologist drafted in 1915 to work with traumatised English officers at Craiglockardt in Scotland—distinguished between repression and suppression, after reading Freud and modifying his technique, as he discovered another mode of transference. Novelist Pat Barker brought him to life in her Trilogy,[11] based on his clinical and ethnographic notes. When one of his patients, rendered mute after seeing his buddy die in an explosion, finally starts to speak, he asks his analyst about his stuttering in stressful situations. Rivers suggests that they change places and questions himself earnestly about what happened to him at the age of five, when he started to stutter.

Like uncle Toby, captain Rivers deals with war traumas and at the same time with a terrorised child, himself, as it happens. At age five, he had his first haircut and got into a fit of anger at the barber shop. When they returned home, his father forced him to look at a painting showing the amputation, on a ship, performed on a young seaman called William Rivers like him— an ancestor who killed Admiral Nelson's assassin on the *Victory* at the Battle of Trafalgar. As they looked at the painting, the boy's father said: "Look at him, he didn't make a sound". Thanks to his patient, Rivers discovered that his symptom was also a resource which prompted him to help other warriors break through their silence.

Unless such transference takes place, solitude is absolute. To survive, our reptilian brain—common to all mammals—dissociates from the neocortex, which gives access to language and to time perception. Toby relives in the present the danger he faced and is afraid he will look like a moron, unable to express himself logically:

> [...] the ground was cut and cross-cut with such a multitude of dykes, drains, rivulets and sluices on all sides —, and he would get so sadly bewilder'd and set fast amongst them, [...] and was oft times obliged to give up the attack upon that very account only. These perplexing rebuffs gave my uncle Toby Shandy more perturbations than you would imagine; and as my father's kindness to him was continually dragging up fresh friends and fresh enquirers, — he had but a very uneasy task of it. No doubt my uncle Toby had great command of himself [...]; — yet anyone may imagine that when he could not [...] get out of the covered way without falling down the counterscarp [...], he must have fretted and fumed inwardly.

Dredging up the past at the victim's bedside worsens his state by triggering regression. Sterne is a child of war, familiar with the psychic wounds of his father, ensign Roger Sterne. To better understand them, he has read Hippocrates and Dr. James Mackenzie, who describe the influence of the passions of the mind on digestion, and he asks: "Why not [on] a wound as well as [on] a dinner"? Had he read Claude Barrois,[12] psychoanalyst and head of psychiatry at the Val de Grâce military hospital in Paris, as well as Jonathan Shay,[13] psychiatrist at the Veterans' Clinic in Boston, he would have discovered the connection they both make between the "paroxystic exacerbation" of wounds and "betrayal by one's command" or by civilians, who have no idea what war is like.

Having gone to war, Wilfred Bion[14] knows about "thoughts without a thinker", when "words become things", when there is no "other" to claim them. He writes that at such times, "thoughts are things, things are thoughts, and they have personality". He also speaks of "thoughts-without-a-thinker in search of a thinker" to think them. For Toby, the word "wound" calls up the "sound" of the falling stone and reactivates the imminence of death: "My uncle Toby could not philosophize upon it;—'twas enough he felt it was so, —and having sustained the pain and sorrow of it for three months together, he was resolved some way or other to extricate himself".

The link between sensations that invade the present and the words that set time in motion again is created by using an eloquent map.

Map of the citadel of Namur

Wittgenstein faced the same impasse when he concluded his *Tractatus Logico-Philosophicus*, written on the Eastern front, with the words: "Whereof one cannot speak, thereof one must be silent". After his return to Cambridge, he changed his formulation. In his *Philosophical Investigations*,[15]

the sentence became: "Whereof one cannot speak, one cannot help showing what is silenced"; he called this "an ostensive definition". In 1936, Wittgenstein told his Irish student Maurice O'Drury,[16] whom he encouraged to
study medicine instead of philosophy: "Now a book I like greatly is *Tristram
Shandy*. That is one of my favourite books. [...] I am particularly fond of
the character of Corporal Trim in *Tristram Shandy*, and especially of the
sermon he read out"—at the end of Volume 2.

To come out of the silence where he tends to take refuge, Toby turns to
Trim, "his man". They have the idea of displaying a map of the Citadel of
Namur on the wall. I recommend his solution to analysts who work with disturbed children coming from foreign countries: "Show them a map of their
country; it will name places familiar to their parents, of which they cannot
speak". This advice goes for our native populations as well.

Many maps of a territory stretching from the Baltic States to the Ukraine
are displayed in historian Timothy Snyder's book *Bloodlands*,[17] on which 14
million civilians were massacred between 1933 and 1945 by Stalin and Hit-
ler. For their descendants, who emigrated to faraway countries, these maps
rescue from oblivion the homelands of their vanished ancestors, "each of
whom died a unique death".

Toby is trying to rescue from oblivion the stranger he has become to himself. One morning, while lying on his back:

> the anguish and nature of the wound upon his groin suffering him to lie
> in no other position, [...] a thought came into his head that if he could
> purchase, and [paste] down upon a board, a large map of the fortifica-
> tions of the town and citadel of Namur with its environs, it might be a
> means of giving him ease.

He could then show the military attacks made by the English and the
French, "— the gallantry of the French officers, who exposed themselves
upon the glacis sword in hand"—during the siege between the gate of
St. Nicolas and St. Roch. For never in his four-year confinement had my
uncle been able to describe to anyone "the principal attack of which [he] was
eye-witness at Namur".

This map constitutes an initial form of alterity and gives a third dimension to the event that flattened him under the stone. Toby takes heart when
he anticipates being able to stick a pin on the spot where he was standing at
the foot of St. Roch church just before being pinned to the ground, helpless,
like an insect exposed to scrutiny. On the contrary, the pin will allow an
"ostensive definition". When asked: "Where were you wounded?", he can
answer: "Here", pointing to a place everyone can see.

The transference to the map is made possible by Corporal Trim, who
brings it and hangs it on the bedroom wall, to contribute to Toby's recovery.
Its effect on the captain is spectacular: he regains his eloquence and is able

to recount clearly the details of the occurrence "where he had the honour to receive his wound".

"All this succeeded to his wishes, and not only freed him from a world of sad explanations, but, in the end, it prov'd the happy means, as you will read, of procuring my uncle Toby his HOBBY-HORSE".

Two analytic techniques have been presented here successively. The first had Toby lying down for a year, like a patient on a couch. The second allowed him to regain self-esteem and discover his hobby horse that Winnicott would call "transitional object".

During World War II, a similar event took place on a Pacific island.

Psychoanalysis of a battle[18]

Island Victory, a book published after World War II by Lieutenant Colonel Marshall, describes "how the truth of battle is found". The story takes place in 1944 on Kwajelein Atoll in the Marshall Islands, where war is raging. The author, an officer and military historian, had the same idea as Toby to help the men recover from the hell of the victory wrested from the Japanese.

Convinced that all those who fought wanted the truth about the battle to be revealed, he pasted a map of the island on the wall, "so they could find their bearings in the impenetrable night of combat". In the course of four days of six-hour a day meetings, they were amazed to discover that many events of the battle could be recalled. The facts lying dormant in each man's mind were waiting for the testimony of other men to come to light. Marshall writes: "All of them are equally good witnesses", regardless of rank, failure or success. They have a common aim: to stand up and speak, to correct or complete what the others have said. A blackboard was placed beside the map, so that each man could indicate his position during the battle and connect what he felt with what the others had said.

Traumatic memory proved to be, as they all saw, "strangely precise and indispensable" to their companions. Until then, none of the soldiers had been able to understand the personal role he had played, since he had not been able to relate his part to anything else. He knew, like Toby, what he had done and felt, but rarely remembered what he had said in the thick of battle. Only the soldier who heard him could recall his words and let him know. Second-hand information was only mentioned if it came from buddies who had died or were severely wounded.

The book was interspersed with maps and names, which would otherwise remain stuck in traumatic revivals. A man who thought he had fatally wounded his companion learned that his comrade was alive. Another soldier, hidden in the bushes not far from his fallen buddy's corpse, thought his last hour had come when Japanese soldiers appeared and stopped nearby, but only to perform a ritual on the body, covering it with branches and saying a prayer. The most fearful of the men was seen rushing forth under machine gun fire to pull a wounded man to safety.

Still, can we call this dialogue, conducted with the helpful intervention of a map psychoanalysis, without provoking indignation among established institutions? Sterne does not let us ponder the question, since he brings the narration of Toby's psychotherapy to an abrupt end. As we have seen, he has a knack for interrupting the narrative to talk about himself. I don't blame him because I do the same thing, especially at critical moments, in spite of orthodox recommendations to keep my mouth shut. Indeed, one day a patient who had, at different times, been Satan and Mother Earth, and who, after our work together had gone on to live her life without medication for several years, told me: "Your theories were not what interested me most; it was, rather, the fragments of your own story that you sometimes told". I don't dare talk about this too much, for fear of angering the Critics.

Critics![19]

The church hierarchy was extremely critical of Sterne when it became known that, after the immediate success of the first two volumes published in London in 1760, the author of *Tristram Shandy* was a parson. The freedom of his style was unacceptable. What was Sterne to do in the face of such fierce attacks? Let us read this passage and take a lesson from it:

> I guard against...leaving them out of the part. [...] I have left half a dozen places purposely open for them; — and [...] I pay them all court, —Gentlemen, I kiss your hands, — I protest no company could give me half the pleasure, —by my soul I am glad to see you, —I beg only you will make no strangers of yourselves, but sit down without any ceremony and fall on heartily. [One of them sets to:] —How, in the name of wonder! Could your uncle Toby, who, it seems, was a military man, and whom you have represented as no fool, — be at the same time such a confused, [...] muddle-headed fellow [...]. —So, Sir Critic, [...]. 'Tis language unurbane —and only befitting the man who cannot give clear and satisfactory accounts of things or dive deep enough into the first causes of human ignorance and confusion.

The analyst who has no idea of the traumatic origins of human confusion is advised to consult one of Freud's predecessors:

> Pray, sir, [...] did you ever read such a book as Locke's *Essay upon the Human Understanding?*—Don't answer me rashly, because many, I know, quote the book who have not read it, —and many have read it who understand it not: [...]—as I write to instruct, I will tell you in

three words what the book is.—IT IS A HISTORY. [The critic takes the bait.] —A history! of who? what? where? —Don't hurry yourself. It is a history book, sir [...] of what passes in a man's own mind; and if you will say so much of the book and no more, believe me, you will cut no contemptible figure in a metaphysic circle.

Sterne leaves Locke[20] for the moment, to quote Plato's *Theaetetus*,[21] where Socrates compares the mind with more or less soft wax on which the impressions received through the senses are imprinted. Psyches that are too hard, retain no impression, while those that are too soft let everything be imprinted on them. But Toby is neither one nor the other. Sterne wants "to shew the world" that his confusion did not arise from a cognitive or psychic pathology.

"[...despite the discourse] in the SCHOOLS of the learned, 'twas not by ideas, — by Heaven! his life was put in jeopardy by words".

This assertion makes me want to show off in some psychoanalytic SCHOOL by telling Toby's story. After all, psychoanalysis also uses military terms: defence, resistance, attacks on linking and so on. But I hesitate for fear of increasing the captain's humiliation, should his words be taken for signifiers of repressed sexual desire, with fantasies of impotence and castration related to his groin injury. Foreseeing such interpretations, Sterne defends the vocabulary of ensign, Robert Sterne, his father:

> What confusion in greater THEATRES from words of little meaning and as indeterminate a sense;—when thou considers this, thou wilt not wonder at my uncle Toby's perplexities, —thou wilt drop a tear of pity upon his scarp and his counterscarp;—his glacis and his covered way;— his ravelin and his half-moon.

The captain's words are now connected to his physical survival response, but his psychotherapy has just started and will have the ups and downs that are to be expected.

Manic Phase[22]

First, the patient became "master of his subject [...] able to talk upon it without emotion", but this state of balance did not last. Soon, he was gripped by a "desire of knowledge" resembling a manic episode. For the moment, Trim's role is to obtain the books Toby devours in a fortnight, with the same thirst as that of Don Quixote for books on chivalry:

> The more my uncle Toby pored over his map, the more he took a liking to it;—by the same process and electrical assimilation, as I told you, thro' which I ween the souls of connaisseurs themselves, by long friction

and incubation, have the happiness, at length, to get all be-virtu'd, —
be-*pictur'd*, —be-*butterflied* and be-*fiddl'd*.

I understand him well. My first hobby horse during the war, in a combat
zone in Savoie, was a book I found in an attic. I was told that I took it
everywhere with me, calling it "my bada". It was a colouring book published
in 1944, with a bright red cover, whose drawings, scribbled over furiously,
depicted Don Quixote and Robinson Crusoe's adventures. One "bada" led
to another, and finally to *Tristram Shandy*, who left me "all shandied".

In Toby's case, as "the desire of knowledge, like the thirst of riches,
increases ever with the acquisition of it", he undertook to study geometry
and ballistics, in order to calculate the path taken by the stone to reach his
groin; he also studied physics, projective geometry, map-making, mathe-
matics and history. Two months later, he was able to recount eloquently the
attack on the counterscarp, "to cross the Maas and Sambre", and even to
analyse all possible attacks knowledgeably:

> [...] before the first year of his confinement had well gone round, there
> was scarce a fortified town in Italy or Flanders of which [...] he had not
> procured a plan, reading over [...] and carefully collating therewith the
> histories of their sieges, their demolitions, their improvements [...], all
> which he would read with that intense application and delight that he
> would forget himself, his wound, his confinement, his dinner.

We are well acquainted with such enthusiasm. Many an analyst has thrown
himself with delight into the study of topology, the theory of knots, Freudo-
Marxism and even the Mandarin language, without making the psychoanalysis of trauma advance in the least.

In the second year, Toby buys books on military architecture by Maréchal
Vauban, Monsieur Blondel, Stevinus and the Count of Pagan in an "endless
Search of Truth"!

In the third year, Toby runs into an impasse. In August 1699, time comes
to a standstill again. When he discovers that the fatal trajectory is not a
straight line, but rather a PARABOLA—or else a HYPERBOLA—he
undertakes the study of conic sections as well as the geometry of Galileo
and Torricelli until the reviviscence of his trauma catches up with him.

Sterne's compassion for him is as great as that Don Quixote would have
deserved when the barber and the priest invaded his library to burn his
books.[23] Sterne identifies with the captain.

In 1759, when the self-published anonymous edition of the first two volumes of *Tristram Shandy* came out in York, copies of Sterne's comic novel *A
Political Romance* were burned at the request of the Archbishop of York. We
see looming on the horizon the Inquisition's burning at the stake appearing
in the second *Don Quixote*, and soon in this Volume we are reading in the

sermon to be read by Trim. Foreseeing imminent regression, the author tries to stop his hero:

> —stop! my dear uncle Toby, —stop!—go not one foot further into this thorny and bewilder'd track, —intricate are the steps! Intricate are the mazes of this labyrinth! Intricate are the troubles which the pursuit of this bewitching phantom, KNOWLEDGE, will bring upon thee. —O my uncle! fly—fly from it as from a serpent.—Is it fit, good-natur'd man! thou shouldst sit up, with the wound upon thy groin [...]? Alas! 'twill exasperate thy symptoms, —check thy perspirations, —evaporate thy spirits, —waste thy animal strength, [...]—and hasten all the infirmities of thy old age.

What happened to make Toby's symptoms flare up again? His physiological reactions are described by military psychologist Dave Grossman in his book *On Combat*,[24] after he observed them in men who had come face to face with death.

"He looks tired and pale, he suffers from constipation, stomach pain, backache, sore throat, narrowing of the arteries, insomnia; his blood boils, the humidity of his body dries up".

Something similar occurs in an analysis when we explore the past but neglect the interaction in the present of the session. The setback, which is always unexpected, occurs when the patient is doing better. It is as if the lawless agency he is fighting takes advantage of this respite to attack again. Sterne can only exclaim: "O my uncle! my uncle Toby". This is not an expression of helplessness, but is inserted:

> for the sake of letting the apostrophe cool, [since] the best plain narrative in the world, tack'd very close to the last spirited apostrophe to my uncle Toby, —would have felt both cold and vapid upon the reader's palate, —therefore I forthwith put an end to the chapter.

Sterne refuses to diagnose Toby's ups and downs, to which he is subject himself, as pathology, seeing them rather as the source of his creativity. Nothing resembles a demolition site more than a construction site.

Negative therapeutic reaction[25]

This paradox has been known since the Middle Ages, when madness was recognised as "*engin* – from the latin *ingenium,* intelligence, rather than *destin,* fate". In the 19th century, President Lincoln's melancholic episodes[26] were fertile ground for daring decisions, such as the 1864 amendment abolishing slavery, a position strongly supported by Sterne, as we shall see in Volume 9.

Toby's discouragement is followed by a new phase of enthusiasm and then by a negative therapeutic reaction. At the end of the third year, he abandons the study of ballistics and returns to his initial interest: the practical aspects of fortifications. Sterne's analysis of his symptoms should be included in training manuals, to replace the discourse on the unforgiving cycle of bipolarity. He compares the "excessive pleasure" Toby experiences to "a spring held back, [which] returned upon him with redoubled force".

This time, Toby is unrecognisable; his rebellious attitude worries those around him. He regresses with lightning speed. He sighs deeply, complains to his brother, is impatient with the surgeon, criticises the protracted duration of his treatment:

> [...] my uncle began to break in upon the daily regularity of a clean shirt, —to dismiss his barber unshaven—and to allow his surgeon scarce time sufficient to dress his wound, [...] when, lo!—all of a sudden, [...] he began to sigh heavily for his recovery, —[...] grew impatient with the surgeon;—[...] expostulate[d] with him upon the protraction of his cure, [...]—he dwelt long upon the miseries he had undergone and the sorrows of his four years' melancholy imprisonment;—adding that, had it not been for the kind looks and fraternal cheerings of the best of brothers, —he had long since sunk under his misfortunes. [...]—My uncle Toby, by nature, was not eloquent [...];—he had never once dropp'd one fretful or discontented word [...].—We lose the right of complaining sometimes by forbearing it [...]: the surgeon was astonished [...] when he heard my uncle Toby go on and peremptorily insist upon his healing up the wound directly, —or sending for Monsieur Roujat, the King's Serjeant Surgeon...

This unexpected tirade brought tears to Walter's eyes. The doctor was flabbergasted. Ever since the Middle Ages,[27] in these circumstances the medical decision has been the blow on the head—a method rendered less brutal today by the use of chemicals and electricity under anaesthesia. Even in those days, Folly took refuge in literature where she entered the "space of the marvel", where her hobby horse could gallop freely, since episodes of "madness", as Cathy Caruth says, are life crises.[28] Sterne agrees with her:

> The desire of life and health is implanted in man's nature; — the love of liberty and enlargement is a sister passion to it [...]; — but I have told you before that nothing wrought with our family after the common way. [...] [Toby's] hobby-horse [grew] headstrong. When a man gives himself up to the government of a ruling passion, — [...] farewell to cool reason and fair discretion! [...] The succession of his ideas was now rapid [...] — and so, [he stopped] consulting further with any soul living.

The surgeon did what he could and said the wound would be dried up in six weeks, for it had miraculously started to heal well. But too late! Trim steps in to act as a wise *therapon*—the second in combat in *The Iliad*—and helps his master organise his get-away. What triggered this decision? Sterne describes the critical moment in analysis of trauma and madness when the patient rejects his analyst's theories: "The reason, or rather the rise, of this sudden demigration, was as follows". More and more agitated, Toby accidentally threw down the books and instruments piled on the table. Reaching for his tobacco box, he threw down his compass, with his sleeve he caused his case of instruments to fall and, trying to catch it, he threw Monsieur Blondel and Count of Pagan off the table. Unable to pick them up because of his wound, he rang for Trim:

> Trim! [...] prithee see what confusion I have here been making.—I must have some better contrivance, Trim. Canst not thou take my rule and measure the length and breadth of this table, and then go and bespeak me one as big again?

The corporal hastens to carry this out immediately, anticipating the principles of Thomas Salmon's "forward psychiatry".

In 1917, Thomas Salmon was sent to the front by the American army which was about to enter the war; his mission was to bring back recommendations serving to prevent psychic casualties. Salmon was not a military man; he had been a physician on Ellis Island, where he showed therapeutic skill in dealing with immigrants with mental illness. After a visit to England, no doubt inspired by William Rivers, he formulated his famous principles, which he subsequently applied in France, on the frontline in the Vosges, when he was drafted by the American army.

Salmon's four principles, "proximity, immediacy, expectancy and simplicity", are followed by two corollaries: do not diagnose and do not prescribe long-term medication. These principles, we came to see, express clearly the function of transference in a context of madness and trauma.

The Salmon principles[29]

Immediacy: Trim suggests to his master that it is high time for him to leave behind brotherly, friendly, medical and bookish discourses in the *Expectancy* of putting an end to recurrent reviviscences.

"I hope Your Honour will be soon well enough to get down to your country seat, where —as Your Honour takes so much pleasure in fortification, we could manage this matter to a T".

Sterne deems it important to inform us of their *Proximity*. The corporal, whose real name is James Butler, served in Toby's regiment. His nickname

Trim means orderly, and his multiple talents bring to mind *The Servant of Two Masters* by their contemporary Carlo Goldoni[30]:

> [...] my uncle Toby [...] would never call him by any other name. [...] The poor fellow had been disabled for the service by a wound on his left knee by a musket bullet at the Battle of Landen [in 1963], which was two years before the affair of Namur;—and as the fellow was well beloved in the regiment, and a handy fellow into the bargain, my uncle Toby took him [...] as valet, groom, barber, cook, sempster and nurse, [...] [waiting] upon him and [serving] him with great fidelity and affection. My uncle Toby loved the man in return.

This love, *philia*, for one's comrades-in-arms is no small matter. It originates in their shared war experience and in "the similitude of their knowledge". Trim has pried into the plans of sieges that fascinate the captain, and little by little he "had become proficient in the science" that was Toby's hobby horse.

The same thing happens in transference with madness and trauma, where by peering over the patient's shoulder and rummaging through his incomprehensible plans, the analyst finally deciphers the sanity of his insanity and the patient finally "gets" his analyst's theoretical obsessions. Trim acquires a reputation as a strategist in the eyes of the cook and the chambermaid, a skill in which he sometimes surpasses his master. In fact, Trim had but one fault:

> The fellow lov'd to advise, —or rather to hear himself talk; [...] he was voluble; [...] My uncle Toby, as I said, loved the man;—and besides, as he ever looked upon a faithful servant—but as an humble friend, —he could not bear to stop his mouth,

as Don Quixote repeatedly stopped Sancho's. But Trim's eloquence was truly impressive on this occasion.

This passage reassures me. In a session, when I feel I can't control my tongue, I often tell myself that ideally an analyst should keep silent, and because I can't, I take the next chapter as a model instead. In it, Trim literally spells out an art of the fugue: "If I durst presume [...] to give Your Honour my advice and speak my opinion in this matter. —Thou are welcome, Trim, quote my uncle Toby, —speak, —speak what thou thinkest upon the subject".

Brushing his hair back and standing erect as before his division, the corporal says: "I think".

This "I think" indicates the need to find a method when impulse is driving one to flee. "I think, therefore I am", Descartes[31] wrote in his *Discourse on Method* in 1637. His method is explicitly linked to his sudden "demigration" from the army, in his youth. On 10 November 1619, he spent the night in the solitude of a stove heated room near Ulm. At twenty-three, he was a soldier in the troops of the Duke of Bavaria during the Thirty Years' War. That night, he decided to embark on a journey through Europe, after he had two terrifying dreams we could call traumatic, followed by a third one showing him the way to "the foundation of an admirable science". The same enthusiasm as Toby's took hold of him that night. Transcribing the dreams, his biographer Adrien Bayet swears that young Descartes was not drunk, although the date was 10 November, St. Martin's Eve, celebrated with much libation in Germany and France.

Sterne describes Trim's method as follows:

> advancing his left, which was his lame leg [...] — and pointing with his right hand open towards a map of Dunkirk [...]: I think, quoth Corporal Trim, with humble submission to Your Honour's better judgement, — that these ravelins, bastions, curtains and hornworks make but a poor, contemptible, fiddle-faddle piece of work of it here upon paper, compared to what Your Honour and I could make of it were we in the country by ourselves, and had but a rood or a rood and a half of ground to do what we pleased with.

But, as Descartes put it at the beginning of his *Discourse*: "It is not enough to have a good mind, the main thing is to use it well". Trim's method includes giving his master's hobby horse a third dimension.

Potential space

When the map acquires a third dimension, it opens a "potential space", as Winnicott[32] would later call it; this space attracts Toby at once: "Speak, speak". The corporal launches into a discourse interspersed with "I thinks" at each breath—following the rhythm of Toby's reiterated "speak" in the conditional form used by children at play and reminiscent of Sancho's distortion of words: "As summer is coming on [...], Your Honour might sit out of doors and give me the nography — (call it iconography, quoth my uncle), —and I will [...] fortify it to Your Honour's mind".

According to Gregory Nagy, Professor of Hellenic Studies at Harvard, the third dimension is imperative for emerging from the *filmy*, two-dimensional sphere of trauma. Nagy illustrates his statement by citing Virgil's[33] verse spoken by Aeneas to his friend Achates after they landed in Carthage, like the boat people, fleeing from Troy. Aeneas waits for the queen, looks at the temple she has built and suddenly recognises himself on the bas reliefs representing the Trojan War. Only then can he weep for the first time, as he pronounces the famous verse: "*Sunt lacrimae rerum et mentem mortalia tangunt* — There are tears in the universe, and mortal things touch the mind".

In his translation, Nagy insists on the word *mentem*. Tears touch not only the heart, but also the mind with its capacity to learn.

Toby's mind is deeply touched by the relief Trim wants to give to their battles by building models that give shape to what they felt. "I will be shot by Your Honour upon the glacis of [the citadel] if I did not fortify it to Your Honour's mind. —I dare say thou wouldst, Trim, quoth my uncle". The plan of the fortifications is visualised and translated into instructions. "—For if Your Honour [...] could but mark me the polygon, with its exact lines and angles, —That I could do very well, quoth my uncle".

The corporal promises to measure to a hair's breadth the angle and the depth, requested by Toby, by throwing shovelfuls of earth upon one hand towards the town for the scarp and upon the other hand towards the countryside for the counterscarp. The captain starts to regain his strength at the prospect of building fortifications in the French style. "The best engineers call them gazons, Trim, said my uncle Toby, —Whether they are gazons or sods is not much matter, replied Trim, Your Honour knows they are ten times beyond a facing either of brick or stone". Toby nods his approval. The plan shall be put into action:

> [...] would Your Honour please to let the bespeaking of the table alone and let us but go into the country, I would work under Your Honour's directions like a horse, and make fortifications for you like a tansy, with all the batteries, saps, ditches and palisades, that it should be worth all the world's riding twenty miles to go and see it.

For these two big kids, the conquest of a potential space brings into being a "transitional subject", as Benedetti[34] was to say, which emerges from a "zone of death". The birth of the subject on the site of the trauma is enacted by Sterne through a canon for two voices.

Cadence

Their enthusiasm bursts out with trance-like rhythm, put into words by Sterne as he would improvise a cadence on his bass viola de gamba.

"My uncle Toby blushed as red as scarlet as Trim went on;—but it was not a blush of guilt, —of modesty—or of anger;—it was a blush of joy". Toby is energised again: "Say no more, Trim". The imperative will be repeated four times, with the added phrase: "Thou hast said enough", to punctuate each instance by addressing the recovered "thou", whose loss had sent the veteran into extreme solitude. The two men combine forces to engage in a war game which is far from virtual. It is announced joyfully with a fugue whose final chord reinstates the captain's rank and does away with the dissociation between body and mind:

> We might begin the campaign [...] on the very day that His Majesty and the Allies take the field, and demolish 'em town by town [...] —Trim, quoth my uncle Toby, say no more. — Your Honour [...] might sit in your armchair [...] giving me your orders, and I would—Say no more, Trim, quoth my uncle Toby, —Besides, Your Honour would get not only pleasure and good pastime, —but good air and good exercise, and good health, —and Your Honour's wound would be well in a month. Thou hast said enough Trim, [...]—I like thy project mightily.

Trim is ready to run and buy the material: spade, shovel, pickaxe and wheelbarrow. The description of the scene conveys unspeakable ecstasy; Toby leaps up on one leg overwhelmed with joy and thrusts a guinea into Trim's hand: "Trim, [...] go down this moment, my lad, and bring up my supper this instant". Trim hurries to do as he is asked, but Toby can't eat a thing. "—Trim, [...] get me to bed". But he could not shut his eyes since the corporal had fired his imagination; "The more he consider'd it, the more bewitching the scene appeared to him".

Two hours before daybreak, Toby decides to leave at dawn. He instructs Trim to pack up his things, including bandages and dressings, and to hire a four-in-hand to come for them at noon when Walter would be at the Stock Exchange. Finally, after packing up his books of fortifications and his instruments, Toby left a banknote on the table for the surgeon and a letter of tender thanks for his brother, then, "by the help of a crutch on one side and Trim on the other, — my uncle Toby embark'd for Shandy Hall", the family mansion inherited by Walter, the eldest son.

This departure replicates the exodus of Laurence's family when he was six months old, from military barracks in Ireland to the Sternes' family mansion in Yorkshire, owned by Richard, his father's eldest brother. Roger Sterne hoped to find help there, but they met with a cold reception and came back disappointed. This time, the military cadet's hopes are realised when he and Trim find a space offering safe shelter.

The bowling green

The psychotherapy of trauma is as old as wars, but must be reinvented each time the guarantee of the world collapses. During World War I, this therapy was discovered by an eighteen-month-old baby who healed his grandfather, Sigmund Freud. One day when the baby's mother was absent, this "excellent child" played at making appear and disappear a spool attached to his crib with a string. He flung it "with considerable skill" over the side of the crib joyfully shouting "Oooo" when he threw it away and "Aaaa" when he brought it back This war child, as Cathy Caruth[35] calls him, got Freud thinking, in this dark period—when he was suffering the privations of wartime, saw the number of his patients shrinking and most of all, worried about his two sons who had been sent to the front. In the opposition of the baby's sounds, Freud recognised the words *Fort* (there) and *Da* (here) symbolising absence and presence, and published these reflections after the war in *Beyond the Pleasure Principle*,[36] in the chapter entitled "Children's Games".

The game of demolition and construction of fortification models invented by Trim serves the same purpose, as long as it can take place in a protected space. There, for several years—until the 1713 Utrecht Peace Treaty when the armies were disbanded—was carried out what Sterne called "the ceremony of the name". Wittgenstein,[37] Sterne's admirer, would later conclude: "One could almost say that man is a ceremonial animal". As with all ceremonies, the space had to be strictly delimited. The captain possessed a small cottage reminiscent of the hut of the old man of Tarente, the veteran portrayed by Virgil in *The Georgics*[38]:

> My uncle Toby had a little neat country house of his own, in the village where my father's estate lay at *Shandy*, which had been left for him by an old uncle, with a small estate of about one hundred pounds a year. Behind his house [...] was a kitchen garden and cut off from it by a tall yew hedge, was a BOWLING GREEN, containing jut about as much ground as Corporal Trim wished for.

Today, a street in Lower Manhattan still bears the name Bowling Green. This name has a magical effect on Toby. When he knocked his maps and books off the table in an avalanche, the thought of the bowling green presented itself to him like a "surviving image"—a term coined by Aby Warburg[39]:

> [...] as Trim uttered the words 'a rood and a half of ground to do what they would with', —this identical bowling green instantly presented itself and became curiously painted [...] upon the retina of my uncle Toby's fancy;—which was the physical cause of making him change colour.

Surviving images play a crucial therapeutic role. During World War I, historian Aby Warburg, expert in Renaissance Art, had to abandon the vast library in his house, where, in Quixotic fits of delirium, he was proclaiming to be commander-in-chief of the German armies. He was hospitalised in the clinic run by Ludwig Binswanger, Freud's pupil. In 1924, he was released after presenting a "Lecture on Serpent Ritual" among the Hopi Indians of North America—in which they dance for half an hour, each one holding a rattlesnake in his mouth and then throwing it away—"Fort"—into the desert. Warburg's feat, accomplished with the help of his disciple Fritz Saxl, who provided his unswerving support when he returned from the front, was itself a ritual of regeneration.

Similarly, mathematician René Thom invented his "morphogenesis – the creation of forms – on the edge of a catastrophe"[40] after a breakdown following his winning of the Fields Medal in 1958. Cervantes saw Don Quixote appear before him in 1597 in his Seville prison cell, where he had been unjustly imprisoned; and in the same way, Uncle Toby appeared to Sterne in 1759, when he was at his wits' end. The image surviving the disaster drove him to "to turn author", like his role model.

The captain regains his strength thanks to the transferential quadruped which allowed Don Quixote to hallucinate the wars fought by "his father", as Cervantes calls himself in the Preface of his first novel. Toby as Don Quixote, Trim as Sancho Panza and the hobby horse as Rocinante—the vector of transference—allow Roger Sterne's son to "mend his father's injuries", in the words of his biographer.[41] As for the fourth pillar of the transference, Dulcinea, the reader, is soon prompted to think of her: "Never did lover post down to a belov'd mistress with more heat and expectation than my uncle Toby did to enjoy this selfsame thing in private".

An analysis must take place in a clearly delimited frame. Toby's enclosed garden is a "Garden of the Rose"[42]—the title of a famous book of the Medieval Period—where his wounded psyche finds refuge. The idea that the garden is sheltered from sight is essential to Toby. It is enclosed by a tall yew hedge on one side and on the two others by hawthorn and briar rose shrubs. The escape from London takes place in the merry month of May when the Green Man, the symbol of regeneration, awakens Eros and Psyche.

In Apuleius's *Metamorphoses*,[43] Eros saves Psyche from the marine monster to whom she has been offered as sacrifice by carrying her away from the rock on which she languishes, exposed, and bringing her into a garden only he knows on condition that she does not try to see him. But she breaks her promise and is ousted from the garden; after escaping Venus's attempts to kill her, she is finally reunited with Eros and welcomed among the gods.

The threat of soul murder always hovers over a psychoanalysis of trauma, when new catastrophes destroy the potential space of play. This misfortune befell Cervantes when authors, jealous of his success, paid a forger to destroy the bowling green of his first *Don Quixote* by writing a sinister sequel in order to disgrace his heroes. Sterne is well aware of the danger and takes on a Cassandrian tone to announce the break in the fence of the bowling green, behind which Toby thinks he is safe: "Vain thought! However thick it was planted about, —or private soever it might seem, — to think, dear uncle Toby, of enjoying a thing which took up a whole rood and a half of ground, —and not have it known"!

Behind the fence lurks a pseudo Dulcinea, the widow Wadman. She will manipulate Toby as skilfully as the Duchess tricked the knight in the second volume of *Don Quixote*. At the end of Sterne's Volume 8, dedicated to "Toby's amours", the captain also says no to perversion. The "shock" he received in that affair in 1714 will be alluded to here in Chapter 7 and narrated in Volume 9, where Toby's trance will be broken thanks to Trim's watchfulness.

Another shock awaits the reader, who must suddenly leap over about twenty years, from 1699 to 1718, to begin the next chapter. I mention the dates because the story falters, ignoring the sequence of events.

Trauma speaks to trauma[44]

The Time of catastrophes imposes itself as the major protagonist of the novel. Having started in 1718, the story of Tristram's half-failed conception will end in Volume 9, which is set four years earlier in 1714, and recounts Toby's rebellion.

Its rhythm is that of the psychoanalysis of madness and trauma, long considered impossible due to frequent returns to square one—taken to be failures—after each advance. For Sterne, on the contrary, these chronological overlaps provide an opportunity to analyse another disaster—what American novelist Kurt Vonnegut, prisoner in a slaughterhouse during the 1945 bombardment that destroyed Dresden, calls a "timequake".[45]

Now, the reader is suddenly propelled from May 1699 to 18 November 1718, when Tristram's birth—for which we have to wait until we get to chapter XIII of Volume 3—is already causing a stir.

Change of scene: we return to the parlour, where we left the two brothers in Volume 1, chapter XXI. They were lost in thought before the fireside, when Walter asked: " —What can they be doing, brother"? Toby answered: "—I think...", striking the ashes out of his pipe. At that point, Sterne cuts him off to paint his portrait and discuss his hobby horse and to give an account of the wound he received in battle.

Now, Sterne brings us back to Toby's "I think". Walter asks: "What can they be doing, brother"? "I think...replied my uncle Toby, — taking, as I told you, his pipe from his mouth and striking the ashes out of it". The captain thinks of the imminent birth, which he seems to be the only one to keep in mind. His third "I think" finally expresses his thought: "I think [...] it would not be amiss, brother, if we rang the bell". Ring, ring... Obadiah arrives and Walter repeats his question: "Pray, what's all that racket over our heads, Obadiah?—my brother and I can scarce hear ourselves speak":

> Sir, answer'd Obadiah, making a bow towards [them], —my mistress is taken very badly. —And where's Susannah running down the garden there, as if they were going to ravish her. —Sir, she is running [...] to fetch the old midwife.

Nothing could be more normal in such circumstances. What is unusual is Walter's reaction. He has a plan of his own, which must be carried out faster than Susannah's. He orders Obadiah to saddle a horse and let Dr. Slop know he must come at once. The race between the two servants is on—a race against the clock that Toby tries to discourage, defending his sister-in-law's choice and bringing his brother back to reality: if the mother and the baby should die, he will probably be unable to father other children at his age. But, once again, a word ruins his whole argument: "Mayhap, brother, [...] [she] does it to save the expense. [...] —Then it can be out of nothing [...]—but MODESTY. —My sister, [...] added he, does not care to let a man come so near her ****".

Words fail before *The Origin of the World*, which Courbet would paint in the next century. The reader, hastening to finish the sentence, speaks the left out word under his breath and is severely scolded by Sterne, who lectures him on stylistics after the fashion of Marc Antony in Shakespeare's *Julius Caesar*: "O my countrymen!—be nice;—be cautious of your language. [...]—the insensible MORE or LESS, determine the precise line of beauty in the sentence, as well as in the statue"![46]

Indeed, one MORE word is introduced in the repetition of Toby's sentence: the verb "to choose", which triggers Walter's wrath:

> —My sister, mayhap, quoth my uncle Toby, does not "choose" to let a man come so near her ****. Make this dash, —'tis an Aposiopesis.—Take the dash away, and write 'backside', —'tis Bawdy.—Scratch 'backside' out and put 'cover'd way' in, —'tis a Metaphor; [...] But [...] whether the snapping of my father's tobacco pipe so critically happened thro' accident or anger, —will be seen in due time.

And seen it is. Besides being a businessman, Walter is a phallocrat for whom all women are hysterics, his wife included. Therefore, after his pipe snapped in two, he stood up and threw the pieces in the fire "with all the violence in the world" upon hearing the words: "My sister does not choose..." His wife has no choice, it's perfectly clear:

> Not choose, quoth my father [...], to let a man come so near her!—By Heaven, brother Toby! you would try the patience of a Job; [...]. —Why?—Where? —Wherein? —Wherefore? [...] —To think, said my father, of a man living to your age, brother, and knowing so little about women! —I know nothing at all about them, — replied my uncle Toby; and I think [...] that the shock I received the year after the demolition of Dunkirk in my affair with widow Wadman [...] —I should not have received but from my total ignorance of the sex.

Walter attempts to calm down by lecturing his brother on female sexuality: "—Methinks, brother [...], you might, at least, know so much as the right end of a woman from the wrong".

Calmer than his brother, the veteran lets the unconscious wander, as he stares blankly at "a small crevice form'd by a bad joint in the chimney piece", muttering:

—Right end of a woman! —I declare [...], I know no more which it is than the man in the moon; —and if I was to think [...] this month together, I'm sure I should not be able to find it out.

Toby's apparent candour hides a true Don Quixote who defends the honour of women, maidens and children throughout the novel. But his older brother knows about the female sex, and undertakes to enlighten his innocent sibling:

Then brother Toby, [...] I will tell you. Everything in this world, [...]—has two handles —Not always, quoth my uncle Toby. —At least, replied my father, everyone has two handles. [...]—Now, if a man was to sit down coolly and consider all the parts which constitute the whole of that animal call'd Woman, and compare them analogically —I never understood rightly the meaning of that word, — quoth my uncle Toby. —ANALOGY, replied my father, is the certain relation and agreement which different...

Here, another catastrophe interrupts his lesson.

Psychic time[47]

Imagine an analyst comfortably ensconced in his chair, going on from session to session, when suddenly his patient changes into a horseman of the Apocalypse. The analyst is thrown off balance. This is the effect produced by a "devil of a rap at the door" on Walter's presentation. Here, we have another *coitus interruptus*. This "devil of a rap" "crushed the head of as notable and curious a dissertation as ever was engendered in the womb of speculation;—it was some months before my father could get an opportunity to be safely deliver'd of it".

This impromptu event or "cross accident" also complicates the construction of the novel. Sterne is at his wits' end. Overwhelmed by "the confusion and distress of [the Shandys'] misadventures", he asks himself whether he "shall be able to find a place for [the dissertation] in the third volume or not". Meanwhile, our author vents his frustration by suspecting the reader of accusing him of "a breach in the probability of time", since between the ringing of the bell to call Obadiah and the rap at the door, the time interval was "no more than two minutes, thirteen seconds and three fifths", while in actual fact Obadiah's errand took an hour and a half. "No one can say, with reason, that I have not allowed Obadiah time enough, poetically speaking and considering the emergency too", ignoring the probability of time which breaches "the true scholastic pendulum". Sterne calls us "hypercritics" who want to measure every little lapse of time, as if we knew nothing about psychic time.

But we do know that the tuberculosis he contracted in Cambridge has come back, and so we overlook his bad humour. He is relentless and goes on to accuse us of not acknowledging all the trouble he took:

> I have brought my uncle Toby from Namur, quite across all Flanders, into England:— that I have had him ill upon my hands near four years; and have since travelled him and Corporal Trim, in a chariot and four, a journey of near two hundred miles down into Yorkshire, —all which put together must have prepared the reader's imagination for the entrance of Dr Slop upon the stage, —as much, at least (I hope), as a dance, a song or a concerto between the acts. If my hypercritic is intractable, — alleging that two minutes and thirteen seconds are no more than two minutes and thirteen seconds.

So much the worse for him.

At least, his negative transference against us has the benefit of calming him down:

> —when I have said all I can [on the subject];—and [knowing] that this plea, tho' it might save me dramatically, will damn me biographically; [...]—I then put an end to the whole objection and controversy [...] at once—by acquainting [the reader] that Obadiah had not got above three-score yards from the stable yard before he met with Dr Slop.

And he promises proof of this and even "tragical proof".

The timequake described in the scene that follows is factual—evidence-based, as we might say today. "This had better begin a new chapter", Sterne tells us. I transcribe his words faithfully, for fear of another scolding.

Timequake[48]

The doctor arrives on a dirt road on a "little diminutive pony", scarcely able to advance under the rider's weight even "had the roads been in an ambling condition".

The doctor's portrait is drawn in three brushstrokes: "a little, squat [...] figure [...] of about four feet and a half [...], with a breadth of back and sesquipedality of belly [of] a sergeant in the Horse Guards". His figure offers the eye the "serpentine line" that William Hogarth describes in *The Analysis of Beauty*,[49] which Sterne advises us to read if we have not done so already. This line can be seen a little later in the book in the engraving illustrating the episode of Trim's reading of a sermon.

As we were saying, Dr. Slop is warily making his way towards the par-
turient woman, when Obadiah suddenly erupts, galloping in the opposite
direction. Dr. Slop:

> had approach'd to within sixty yards of [Shandy Hall], and within five
> yards of a sudden turn made by an acute angle of the garden wall, —
> and in the dirtiest part of a dirty lane, —when Obadiah and his coach
> horse turn'd the corner, rapid, furious, —pop, —full upon him! [...]—
> splashing and plunging like a devil thro' [...] a vortex of mud [...] moving
> along with it round its axis [...] at [a] monstrous rate.

The nearly fatal clash produces a freeze-frame focusing on a fantastic horseman, like Yorick was in Volume 1, with the difference that Obadiah's mount
is not a skinny nag, but rather a furious coach horse, advancing at a "monstrous rate".

Sterne borrows the style of the Scriptures to describe the terrible "ren-
counter" for which Slop is in no way prepared:

> What could Dr Slop do?—He crossed himself (the sign of the cross is
> drawn in the text). —Pugh! [exclaims the Protestant reader]—but the
> Doctor, sir, was a papist.—No matter [objects the pragmatic Anglo-
> Saxon]; he had better have kept hold of the pummel.—He had so;—nay,
> as it happen'd, he had better have done nothing at all.

The apotropaic gesture causes an avalanche of catastrophes. When he crossed
himself, Slop let go of his whip, and trying to retrieve it, he lost his stirrups:

> ... —and in the multitude of all these losses [...], the unfortunate Doctor
> lost his presence of mind (which, by the by, shews what little advantage
> there is in crossing.) So that, [...] he left his pony to its destiny, tumbling
> off it diagonally, [...] in the style and manner of a pack of wool, [...] the
> broadest part of him [sinking] about twelve inches deep in the mire.

All the while, Obadiah was spinning around him. He would gladly have
helped him if the accelerated MOMENTUM of his horse had not prevented
it. He needed to ride three circles around the doctor before slowing down,
and then he stopped his beast with an explosion of mud that covered the
doctor from head to foot. The result is described by a papist metaphor: Slop
is "transubstantiated", changed into a substance of a different kind, as the
body of Christ was changed into bread in the Eucharist, before he makes his
entrance into the anti-papist household, following the loud rap on the door
which interrupted Toby's initiation into feminine sexuality.

In an analysis of madness and trauma, timequakes often announce a
past experience left unacknowledged. "The time is out of joint", Hamlet[50]

says after the visit of the ghost brings into the present a crime cut out of transmission.

Writing is but a different name for conversation[51]

The reference to Shakespeare is explicit: Slop appears in the doorway holding Obadiah by the hand, "like Hamlet's ghost, motionless and speechless, for a full minute and a half [...], with all the majesty of the mud [...], *unwiped, unappointed, unanelled*".

These adjectives describe the former King of Denmark, when he reveals to his son how he was deprived "of life, of crown [...], *unhous'led, disappointed, unanel'd*",[52] murdered by his brother. The figure of the doctor also brings to mind the genesis of the first man shaped out of clay as well as the "true man without rank" described by Zen master Lin-Chi[53]:

> Here was a far opportunity for my uncle Toby to have triumph'd over my father in his turn; [for it was easy to agree] that mayhap his sister might not care to let such a Dr Slop come so near her ****. [...] But—'twas not his nature to insult.

Walter, however, was thinking "like the hypercritic". A hypercritic might ask what business have I in Sterne's novel. Fortunately, Sterne comes to my rescue by laying out the precept of literary democracy I cited at the beginning of this Volume to enter into a dialogue with him. I repeat:

> Writing, when properly managed [...] is but a different name for conversation: as no one [...] would venture to talk all; — so no author who understands the just boundaries of decorum and good breeding would presume to think all: the truest respect which you can pay to the reader's understanding is to halve this matter amicably and leave him something to imagine in his turn.

Of course, Sterne constantly interrupts our conversation. But I don't blame him, for these interruptions are familiar to me. Sometimes, after work with a patient has been going well, suddenly in the middle of a session he proclaims that psychoanalysis is useless. When such a breaking off occurs, *the psychoanalyst's progress* consists of confronting the agency which kills alterity. This agency is ubiquitous in the work of Sterne's friend William Hogarth, a painter also famous for his art of conversation.

Indeed, the series of paintings *A Harlot's Progress, The Rake's Progress* and *Marriage À-la-Mode* portray breaks in the conversation. In *A Harlot's Progress*, a young country girl is shown arriving in London; in the background, a scoundrel is watching her, ready to lure her into prostitution; finally, she dies in a poor house of venereal disease. In *The Rake's Progress*—turned into an opera by Stravinsky in 1951—a young man from a prosperous family follows the same declining path, from gambling to debauchery and finally to crime and prison. *Marriage À-la-Mode* depicts a similar downfall, ending in a burst of violence.

While I'm preparing my imagination for the next twist in the plot, Sterne is already way ahead of me:

> Let the reader imagine then that Dr Slop has told his tale; [...]—let him suppose that Obadiah has told his tale also, and with such rueful looks of affected concern [...] that my father has stepp'd upstairs to see my mother:—and, to conclude [...], —let him imagine the Doctor wash'd, —rubb'd down, [...]—got into a pair of Obadiah's pumps...

Pumps are also called court shoes. After this trivial detail, Walter Sterne launches into a speech with sermonlike overtones. "Truce!—truce, good Dr Slop! [...]—little dost thou know what obstacles [...], what hidden causes retard thy obstetrical hand. [...]—Art thou aware that [...] a daughter of Lucina is put obstetrically over thy head"?

Slop loses the first round of the covert battle against the midwife, who has the goddess of childbirth for an ally, for he has forgotten to bring all his obstetric equipment: forceps, cannulas and syringes—still indispensable tools of the psychiatric arsenal today.

The Indo-European triad[54]

Toby brings the conversation back to the book he cited out of nowhere. The three men are seated at the fireside, shrouded in the billowing pipe smoke seen in Hogarth's engraving. The woman in labour upstairs can wait, for Obadiah has been sent to Dr Slop's house to fetch his bag with the promise of a tip. He is to reappear six chapters later.[55] The three men personify the Indo-European triad defined by Georges Dumézil and by Cervantes[56]: *laborantes, milites et orantes*: business for the oldest son, war for the second and the church for the third. Slop is given the role of barber and priest. The captain tells the doctor: "Your sudden and unexpected arrival [...], —instantly brought the great Stevinus into my head, who you must know, is a favourite author with me".

No one knows what he is talking about. Walter bets twenty guineas to a crown that Stevinus wrote something on fortifications. A sure bet, which Toby confirms. "—I knew it, said my father", saving his anti-war discourse for the right moment. The doctor and the businessman assail the military man, each in his own way. Undisturbed, Toby continues his lecture on fortifications and military works: "—the common men [...] confound the ravelin and the half-moon together, —tho' they are very different things; [...]—Where then lies the difference? (quoth my father, a little testily). [...]—I think[...] that the noble science of defence has its weak sides". But Toby continued, ignoring his sarcastic remarks about horn-works: "— they are called by the French engineers *ouvrages à corne*".

In those days, the French language competed with English in the military and medical spheres. When Walter referred to Dr. Slop as a "man-midwife", the latter corrected him: "—*Accoucheur*, —if you please". The word was new, in a profession previously reserved for midwives.

"High! Ho! Sigh'd my father", for Toby has set off again to give half a page of definitions. Walter stops him at the term "double tenaille" in an explosion of rage, brandishing the banner of pacifism and suddenly remembering his wife, who is still in labour:

> —By the mother who bore us! —brother Toby [...], you would provoke a saint; —here have you got us [...] tho' my wife is this moment in the pains of labour —and you hear her cry out, —yet [you] carry off the man-midwife. [...]—I would not [...] have my brains so full of [...] ravelins, half-moons and such trumpery to be proprietor of Namur and of all the towns of Flanders with it.

The heated discussion becomes outright sacrilegious, reminiscent of the song "Auprès de ma blonde". Now sung by every child in France, it was popular during the Franco-Dutch War led by Louis XIV. It was also well known in Toby's army under the title "The prisoner of Holland". The blond who demands the return of her husband, a prisoner in Holland, is asked: "What would you give, my fair one to have your husband back"? and answers: "I would give Versailles, Paris and Saint Denis, the towers of Notre Dame and the streets of my country". Like her, Walter is ready to give up Namur, not for love, but rather to destroy his brother's hobby- horse.

Caught in a vice between his brother's attacks and the medic's jokes, Toby is saved by the author, who gets him out of this bind by telling two clinical stories in which the captain acts as an analyst. This is not surprising, since Cervantes did the same to save Don Quixote from the attacks of the prisoners he had just freed from their chains. Fleeing into the mountains, Don Quixote became the analyst of Cardenio, the madman of the Sierra Morena.[57]

These two healing stories are presented at the same point in the narration, even though they occurred ten years apart. The first involves Tristram when he was a boy of ten and the second is Walter when his son was born. In the first case, Toby's intervention allows the child to overcome the dissociation of his emotions, while in the second Toby reminds his brother of the symbolic order of their lineage.

Psychoanalysis of the cut-out unconscious

Indeed, speaking as an adult and with no transition, Tristram sings the praises of his uncle Toby, in which an attentive ear can hear the condemnation of Laurence's uncles on the Sterne side of the family. Richard, the eldest, had been chosen as the eleven-year-old Laurence's tutor, and the boy was taken by his father from Ireland to the Sterne estate in Yorkshire to attend a school founded there by Richard Sterne. He not only neglected Laurence, but demanded to be reimbursed for his educational expenses. As for Jaques, the youngest uncle, archdeacon of Cleveland, he used his nephew's writing talent under the guise of protecting him and then pursued him with his hatred when Laurence refused to serve his fanatical "party writing". Toby is their total opposite:

> My uncle Toby was a man of patient injuries;—not from want of courage—[...] where just occasion presented or called forth, —I know no man under whose arm I would sooner have taken shelter; nor did this arise from any insensibility or obtuseness of his intellectual parts;— for he felt this insult of my father's as feelingly as a man could do;—but he was of a peaceful, placid nature, —no jarring element in it, —all was mix'd up so kindly within him; my uncle Toby had scarce a heart to retaliate upon a fly.

This reference to the fly was to resonate in the consciousness of Aaron Burr at the start of the next century. In 1804, this libertine and mediocre politician killed Alexander Hamilton in a duel. Although he never showed any regret for having assassinated the founding father of American democracy, in his old age he admitted in one of his letters: "Had I read Sterne more and Voltaire less, I should have known the world was wide enough for Hamilton and me".[58]

The scene Burr regrets not having read takes place during a dinner around the year 1728, where Toby finally catches a fly that has been buzzing around his nose. He speaks to it using the dignified "thee":

> —Go, —says he, lifting up the [window] sash and opening his hand as he spoke, to let it escape; —go, poor devil, get thee gone, why should I hurt thee?—This world surely is wide enough to hold both thee and me.

The child, Tristram, who heard these words and witnessed this scene, is undoubtedly Laurence. When he was ten, he and his family were generously welcomed for a year by a distant cousin of Laurence's father, Brigadier General Robert Stearne, who, like Toby, had fought at Namur. After surviving fifteen more sieges and seven great battles, he founded a military hospital near Dublin on the model of Les Invalides Hospital in Paris.[59] Sterne analyses his childhood impressions:

> ...Whether it was that the action itself was more in unison to my nerves at that age of pity, which instantly set my whole frame into one vibration of most pleasurable sensation, —or how far the manner and

expression of it might go towards it;—or in what degree, or by what secret magic, —a tone of voice and harmony of movement, attuned by mercy, might find a passage to my heart, I know not.

His "nerves at that age" had already been shaken by the death of his younger siblings in Ireland, in the miserable military barracks in which the family lived, moving often while his father followed the movement of the troops from assignment to assignment. The therapeutic effect of Toby's words and movements, "attuned" to his heart, is described on the musical mode of a vibration running through his whole frame in "one most pleasurable sensation".

This "secret magic" exerts its effect each time the memory of the body, recorded in the solitude of an unyielding present, resonates with another person, thanks to an interference that gives access to speech and sets time in motion. The buzzing fly is also to be found in Wittgenstein's *Philosophical Investigations*: "What is your goal in philosophy? — To shew the fly the way out of the bottle".[60]

After fighting in World War I and being held captive at Mount Cassino, Wittgenstein endured situations where he could say: "I turn to stone, and my pain goes on".[61] The way out can only be shown by another, whose tone of voice or fugitive expression resonates with an element of the petrified state.

We come upon "frozen words" in Rabelais—Sterne's master—in two chapters of the *Quart-Livre*. Pantagruel warms them in his hand as they fall onto the deck of his ship like candies of various colours, while the ship sails across a zone where the previous winter there had been "a great and bloody fight" on the frozen sea. When Toby opened the window to free the fly while addressing it, he warmed in his hand the frozen words of the child. The scene left an indelible impression on Tristram. A hand with a pointing index, drawn beside the text, points to what Wittgenstein would call an "ostensive definition":

> ... tho' I would not [...] discredit the other helps of an expensive education bestowed upon me [...]—yet I often think that I owe one half of my philanthropy to that one accidental impression. This is to serve for parents and governors instead of a whole volume upon the subject.

And also for psychoanalysts seeking access to the child imprisoned in the adult by traumatic experiences. The passage can be opened by someone who accidentally finds the word "in unison with his nerves". In her book subtitled *Overcoming Internal Self-Alienation*, Janine Fisher,[62] who worked with Bessel Van der Kolk, becomes an ally to the adult before her, so they can both address the neglected child, praising him for his courage and telling him that he is striving to gain recognition for his reactions of fight and flight, of retreat or submission—not registered in the past—which are shared by all living beings in the face of a death threat.

Toby's second analytic intervention is more orthodox.

Psychoanalysis of the repressed unconscious

In the second clinical example, Toby brings out the symbolic overtones in his brother's constant provocation. Although Walter was "frank and generous in his nature", he prodded Toby when it came to "the little vexations of life":

My father [...] had a much more acute and quick sensibility of nature, attended with a little soreness of temper [...] and in [...] this subacid humour towards [...] my uncle Toby", attacked his hobby-horse under the breast-plate. [...] I need not tell the reader [...] that a man's HOBBY-HORSE is as tender a part as he has about him; [...] these unprovoked strokes at my uncle Toby's could not be unfelt by him. —No [...]; my uncle Toby did feel them, and very sensibly too.

The reader must have been puzzled by Toby's lack of reaction when his brother, in the heart of his argument, was ready to hand Namur over to the French. Sterne's answer is quite emphatic:

Pray, sir, what said he?—How did he behave?—Oh, sir!—it was great: for as soon as my father had done insulting his HOBBY-HORSE, — he turned his head [...], and look'd up into my father's face with a countenance spread over with so much good nature;—so placid;—so fraternal;—so inexpressibly tender towards him, —it penetrated my father to his heart. He rose up hastily from his chair and [seized] hold of both my uncle Toby's hands...

Given his expertise in the art of combat, Toby does not respond in kind. When his brother, mindful of his self-image, tearfully shows contrition, the captain's reply cuts to the core, making the name of their lineage ring out amidst the tearful jabber of excuses and apologies:

Brother Toby, [...]—I beg thy pardon;—forgive, I pray thee, this rash humour which my mother gave me. —My dear, dear brother, answer'd my uncle Toby [...], say no more about it. [...] But 'tis ungenerous, replied my father, [...] to hurt a brother of such gentle manners, —[...] tis base:— by Heaven, 'tis cowardly. —You are heartily welcome, brother, quoth my uncle Toby, —had it been fifty times as much. —Besides, what have I to do [...] wither with your amusements or your pleasures, unless it was in my power [...] to increase their measure?—Brother Shandy [note the use of the patronymic], answer'd my uncle Toby, looking wistfully in his face, —you are much mistaken in this point;—for you do increase my pleasure very much in begetting children for the Shandy family at your time of life. —But by that, sir, quoth Dr Slop, Mr Shandy increases his own. —Not a jot, quoth my father.

Toby's two modes of transference, towards his nephew and towards his brother, apply to the unconscious, which can be either suppressed or repressed, according to the distinction made by William Rivers[63] in his presentation to the Royal Society of Medicine at the end of 1917. Winnicott,[64] who had also read Tristram Shandy, makes the same distinction when speaking about traumatised patients: "In this special context, the unconscious thing the patient needs to 'remember' is not repressed, because he was not there for it to happen to". Dori Laub, who founded the Video Archives of the Holocaust at Yale with Steven Spielberg, speaks of "events without a witness".[65]

When the dissociation is lifted in the present of the transference, Winnicott adds, "in reaction to the analyst's failures and mistakes" and, as we well know, in reaction to events such as the freeing of the fly by Tristram's uncle, which showed the child that an other was there to open the window through which his psyche could soar towards the future—as the psyche of the captain did after four years of confinement. By contrast, in the transference towards his brother who infantilises him, Toby invokes the agency of the name of their forefathers.

The first mode of transference provides an answer to Wittgenstein's "Now suppose that the tool with the name is broken....What shall we do".[66] His answer is to create a language game which makes a place for the broken tool. Sterne adopts the same solution when he invents the language game of the reading of the sermon, to show the circumstances in which the tool with the name will break.

Renewable energy[67]

Before fighting against perversion, Sterne foresees the fight against climate change. The trio comes together around the question of renewable energy.

In the parlour at Shandy Hall, the two brothers call a truce, as Brutus and Cassius did in *Julius Caesar*,[68] on the eve of the Battle of Philippi. Still, Toby refuses to drop the matter and rings for Trim, to ask him to bring the book by Stevinus, to show his brother that "he has no resentment". Stevinus is an engineer who in the previous century had invented a sailing chariot that could "carry half a dozen people thirty German miles in I don't know how few minutes".

Fortunately, unanimity was reached about this chariot. Dr. Slop had even made a detour to see it on his way from Leyden to The Hague. Toby knows better: "That's nothing [...] to what the learned Peireskius did, who walked a matter of five hundred miles". And even Walter, who would not have bet a penny on Stevinus an hour earlier, begins to praise the "very mechanical head" of the inventor, and becomes curious about his prototype. Dr. Slop praises the winds on the shores of the North Sea and imagines the benefit that an "accoucheur" carried by their strength over Yorkshire plains could offer English women in labour. In anticipation of the wind farms that would spring up on the beaches of the North Sea, he sees the economic advantage in replacing the care and feeding of horses with wind power. No less prophetic, Walters counters this argument with the implacable law of the market:

> 'Because they cost nothing' [...]—the scheme is bad; [...]—if I was a prince, I would generously recompense [this] scientific head [...];—yet I would as peremptorily suppress the use of [...] such contrivances, [to protect] the consumption of our products, [...] which gives bread to the hungry, [...] supports the value of our lands, [...] and circulates trade.

This literally neoliberal doctrine would have demolished the arguments of the two others, if, fortunately, "the destinies had [not] decreed" that no such thing would take place that day. When Trim burst into the room carrying Stevinus, "the discourse [...]" was running into "a new channel", due to a coincidence Sterne calls "a cross accident", which the Ancient Greeks called a *kledon* and considered to be a sign from the gods, while Freud spoke of the "undeniable compliance of chance"[69] and the Surrealists of "objective chance". The list would not be complete without Lewis Carroll's White Rabbit[70] pulled out of *Alice in Wonderland*, as we shall see.

The lost sermon[71]

Playing and Reality[72] could only have been written by an English analyst. When Toby nods to Trim to take the book away, Walter asks the corporal in a playful tone: "But [...] look first into it, and see if thou canst spy aught of a sailing chariot in it". Playing the game of obeying orders, the corporal runs over the pages and then shakes the book holding it by the covers to make the imaginary chariot drop out. Fiction meets reality when something actually falls out of the book:

> '... but it is not a chariot or anything like one. [...] —Prithee, corporal, said my father smiling, what is it then? —I think, answered Trim [...], —'tis more like a sermon, —for it begins with a text of scripture [...];—and then goes on not as a chariot, —but like a sermon directly.' The company smiled.

The energy of the smile freed by this coincidence lightens the mood of the three men nervously awaiting the birth. Although Toby is familiar with surrealism—a word invented by Apollinaire during World War I when the incredible was a daily occurrence—he is the first to be surprised: "I cannot conceive how it is possible [...] for such a thing as a sermon to have gone into my Stevinus". Trim offers to read a page of it, "for [he] loved to hear himself read almost as well as talk". Toby supports Trim's candidature to the position of "public reader": "He can read it [...] as well as I can, —Trim, I assure you, was the best scholar in my company, and should have had the next halberd but for the poor fellow's misfortune".

Beyond the misfortune of his wounded knee at the battle of Landen in 1613, Trim's fate is going to take on a political dimension thanks to the lost sermon, found again by chance. The name of its author is not revealed until Trim finishes reading. It was Parson Yorick, a close friend of the Shandy family and the double of Laurence Sterne, who preached this sermon in the York cathedral in July 1750 under the title "The abuses of conscience". The sermon was to be published in a book entitled *The Sermons of Mr. Yorick* in 1760, the year when the first two volumes of *Tristram Shandy* came out in London.

The loss of a manuscript is a recurrent theme in texts dealing with trauma. Two centuries earlier, the manuscript of the first *Don Quixote*[73] was lost in Chapter 8 and found again in Chapter 9 in Arabic, the language of slavery that Cervantes preferred not to remember.

Two centuries later, the diary Wilfred Bion was writing on the frontlines in lieu of letters to his parents would also be lost, found and lost again, before resurfacing during the author's exile in Los Angeles in 1968. Published after Bion's death under the title *War Memoirs*,[74] it is the source of his three autobiographical books about a war he, like Cervantes, no longer wanted to remember, but could not forget. It comes back to him in his California exile, prompted perhaps by the American accent—that of soldiers who had fought alongside him—as well as by Kurt Vonnegut's bestseller *Slaughterhouse-Five*,[75] published the year Bion arrived in the US. In that book, which describes the author's captivity in a Dresden slaughterhouse during the destruction of the city in February 1945, Vonnegut uses the expression "a memory of the future" several times. Interestingly, Bion's third autobiographical book, written in the form of Shandean dialogues, is entitled *A Memoir of the Future*.

How often have I seen brought to my office war diaries and letters found by chance in an attic or in the back of a drawer, which would have remained lost—an unclaimed experience,[76] to use Cathy Caruth's term—had I not asked for them. Yorick's sermon had the same fate as these writings. After being found the first time, it fell out of its author's torn pocket before finally finding its way into Sterne's novel:

> Ill-fated sermon! Thou was lost, after this recovery of thee, a second time, dropp'd thro' an unsuspected fissure in thy master's pocket

[...], —trod deep into the dirt by the left hind foot of his Rocinante, inhumanly stepping upon thee as thou falledst;—buried ten days in the mire, [...]—not restored to his restless MANES till this very moment that I tell the world the story. [...] this sermon of Yorick's was preach'd [...] in the cathedral of York [...], by a certain prebendary of that church, and actually printed by him [...] within so short a space as two years and three months after Yorick's death.—Yorick, indeed, was never better served in his life!—but it was a little hard to maltreat him before, and plunder him after he was laid in his grave.

In order to give the sermon back to the parson's worried Manes, Sterne decided to put it in a safe place, so that, as he says: "I may give rest to Yorick's ghost;—which, as the county people—and some others believe, — still walks".

I can say the same about the publication of Jean-Max Gaudillière's seminars[77] at the EHESS (School for Advanced Studies in the Social Sciences), which would have been lost forever—since he spoke without a written text— if not for the invitation extended by Jane Tillman, Director of the Erikson Institute of Research at Austen Riggs Center, for me to transcribe my notes of the seminars so as to render justice to their author.

The serpentine line of beauty[78]

Trim delivered the sermon with deep feeling, becoming entirely possessed by it as he read. Sterne describes his stance precisely:

He stood before them with his body swayed and bent forwards just so far as to make an angle of 85 degrees and a half upon the plane of the horizon;—which sound orators [...] know very well to be the true persuasive angle of incidence;—in any other angle you may talk and preach;—'tis certain, —and it is done every day;—but with what effect, —I leave the world to judge.

We see him from the back in Hogarth's engraving, standing in the fore-ground, facing the three men seated by the fireplace. The famous "serpentine line of beauty"[79] follows Slop's belly and the billowing pipe smoke, avoiding, Hogarth says, the "fixity of the straight line". Before the reading of the sermon begins, Sterne wonders about the intelligence of Trim's body:

How the deuce Corporal Trim, who knew not so much as an acute angle from an obtuse one, came to hit it so exactly? [...] He stood [...] with his body sway'd and somewhat bent forwards, —his right leg firm under him, sustaining seven eights of his whole weight, —the foot of his left leg [...] advanced a little, [...];—his knee bent, but not violently, —but so as to fall within the limits of the line of beauty.

The index of a hand drawn in the margin of the text indicates this posture to painters and orators, who must practice it in order to avoid falling over. Trained in soldiering, Trim knows as much as the slave Meno questioned by Socrates[80]:

> He held the sermon loosely, —not carelessly, in his left hand, raised something above his stomach and detach'd a little from his breast [as one would hold a sword or the reins of a horse];—his right arm falling negligently by his side, as nature and the laws of gravity order'd it [...]. Corporal Trim's eyes and the muscles of his face were in full harmony with the other parts of him;—he look'd frank, —unconstrained, —something assured, [...] with such an oratorical sweep throughout [his] whole figure.

T. S. Eliot[81] would write much later: "You are the music while the music lasts". Little by little, the music of the sermon starts to resonate with a traumatic memory whose musical score is inscribed in the corporal's body.[82]

Wittgenstein[83]: I am fond of corporal Trim in *Tristram Shandy*, especially the sermon he read

The sermon entitled "The abuses of Conscience" is punctuated by the relentless upswing of an agency that destroys all alterity. We encounter this agency in the critical stages of an analysis of madness or trauma. Here, what is needed is not the lifting of unconscious repression Lacan[84] calls "the discourse of the Other", since there is no otherness, but the introduction of a witness bringing into the present psychic murders orchestrated by a good conscience for which the other does not exist.

Trim's reading to the other three men resembles a martial arts session in which the corporal confronts successive enemies. "Trim made a bow and read as follows". The battle starts at once, with Paul's epistle to the Hebrews 13:18: "For we trust we have a good conscience". "To trust" means to rely on someone. The first sentence of the sermon challenges the existence of good faith—something Walter sees at once in Trim's attitude, on which he comments, interrupting the reading:

> Certainly, Trim, [...] you give that sentence a very improper accent; for you curl up your nose, man, and read it [...] as if the parson was going to abuse the Apostle. —He is, and please Your Honour, replied Trim. —Pugh! Said my father, smiling.

Things will get heated between the Catholic and the Anglicans. Slop attacks first, Walter counterattacks and Toby gets to the heart of the matter by asking a seemingly naïve question:

> Sir, quoth Dr Slop, Trim is certainly in the right; for the writer [...] I perceive is a Protestant, by [his] snappish manner [...]. But from whence, replied my father, have you concluded so soon [...]?—For aught I can see yet, —he may be of any Church. —Because, answered Dr Slop, if he was of ours, —he durst no more take such a licence—[...] to insult an Apostle, — a saint, [...]—he would have his eyes scratched out. —What, by the saint? Quoth my uncle Toby. Slop falls into his snare. —No [...] he would have an old house over his head. —Pray, is the Inquisition an ancient building, answered my uncle Toby, or is it a modern one?

Now, the word has been spoken. The tribunals of the Inquisition, founded in the 12th century, took up their activities again in the 1800s after a period of calm in the previous century. A totalitarian agency takes centre stage, just as it does at critical stages in an analysis, when the aim of the transference is to fight it and introduce a reliable alterity in the very place where it has been destroyed. In the meantime, denial runs rampant. Slop wants to drop the whole thing: "I know nothing of architecture". Walter tries to gain time. Trim exclaims: "—An' please Your Honours [...], the Inquisition is the vilest—[...] for, Heaven above knows, I have a poor brother who has been fourteen years a captive in it".

A dramatic twist! The theoretical discussion takes a personal turn, thanks to a particular story—the kind we were taught to avoid in our youth, since personal stories serving to illustrate theories were considered anecdotal evidence. But, in fact, Trim's story opens the way to a suppressed account of political terror no one had been aware of. The corporal promises his master to tell him the story later, while they build fortifications together. The narration which will unfold in Chapters V and VI of Volume 9 is summarised here. Tom, Trim's brother, was working as a servant in Lisbon when he married the widow of a Jew who owned a sausage shop. This, "somehow or other", caused his arrest in the middle of the night, when he was pulled from his bed in front of his wife and his two small children, to be carried off to the Inquisition, where, Trim lamented, "the poor honest lad lies confined at this hour".

The revival of the scene made tears trickle down Trim's face faster than his handkerchief could wipe them away. A dead silence ensued in the room, long enough to give us time to remember nocturnal arrests in our own time. Of course, one can't make an omelette without breaking eggs, says Dr. Slop, whose generalisation covers all eras. Walter's solution is to think of something else: "Come, Trim [...], —read on—and put this melancholy story out of thy head.—I grieve that I interrupted thee".

After wiping his face and putting his handkerchief back in his pocket, the corporal bows again, not knowing that traumatic memory would interrupt him once more now that it has found an audience for its testimony. The word "trust" is spoken again, twice:

> TRUST!—Trust we have a good conscience! [...] If a man thinks at all, he cannot well be a stranger to the true state of this account;—he must be privy to his own thoughts and desires;—he must remember his past pursuits and know certainly the true springs and motives which [...] have governed the actions of his life.

The sermon opens the way to the unconscious that is "a stranger" to itself, since it has been cut out by the destruction of speech. In *Gradiva*,[85] Freud wrote: "Everything that is repressed must remain unconscious, but [...] let us state that the repressed does not comprise the whole unconscious". The agency responsible for this cutting out is identified in the sermon:

> Did no such thing ever happen that the conscience of a man, by long habits of sin, might insensibly become hard [...] Did this never happen;—or was it certain that self-love could never hang the least bias upon the judgement [...]—or, lastly, were we assured that INTEREST stood always unconcern'd. [...]—so that the common consolation—that [a man] has a good conscience, because he has a quiet one, —is fallacious. [...]—the principle upon which it goes [is] so often perverted.

The perverted principle is presented as an escalation, through the "banalisation of evil", a term that would be introduced later by Hanna Arendt in her analysis of perverted social links leading to totalitarianism.

The four stages of perversion

The first case is that of a "vicious and utterly debauched" man who shamelessly ruins and dishonours his partner, "robs her of her best dowry, and not only covers her own head but her whole family with shame and sorrow": "Surely you will think [...] such a man can have no rest at night from [the] reproaches of his conscience [...]. Perhaps CONSCIENCE has something else to do", [...] talking loud against petty larceny and [...] some puny crimes as his fortune and rank in life secured him against..."

On this point, the papist and the anti-papists agree. But Dr. Slop argues that such a case could not occur among Catholics, who have confession, after Walter promptly admits that "It happens in our [church] but too often"; the doctor then concedes that in the Roman Catholic faith, "a man may live as a badly, but then cannot easily die so. —'Tis little matter, replied my father [...], —how a rascal dies".

The brief truce is soon over; the war of religion is ignited again by Toby's falsely naïve question about the number of sacraments in the Catholic faith:

> Seven, answered Dr Slop. —Humph!—said by uncle Toby; [...]—Doctor Slop, who had an ear, understood my uncle Toby as well as if he had wrote a whole volume against the seven sacraments [...] —Humph! [...]—Why, sir, are there not seven [...] mortal sins?....

And he goes on to list all things that go by sevens. Walter cuts him short and asks Trim to go on.

"Another is sordid, unmerciful..." The second stage of cruelty portrays "a strait-hearted, selfish wretch", incapable either of private friendship or public spirit. Trim interjects:

> And please Your Honours, [...] I think this is a viler man than the other. [...] Take notice how he passes by the widow and orphan in their distress [...]. Shall not conscience rise up and sting him on such occasions? — No; thank God there is no occasion; *I pay every man his own;—I have no fornication to answer to my conscience;—no faithless vows or promises to make up;—I have debauched no man's wife or child; thank God, I am not as other men [...]or even as this libertine who stands before me.*

The man illustrating the third stage of cruelty is "crafty and designing", takes advantage of "the ignorance and perplexities of the poor [...] man" and of the inexperience of youth, to build his fortune. This man inspired Diderot—who read *Tristram Shandy* in the original—to write in *Rameau's Nephew*[86]:

> Be as miserly as you like, but don't talk like the miser. [...] be a hypocrite, if you like, but don't talk like a hypocrite. Keep the vices which are useful, but don't assume a tone or an appearance which will make you ridiculous.

At the end of his life, the crafty man's conscience is as clear as that of the ones described earlier:

> CONSCIENCE [...] finds no express law broken by what he has done;— [...] sees no [...] prison opening [its] gates upon him. [...] Conscience has got safely entrenched behind the letter of the Law; [...] fortified with CASES and REPORTS (in Gothic script) so strongly on all sides—that [no] preaching can dispossess it of its hold.

Hearing the reference to fortification, Toby and Trim exchange meaningful glances. Walter senses their hobby horse chomping at the bit and tries to head it off. But to no avail:

> Aye, —aye, Trim! quothe my uncle Toby, shaking his head, —these are but sorry fortifications, [...]. —Go on, Trim, quothe my father, or Obadiah will have got back before thou hast got to the end of thy sermon. —'Tis a very short one, replied Trim. —I wish it was longer, quothe my uncle Toby, for I like it hugely.

This unexpected admission confirms the captain's resemblance to the Don Quixote of *The Second Part*,[87] who fought against perversion at the ducal castle. A paroxysm of violence is reached in the fourth stage of cruelty, in which cheating, lying, perjury, robbery and murder are committed openly. "Horrid"! The Shakespearian adjective underlines the impunity of terror. If he is godly, the pervert will always find a bigot to excuse him and give him absolution: "—the poor man was in the dark"! or he had an unhappy childhood, it was not his fault. Sterne is not impressed by these self-satisfied egos by the man who is "such a bubble to himself" that his wicked actions:

> are generally dress'd out and painted with all the false beauties which a soft and a flattering hand can give them. [...] This unwary traveller [is] too apt, God knows, to [...] confidently speak peace to himself when there is no peace.

The sermon continues with a quote from Ecclesiastics: "Blessed is the man, [...] whether he be rich or whether he be poor, if [...] his mind shall tell him more than seven watchmen that sit upon a tower on high". While the two veterans discuss the number of sentinels needed to guard such a tower, I hear Bach's chorale in Cantata No. 140 ("Awake, the Voice Is Calling"), composed in Leipzig in 1731. Here, pastor Yorick, who composed his sermons like music, slows down the tempo, *ma non tropo*, before launching into his last movement, *con furia*. He gives two examples, taken from the rising ranks of physicians, bankers and lawyers whose pompous discourses mask pride and personal interest:

> I know the banker I deal with or the physician I usually call in [...] to be neither of them men of much religion[...]. Well, —notwithstanding this, I put my fortune into the hands of the one; —and [...] I trust my life to the honest skill of the other. [...]—Why, in the first place, I believe there is no probability that either of them will employ the power I put into their hands to my disadvantage? [...] What is my reason for this great confidence? [...] I know their success in the world depends upon the fairness of their characters. [...] I must lay at the mercy of HONOUR.

The army is not spared either. Trim waves his right arm when the sermon takes up the topic of:

> ...the crusading sword of this misguided saint-errant [who] spared nei-
> ther age or merit, or sex, or condition [...]; under the banners of a reli-
> gion which set him loose from justice and humanity, —and he shew'd
> none. [...] —I have been in many a battle [...], quoth Trim, sighing, but
> never in so melancholy a one as this.—I would not have drawn a tricker
> in it, against these poor souls, —to have been made a general officer. —
> Why, what do you understand of the affair? Said Doctor Slop, [...] with
> something more contempt than the corporal's honest heart deserved.

Roger Sterne's son shatters the good conscience of civilians like Dr. Slop—the same good conscience which caused Captain Bion,[88] when he was on leave in London, to want to desert towards the frontline. The corporal forces the doctor to face his ignorance:

> —What do you know, friend, about this battle you talk of? —I know,
> replied Trim, that I never refused quarter in my life to any man who
> cried out for it;—but to a woman or a child [...].

Impatient with this outpouring of emotion, Walter prompts Trim to finish reading the last two pages, in which the ultimate stage of cruelty is reached.

Traumatic revival

The sermon takes them into a prison of the Inquisition full of instruments of torture, where they hear the Shakespearean injunction: "Hark!—hark! What a piteous groan!" The close-up shows the tortured man. Trim's face "turns as pale as ashes". He can't fight back his tears. "D—m them all". He has forgotten all about the sermon, and goes from ashen to blood-red. Suddenly alone, he beholds:

> this helpless victim delivered up to his tormentors, [...] just brought forth
> to undergo the anguish of a mock trial and endure the utmost pains that
> a studied system of cruelty has been able to invent. [...] [Oh! 'tis my
> brother, cried poor Trim [...] dropping the sermon upon the ground and
> clapping his hands together—I fear 'tis poor Tom].

Sterne too probably had to hold back tears and stifle his own cry: "Oh, 'tis my brother, 'tis my sister"! when his pastoral duties took him to the bedside of dying children, bringing back his own siblings' dying moments. In the presence of the three shaken men, corporal Trim can finally shed the tears long held back in a cut-out portion of his memory. Walter tries to calm him by bringing him back to reality: "—Why, Trim [...], this is not a history, —'tis a sermon thou art reading;—prithee begin the sentence again".

But the corporal is unable to continue reading. Entrapped in the unbearable scene, he cannot stop himself from enduring the tortures inflicted on defenceless victims in all the jails of the planet. We are reminded of Kafka's machine in *The Penal Colony*,[89] which etches the sentence received into the flesh of the prisoner:

> Behold the helpless victim [...], —his body so wasted [...] you will see every nerve and muscle as it suffers. Observe the last movement of that horrid engine! [...]—See what convulsions it has thrown him into!—Consider [how] he now lies stretched, —what exquisite tortures he endures by it!—[...]—'Tis all nature can bear! Good God! See how it keeps his weary soul hanging upon his trembling lips! [...]—I fear [...] all this is in Portugal, where my poor brother Tom is.

Time and space are unhinged. Like an analyst shaken by a scene of reviviscence, Walter tries to minimise once again: "I tell thee, Trim, again [...], 'tis not a historical account;—'tis a description —[...] there's not a word of truth in it, quoth Slop. —That's another story, replied my father".

History has entered the novel through an opening other than that offered by Toby and Trim's wars, which will be recounted in Volume 9, when Tom's story will be told in the context of slavery.

Catharsis[90]

Cruelty can also insinuate itself into therapies that promote regression. Walter is aware of the corporal's distress and does not want him traumatised any further; for once, he plays the role of *therapon* and offers to continue the reading himself:

> Trim reads [the sermon] with so much concern, —'tis cruelty to force him to go on with it.—Give me hold of the sermon, Trim, —[...]—Behold the unhappy wretch led back to his cell! [Then thank God, however, quoth Trim, they have not killed him]—See him dragged out of it again to meet the flames, and the insults in his last agonies, which this principle—this principle that there can be religion without mercy has prepared for him. [Then, thank God, —he is dead, quoth Trim, —he is out of his pain, [...].

The reading of the sermon cools down emotions, until we come to the word *FINIS* written in capital letters:

> In a word, —trust that man in nothing who has not a CONSCIENCE in everything. [...] conscience [has been] placed within you to determine

[...] his own passions, —[...] like a British judge [...] who makes no new law in this land of liberty and good sense, but faithfully declares that law which he knows already written.

Walter congratulates Trim for his reading of the sermon, saying that it should be preached the world over without meeting with the fate of French politicians, who "lose in the field what they gain in the cabinet".

Let us overlook the treacherous remark of France's traditional enemy, since we have just taken part in a ritual performance. The reading of the sermon not only denounces perversion, but goes beyond the text heard in the cathedral of York. It brings into play the "fearful imagination" of those who have not experienced such tortures but affirm their truth and can testify—as Hannah Arendt[91] has written:

> Only the fearful imagination of those who have been aroused by reports but have not actually been smitten in their own flesh, of those who are consequently free from the bestial, desperate terror which [...] inexorably paralyzes everything that is not mere reaction, can afford to keep thinking about horrors.

Once this catharsis has taken place, chronology can resume its function and cut-out memory be inscribed: "There are now in the possession of the Shandy family as many [sermons] as will make a handsome volume, at the world's service..."

The aim of a psychoanalysis of madness and trauma is to inscribe the "historical truth" destroyed by a totalitarian agency, Freud wrote in *Moses and Monotheism*[92] after his books were burned by the Nazis in 1933. This analysis creates a political subject who asserts himself grammatically in the "I wish" that introduces the novel and is repeated like a leitmotif throughout the book, up to its conclusion: Toby's "no" to perversion.

Toby's *I wish*[93]

The event of the birth of the hero, which will only occur in Volume 3, will provoke a clash of the "fates" gathered around him, like in fairy tales. Trim exits the scene just as Obadiah enters—with Dr. Slop's bag which he was sent to fetch in chapter VI—and is given the two crowns. He comes in accompanied by the jingling of the obstetrical instruments in the bag slung across his chest. The doctor is about to go into action when Walter reveals the pact he made with his wife to call in the midwife as well in an effort to minimise the conflict between the sexes:

> Women have their particular fancies, and in points of this nature [...], where they bear the whole burden and suffer so much acute pain for the advantage of our families and the good of the species, —they claim

a right of deciding, *en souveraines* [...]. —They are in the right of it, — quote my uncle Toby [in Quixotic fashion].

Dr. Slop intercedes to defend patriarchal law:

They had better govern in other points. [...] it would astonish you to know what improvements we have made of late years in all branches of obstetrical knowledge, but particularly in [...] the safe and expeditious extraction of the fetus...

The captain interrupts the inexorable progress of enlightenment with a discordant "I wish", echoing that of the embryo, which leaves the two other men speechless: "I wish you had seen what prodigious armies we had in Flanders".

This phrase will be repeated three times, in chapters I, II and VI of Volume 3, with no explanation, like the striking of a gong. The scene ends there. Curtain! We are left to guess about Toby's out-of-the-blue interjection. Is it the ramblings of an old soldier? Or the regret of Sterne's father, expressed when he was demobilised by the Treaty of Utrecht in 1713, the year of Laurence's birth? Or Toby's post-traumatic reaction after Trim's breakdown? In those days, PTSD (post-traumatic stress disorder) was called "nostalgia".

Jean-Jacques Rousseau[94] speaks of nostalgia in the ranks of the Swiss soldiers who threw their weapons away and cried when they heard "*Le Ranz des vaches*" ("The Cow's Song"), a beloved anthem from the mountains of their homeland. I heard it at the Winegrowers' Festival in Vevey (Switzerland), celebrated five times in a century since Sterne's era. The term "nostalgia" was also used by Baron Larrey, surgeon in Napoleon's *Grande Armée*, to describe traumatised soldiers.

In any case, Sterne brushes aside all our speculations about Toby's "I wish" and interrupts his narrative to introduce a memory of the future.

The wing of a butterfly and the location of the psyche in the brain[95]

When Toby expresses his nostalgia for the "prodigious armies in Flanders", the narration is suddenly interrupted: "I have dropp'd the curtain over this scene for a minute—to remind you of one thing —and to inform you of another [...]; [that] should have been told a hundred and fifty pages ago." Sterne's reminder concerns Walter's foresight, a gentleman ahead of his time, "odd and whimsical" in his opinions, which were very far from "the highway of thinking" and even very contemporary:

[...] he placed things in his own light;—he would weigh nothing in common scales. [...] Knowledge, [...] he would affirm, was divisible *in infinitum*;—that the grains and scruples were as much a part of it as the gravitation of the whole world. (Newton was Toby's contemporary.) [...] a mistake in the dust of a butterfly's wing [was of equal consequence with a mistake] in the disk of the sun, the moon, and all the stars of heaven put together.

In 1972, Edward Lorenz was to formulate the metaphor of "the flap of a butterfly's wings in Brazil setting off a tornado in Texas" to describe the sensitive dependence on initial conditions in chaos theory. Walter understands the political and economic dimensions of such a metaphor:

> He would often lament that it was for want of considering this properly and applying it skillfully to civil matters [...], that so many things in this world were out of joint (as Hamlet says), [...]—that the very foundations of our excellent constitution [...] were so sapp'd [...]. You cry out, he would say, we are a ruined, undone people.—Why? [...]—Why are we a ruined people?—Because we are corrupted.—Whence is it, dear sir, that we are corrupted?—Because we are needy;—our poverty, and not our wills, consent.—And wherefore [...]—are we needy?—From the neglect [...] of our pence and our halfpence.

On what does he base his vision of micro funding? In our history courses, we learned about events in 1720 known as "Law's bankruptcy". John Law was a Scottish economist appointed to restore finances in France. He directed the Mississipi Company when it went bankrupt concurrently with the collapse of the South Sea Bubble in England. This financial crash revealed the underside of British prosperity, whose victims were, first and foremost, children, as we can see in William Hogarth's paintings. Born in 1697, as a boy between the ages of ten and fifteen, Hogarth lived in debtors' lodgings near the Fleet Street Prison, where his father was imprisoned for debt. Sterne, who experienced the same precarious circumstances as a child, befriended the painter who, before his death in 1764, gave him three more etchings to illustrate in his book, in addition to "Corporal Trim Reading a Sermon".

Once we have been reminded of Walter's visionary perspectives in physics and economy, Sterne ventures into the neurosciences to teach us something about the location of the soul in the brain.

Going beyond the 17th-century belief that the seat of the soul was in the pineal gland, Walter foresees the advances put forth by Antonio Damasio in his book *Descartes' Error*.[96] The neurologist describes the famous case of Phineas Gage, who continued to reason after his frontal lobe was destroyed by an iron rod that went through his skull, at the end of the 19th century. Well, Toby already knew of such a case in the 18th century, and told a similar story about a:

> Walloon officer at the Battle of Landen in 1693, who had one part of his brain shot away [...]—another part of it taken out after by a French surgeon; and, after all, recovered and did his duty very well without it.

Ergo, the seat of the soul is not located in the frontal lobe.

Walter also rejects the theory of an Italian physician:

> As for [...] Coglionissimo Borri, [he] affirms [...] to have discovered [it] in the fragrant juice of the occipital parts of the cerebellum [...]. The very idea [of] the *anima* [...] dabbling like a tadpole [...], both summer and winter, in a puddle [...] shock'd [my father's] imagination.

He also disagrees with Dutch anatomists who place the headquarters of the soul somewhere near the *medulla oblongata*. Their descendants, Bassel Van der Kolk in Boston and Onno Van der Hart[97] in Amsterdam, locate in this vicinity the seat of traumatic revivals dissociated from the area of language and temporality in the brain. But Walter has drawn no conclusion yet, and prefers to arrive at one by formulating his Shandean hypothesis concerning the catastrophes to which the newborn could be exposed.

The hypothesis concerns, first of all, the importance of the act of procreation for establishing in each individual "this incomprehensible contexture in which wit, memory, fancy, eloquence do consist". The second point has to do with the meticulous choice of a Christian name, a failed endeavour in Tristram's case. And finally, the third circumstance, called *causa sine qua non* by logicians, depends on the "lucky or unlucky organization of the body in that part where the soul principally took up her residence". Walter is convinced that the seat of the soul is in the brain, even if we cannot pinpoint it exactly. Therefore, he is determined to protect his child's brain from the havoc caused "by the violent compression and crush which the head was made to undergo by the nonsensical method of bringing us into the world". This intuition struck him like a lightning bolt:

> My father, who dipp'd into all kinds of books [...], had found out that the lax and pliable state of a child's head in parturition [...] was compressed and moulded into the shape of an oblong conic piece of dough [...].—Angels and ministers of grace defend us! Cried my father, —can any soul withstand this shock?—No wonder [...] that so many of our best heads are [...] all perplexity, —all confusion within side.

The hypothesis accounted for everything. "—it accounted for the eldest son being the greatest blockhead in the family."

In Sterne's novel, the eldest sons do not have an easy time of it. This one, named Bobby, will appear briefly in Volume 5 before departing from this life. Mrs. Shandy is treated no better. Her husband considers her incapable of understanding a reasonable argument, especially as she almost faints at the prospect of a caesarean without anesthesia: "But when my father [learned] that a child [could be] turned topsy-turvy [...] and extracted by the feet", he tried to persuade his wife to have a caesarian section. He talked to her one afternoon of the:

> incision of the abdomen and uterus, [saying] that wounds in the epigastrium and those in the matrix were not mortal [...], —but seeing her turn as pale as ashes [...], he thought it as well to say no more of it.

This explains Slop's arrival on the scene, with his forceps, which in the 18th century were at the centre of a veritable mystery. The instrument had been invented in the 17th century by Peter Chamberlain, and was hidden in a large wooden box, remaining a family secret for a hundred years, until Hugh, the inventor's son, decided to make his fortune by leaking the secret in France. The first to use forceps, male "accoucheurs", started rivalling midwives, a situation illustrated by the dispute between Walter Shandy and his wife.

Volume 2 ends with the announcement of the stand that Toby, "a plain man, with nothing but common sense", would have to take in opposition to the two proponents of science allied against him. How he bore up is left to the reader's imagination until the end of the following year, "when a series of things will be laid open which he little expects". Suspense! The battle between brain and psyche is far from over.

Notes

1 Sterne, L., *Tristram Shandy*, op. cit., Vol. 2, ch. II.
2 Freud, *Delusions and Dreams in Wilhelm Jensen's Gradiva*, S.E. 9, London: Hogarth, 1907.
3 Sterne, L., *Tristram Shandy*, op. cit., pp. 90–91.
4 Fuentes, C., *Christopher Unborn*, New York: Farrar, Straus and Giroux, 1989.
5 Bion, W., *A Memoir of the Future*, London and New York: Routledge, 2018.
6 Sterne, L. *Tristram Shandy*, op. cit., Vol. 2, ch. I.
7 Sterne, L. *Tristram Shandy*, op. cit., pp. 64–65.
8 Van der Kolke, B., *The Body Keeps the Score*, Penguin Books UK, 2015.
9 Wittgenstein, L., *Philosophical Investigations*, op. cit.
10 Gaudillière, J.-M., *Madness and the Social Link*, London and New York: Routledge, 2021.
11 Barker, P., *The Regeneration Trilogy*, Hamish Hamilton UK, 2014.
12 Barrois, C., *Psychanalyse de guerre*, Paris: Hachette, 1993.
13 Shay, J., *Achilles in Vietnam*, New York: Simon & Shuster, 1995.
14 Bion, W., *A Memoir of the Future*, op. cit., p.168.
15 Wittgenstein, L. *Philosophical Investigations*, op. cit.
16 Drury, M. O'C., *The Selected Writings of Maurice O'Connor Drury*, London, Oxford, New York, New Delhi, Sydney: Bloomsbury Academic, 2017.
17 Snyder, T., *Bloodlands*, New York: Basic Books, 2012.
18 Marshall, S. L. A., *Island Victory*, Washington, DC: Zenger, 1982.
19 Sterne, L., *Tristram Shandy*, Vol. 2, ch. II.
20 Locke, J, *An Essay Concerning Human Understanding*, Penguin Books UK, 1997.
21 Plato, *Theaetetus*, New York: The Liberal Arts Press, 1955.
22 Sterne, L., *Tristram Shandy*, Vol. 2, ch III.

23 De Cervantes, M., *Don Quixote I* (1605); Don Quixote II (1614), op. cit.
24 Grossman, D. and Christensen, L. W., *On Combat: The Psychology and Physiology of Deadly Conflict in War and Peace*, Illinois: PPCT Research Publications, 2004.
25 Sterne, L., *Tristram Shandy*, op. cit., Vol. 2, ch. IV.
26 Shank, J.W., *Lincoln's Melancholia*, Boston: Houghton Mifflin Company, 2005.
27 Fritz, J. M., *Le discours du fou au Moyen Âge*, Paris: PUF, 1992.
28 Caruth, C., *Unclaimed Experience*, Baltimore: John Hopkins University Press, 2016.
29 Sterne, L., *Tristram Shandy*, Vol. 2, ch. V.
30 Goldoni, C., *The Servant of Two Masters*, New York: Broadway Play Publishing, 2006.
31 Descartes, R. (1637) *Discourse on Method and Meditations*, New York: Dover Philosophical Classics, 2003; Baillet, A., "Olympica", in *La Vie de Monsieur Descartes*, Books LLC, 2011.
32 Winnicott, D., *Playing and Reality*, London and New York: Routledge Classics, 1971.
33 Virgil, *The Aeneid of Virgil*, New York: Charles Scribner's Sons, 1952.
34 Benedetti, G., *Todeslandschaften der Seele* (Landscapes of Death of the Soul), Göttingen: Vandenhoeck & Ruprecht, 2003.
35 Caruth, C., *Literature in the Ashes of History*, Baltimore: John Hopkins University Press, 2012.
36 Freud, S., *Beyond the Pleasure Principle*, S.E. 18, London: Hogarth.
37 Wittgenstein, L., *Remarks on Frazer's Golden Bough*, op. cit.
38 Virgil, *The Georgics*, New York: Cambridge University Press, 1988.
39 Binswanger, L. and Warburg, A., *La guérison infinie*, Paris: Rivages, 2011.
40 Thom, R., *To Predict is Not to Explain*, Tsatsanis, S. P. (Ed.), Toronto: Thombooks Press, 2016.
41 Ross, I. C., *Laurence Sterne: A Life*, op. cit.
42 De Lorris, G. and De Meun, J., (13th C.) *The Romance of the Rose*, Horgan, F. (Trans.) Oxford Paperbacks, 2008.
43 Apuleius (2nd c). *Metamorphoses*, Cambridge: Harvard University Press, 1996.
44 Sterne, L., *Tristram Shandy*, op. cit., Vol. 2, chs. VI to VIII.
45 Vonnegut, K. *Timequake*, New York: Berkeley Books, 1997.
46 Sterne, L., *Tristram Shandy*, op. cit., p. 84.
47 Sterne, L., *Tristram Shandy*, op. cit., Vol. 2, ch. VIII.
48 Sterne, L., *Tristram Shandy*, op. cit., Vol. 2, ch. IX.
49 Hogarth, W. (1753). *The Analysis of Beauty*, New York: Cosimo Classics, 2010.
50 Shakespeare., *Hamlet*, New York: Dover Thrift Editions, 1992.
51 Sterne, L., *Tristram Shandy*, op. cit., Vol. 2, chs. X, XI.
52 Shakespeare, W., *Hamlet*, op. cit., Act 1, sc. 5, vs. 75, 77.
53 Lin-Chi, *The Zen Teachings of Master Lin-Chi*, Watson, B. (Trans.), New York: Columbia University Press, 1999.
54 Sterne, L., *Tristram Shandy*, op. cit., Vol. 2, ch. XII.
55 Sterne, L., *Tristram Shandy*, op. cit., Vol. 2, ch. XVIII.
56 De Cervantes, M., *Don Quixote I*, op. cit., ch. 39.
57 De Cervantes, M., *Don Quixote*, op. cit., ch. 22.
58 Chernow, R., *Alexander Hamilton*, Penguin Books UK, 2004, pp. 721–722.
59 Ross, I.C., *Laurence Sterne, A Life*, op. cit., p. 28.
60 Wittgenstein, L., *Philosophical Investigations*, op. cit., § 309.
61 Ibid., § 288.
62 Fisher, J., *Healing the Fragmented Selves of Trauma Survivors*, Routledge, 2017.

63 Rivers, W., "An Address on the Repression of War Experience", *The Lancet*, April 1918.
64 Winnicott, D., "Fear of Breakdown", *International Review of Psychoanalysis*, 1974, No. 1.
65 Laub, D. and Felman, S. *Testimony*, London: Routledge, 1992.
66 Wittgenstein, L., *Philosophical Investigations*, op. cit., § 41.
67 Sterne, L., *Tristram Shandy*, op. cit., Vol 2, chs. XIII, XIV.
68 Shakespeare, W., *Julius Caesar*, New York: Dover Publications, 1991.
69 Freud, S. and Jung, C., *The Freud/Jung Letters*, Princeton University Press, 1994.
70 Carroll, L., *Alice in Wonderland*, Hertfordshire, UK: Wordsworth Editions, 2018.
71 Sterne, L., *Tristram Shandy*, op. cit., chs. XV–XVII.
72 Winnicott, D., *Playing and Reality*, London and New York: Routledge Classics, 1971.
73 De Cervantes, M., *Don Quixote I*, op. cit., chs. 8, 9.
74 Bion, W., *War Memoirs 1917–1919*, London and New York: Routledge, 1997.
75 Vonnegut, K., *Slaughterhouse-Five*, New York: Dell, 1991.
76 Caruth, C., *Unclaimed Experience*, op. cit.
77 Gaudillière, J-M., *Madness and the Social Link Seminars* (Book 1, Book 2), London and New York: Routledge, 2021.
78 Sterne, L., *Tristram Shandy*, op. cit., ch. XVII.
79 Hogarth, W., *The Analysis of Beauty*, op. cit.
80 Plato, *Meno*, London: Macmillan Publishing, 1949.
81 Eliot, T.S., *Four Quartets*, Boston: Mariner Books, 1968.
82 Van der Kolk, B., *The Body Keeps the Score*, op. cit..
83 Hays, J. and Monk, J. (Eds.), *The Selected Writings of Maurice O'Connor Drury: On Wittengenstein…*, London, Oxford, New York, New Delhi, Sydney: Bloomsbury Academic, 2018, p. 93.
84 Lacan, J., *Écrits*, Paris: Seuil, 1966, p. 265.
85 Freud, S. *Delusions and Dreams in Jensen's Gradiva*, op.cit.
86 Diderot, D., *Rameau's Nephew*, Oxfordshire: Benediction Classics, 2011.
87 De Cervantes, M., *Don Quixote II*, op. cit.
88 Bion, W., *The Long Week-End*, op. cit.
89 Kafka, F., *The Penal Colony*, London: Penguin Classics, 2011.
90 Sterne, L., *Tristram Shandy*, op. cit., Vol. 2, chs. XVII–XVIII.
91 Arendt, A., *The Origins of Totalitarianism*, Cleveland: The World Publishing Company, 1951, p. 441.
92 Freud, S., *Moses and Monotheism*, London: Vintage Books, 1955.
93 Sterne, L., Tristram Shandy, op. cit., Vol 2, ch. XVIII.
94 Rousseau, J.-J., *A Dictionary of Music*, Waring, W. (Trans.), Gale ECCO, 2010.
95 Sterne, L., *Tristram Shandy*, op. cit., Vol. 2, ch. XIX.
96 Damasio, A., *Descartes' Error*, Penguin Books UK, 2005.
97 Caruth, C., *Listening to Trauma. Conversations with Leaders in the Theory and Treatment of Catastrophic Experience*, Baltimore: Johns Hopkins University Press, 2014.

3

Theatre of fools[1]

Volume 3 starts with two mysterious phrases. The first is a 12th-century Latin epigraph quoting John of Salisbury, Bishop of Lyon. The Primate of the Gauls defends the proximity between laughter and gravity:

> I do not fear the opinions of the ignorant mob, but I ask that they spare my little book, in which I always proposed to pass from the mirthful to the serious, and from the serious to the mirthful again.

The second phrase is the one repeated by Toby[2]: "I wish, Dr Slop, [...] you had seen what prodigious armies we had in Flanders". Slop and Walter stare at him in disbelief. This desire, repeated a second time "with a degree of more zeal and earnestness [...] than he had wished it at first", cuts short the praises of the Caesarean section by Walter and the promotion of forceps presented by Slop as "the safest instrument of deliverance".

Toby's wishful sentence, repeated four times, could suggest a "psychic automatism", as defined by Gaetan Gatian de Clérambault, Lacan's master. But Sterne saves Toby from such a diagnosis. By beating the drum of "our prodigious armies", the captain unknowingly becomes a "wisher" whose power stuns the doctor: "My uncle Toby's wish did Dr Slop a disservice [...], —sir, it confounded him..."

After addressing the "sir", Sterne turns to me; in his country parish, he must have met some women about my age accused of witchcraft, for he has drawn certain conclusions:

> Nothing is more dangerous, madam, —whether for honour, for profit or for love, — [...] than a wish coming sideways in this unexpected manner upon a man. The safest [response] is, for the party wished at, instantly to get upon his legs—and wish the *wisher* something in return of pretty near the same value.

DOI: 10.4324/9781003224907-3

The "wished" tries to gather his thoughts, but to no avail:

> Dr Slop did not understand the nature of this defence, —[...] my father saw the danger—the dispute was one of the most interesting disputes in the world [...], he waited to the last moment to allow Dr Slop, in whose behalf the wish was made, his right of returning it; but perceiving that he was confounded [...], —my father thought there was no time to lose with my uncle Toby...

Sterne promises us, in passing, a "chapter on wishes", a topic he continues to discuss as if it were a martial art. By launching the prodigious armies he had in Flanders against Dr. Slop, the captain never intended any harm, but he achieved his aim. In his book *Zen in the Art of Archery*, Eugen Herrigel[3] quotes his Zen master: "The arm which shoots the arrow must do so without purpose, without attaching importance to whether or not the arrow hits the target".

Captain Toby's traumatic memory has registered the historical truth of his wars, and he testifies in the present through reviviscences which unwittingly hit the target of medical discourse.

Another War Scene[4]

Walter favours the classical approach where the analyst echoes his patient's words back to him, so he repeats his brother's sentence: "What prodigious armies you had in Flanders! — brother Toby". But the gestures accompanying the phrase do not escape the veteran's vigilant eye. Walter argued the point "taking his wig from off his head with his right hand, and with his left pulling out a striped India handkerchief from his right coat pocket in order to rub his head". The author explains the historical reason for this twist.

Just after Sterne's birth, in 1714, George of Hanover ascended the throne, succeeding Queen Anne, the last of the Stuart monarchs. This brought about political contortions which the author illustrates through Walter's twisting, in "image-thinking"—the title of Mieke Bal's book[5]—as "coat pockets were cut very low down in the skirt", after the fashion of the times. Thus, in 1718, "it was not an easy matter in any king's reign [...] to have forced your hand diagonally quite across your whole body, so as to gain the bottom of your opposite coat pocket".

Walter does not suspect that his contortion could trigger a resurgence of the battle of Namur: "When my uncle Toby discovered the transverse zig-zaggery of my father's approaches [...], it instantly brought into his mind those he had done duty in before the gate of St Nicholas". His reaction is immediate:

> He had got his right hand to the bell to ring up Trim to go and fetch his map of Namur [...].—My father knit his brows and [...] all the blood in his body seemed to rush up into his face—my uncle Toby dismounted immediately.

Enacting the frantic struggle to escape from death on the battlefield requires help from the map which has already saved him earlier. The confusion transmits itself to the reader, making him lose sight of the metaphor: "I did not apprehend your uncle Toby was o'horseback". Disheartened, Sterne also "dismounts", unable to go on.

It is a fact that metaphors do indeed disappear when "thoughts without a thinker"—as Bion[6] calls them—emerge in search of a thinker to think them. The analyst must adopt a different strategy to face the formidable agency which destroys all symbolic links and swoops down from all directions, like the strange creature in the Japanese tale "The Woodcutter and the Satori".

Satori, a murderous monster who can read man's thoughts, attacks a woodcutter in the forest. Whatever thought of escape comes to his mind, the monster can read it. So, expecting to die, the woodcutter decides to ignore the threat and go on with his work. Suddenly, the blade flies out of his axe, knocking out Satori, unaware. In a similarly hopeless situation, the analyst must count on coincidences stemming from his own history intersecting with the story of the person in deadly peril. Sterne follows the same procedure as a template for Shandean psychoanalysis.

"Live or write...in my case means the same thing"[7]

The reviewers thrashed his writing, outraged by his supposedly "bawdy" style. They fell upon him "pell-mell, helter-skelter, back stroke and fore stroke, side way and long way"—and other obscure adverbs borrowed from British military jargon. Returning to his metaphoric style, Sterne dissociates. In fact, dissociation is his method of survival; he goes on with a tailoring metaphor:

> A man's body and his mind [...] are exactly like a jerkin and a jerkin's lining;—rumple the one—you rumple the other, [unless] you are so fortunate a fellow as to have had your jerkin made of a gum-taffeta and the body lining to it of [...] thin Persian.

Among these fortunate fellows, Sterne counts "a score and a half of good Shandeans", along with the Greek and Roman Stoics and "Montaigne among the Christians". But, in spite of appearances, he is as enraged as Cervantes was against the forger of his first novel, whom he firmly put in his place without stooping to argue with him. "Don't feed the trolls", says an old Norwegian proverb: "Never poor jerkin has been tickled off at such a rate as [mine] has been these last nine months together"—while he worked on Volumes 3 and 4, published in 1761. Sterne is not indifferent to his colleagues' ferocity, but he ignores them so that he can live and write, as he explains in the famous statement which Aaron Burr regretted not having read sooner:

> —You Messrs the monthly Reviewers!—how could you cut and slash my jerkin as you did?—how did you know but you would cut my lining too? [...]—so God bless you; don't be exasperated if I pass it by with good temper, —being determined as long as I live or write (which in my case means the same thing) never to give the honest gentleman a worse word or a worse wish than my uncle Toby gave the fly which buzz'd about his nose all dinner time, —'Go, —go, poor devil... This world is surely wide enough to hold both thee and me.'

Having made this point, Sterne takes up the narrative again, addressing his feminine reader promoted to the rank of Lady of thoughts:

> Any man, madam, [...] observing the prodigious suffusion of blood in my father's countenance [...], —any man madam, but my uncle Toby, who had observed this, together with the violent knitting of my father's brows and the extravagant contortion of his body during the whole affair, —would have concluded my father in a rage; [...]—the whole piece, madam, must have been played off like the sixth Avison's Scarlatti—con furia, —like mad.

After these injurious attacks, music restores the breath of life. Sterne played the bass viol before this instrument ceased to exist. My grandfather played the horn and the trumpet in the orchestra of his small town. His musical talent helped to cheer up his companions, as they later told my father. I still have his hunting horn, brought back from the front all dented.

The therapeutic value of Sterne's musical rhythm is clearly indicated in the scansion of his sentences by his famous dashes, breathing life in the apnea of anguish and rage—which Toby also knows how to calm:

> Any man, I say, madam, but my uncle Toby, [...] would have concluded my father angry and blamed him too. My uncle Toby blamed nothing but the tailor who cut the pocket hole;—so, sitting still till my father had got his handkerchief out of it and looking all the time up in his face with inexpressible good will.

More aggressive than the military man, Walter, the pacifist, repeats the fateful phrase a fourth time, to rekindle the quarrel:

> What prodigious armies you had in Flanders!—Brother Toby, [...] I do believe thee to be as honest a man, [...] nor is it thy fault, if all the children which have been [...] begotten come with their heads foremost into the world:—but believe me [...]—little need is there to expose them to unnecessary [dangers].

Toby halts the adrenaline rush by placing his hand on Walter's knee, asking, as he looks into his face: "Are these dangers greater now o'days, brother, than in times past"? Walter concedes:

> Brother Toby [...], if a child was but fairly begot and born alive, and healthy, and the mother did well after it, —our forefathers never looked further.—My uncle Toby instantly withdrew his hand from off my father's knee, reclined his body gently back in his chair, raised his head till he could just see the cornice of the room and then, [...]—he whistled *Lillibullero*.

This time, it sounded like a song of victory after the return of peace.

Still, we know that it is unwise to celebrate victory too. After a session which restores the symbolic order, a new catastrophe is likely to occur in order to be inscribed in the flow of time.

Charivari, Rough Music[8]

Without delay, Toby's *Lillibullero* is drowned out by the insults Slop hurls at Obadiah, who seems unable to untie the knots he made around the doctor's bag: "Dr Slop was [...] cursing and damning at Obadiah at a most dreadful rate".

In Sterne's time, insolence was part of public discourse. "Masters of the quip" counted among their "learned wits" Samuel Johnson, author of an English language dictionary as well as a *Dictionary of Insults*.[9] Famous for his mood swings, he would be labelled "bipolar" today, along with Groucho Marx. Indeed, the scene of the tying of the knots is worthy of the Marx Brothers.

As he was riding, Obadiah was greatly incommodated by the noise of obstetrical instruments in the bag:

> Lest anything should bolt out in galloping back at the speed Obadiah threatened, [he] had taken the two strings (out of his hat) and tied them close [...] with half a dozen hard knots, each of which [he] [...] had twitched and drawn together with all the strength of his body [...] Such a terrible jungle, what with the *tire-tête*, *forceps*, and *squirt* [...] would

have been enough, had Hymen been taking a jaunt that way, to have frightened him out of the country.

The reference to "rough music"[10] is explicit. Traditionally, this was a ruckus raised using pots and other metallic objects under the window of greybeards who married young maidens as a means of demanding compensation for the youths thus deprived of damsels of their age. If the old husband refused to pay, he was placed backwards on a mule and paraded through town. Sterne concurs:

> As Obadiah had a wife and three children—the turpitude of fornication and the many other political ill consequences of this jingling never once entered his brain;—he had however his objection [...].—The poor fellow, sir, was not able to hear himself whistle.

He belonged to the English militia, whose training consisted of learning to march in step and to shoot and above all to sing in the midst of merry toasting with plenty of drink. Like most men of earlier times, including my grandfather and Wittgenstein, who was a prodigious whistler, "Obadiah loved [the] music he carried with him" and strove to "put himself in a condition to enjoy it".

A race begins between the delivery of the bag and NATURE: "Had the goddess been in one of her nimble moods that day, and in humour for such a contest, [...] my mother, madam, had been delivered sooner than the green bag infallibly—at least by twenty knots".

Sterne now addresses his hero, to predict that he will have the same fate as his own:

> Sport of small accidents, Tristram Shandy! That thou art and ever will be! Had that trial been made for thee, and it was fifty to one but it had, — thy affairs had not been so depress'd— (at least by the depression of thy nose) as they have been; nor had the fortunes of thy house [...] been so often [...] abandoned [...]—but 'tis over, —all but the account of 'em, which cannot be given to the curious till I am got out into the world.

At the end of this prophecy, the "I" of the author merges with that of Tristram on the verge of being born. When everything seems hopeless, a "transitional subject" shared by them both[11] can thwart the fate by inscribing the silent traumas in the novel. Likewise, had they not been acknowledged and told to his nephew by Toby, the death wishes raining down on the unborn baby would have remained buried in the cut-out unconscious, instead of being transformed by the power of laughter.

While Obadiah tries to unknot the bag, Slop thanks Heaven "that Mrs Shandy has had so bad a time of it". "Great wits jump"! comments the author at the doctor's malicious joy—*Schadenfreude*—just as Sterne's enemies were pleased about the critics of his work. "The thought floated only in Dr Slop's mind", when suddenly the thing—*Das Ding*—broke in through the "trampling in the room above, near my mother's bed", making Slop exclaim: "By all that's unfortunate, unless I make haste, the thing will actually befall me as it is".

Worse than a stillborn infant, "the thing" he fears is the loss of his reputation, endangered by the knots which resist his efforts. Having no teeth or nails to use, he borrows a penknife, shouting out "pugh!—psha"! as he cuts his thumb to the bone and cursing: "I wish the scoundrel hang'd—I wish he was shot—I wish all the devils in hell had him for a blockhead".

His murderous wishes remind Tristram of the "slip knots" of the sinister Judge Goerge Jeffreys, who sentenced his great uncle Hammond Shandy to hang in 1685—with hundreds of others whose heads were displayed on spikes along the roads—for having participated in the Rebellion of Monmouth, Charles II's illegitimate son, who was himself beheaded by five blows of the axe. Nor are Obadiah's knots Borromean, borrowed by Lacan from the Borromée family's coat of arms, and having the particularity of coming apart when one of the three rings is cut. They are "good, honest, devilish tight, hard knots", made *bona fide*. Slop attacks Obadiah in bad faith and Walter, taking it personally, asks him to read aloud a 12th-century form of excommunication of the Church of Rome, a copy of which hung framed above the chimney.

The furious doctor's "thoughts without a thinker"[12] are about to find a thinker from the distant past to think them.

The round of curses[13]

This outburst of rage triggers another "timequake", Kurt Vonnegut's expression,[14] just at the moment of Tristram's birth. We are in 1719, and the reproduction of the medieval text would only be published in 1746—the year of the defeat of the Catholic pretender to the throne by the forces of the reigning monarchy. The defeated troops retreated towards York, where papist obstetrician John Burton was suspected of conspiring with the enemy and barely escaped hanging. That year, Protestant families could purchase for three pence a text to be framed, reproducing pontifical excommunication formulas transcribed in the 12th century by Ernulf, Bishop of Rochester.

Nevertheless, twenty-seven years earlier, in November 1719, Walter takes down this medieval list of curses "suitable to all cases" and hands it to Slop, "with the most Cervantic gravity [...] which might have cajoled ERNULPHUS himself". The doctor is duly impressed:

I beg your pardon—answered my father; I was reading one [...] to my brother Toby this morning whilst he pour'd out the tea [...]. but if I remember right, 'tis too violent for a cut of the thumb. —Not at all, quoth Dr Slop [...]. —'Tis much at your service [...]—on condition you will read it aloud.

The reading performance is turned into a musical comedy to the tune of Lillibullero, which Toby whistles as loudly as he can, adding to the irony, since some lyrics to the tune of this old Irish ballad are scarcely any kinder: "O brother Sawney, hear you the News, Twang'em, we'll bang'em, and hang'em all". Dr. Slop wraps his handkerchief around his thumb and "without any suspicion" starts to read the list softly. Walter asks him to speak louder, so he raises up the paper to his face and asks my uncle to accompany him, "as he might as well read [it] under that cover, — my uncle Toby whistling Lillibulero, though not as loud as before".

The original text entitled EXCOMMUNICATION is on the left-hand page in Latin, with a translation on the right-hand page. The enactment speaks out "Obadiah" where a space is left blank to insert the name of the man being excommunicated. Here are some examples needing no comment: "May he (Obadiah) be damn'd, (for tying these knots). May the Father [...]— May the Son [...]—May the Holy Ghost [...] curse him (Obadiah). (...) — The captain is shocked: 'Our armies swore terribly in Flanders, cried my uncle Toby, —but nothing to this... I could not have a heart to curse my dog so'"; and he went on whistling.

Let us bypass the company of martyrs and saints and the choir of holy virgins whose names are invoked in the curses and quote the attacks on the body of the excommunicated:

> May he be cursed inwardly and outwardly [...] May he be cursed in his brains, and in his vertex. [...] May he be damn'd in his mouth [...] and in his groin, (God in heaven forbid, quoth my uncle Toby)—in his thighs, in his genitals, (my father shook his head) [...]. May he be cursed in all the joints and articulations of his members, from the top of his head to the sole of his foot! May there be no soundness in him...

His patience exhausted, "Toby [...] gave a monstrous, long, loud Whew-w-w", just before the arrival of godly beards of Antiquity:

> By the golden beard of Jupiter—and of Juno (if Her Majesty wore one), and by [...] the beards of your celestial gods [...], of town gods and country gods, [...]—all which beards [...] made no less than thirty thousand effective beards upon the pagan establishment—

We recognise the ballet of the bearded duennas in the Second Part of *Don Quixote*[15] and Cervantes's voice in *basso continuo*. Sterne admits it readily:

> I vow and protest that of the two bad cassocks I am worth in the world I would have given the better of them as freely as ever Cid Hamet

offered his—only to have stood by and heard my uncle Toby's accompaniment.

The quote is accurate: "Cide Hamete Benengeli"—*Don Quixote*'s Arabic author—"would have given his best burnous" to be present at the Knight's secret meeting with duenna Rodriguez.

Toby has had enough: "I declare, [...] my heart would not let me curse the Devil himself with so much bitterness". But suddenly the door bursts open, "putting an end to the affair". Before we know who rushes through the door, we have to read Chapter XII about the ownership of speech.

Language games belong to everyone[16]

"I cannot choose the mouth with which I say 'I have toothache'",[17] Wittgenstein was to declare later—nor the mouth with which I hurl insults, Sterne wrote a century and a half earlier. Curses can be borrowed from anyone, even from our worst enemies:

> Now, don't let us give ourselves a parcel of airs and pretend that the oaths we make ...are our own and because we have the spirit to swear them, imagine that we have the wit to invent them too. My father [...] consider'd Ernulphus's anathema as an institute of swearing.

Of course, curses do get stale from overuse: I curse today with words that would have horrified my grandmother and me too. Sterne also points out that the notorious *God damn!*—soon to be proffered in France by Figaro[18]— was a much stronger expression in Ernulphus's era. Never mind! He throws it in the face of critics scandalised by his freedom of style.

Incidentally, such transfers may also distort meaning. While Sterne quotes *Candide* faithfully, Voltaire, in his 1764 *Philosophical Dictionary*[19] under the heading "Of a Deceitful Conscience", calls Sterne *un curé*—a Catholic priest—and speaks of two captains, Toby and Walter, forgetting all about Trim, and portraying Slop as a strong opponent of Catholicism.

But Sterne would not have minded, since Voltaire's *Dictionary* had a favourable impact on the reputation of his book.[20] He knows the worth of his novel, described by young James Boswell, Samuel Johnson's friend, as a "damned clever book". But he is merciless when it comes to "admirable connoisseur[s] befetish'd with the bobs and trinkets of criticism":

> [...] a work of genius had better go to the devil at once than stand to be prick'd and tortured to death by 'em. [...] Of all the cants which are canted in this canting world, —though the cant of hypocrites may be the worst, —the cant of criticism is the most tormenting!

And he adds:

> I would go fifty miles on foot, [...] to kiss the hand of that man whose
> generous heart will give up the reins of his imagination into his author's
> hands, —be pleased he knows not why and cares not wherefore.

Since he mocks those who measure everything by "rules and compasses",
I wonder what Sterne would think of ten-minute sessions and the jargon
serving to justify them.

The thing[21]

Having taken the time to vent his vexations, Sterne returns to his narrative,
when the door suddenly opens and Suzannah rushes in:

> Bless my soul!—my poor mistress is ready to faint, —and her pains are
> gone, [...]—and the bottle of julep is broke, —and the nurse has cut her
> arm, [...]—and the midwife has fallen backwards upon the edge of the
> fender and bruised her hip as black as your hat.

Slop makes a show of concern for the poor woman when Susannah tells him:
"You had better look at my mistress [but]—the midwife would gladly first
give you an account how things are, so desires you to go upstairs and speak
to her this moment".

The doctor hesitates, and Sterne comments: "Human nature is the same
in all professions". Ours is no exception. Slop demands that the midwife
come down to see him, at the risk of losing the mother and the baby. Simu-
lating approval, Toby comments wryly: "I like subordination". Not grasp-
ing the irony, the Doctor "parodies my uncle's hobby horsical reflection"
and invokes "the subordination of fingers and thumbs to ***** [...], without
[which] the cut upon my thumb might have been felt by the Shandy family as
long as [it] had a name".

Both Sterne and the reader translate the ***** *in petto*, before it appears—
pop!—at any moment. It can be anything: "a scar, an axe, [...] a pink'd dou-
blet, a rusty helmet [...], —but, above all, a tender infant royally accoutred".
We hear echoes of *Titus Andronicus* and of recent wars of succession. To
solve the mystery, Sterne goes back to Antiquity:

> It is a singular stroke of eloquence (at least it was so in Athens and
> Rome where orators [wore] mantles). [...] when the orator has [...] hid
> the BAMBINO [...]—and produced it so critically that no soul [saw it
> coming], —Oh sirs! It has done wonders. It has open'd sluices ...and
> turn'd the brains, and shook the principles and unhinged of half a

nation. ... All of which plainly shews [...] that the decay of eloquence [...] is owing to [...] short coats and the disuse of trunk-hose.—We can conceal nothing under ours, madam, worth shewing.

I am asked to witness again the relation between fashion and politics in the future history of the upheavals that would unhinge most of Europe and America—and in psychoanalysis too. After all, the BAMBINO pulled out—*pop!*—in some critical sessions of madness and trauma psychotherapy, may be called, as I have said, a political subject[22] capable of turning brains upside down and shaking up principles.

Off with his head![23]

"The thing" at last extracted by Slop from the bag on his knees is the famous forceps, which he pulls out with a syringe. Toby cries—echoing Agnes's question in Molière's *The School for Wives*[24] "Are children made through the ears"?—"Good God! [...] are children brought into the world with a squirt"?, while screaming at once: "Sir, you have torn every bit of skin quite off the back of both my hands [...] and you have crushed all my knuckles". We surmise that the doctor used the captain's fist to simulate the action of the forceps on the head of the baby. The doctor's classic answer: "'Tis your own fault" frightens Walter, who reflects out loud: "'Tis well, [...] that the experiment was not first made upon my child's headpiece".

His reiterated wish that the baby be delivered by his feet is disqualified by the two specialists, who agree for once. The midwife thinks it impossible, since the baby's feet do not present first, and Slop whispers to "my father" that "if the hip is mistaken for the head, — there is a possibility (if it is a boy) that the forceps ***". A whole line of asterisks suggests the extent of the consequences. "You may as well take off the head too", roared Walter, in the tone of *Alice in Wonderland*'s Queen of Hearts.[25] Sterne reassures us: "It is morally impossible the reader should understand this, —'tis enough Dr Slop understood it;—so, taking the green bag in his hand, [...] he tripp'd pretty nimbly, for a man of his size [...] to my mother's apartment".

An endless wait begins at this point. Walter looks at his watch, as is to be expected on such occasions. "It is two hours and ten minutes—and no more [...]—since Dr Slop and Obadiah arrived, —and I know not how it happens, brother Toby, —but to my imagination it seems almost an age". What is totally unexpected is Toby's reply.

To prepare us for the jester's retort, Sterne suggests: "Take hold of my [fool's] cap, —nay, take the bell along with it, and [the] pantofles too"—so that we are in condition to hear the "foliysophy" which leaves Walter speechless:

—Tis owing entirely, quoth my uncle Toby, to the succession of our ideas. My father [...] who proposed infinite pleasure to himself in

[...] reasoning upon this [...] and had not the least apprehension of having it snatch'd out of his hands by my uncle Toby, who [...] troubled his brain the least with abstruse thinking [...] was disappointed with my uncle's fortuitous solution.

Freud must have turned over in his grave, so clear was it that Toby's reply came straight from the unconscious. Walter asked his brother:

Do you understand the theory of that affair? —Not I, quoth my uncle. —But you have some ideas [...] of what you talk about. —No more than my horse [...]. Gracious Heaven! cried my father, [...] clapping his two hands together, —there is a worth in thy honest ignorance [...], —'twere almost a pity to exchange it for a knowledge.

Yet he can't help spoiling this worthy ignorance with a learned quotation from *An Essay Concerning Human Understanding*,[26] in which Locke analyses the time it takes to associate successive ideas, contrasting this duration with the immediate effect of a cannonball—when it destroys our houses or tears off a part of our body—or with the mixed-up chronology of our dreams that we set right in our waking state, thanks to "computations of time [...] and [the chronology] of clocks".

We recognise here the difference between the immediacy which takes place in an analysis of traumatic revivals and the chronology of clocks demanded by the anamnesis of repressed desires in dreams. As a matter of fact, the word "clock" suddenly revives Walter's initial *coitus interruptus*: "I wish there was not a clock in the kingdom [...]—'twill be well if in time to come, the succession of our ideas be of any use or service to us at all".

At this, Freud may turn over in his grave once again.

Brouhaha[27]

Sterne's two heroes are now asleep and so "off my hands", as he says. He is therefore able to write his Preface with the help of his favourite spirits: "by the tombstone of Lucian [...], by the ashes of my dear Rabelais, and dearer Cervantes"! The "Author's Preface" makes its entrance in the middle of the page:

No, I'll not say a word about it, —here it is;—in publishing it, —I have appealed to the world, —and to the world I leave it;—it must speak for itself. [...] All I know of the matter is, —when I sat down, my intention was to write a good book; [...]—a wise, aye, and a discreet, —[with] all the wit and the judgement (be it more or less) which the great author and bestower of them had thought fit originally to give me—so that t'is just as God pleases.

Sterne's Preface was to inspire Wittgenstein when he wrote his own Preface to *Philosophical Investigations* in 1945[28]:

> I make [my remarks] public with mixed feelings. It is not impossible that it should fall to the lot of this work, in its poverty and in the darkness of this time, to bring light into one brain or another — but, of course, it is not likely. I should not like my writing to spare other people the trouble of thinking. But, if possible, to stimulate someone to thoughts of his own. I should have liked to produce a good book [...], but the time is past in which I could improve it.

In addition to *Tristram Shandy*, he may have read the Prefatory Note of Freud's *Moses*,[29] dated "before March 1938":

> We find with astonishment that progress has concluded an alliance with barbarism. In Soviet Russia the attempt has been made to better the life of a hundred million people [...] robbed of every possibility of freedom of thought. [...] In the case of the German people, [...] regression into all but prehistoric barbarism can come to pass. [...] I know that this external danger will deter me from publishing [...] this essay. But that need not hinder me from writing it. [...] Thus it may lie hid until the time comes when it may safely venture into the light of day, or until someone else who reaches the same opinions and conclusions can be told: 'In darker days there lived a man who thought as you did'.

Sterne's preface speaks of the dark time when his *Political Romance* was condemned to be burnt by Agelastes, who never laughs and who attacks his novel by saying that "there may be some wit in it, but no judgement at all". Hence the question:

> "How is it possible [...] that wit and judgment in this world never go together; inasmuch as they are two operations differing from each other as wide as east is from and west. —So, says Locke [30] —so are farting and hickuping, say I.

His preface goes on to mock the church lawyer Didius—alias Francis Topham—already satirised in *A political Romance* as the author whose treatise "*de fartendi et illustrandi* doth maintain that an illustration is no argument".

This statement sounds familiar to me, since in my youth we were taught not to spoil theory with anecdotes. I am stunned to hear Sterne saying that this was already the rule in the 18th century. Had I read *Tristam Shandy* at the time, I could have used his demonstration:

> ... an illustration is no argument, —nor do I maintain the wiping of a looking glass clean to be a syllogism;—but you all, may it please Your

Worships, see the better for it, —so that the main good these things do is only to clarify the understanding by freeing] it from any little motes or specks of opacular matter which [...] might hinder a conception and spoil all.

After presenting a whole list of famous anti-Shandeans, Sterne declares that he feels no resentment towards them. Indeed, instead of heaping grievances upon his colleagues, he draws them into a "Brouhaha"—from the Hebrew "Baruch haba" (blessed is the one who comes)—introduced into the French language in Rabelais's era:

> My most zealous wish and fervent prayer [...]—is that the great gifts and endowments both of wit and judgement, [...] may [...] be poured down warm as each of us could bear it, —scum and sediment an' all; [...]. Bless us!—what noble work we should make! And what spirits should I find myself in. [...] Heaven! [...]—but 'tis too much, —'tis more than nature can bear!—[...] lay hold of me, —I am giddy, —I am stone-blind, —I am dying, —I am gone.—Help! Help! Help!

I have experienced such states of saturation, but not to that extent. Was Sterne high? He insists he only infused a *quantum* of the wit—yes, he uses the word—available to all mankind. But this *quantum* produces explosive effects:

> I am beginning to foresee [...] that as we shall all of us continue to be great wits, —we should never agree amongst ourselves one day to an end:—there would be so much satire and sarcasm [...]. Chaste stars! What biting and scratching, and what a racket and a clatter we should make...

Those were the good old days before mood stabilisers, when carnivals and dancing in the streets acted as antidepressants, in the same way that reading Rabelais, Cervantes and Sterne does for me today.

Mission accomplished, he sees fit to cool down his pen by taking us to Lapland, where playwright Jean-François Regnard[31] had travelled a century earlier. But I find his portrayal of the *Kalevala* people[32] extremely unfair:

> Man's concerns lies for near nine months together within the narrow compass of his cave, —where the spirits are compressed almost to nothing, —and where the passions [...] are frigid [...];—there the least quantity of judgement [...] does the business, —and of wit, [...] not one spark is given.

This is what happens when one has never visited a sauna, where wit and judgement are given free rein.

Making good use of bipolarity

Sterne heard me and hastens to take us "home again", to his native island where:

> our air blows hot and cold;—so that sometimes, for near half a century together, there shall be very little wit or judgement [...] amongst us:—the small channels of them shall seem quite dried up, —then all of a sudden the sluices shall break out and take a fit of running again like fury [...]—and then it is that in writing and fighting, and twenty other gallant things, we drive all the world before us.

Thus, British imperialism stems from bipolarity. Sterne apologises to French readers, for whom "the progress wrought by the Enlightenment is an article of faith", and also to others, since his "caressing preface" fooled us into believing that wit and judgement always shine with the same intensity. On the contrary:

> of these two luminaries, [only] so much of their irradiations are suffered from time to time to shine down upon us. For alas! [...] I tremble to think how many thousands for it or benighted travellers (in the learned sciences at least) must have groped and blundered on in the dark all night of their lives, — running their heads against posts and knocking out their brains... [...] What confusions!

No wonder the critics are outraged when they read the following antiphrases:

> What mistakes!—fiddlers and painters [...]—trusting to the passions excited in an air sung or a story painted to the heart, —instead of measuring them by a quadrant. [...]—a statesman turning the political wheel, like a brute, the wrong way round—against the stream of corruption, —by Heaven!— [...] a son of the divine Aesculapius [...] feeling his patient's pulse instead of his apothecary's—a brother of the faculty [...] In that spacious HALL [...], —a litigated point fairly hung up rashly determined [...] in five-and-twenty minutes, which [...] might have taken up as many months ...

The same rhetorical device is applied to military campaigns.

After this attack on the army, we expect one on the church. But there, Sterne draws the line: "As for the clergy—No—If I say a word against them, I'll be shot. [...]—I durst not for my soul touch upon the subject;—with such weak nerves and spirits [...]". And he concludes: "...it comes to pass that your men of least wit are reported to be men of most judgement.—But mark,

[...] I maintain [this] to be a vile and a malicious report". Then, he asserts: "I hate set dissertations".

This statement catches my attention since I hated them too when I had to take competitive exams in my youth. Had I read the sentence below, I would have felt less alone:

> ...'tis one of the silliest things [...] to darken your hypothesis by placing a number of tall, opaque words one before another [...] betwixt your own and your reader's conception, —when in all likelihood, if you had looked about, you might have seen something standing or hanging up which would have cleared the point at once.

As I became an analyst, I ran into these tall, opaque words again. But in the common room of the psychiatric hospital where I learned my job, I noticed that people confined there searched for something that stood out in my face, my posture, my clothes and the tone of my voice. When I confirmed their observations, a co-research could begin to explore traumatic zones in their story, resonating with catastrophes in my own life experience. Things speak, when "the tool with the name is broken",[33] if we are able to see what they show on both sides of the transference. Sterne lists a number of trifles: "a sot, a pot [...], a winter mitten [...], an old slipper or a cane chair".

Sterne makes use of the two knobs on the back of his cane chair to demonstrate this idea: "They are fasten'd on [...] to answer one another [...]—as wit and judgement [do]". We are now asked to stand up and involve our own bodies—too often absent from the reasoning process—in understanding the relationship between wit and judgement:

> Now, for the sake of an experiment [...], —let us [...] take off one of these two curious ornaments (I care not which) from the [...] pinnacle of the chair [...];—nay, don't laugh at it [...] Do, —pray, [...] lay your hands upon your hearts and answer this plain question, whether this one single knob which now stands here like a blockhead by itself can serve any purpose upon earth but to put one in mind of the want of the other...

I infer from this sentence that wit is not limited to puns, so dear to Lacan, who refused to address the question of transference with people labelled psychotic. He had his limits, like Sterne's beloved philosopher:

> The great Locke, [who] free[d] the world from the lumber of a thousand vulgar errors, [...] took the cry [...] against the poor wits for granted and so joined in with the cry and halloo'd it as boisterously as the rest.

Sterne calls this ignorance the beginning of the "Magna Carta of stupidity". But, like Cervantes in the Preface to the Second Part of his novel, he advises us not to confront it directly, but to simply walk away:

> As for the great wigs, upon which I may be thought to have spoken my mind too freely, —I beg leave to qualify whatever has been unguardedly said to their dispraise or prejudice by one general declaration [...]— peace be with them;—(emphasized by a pointing index) mark only, —I write not for them.

I dare say that he writes for analysts open to this kind of transference— overlooked by the great psychoanalyst at the end of his chapter "On the possible treatment of psychosis"[34]—which Sterne now illustrates by giving an example.

Hinges: "The time is out of joint"[35]

It's time to wake up the two brothers. "Had the parlour door open'd and turn'd upon its hinges as cleverly as our government", we could make no sense of the next scene, where corporal Trim arrives in the parlour with two mortar pieces, "delighted with his handiwork [...]; and knowing what a pleasure it would be to his master". Note the political reference. The door in Shandy's house is probably not as unhinged as the time in the kingdom of Denmark, but it is badly in need of attention:

> No family but ours would have born it an hour [...];—three drops of oil with a feather, and a smart stroke of a hammer [would have ended it]. [On this subject], Walter's rhetoric and conduct were at perpetual handicuffs. [...] Every day for at least ten years [...] did my father resolve to have it mended.

Contrary to Walter, modern medicine does not procrastinate. When the symptoms creak, it instantly pours three drops of something on the synapses or delivers an electrical shock to stop the noise. But Sterne sees this nuisance as an opportunity: "Had the parlour door open'd and turn'd upon its hinges as a door should do", we would have missed an essential scene. Seeing Walter and Toby fast asleep, Trim "would have retired as silent as death". The essential scene will address the intergenerational transmission of trauma.

First, the creaking of the door allowed "my father," who was only half asleep, to remain alert to any move in his house: "Pray, what's the matter? Who is there"? he cries out when Trim enters the room. His misunderstanding the word "mortar" does not lead to repressed desires but opens the door to History. He orders that it be taken to the kitchen so drugs can be crushed in it. Trim explains that he is talking about mortar pieces for a siege made out of a pair of jackboots.

Hearing this last word, Walter jumps up and wakes his brother: those boots were worn by their ancestor Sir Roger Shandy in 1644 at the battle of Marston Moor, where Cromwell defeated the Royalist troops. And he affirms his birthright loud and clear: "they were *hereditary*". There follows the classic squabble between the businessman and the soldier about the uses of money.

When Walter claims the worth of the boots to be £10, his brother puts his hand in his pocket, only to be accused of throwing money away. Toby objects: "Have I not a hundred and twenty pounds a year besides my half-pay"? And he offers a tenth of it to repay his brother. Walter quickly estimates the cost of Toby's sieges erected on the bowling green: "Dear brother Toby [...]—these military operations of yours are above your strength; [...]— and take my word, —they will in the end quite ruin your fortune and make a beggar of you". But that reasoning is instantly wiped out by Toby's hobby-horsical gallantry: "What signifies it if they do, brother, [...], so long as we know 'tis for the good of the nation? —Generous soul!—God prosper you both, and your mortar pieces too, quoth my father to himself".

At this point, the unconscious produces another signifier, suspended between repressed desires and indelible traumatic memory. "Hinges" rhymes with "bridges", which word sends us flying five years back, to 1713, date of the Treaty of Utrecht and of Toby's *amours*—and also a century earlier, to Tristram's great-grandmother's time.

Bridges: The crossway to the beyond[36]

Ever watchful, Walter detects another unusual sound: "All is quiet and hush [...], at least above stairs [...].—Prithee, Trim, who is in the kitchen"? Hearing that Dr. Slop has come down to make a bridge, he is alarmed again, for "not one single thing has gone right this day"! The captain believes that the doctor is putting together a bridge for his bowling green and asks Trim to thank him heartily. The author enlightens us: "You must know my uncle Toby mistook the bridge as widely as my father mistook the mortars". Suspense! The clue to the mystery will be revealed three chapters later, since we are now on the perilous bridge of speech, where the words we take for signifiers are changed into things.

Now Sterne dons his fool's cap as he is caught in a double bind that maddens him. In order to explain the reason for Toby's misunderstanding, he is forced to reveal Trim's role at the time of his master's amours, "in which [he] was no mean actor". But this story is out of place here. Yet, if he reserves it for later, he ruins the story he is telling now, and if he tells it now, he ruins the subsequent story. "—What would Your Worships have me do in this case"? The readers only confuse him with contradictory advice: "—Tell it, Mr Shandy, by all means. —You are a fool, Tristram, if you do".

Raging against us, Sterne appeals to the Powers Beyond:

> O ye POWERS! [...] which enable mortal man to tell a story worth the hearing, —that kindly shew him where he is to begin it—and where he is to end it, —what he is to put into it— and what he is to leave out [...], I beg and beseech you [...] that wherever [...] it so falls out that three several roads meet in one point, as they have done just here, —that at least you set up a guide post [...] in mere charity to direct an uncertain devil which of the three he is to take.

The Powers Beyond answer his plea.

The lady of the bridge: Bridget[37]

Sterne decides to take his story back to 1714, one year after:

> the shock my uncle Toby received [...] in his affair with widow Wadman [which] fixed him in a resolution never more to think of the sex [...]—yet Corporal Trim made no such bargain with himself. [...] When therefore my uncle Toby sat down before the mistress, —Corporal Trim incontinently took ground before the maid.

The parallel love affair of master and servant is a device as old as theatre. In Cervantes's time, it took the concrete form of a two-tiered stage, which can still be seen in Spain at the Almagro Comedy Theatre. Likewise, at widow Wadman's house, Toby was paying court in the parlour, while Trim did the same one storey below, in the kitchen, albeit with opposite results. After nine months of diligent visits, Toby grew indignant enough to raise the siege. But Trim continued courting Bridget, "turning his own siege into a blockade" away from prying eyes:

> He never met Bridget in the village but he would either nod or wink or smile or look kindly at her, —or (as circumstances directed) he would shake her by the hand, —or ask her lovingly how she did, or would give her a ribbon [...] but [only] when it could be done with decorum.

Four years later, in 1718, "about six or seven weeks before Tristram's birth", Bridget would break Toby's bridge. In 1719, according to Sterne's biographer, "all became unhinged again" in the author's life.[38] In Chapter I, I already mentioned that Laurence was six years old when his father embarked on an expedition to Spain from the Isle of Wight where he was stationed. Laurence's brother Joram, who was four, died of smallpox, while their mother was pregnant with Anne who would be killed by a fall in a Dublin barracks when she was three. In the meantime, after Roger Sterne had returned to Ireland, such a fierce storm unleashed its fury upon the ship bringing his family back from England that he thought he may never see them again.

Let us come back to the novel. On a moonlit night, the corporal "courteously and gallantly took [Bridget] by the hand" in the lane with flowering shrubs leading to the fortifications on the bowling green:

> This was not done so privately but the foul-mouth'd trumpet of Fame carried it from ear to ear, till at length it reached my father's, [...] that my uncle Toby's [...] drawbridge [...]—was broke down, and [...] crush'd all to pieces.

Walter could not avoid making fun of his brother's hobby horse:

> He thought it the most ridiculous horse that ever gentleman mounted [...]—so that [...] this accident [...] proved an inexhaustible fund of entertainment to him.—Well, —but dear Toby! [...] do tell me seriously how this affair of the bridge happened.

This sets off a round of ambiguous sexual repartee, in which *Witz*, stemming from the repressed unconscious, plays its part.[39]

Sensing the trap, Toby avoids metaphors: "How can you tease me so much about it? [...] I have told it you twenty times, word for word..." But Walter won't give up, any more than a psychoanalyst would:

> Prithee, how was it then, corporal? [...] —It was a mere misfortune [...], —I was shewing Mrs Bridget our fortifications, and in going too near the edge of the fossé, I unfortunately slipped in. —Very well, Trim! My father would cry—(smiling mysteriously and giving a nod...).

In the background, I can hear François Couperin's *Les Barricades mystérieuses* composed one year before this conversation—played by Jean-Max on the harpsichord.

Trim continues, unsuspecting: "And being link'd fast, [...] arm in arm with Mrs Bridget, I dragg'd her after me, by means of which she fell backwards soss against the bridge". The fact that the dragging led to a pile-up does not escape Walter, while his brother sticks to a literal description given in military terms:

> It was a thousand to one [...] that the poor fellow did not break his leg. — Ay truly! My father would say, —a limb is soon broke, brother Toby, in such encounters. [...]—When my uncle Toby was so unfortunate as to say a syllable about cannons, bombs or petards, —my father would tell him [...]—but what are these to the destructive machinery of Corporal Trim?

Assailed by interpretations, Toby draws on his pipe vehemently, filling the room with smoke and causing his brother to go into a fit of coughing which Toby, jumping up despite the pain in his groin, appeases by wiping his brother's eyes with a clean cambric handkerchief. Walter relents, though he savours his victory: "May my brains be knock'd out with a battering ram or a catapulta [...] if ever I insult this worthy soul more".

Six weeks later, he would lose his crown of laurels, catapulted from the Tarpean rock not far from the Capitol. Such disappointment is familiar to me. When I enjoy a moment of triumph in a session, the cut-out unconscious seizes the opportunity to make its entrance and I fall off my analyst's chair, completely defeated.

The Shandy brothers make plans for the reconstruction of the drawbridge. They do not know yet that after Tristram's birth, the word "bridge" would be banished from the symbolic chain and transformed into a word-thing, unfit to be used metaphorically. "My father [...] was infinitely the better politician and took the lead in the cabinet as my uncle Toby took it of him in the field". Against his brother's advice to choose a Flemish one, "my uncle Toby [...] determined upon an Italian drawbridge, [built] upon the old model", and his choice proved to be right.

As they are talking, Walter detects "a train of military ideas" in his brother's brain:

> Had my uncle Toby's head been a Savoyard's box and my father peeping in all the time at one end of it, — it could not have given him a more distinct conception of the operations in my uncle Toby's imagination.

Here, there is also a misunderstanding. Let me explain that a Savoyard's box is not a magic lantern, but simply a box with holes, in which my countrymen carried their marmots to show to passers-by. Of course, this can lead to innuendos, but we have no time to lose, since the bridge of Bridget's amours suddenly changes into a bridge of sighs for Walter.

The reader must now run back to events that occurred three chapters earlier.[40] So we find ourselves out of breath, in the parlour again, on the day of Tristram's birth.

The bridge of the nose[41]

Let us remember that Walter had asked who was making noise in the kitchen. The corporal's answer had catastrophic effects:

> God bless Your Honour, [...] 'tis a bridge for master's nose.—In bringing him into the world with his vile instruments, [the doctor] has crush'd his nose, Susannah says, as flat as a pancake to his face, and he is making a false bridge with a piece of cotton and a thin piece of whalebone out of

[her] stays to raise it up. — Lead me, brother Toby, cried my father, to my room this instant.

Walter falls into a cataleptic state, which causes the author to be assailed by traumatic revivals. Crossing the threshold of autobiography, Sterne merges into the fictional "my father":

> From the first moment I sat down to write my life for the amusement of the world and my opinions for its instruction, has a cloud insensibly been gathering over my father.—A tide of little evils and distresses has been settling in against him.—Not one thing [...] has gone right: and now is the storm thicken'd and going to break, and pour down full upon his head. I enter upon this part of my story in the most pensive and melancholy frame of mind.—Every line I write, I feel an abatement of the quickness of my pulse and of that careless alacrity [...] which [...] prompts me to say and write a thousand things I should not.

Sterne's biographer[42] provides us with the key to this *shandied* fusion of Walter with his author. Some fifteen years earlier, his servant, Richard Greenwood, saw his master devastated, lying in his bed for eight days after the death of his first son, who was three weeks old, and then the death of his first Lydia, who only lived one day in 1745. His second Lydia was the only one who survived a series of stillbirths. Such reviviscences are probably at the root of the following sentence: "And this moment that I last dipp'd my pen into my ink, I could not help taking notice what a cautious air of sad composure and solemnity there appear'd in my manner of doing it".

Sterne has read Robert Burton's *The Anatomy of Melancholy*,[43] published a century earlier. But this time, Shandean analysis takes over in a scene of transference between the brothers, in which Walter shows Toby what he cannot say. His word games have stopped since he is no longer dealing with the repressed unconscious, but rather, as we shall soon learn, with a ruthless agency attacking the rules of alliance in the Shandy family.

Turning to stone[44]

"My father" enters a state summed up by Wittgenstein's question: "Couldn't I imagine having frightful pains and turning to stone while they lasted"?[45] The belief that psychoanalysis is useless in such cases since transference cannot occur was contradicted during World War I by analysts working in military hospitals with traumatised soldiers.

Sterne challenges his feminine reader on this issue:

> I won't go about to argue the point with you, 'tis so, —and I am persuaded of it, madam, as much as can be, that both man and woman bear

pain or sorrow (and, for aught I know, pleasure too) best in a horizontal position. The moment my father got up into his chamber, he threw himself prostrate across his bed in the wildest disorder imaginable, but at the same time in the most lamentable attitude of a man borne down with sorrow.

This state of prostration is not considered a pathology, but rather as Walter's only way to survive the blow he received. His attitude is described with the clinical precision of Sterne's own traumatic memory:

The palm of his right hand, as he fell upon the bed, receiving his forehead and covering the greatest part of both his eyes, gently sunk down with his head (his elbow giving way backwards) till his nose touch'd the guilt;— his left arm hung insensible over the side of the bed, his knuckles reclining upon the handle of the chamber pot, which peep'd out beyond the valence, —his right leg (his left being drawn up towards his body) hung half over the side of the bed, the edge of it pressing upon his shin bone.

Bereft of all feeling, unspeakable distress etched on his face, he sighs without uttering a word. This is when mainstream analysts would diagnose an absence of transference, while Frieda Fromm-Reichmann would say that here "everything is transference", provided one analyses one's own impressions. Wittgenstein can testify to this, from his own experience.

The first page of *Notes for Lectures on Private Experience*[46] recounts that when confronted with a person "with a far away look, a dreamy voice, incapable of conveying inner feelings", the philosopher examines his own reaction. "What is it that puzzles me in this matter? [...] There is something further about it, only you can't say it [...]. It is this idea which plays hell with us". While he analyses himself, he manifests his presence "as a witness for an event without any witness",[47] like Toby who sits in an old armchair close to his brother's head and ponders.

Sterne voices his reflections:

Before an affliction is digested, —consolation ever comes too soon;— and after it is digested, —it comes too late: so that you see, madam, there is but a mark between these two, as fine almost as a hair for a comforter to take aim at. Toby believed [...] he could as soon hit the longitude.

The captain draws the curtains, takes out his cambric handkerchief, sheds a tear he always has "at everyone's service", heaves a great sigh and holds his peace. His silent vigil lasts half an hour, spread over forty pages, until we learn about Walter's recovery in Chapter VII of Volume 4.

Another veteran, psychoanalyst Otto Will, tells us he adopted the same attitude at the bedside of a soldier sunk into catalepsy. A military surgeon at Guadalcanal, Otto had just returned to the US and resumed his work in a military hospital after undergoing stomach surgery. In his ward, he fell into the habit of sitting down to rest next to this unresponsive man's bed. He started saying out loud whatever came into his mind, encouraged, so to speak, by a strange dialogue with the rustling of the sheets. Little by little, the soldier emerged from the clutches of death. Soon afterwards, Otto Will undertook an analysis with Harry Stack Sullivan and, after the latter's death in Paris in 1949, with Frieda Fromm-Reichmann. He became an analyst at Chestnut Lodge, and later the medical director of Austen Riggs Center, where we met him.

So, it is not enough to sit silently next to a patient "borne down with sorrows" to put an end to them. One has to take on the role of the *therapon* depicted in the *Iliad*,[48] the second in combat, like Trim did for Toby.

Tristram's ancestor[49]

Toby, who had remained bedridden at his brother's home for a time, now took on the function of *therapon* at Walter's bedside. But Walter was not returning from the front. Indeed, Shandean analysis concerns not only war trauma, but the transmission of an intergenerational collapse, in this case affecting both brothers:

> No doubt the breaking-down of the bridge of a child's nose by the edge of a pair of forceps, —however scientifically applied, —would vex any man [...], —yet it will not [...] justify the unchristian manner [Walter] abandoned and surrender'd himself up to it. To explain this, I must leave him upon the bed for half an hour—and my good uncle Toby in his old fringed chair sitting beside him.

Shandean analysis raises the question of a source—not of a cause—creating such a stoppage of time. The source of the relation between "my father's" breakdown and the physical injury to his baby is to be found in the breaking of the symbolic law of alliances. Sterne expresses this in a mysterious maxim printed in italics: "*All is not gain that is got into the purse*". This refers to the transmission of an "attack on linking"[50] perpetrated by the great-grandmother of the baby with the flattened nose.

We are now plunged directly into a quarrel between the great-grandmother and her husband. She reproaches him with having "little or no nose, sir". Considering herself cheated in the bargain, she demands a yearly compensation of £300, to be paid each year in two instalments, by their descendants as well.

Although he finds her demand outrageous, her husband defends himself poorly and ends up signing the document requesting that their offspring also pay the jointure to the old woman. "My great-grandmother outlived my grandfather twelve years", and the inheritance being passed up the line instead of down, it can indeed be said that: "All is not gain that is got into the purse". Walter complied, but:

> as soon as he enter'd upon the odd fifty, —he generally gave a loud *Hem!*—rubb'd the side of his nose leisurely with the flat part of his forefinger, — [...]—look'd at both sides of every guinea as he parted with it—and [pulled] out his handkerchief [to wipe] his temples.

At the same time, we are getting an idea of Sterne's mother's greed. Although she had never visited her son in Yorkshire, she made the trip from Ireland twenty years later to claim her part of her daughter-in-law's dowry. Disappointed, she sided with Laurence's hostile uncle Jaques and contributed to Laurence's reputation as an unworthy son, a rumour spread by Byron, Thackeray and Taime, despite the fact that Sterne provided his mother with a pension until her death in 1759.

A reader keen on psychoanalysis might consider these two women phallic, especially the ancestor obsessed with noses. Sterne rejects this interpretation, in the style of his master Rabelais, who nicknamed himself Alcofibras Nasier:

> Now, before I venture to make use of the word *nose* a second time, — [...], it may not be amiss to explain my own meaning and define, with all possible exactness and precision, what I would willingly be understood to mean by the term. [...] Heaven is witness how the world has revenged itself upon me for leaving so many openings to equivocal strictures.

This clarification is illustrated with a story. Near Sterne's Yorkshire parsonage stood Crazy Castle, owned by John Hall-Stevenson, who had been his fellow student at Cambridge and became Eugenius in the novel. Eugenius is pointing out the word "crevice", the crack in the wall that fascinated Toby[51] in the second volume, while Walter was lecturing him on the nature of women. Sterne asks him: "And here are two roads [...], —a dirty and a clean one, —which shall we take? The clean, —by all means, replied Eugenius". Sterne then swears that, laying his hand on Eugenius's breast, "to define —is to distrust".

Indeed, defining the psyche as a normal or a psychotic structure is an act of mistrust of the latter's experience.

A nose is a nose and nothing more[52]

Sterne triumphed over Eugenius as he always did, "like a fool", he says, and also over ready-made interpretations. He thumbs his nose at them:

> I define a nose as follows, —entreating only [...] my readers, both male and female [...], to guard against the temptations [...] of the Devil

[...] to put any other ideas into their minds than what I put into my definition.—For by the word *nose*, [...] in every part of my work, where the word *nose* occurs, —I declare by that word I mean a nose and nothing more or less.

Prefiguring Gertrude Stein's "a rose is a rose is a rose", Sterne declares: "A nose is a nose and nothing more". His great-grandfather's was shaped like an ace of clubs, like that of the people on Rabelais's triangular Island of Ennasin,[53] where alliances were very strange. Here, the reader may wonder what alliances passed down to Roger Sterne condemned him to the perpetual rank of ensign while his brothers enjoyed a lavish life, but whose cruelty their nephew never forgot:

> Defend me, gracious Heaven! from those persecuting spirits who make no allowances for those workings within us. [...]For three generations at least, this tenet in favour of long noses had gradually been taking root in our family.—TRADITION was all along on its side [...]; so that "...) my father might be said to have suck'd this in with his mother's milk.

Prejudices are passed down through generations with:

> the obstinacy of old dogs opposed to learning new tricks. [...] My father stood up for all his opinions: he had spared no pains in picking them up [...].—Accordingly, he [...] would entrench and fortify them round with as many circumvallations and breastworks as my uncle Toby would a citadel.

Walter collected "every book and treatise which had been [...] wrote upon noses", but their numbers were scarce, so that his library on the topic was almost as "ridiculous" as Toby's on fortifications.

Here, Sterne suddenly stops, overwhelmed by an unexpected wave of emotion towards "my uncle". Suddenly, his analysis of perverted transmission flips over, as he unexpectedly becomes the *therapon* who can give his father the funeral rites he missed in Jamaica by performing them for Uncle Toby:

> Here, —but why here—rather than in any other part of my story, —I am not able to tell, —but here it is, —my heart stops me to pay to thee, my dear uncle Toby, once for all, the tribute I owe thy goodness.

Now, Sterne kneels on the ground to sing the elegy he owes his quixotic uncle Toby:

> Thou envied'st no man's comforts, —insulted'st no man's opinions.— Thou blackened'st no man's character [...]: gently with faithful Trim behind thee didst thou amble round the little circle of thy pleasures, jostling no creature in thy way;—for each man's need, thou hadst a

shilling. Whilst I am worth one to pay a weeder, — thy path from thy door to thy bowling green shall never be grown up.—Whilst there is a rood and a half of land in the Shandy family, thy fortifications, my dear uncle Toby, shall never be demolish'd.

The antidepressant psychotherapy, which Rabelais called Pantagruelism and his disciple Shandeism, is a success. In a letter to his friend John Hall Stevenson, Sterne wrote: "the spirit of Shandeism [...] will not suffer me to think two moments upon any grave subject, [or] else I would just now lay down and die".

But this type of therapy takes time. It will take twenty chapters to bring Walter out of his catatonic state. I am familiar with its stages in my practice.

The spirit of Shandeism[54]

First, we can't help searching for the cause of the patient's condition, such as, for instance, the foreclosure of the nose of the father. What has been excluded from the Symbolic returns in the Real, Lacan says[55]—the real baby's crushed nose—which turns into a quasi "hallucinated image"[56] for his father in the third generation. Aby Warburg calls it a "surviving image"; Bion, in his Grid,[57] a "Beta-element"; and Socrates in the *Thaetatus*, an *aloga* element"[58]—without speech or reason. Evidently, in this instance, the "tool with the name" is really broken.[59]

But once the cause is found, the analyst is no further ahead since, in the absence of a symbolic chain, causality loses its function. Going a step further, Sterne focuses on Walter's attempts to repair the tool with the name by collecting books—with the energy of Don Quixote[60] trying to heal his father's war traumas by reading chivalric books before acting them out through hallucinations. Here is Walter's bibliographical research on the theory of noses.

It began with Bruscambille, a French author for whom "my father had a strong fancy", whose real name was Deslauriers. He lived between 1575 and 1634, and became famous for his songs on the *Pont au Change*. In the 17th century, people danced on the bridges, since there was little space within city walls. Charlatans sold their potions and on the Pont Neuf, on which Sterne knelt during his *Sentimental Journey*,[61] songs called *Pont Neuf* were performed; their lyrics, set to a familiar melody called *fredon*, derided the abuses of the times.

Sterne knew them well, since he and his friends from Crazy Castle took a passionate interest in 16th-century French authors. He depicts Walter's excitement when in a bookshop he came across one of Bruscambille's five books, which included the "Prologue upon Noses":

My father flung down the money as quick as lightning, —took the Bruscambille into his bosom, —hied home [...] with it as he would have hied home with a treasure. [...] —There are not three Bruscambilles in Christendom, —said the stall-man.

So, Walter had bought the book for next to nothing and carried it off. Once home, "he solaced himself with Bruscambilles after the manner in which [...] your worship solaced yourself with your first mistress, that is, from morning even unto night".

But in Walter's case, the *inamorato* reader's secret rapture did not last. "My father's eye was greater than his appetite [...], —he cool'd—his affections became divided [...], —he purchased [other books]".

At this juncture, Sterne turns to his feminine reader whom he calls "my dear girl" and ushers her into a medieval theatre of fools he knows well. I can easily identify with the dear girl, since I wrote a book[62] in which I created dialogues between the Fools of a political theatre called *Sotties*—very popular at the end of 15th century after the Great Plague and the Hundred Years' War—and my patients confined in psychiatric hospitals.

Sotties[63]

At the beginning of a "Sottie Judgement", the loud cry of Mother Folly summons onto the stage the *Sots* and the *Sottes*, her children, for a mock trial of tyrannical characters of the time. Here, her cry is replaced by Sterne's warnings. The first to the "dear girl" not to let Satan "get astride of your imagination" at the mention of the least rising ground; the second is promised for later, since he "shall have much to say by and by".

We are indeed in a Sottie, where the jugglers rush on the stage with their verbal and gestural prowess to judge political abuses. Like a filly not yet broken in, the feminine reader is asked "to frisk it, [...] to jump it, to rear it, to bound it", to rid herself of the intruder who wants to put the bit in her mouth and bridle her imagination. The scene refers to Rabelais's Fourth Book (Chapter 13) and concerns his master, the famous poet François Villon, who fled to Paris to avoid hanging and had joined a troupe of jugglers for whom he composed *Sotties et Mystères*. For one of these, Friar Tickletoby refused to lend the poet church garb.

Perched on his filly, he is attacked by jugglers dressed in wolf, calf and ram skins, Spirits of the Land, bursting forth and spooking the mare, so that he is dragged through the bushes, his foot tangled in the stirrup and his backside badly skinned.

This is where Sterne delivers his second piece of advice to the dear girl: "Read, read, read, read, my unlearned reader"! And he tells her why:

> for without much reading, by which Your Reverence knows I mean much knowledge, you will no more be able to penetrate the moral of the next marbled page (motely emblem of my work!) than the world with all its sagacity has been able to unravel the many opinions,

transactions and truths which still lie mystically hid under the dark veil of the black one.

After admiring his two-sided marbled page—*shandied*, we might say—marking the progress of Shandeism from the black page to the advent of colour, I answer that although Walter was an avid reader, he is no more advanced than psychoanalysts who read seminars on psychosis but have no experience of the transference specific to it. Walter continues his research by turning to Erasmus's *Familiar Colloquies*.

The meaning of the meaning[64]

Sterne agrees. Erasmus's dialogue on noses, so carefully scrutinised by Walter, does not provide the expected answers either. The dialogue, entitled *In Pursuit of Benefices*,[65] recounts the meeting between Cocles and his friend Pamphagus, endowed with a huge nose, whom he has not seen for twenty years:

> Cocles: Well then, do you admire that I know you that have so remarkable a Nose.
> Pamphagus: I am not at all sorry for this nose.
> Cocles: No, nor have you any Occasion to be sorry for having a Thing that is fit for so many Uses.
> Pamphagus: For what Uses?
> Cocles: First of all, it will serve instead of an Extinguisher, to put out Candles.
> Pamphagus: Go on.

Three centuries after Erasmus, Cyrano[66] will use Cocles's enumeration to answer his rival De Guiche's insult with his famous monologue about his nose, saying at the end:

> — Such, my dear sir, is what you might have said,
> Had you of wit or letters the least jot:
> But, O most lamentable man! — of wit
> You never had an atom, and of letters
> You have three letters only! — they
> spell Ass!

Walter strives to change the word-thing into a signifier. Studying every syllable with application—"Mayhaps there is more meant than is said"—he dissects the words like a postmodern analyst obsessed with "the agency of the letter". After trying to transform *focum*, the fire, into *ficum*, the fig, in order to draw from Erasmus's text a meaning suitable to his grandfather's fig (penis), he finally gives up, disappointed at "finding nothing more from so able a pen, but the bare fact itself". The curse of the ancestor is unbroken and the ransom is real.

This is when Walter turns to a *faithful Analyser*, a German analyst whose unpronounceable name—Hafen Slawkenbergius—is composed of *Hafen* (pot) and *Slawkenber* (snot). Another analyst I don't know, I think to myself, and whose *Institute of Noses* I haven't heard of. The title brings to mind Jonathan Swift's "Institute of Wits" in *A Tale of a Tub*.[67] Any resemblance to our present-day institutes is entirely fortuitous.

The institute of noses[68]

Walter speaks to Slawkenbergius as he would to a *thou* who can alleviate his distress. Transference works very well:

> O Slawkenbergius! [...]—thou sad foreteller of so many of the whips and short turns which have come slap upon me from the shortness of my nose [...].—Tell me, Slawkenbergius! what secret impulse was it? what intonation of voice? [...]—which first cried out to thee, —go, —go, Slawkenbergius! Dedicate the labours of thy life, —[...] in the service of mankind and write a grand FOLIO for them upon the subject of their noses.

Like all founders, the master has received a calling from the higher Power. A short biographical reference informs the reader that:

> ever since he had arrived at the age of discernment and was able to sit down coolly and consider within himself the true state and condition of man, [...]—or rather *what was what*—and could perceive that the point of long noses had been too loosely handled by all who had gone before [...] he has entered the list with a stronger lance, and [took] a much larger career in it [...].

He has compiled "all that had been wrote or wrangled thereupon in the schools [...] of the learned", and founded, "all alone as he had always been", his own "institute of noses" centuries earlier than anyone else.

But let us be wary of idealisation. As we shall see, the life of the "institute" was regularly disrupted by violent quarrels between the partisans of psychic and organicist causality. The first of these disputes was documented by Prignitz's statistics with supporting evidence: the dissection of 4,000 skulls from an ossuary in Silesia. Prignitz decided in favour of psychogenesis, concluding that "the excellency of the nose is in a direct arithmetical proportion to the excellency of the wearer's fancy".

Scroderus's organicist approach is based on the opposite view: "so far from the truth in affirming that the fancy begat the nose that, on the contrary, —the nose begat the fancy". Scroderus attacked Prignitz violently, invoking "a series of stubborn facts". All their disciples maintained their respective views passionately and ignored each other's.

Ambroise Paré, 16th-century "chief surgeon and nose-mender" to many kings of France, known as the father of modern surgery and inventor of new techniques to treat war wounds, overthrew both systems. Sterne turns to the reader:

> Be witness—[...]—the true and efficient cause of [the size of a nose] was neither this nor that, —but that [it] was owing simply to the softness and flaccidity in the nurse's breast, —as the flatness and shortness of noses was [owed] to the firmness to the firmness and elasticity repulsion of the same organ of nutrition of the same organ of nutrition in the hale and lively [...];—but that in (the other) case [...], —by sinking into it as into so much butter, the nose was plump'd up [...] and set a-growing for ever.

This is how the French surgeon's theory of the "good breast" overthrew not only Prignitz and Scroderus, but also "the system of peace and harmony of our family. [...] For three days together [it] not only embroiled matters between my father and my mother, but turn'd likewise the whole house [...] except my uncle Toby, quite upside down".

Here, we have evidence-based proof of the ravages produced by conflicting theories in domestic life. Sterne is about to give us an example—"necessary to let you know first: My mother, you must know...", when suddenly he feels lost. Is it due to his "not good enough mother"? We have no way of knowing and must await the arrival of Melanie Klein and Winnicott to fill out the suspension points. In the meantime, Sterne is subject to a panic attack: "I have a hundred difficulties which I have promised to clear up, and a thousand distresses and domestic misadventures crowding in upon me [...], —a cow broke in (tomorrow morning) to my uncle Toby's fortifications".

I have known such moments in my practice, when tenses "shandy", mingling verb conjugations in a timequake, where the past interacts in the present with the future.

Five minutes less than no time at all[69]

The memory of the future has been set in action. Later, in Chapter XXXI of Volume 4, Trim will burst into the parlour to announce that a cow has trampled the bowling green. This mischief is announced now in mixed tenses: "A cow broke in (tomorrow morning) and eat up two rations [...] of dried grass, tearing up the sods". The corporal insists on being tried by a court-martial. "—the cow to be shot—Slop to be crucifi'd—myself to be *tristram'd*". The newborn protests: "—I want swaddling —".

What follows will only be revealed in the next volume. Sterne exclaims: "Poor unhappy devils that we all are!—but there is not time to be lost in exclamations". He is overwhelmed—understandably—how can he write with a baby screaming in the background? What's more, he promised the reader to return to Walter's bedside in half an hour, but five and a half minutes have already passed and he has not yet translated the tale from Slawkenbergius' folio, as he promised.[70] "Of all the perplexities a mortal author was ever seen in — this certainly is the greatest [...], and all this in five minutes less than no time at all".

Temporal confusion makes the reader spin like in blind man's buff, skipping from one volume to the next, back and forth, blindfolded. After transferring his panic on to us, Sterne can pick up the thread of his story:

> There was not any one scene more *entertaining* in our family [...]—and I here put off my cap and lay it on the table [...] to make my declaration [...]—that I believe the hand of the Supreme Maker never put a family together where characters of it were cast and contrasted with 'so dramatic a felicity' as ours was.

Noticing the oxymoron, a family therapist could wonder if the adjective "entertaining" is appropriate. Indeed, at this point the tone has changed. The analysis of the Shandy family's system will henceforth be decidedly comical—contrary to therapies which undermine the patients' morale. The fatal spell cast by the ancestor will be foiled by the devastating energy of laughter.

"Je dis: solution (I say: solution), dissolution"[71]

Sterne has donned the fool's cap once again to put forth another of Toby's jumbled remarks, which comes out of nowhere. But first, the reader is provided with a notion that will prove crucial as he proceeds:

> The gift of [...] making syllogisms, —I mean in man, —for in superior classes of beings such as angels and spirits—'tis all done, [...], as they tell me, by INTUITION [...]; — amongst us [...], is the finding-out the agreement or disagreement of two ideas.

One winter night, when Walter closes the book he has been translating painstakingly for three hours, he confesses his discouragement to Toby, paying no heed to his choice of words:

> 'Tis a pity [...] that Truth should shut herself up in such impregnable fastnesses and be so obstinate as not to surrender herself [...] upon the

closest siege. (...)But the word *siege*, like a talismanic power [...] waft-
ing back my uncle Toby's fancy [...], —he open'd his ears—[although
his fancy] had taken a short flight to the bowling green; he was in fact
ignorant of the whole lecture [...] as if my father had been translating [...]
from the Latin tongue into the Cherokee.

Taking the metaphor literally, Toby takes his pipe out of his mouth and
pulls his chair nearer his brother, who repeats his phrase, taking care to
avoid the obsidional reference and its consequences: "'Tis a pity [...] that
truth can only be on one side, brother Toby, —considering what ingenuity
these learned men have all shewn in their solution of noses. —Can noses be
dissolved? replied my uncle Toby".
   Lacan would be excited by this pun, which he used himself to announce
the dissolution of the École freudienne de Paris to its members in January
1980: "... *Je dis solution* (I say solution): *dissolution*". I remember that Louis
Althusser came into the room then, a spectral figure appearing as the fool,
in a scene that he describes in his last book.[72] Knocking his pipe against his
heel, before a silent audience, he opposed the dissolution. Then everybody
rose to gather around a table where drinks were being served. Althusser was
left standing alone in the room. Ten months later, he strangled his wife in his
apartment of the *Ecole normale superieure*, rue d'Ulm.
   Walter's reaction to the word "dissolution" is more virulent, though less
deadly:

My father thrust back his chair, —rose up, —put on his hat, —took
four long strides to the door, —jerked it open [...], shut the door
again, —took no notice of the bad hinge, —returned to the table, —
pluck'd my mother's thread-paper out [...], twisting [it] about his thumb, —
unbutton'd his waistcoat, —threw [the] paper into the fire, [...]—[and
swore] at my uncle Toby's brain.

Fortunately, "my father's passions lasted not long. [...] 'Twas all one to my
uncle Toby:—he smoked his pipe on".
   Unlike the philosopher, Toby achieves Jonathan Swift's desire: to attain
"the serene peaceful state of being a fool among knaves". Indeed:

his heart never intended offence to his brother, —he always gave my
father the credit of cooling by himself.—He was five minutes and thirty-
five seconds about it in the present case. —'By all that's good!' said my
father as he came to himself [...], if it was not for the aid of philosophy
[...], —you would put a man beside all temper. [...] had you favoured me
with one grain of attention [you might have known] the various accounts
which learned men [...] have given the world of the causes of short and

long noses.—There is no cause but one, replied my uncle Toby, because God pleases to have it so.

Like a true man of the Enlightenment, "my father" refutes his brother's outmoded opinion and points to the distinction between religion and science, causing Toby to start whistling his *Lillibullero* "with more zeal (though more out of tune) than usual". Volume 3 ends with Walter's decision to bone up on Slawkenbergius, whose work is like a "canon's prayer book" to him, to the point where he professes that "if all the arts and sciences in the world [...] were lost [...], —and Slawkenbergius only left, —there would be enough in him [...] to set the world a-going again".

When the Nazis were about to enter Vienna, after his books were burned on Berlin Opera Platz in 1933, Freud wrote his *Moses and Monotheism*, asking himself how psychoanalysis could be "set a-going" again. Thirteen years later, Lacan's "Remarks on Psychic Causality", delivered at the Bonneval conference in 1946,[73] set it a-going again in a way that would have delighted Walter but would have disappointed Toby, since Lacan did not mention the war that just ended except in a short paragraph of excuses for having abandoned his practice in the meanwhile.

As an adult, Tristram claims not to be "such a bigot as my father", preferring his uncle's hobby horse, as we can conclude from his translation of the German analyst's tale about a free city caught off guard by the arrival of war.

Notes

1 Sterne, L., *Tristram Shandy*, op. cit., Vol. 3, ch. I.
2 Sterne, L., *Tristram Shandy*, op. cit., Vol. 2, ch. XVIII.
3 Herrigel, E., *Zen in the Art of Archery*, London: Vintage, 1999.
4 Sterne, L., *Tristram Shandy*, Vol. 3, chs. II, III.
5 Bal, M., *Image-Thinking*, Edinburgh University Press, 2022.
6 Bion, W. *A Memoir of the Future*, op. cit., ch. I; "Attack on Linking", in *Second Thoughts*, London: Karnac Books, 1987.
7 Sterne, L., *Tristram Shandy*, Vol. 3, chs. IV–VI.
8 Sterne, L., *Tristram Shandy*, op. cit., Vol. 3, chs. VII–X.
9 Johnson, S. (1755). *Samuel Johnson's Insults*, New York: Walker Company, 2004.
10 Le Goff, J. & Schmitt, J.-C. (Eds.), *Le Charivari*, Paris: Éditions de l'EHESS/ Berlin: Mouton de Gruyter, 1981.
11 Benedetti, G., *Le sujet emprunté*, Erès, 1995.
12 Bion, W., *Second Thoughts*, op. cit.
13 Sterne, L., *Tristram Shandy*, op. cit., Vol. 3, chs. X–XI; reference to song *La ronde des jurons*, by Brassens, G. 1958.
14 Vonnegut K., *Timequake*, New York: Berkley Books, 1997.
15 De Cervantes, M., *Don Quixote II*, op. cit., ch. 48.
16 Sterne, L., *Tristram Shandy*, op. cit., Vol. 3, ch. XII.

17 Wittgenstein, L., Notes for lectures on "private experience" and "sense data". In the *Oxford Handbook of Wittgenstein*, Oxford University Press, 2011.
18 Beaumarchais, P., The *Marriage of Figaro*, Chicago: Ivan R. Dee, 1994.
19 Voltaire, *Philisophical Dictionary*, Mineola, NY: Dover Publications, 2010.
20 Ross, I. C., *Laurence Sterne, A Life,* Oxford University Press, 2001.
21 Sterne, L., *Tristram Shandy*, op. cit., Vol. 3, chs. XIII–XIV.
22 Tweedy, R., *A Political Self,* London: Karnac, 2017; Gaudillière, J.-M., *The Birth of a Political Self*, London and New York: Routledge, 2021.
23 Sterne, L., *Tristram Shandy*, op. cit., chs. XV–XIX.
24 Molière, *The School for Wives* and *The Learned Ladies*, New York: Harper Collins, 1991.
25 Carroll, L., *Alice in Wonderland*, New York: Random House, 2009.
26 Locke, J., *An Essay Concerning Human Understanding*, op. cit.
27 Sterne, L., *Tristram Shandy,* op. cit., Vol. 3, ch. XX.
28 Wittgenstein, L., *Philosophical Investigations*, op. cit.
29 Freud, S., *Moses and Monotheism*, op. cit.
30 Locke, J., *An Essay Concerning Human Understanding*, op. cit.
31 Regnard, J.-F. (1681). *Voyage en Laponie*, Paris: GINKGO, 2010.
32 Lonnrot, E., *The Kalevala*, Oxford Paperbacks, 2008.
33 Wittgenstein, L., *Philosophical Investigations*, op. cit., § 41.
34 Lacan J. Écrits, New York, Norton, 1977.
35 Sterne, L., *Tristram Shandy*, op. cit., Vol. 3, chs. XXI–XXII.
36 Sterne, L., *Tristram Shandy*, op. cit., Vol. 3, ch. XXIII.
37 Sterne, L., *Tristram Shandy*, op. cit., Vol. 3, chs. XXIV–XXV.
38 Ross, I. C., *Laurence Sterne: A Life*, op. cit.
39 Freud, S., *Jokes and their Relation to the Unconscious*, S.E. 8, London: Hogarth.
40 Sterne, L., *Tristram Shandy*, op. cit., Vo.3, ch. XXIII.
41 Sterne, L., *Tristram Shandy*, op. cit., Vol. 3, chs. XXVI–XXVIII.
42 Ross, I.C., *Laurence Sterne: A Life*, op. cit., p. 118.
43 Burton, R., *The Anatomy of Melancholy*, New York: NYRB Classics, 2001.
44 Sterne, L, *Tristram Shandy,* Vol. 3, ch. XXIX.
45 Wittgenstein, L., *Philosophical Investigations*, op. cit., §283.
46 Wittgenstein, L., *Notes for Lectures on «Private Experience» and «Sense Data»*, op. cit.
47 Laub, D., Felman S. *Testimony, New York and London:* Routledge 1997.
48 Nagy, G., *The Best of the Achaeans*, Baltimore: The Johns Hopkins University Press, 1979.
49 Sterne, L., *Tristram Shandy*, op. cit., Vol. 3, chs. XXX–XXXI.
50 Bion, W., "Attacks on Linking", op. cit.
51 Sterne, L., *Tristram Shandy*, op. cit., Vol. 2, ch. VII.
52 Sterne, L., *Tristram Shandy*, op. cit., Vol. 3, chs. XXXI–XXXV.
53 Rabelais, F., *Gargantua and Pantagruel*, op. cit., "The Fourth Book", ch. 9.
54 Sterne, L., *Tristram Shandy*, op. cit., Vol.3, ch. XXXV.
55 Lacan, J., *Écrits*, op. cit.
56 Freud, S. (1895). *Project for a Scientific Psychology*, S.E. 1, London: Hogarth.
57 Bion, W., *Elements of Psychoanalysis*, London: Karnac Books, 1963.
58 Plato, *Theaetetus*, New York, The Liberal Arts Press, 1955.
59 Wittgenstein, L., *Philosophical Investigations*, op. cit., § 41.
60 De Cervantes, M., *Don Quixote I*, op. cit., ch. 1, ch. 8.
61 Sterne, L., A *Sentimental Journey and Other Writings*, Oxford University Press, 2008.

62 Davoine, F., *Mother Folly: A Tale*, Stanford, CA: Stanford University Press, 2014.
63 Sterne, L., *Tristram Shandy*, op. cit., Vol. 3, ch. XXXVI.
64 Sterne, L., *Tristram Shandy*, op. cit., Vol. 3, ch. XXXVII.
65 Erasmus, D. (1725). *The Whole Familiar Colloquies of Desiderius Erasmus of Rotterdam*, Bailey, N. (Trans.), Charleston, SC: BiblioLife, 2009.
66 Rostand, E., *Cyrano de Bergerac*, Mineola, NY: Dover Publications, 2000.
67 Swift, J., *A Tale of a Tub*, op. cit.
68 Sterne, L., *Tristram Shandy*, op. cit., Vol. 3, ch. XXXVIII.
69 Sterne, L., *Tristram Shandy*, op. cit., Vol. 3, chs. XXXVIII and XXXIX.
70 Sterne, L., *Tristram Shandy*, op. cit., Vol. 4.
71 Lacan, J., Letter of Dissolution, Jan. 5, 1980; Sterne, L., *Tristram Shandy*, op. cit., Vol. 3, chs. XXXIX–XLII.
72 Althusser, L., *The Future Lasts Forever*, New York: The New Press, 1995.
73 Lacan, J., *Écrits*, op. cit.

4

Social unrest in Strasburg

The story continues with the a detailed analysis of group psychology among clerics in a situation aimed at pastor Yorick's annihilation—leading to his death, recounted in Volume I.

Along the way, at the crossroads of historical events and Shandy's particular story, the question is raised of the possibility of repairing the damage to the baby's face with a prestigious name.

The story takes place during the month of August 1681 in the free city of Strasbourg just before it fell to the French. I can't help drawing a hobby-horsical parallel with the fall of psychoanalysis into the hands of pharmacologists, as a consequence of its only focus on repressed desires. Both Strasbourgians and psychoanalytic experts neglected taking history into account.

When Sterne analyses Walter's catatonic state with its transgenerational source, he does not diagnose it as pathology, but as a way to survive a catastrophe—something the wounded captain understands well. This paradigm shift away from mainstream and structural analysis has a political dimension, since it allows the emergence of a subject destroyed by lawless agencies for whom the other does not exist. At the end of this volume, Sterne portrays pastor Yorick's persecution by his hierarchy, which led to his death.

The reasons for the reticence shown by mainstream psychoanalysis towards madness and trauma can be traced back to a letter dated October 1867, in which Freud announces to Wilhem Fliess the abandonment of his "Neurotica", that is, his belief in sexual abuse suffered by his patients, attributing their accounts to repressed fantasy, despite the fact that in an earlier letter, written in February, he confided to his friend that his own father "was a pervert" who abused his younger brothers and sisters. Yet Freud kept coming back to the question of an unrepressed unconscious, where sensorial impressions have recorded unspeakable catastrophes. One of the last chapters of *Moses and Monotheism*, written under the Nazi terror, is entitled "The Historical Truth".

DOI: 10.4324/9781003224907-4

Historical truth is the aim of Shandean psychoanalysis through co-research between analyst and patient, which fights the erasure of traces, as we shall see illustrated again in two carnivalesque tales at the start and the end of this volume.

Madness and the social link

Slawkenbergius's tale

A city led by the nose[1]

This German tale, written in Latin, is translated by Tristam and presented in bilingual form, like Ernulf's excommunications. It describes the subversion of desire on a collective scale, enacting Lacan's "*La signification du phallus,*[2] — *Die Bedeutung des Phallus*" in Slawkenberius's tongue and producing "a revolution often spoken of but little understood". Here is its summary.

Towards the end of August 1681, a stranger on a mule, carrying only "a few shirts, a pair of shoes and a crimson-satin pair of breeches", entered the gates of the free city of Strasbourg. He was only passing through, leaving those who saw him confounded by his gigantic nose. The sentinel at the gate and the bandy-legged drummer beside him stared at him in amazement.

Asked about his destination, the stranger answers that he is "going on to Frankfurt—and should be back again in Strasburg that day month, in his way to the border of Crim Tartary". As for whence he has come, "he had been at the Promontory of NOSES". We hear echoes of Cyrano: "A promontory did I say? Nay, it's a PENINSULA"! As he pays the toll, the stranger's gestures reveal, hanging from his wrist, a "naked" scimitar without a scabbard—*vagina* in Latin—as we see plainly written on the opposite page.

Sterne describes the stranger as "courteous" and draws his portrait from the bits of gossip elicited by his nose. The two men at the gate regret that they did not touch it and wonder if it is real. "I heard it crackle, said the drummer. —By dunder, said the Sentinel, I saw it bleed". A trumpeter and his wife enter the scene and continue the argument: "Benedicity! —'Tis as soft as a flute, said she. —'Tis brass said the trumpeter. —[...] I'll know [...], (she insists); for I will touch it with my finger before I sleep".

As the stranger proceeds astride his mule, the burger master's wife hears him speaking to himself, his hands on his breast in a saint-like posture, and catches a few words: "slandered and disappointed as I have been..." Then he vows to Saint Nicolas: "my nose shall never be touched whilst Heaven gives me strength. —To do what? she wonders". Soon, he reaches the great inn in the marketplace where, after his mule is lead to the stable and himself to his room, he takes down his crimson satin breeches with a silver-fringed appendage—from the Greek *perizonate*, on the left-hand page, called "girdle" in English and *"braguette"* in French—a term dear to Rabelais, which Tristram does not dare to translate.

Handsomely dressed, he walks out onto the "grand parade", but seeing the trumpeter's wife there, he returns to the inn at once for fear of having his nose touched, undresses, packs his cloak bag, mounts his mule again and calls out:

> I am going forwards, for Frankfurt, —and shall be back at Strasbourg this day month. [...] —'Tis a long journey, sir, replied the master of the inn, —unless a man has great business.—Tut! Tut! said the stranger, I have been at the Promontory of Noses; and have got me one of the goodliest and jolliest...

Fascinated, the innkeeper's wife reflects, "upon St. Radegunda, —that a dozen of the largest in town could be contained in it"—and she was not just guessing. Her husband was sceptical: 'Tis an imposture, my dear, —'tis a false nose. [...] 'Tis a dead nose [...]. —'Tis a live nose and if I am alive myself, I will touch it".

The same irresistible impulse would take hold of the widow Wadman in Volume 9, with respect to Toby's groin.[3] The young man's fear intensifies. He clasps his hand again, saying:

> I have made a vow to St. Nicolas that my nose shall not be touched till—
> [...] —Till when? said she hastily. —It never shall be touched, said he,
> [...] till that hour —What hour? Cried the innkeeper's wife, —Never!—
> never! Said the stranger, never till I am got... —For Heaven's sake, into
> what place? Said she.—The stranger rode away without saying a word.

Lacanian readers on both sides of the Atlantic have their work cut out for them if they want to understand the structure of this desire. The task is too daunting for me, especially since *Massen Psychologie* is already taking central stage. Even the translator is at a loss, as evidenced by the disappearance of the Latin on the left-hand page:

> [...] the city was like a swarm of bees;—men, women and children [...]
> flying here and there, —in at one door, out at another [...], —up one
> street, down another street [...]. —Did you see it? Did you see it? [...] Oh!
> Did you see it? [...] God help me! I never saw it —I never touch'd it!—
> would I have been a sentinel, a [...] drummer, a trumpeter, a trumpeter's
> wife, was the general cry and lamentation in every street and corner of
> Strasbourg.

Although no one saw anything since they were all busy "going to vespers, washing, scouring or sewing", the lost object of desire produces its subversive effect, of which the young man is unaware as he rides on, speaking to his mule named Julia:

> Whilst all this confusion and disorder triumphed through the great city of Strasbourg, was the courteous stranger going on as gently upon his mule [...] as if he had no concern at all in the affair [...] 'O Julia, my lovely Julia! [...] —that ever the suspected tongue of a rival should have robbed me of enjoyment when I was upon the point of tasting it! [...]— Banish'd from my country, —my friends, —from thee'.

The reader can guess that he is grappling with desires of his own which, given his age, have become overwhelming and disrupted the routine of a whole city. Ignoring the stir he has caused, he goes on speaking to his mule, when they cross a horseman riding towards them: "—O Julia!—What dost thou prick up thy ears at? —'tis nothing but a man". Soon, he stops at an inn, orders an omelette, goes to bed at midnight and falls into a deep sleep.

We guess that what is most essential will take place while he sleeps, just as while Don Quixote slept at the inn, four lovers were reunited, escaping the machinations of an evil lord, thanks to the knight's intervention.

Crowd psychology

During the night, "when the tumult in Strasbourg [...] abated", Queen Mab found another way to stir it up again. Sterne starts with the nuns—hated by Uncle Jaques—whom his nephew describes in Rabelasian fashion. "The abbess of Quedlinberg, [...] with [...] the prioress, the deaness, the sub-chantess, and the senior canoness, had that week come to Strasbourg to consult the University upon a case of conscience relating to their placket holes". The holy woman falls victim to insomnia, since the stranger's nose sits on the pineal gland of her brain. She cannot close her eyes, and neither can the other dignitaries of her chapter. In fact, an epidemic of "possession" was observed in "all of the severe orders of nuns" of the city. "The nuns of Saint Ursula acted the wisest: they never attempted to go to bed at all".

As for the male dignitaries of the Church assembled to consider the case of the "buttered buns" (slang for women of easy virtue), they regret not having followed the example of the Ursulines because that morning the bakers could not bake any buns to be buttered for breakfast. Such a thing had not happened in Strasbourg "since Martin Luther had turned the city upside down".

Could the nose have played the role of the moustache-to-come, foreseen by Freud in his essay on Group Psychology?[4] The difference is that here the person concerned does not care. And the German analyst only carries out his survey among witnesses who all agree that "he is a paragon of beauty, whether his nose is true or false". But since this does not explain the scope of the social movement set off by the untouchable thing, the German analyst launches into the sociology of the media.

Among the elite, the overexcited abbess sends for the trumpeter's wife and they confer together for three days. In the lower classes, the sentinel and his friend give talks to passers-by under the city gates. The innkeeper gives his lecture at the stable door, and "his wife hers more privately in a back room", to those who flocked there "as faith and credibility marshall'd them". They all "came crowding for intelligence, —and every Strasburger had the intelligence he wanted". The enquiry also reveals the rivalry between the leaders. No sooner has the trumpeter's wife left the abbess than she begins to read her notes upon a stool in the middle of the great parade, gaining, thanks to her credentials, the attention of "the most fashionable part of the city" which sets the tone for all the others.

From the historical perspective, the quarrel reawakened the chronic animosity between the Catholic and Protestant universities of the city, set off initially by the transfer of Luther's birthday in 1453 to Saint Martin's day, in order to avoid the damnation predicted by his horoscope.

Having gone this far, Tristram breaks off his translation, "for if I did not I should no more be able to shut my eyes in bed than the abbess of Quedlinburg". But first, Sterne has to bring an important detail to the reader's attention.

Coitus interruptus of a city

The detail concerns the triumph with which Walter reads this passage:

> Now you see brother Toby, [...]—had Luther here been called by any other name but Martin, he would have been damned to all eternity. [This tale] flattered two of his strangest hypotheses together:—his NAMES and his NOSES. [...] [It] hit two nails upon the head at one stroke.

His theory of names shall be brought again to the reader in good time. As for the nose, it continues to divide the city of Strasbourg into Nosarians and Antinosarians, as fiercely opposed as the Big-Endians and the Little-Endians on the Island of Lilliput, ready to kill each other over the best way to break open a boiled egg. The controversy spread among physicians, logicians and lawyers.

It was impossible to guess "on which side of the nose the two universities would split. [...] The less they understood of the matter, the greater was their wonder about it;—they were left in all the distresses of desire unsatisfied". The Parchmentarians believed the nose to be made of cardboard, the Brassarians believed it to be brass, the Turpentarians of turpentine-smelling wood. In the meantime, the "poor Strasburgers were left upon the beach"! Nevertheless, the German analyst praises them:

> I dip [...] my pen into my ink to [...] write your panegyric. Shew me a city so macerated with expectations, —who neither eat or drank or slept or prayed [...] for seven-and-twenty days together, who held out, [for] on the twenty-eighth, the [...] stranger promised to return.

The city's dignitaries prepare a grand entrance for him and leave the city solemnly to meet him, the rest of the population following "higgledy-piggledy", some on horseback, some on foot. "[...] all set out at sunrise to meet the courteous stranger on the road". This is where the catastrophe intervenes. The meeting will not take place, and the long-awaited stranger will remain unaware of the mobilisation which leaves the city exhausted after it has used up all its libidinal resources. Coitus interruptus once again!

After quoting Aristotle, "without whom a tale had better never be told at all", the German analyst expounds on his historical, political, economic and psychological theories.

Theory!

Indeed, Aristotelian catharsis is what the stranger experiences, when the "unwinding [of] the labyrinth [brings] the hero out of a state of agitation [...] to a state of rest and quietness". We are at the inn where the traveller he crossed on the road has arrived while he slept. When the innkeeper mentions the famous nose, the new guest falls upon his knee, exclaiming: "Trifle not with my anxiety [...]. [It is] the end of my pilgrimage!—'Tis Diego"!

The traveller is the brother of Diego's Dulcinea, named Julia, like his mule. She sent him from Valladolid in pursuit of her sweetheart, to give him a letter confessing that her suspicions about his extravagant nose were the reason she asked her duenna to forbid him to appear under her window. We finally understand what the suspension points in Diego's monologue covered over: a spurned lover, he had concluded that she was thinking of another nose. The next morning, he reads in her letter that she regrets her decision: "How could I know so little of myself"? she asks, acknowledging the role played by unconscious repression.

Wasting no time, they hasten to Valladolid, where they arrive in three days. The reunion of the lovers is described as a "lambent pupilability of slow, low, dry chat",[5] whispered in precious language difficult to translate, but insinuating that the "naked scimitar" has found its "scabbard".

As for the historical events, "the cavalcade moved to and fro on the road to Frankfurt", where the citizens were gathered outside the city walls. The analyst of this "revolution" specifies the political context to be "the grand

system of Universal Monarchy wrote by order of Mons. Colbert and put
[...] into the hands of Louis the Fourteenth in the year 1664". Gaining possession of Strasbourg allowed the French king to enter Swabia in order to
disturb the quiet of Germany. His victory would be facilitated by the sudden
economic crisis in the city:

> Trade and manufactures have decayed and gradually grown down ...
> [Strasbourgers] brought themselves under taxes, [...] and, in the end,
> became so weak a people they had no strength to keep their gates shut,
> and so the French pushed them open.

But to political and economic arguments, Slawkenbergius adds the paramount subversive power of the unconscious:

"Alas! Alas! [he] cries, 'twas not the *French* [...]—it's not the first, —and
I fear will not be the last, fortress that has been either won—or lost by
NOSES". The city was led by the nose towards a catastrophe no one saw
coming.

END of Slawkenbergius's tale.

Walter's catatonic state[6]

Against the backdrop of this "often spoken of but little understood revolution", Sterne dons the fool's cap again to analyse Walter's breakdown.

Toby is sitting next to his brother, who lies spread out on his bed "as
still as if the hand of death had pushed him down". Sterne agrees, from
experience, with Bessel van der Kolk's future statement that in response
to lethal danger, our animal brain disconnects from the prefrontal sites of
thought and time perception: "... in [no] other posture could [a man] bear
the shock [in] the region of the heart.—The brain made no acknowledge-
ment.—There's often no good understanding betwixt 'em". To put theory
into practice, we are urged to "throw [ourselves] down upon the bed, a dozen
times [...], nose upon the quilt". This allows the heart rate to slow and the
parasympathetic nervous system to restore energy, as will say also military
psychologist Dave Grossman.[7]

Walter's method seems to work. "My father" comes to his senses little by
little. After an hour and a half, he draws up his left hand slowly to his chest
and gives a sigh. Toby answers it "with infinite pleasure", until his brother
cries out: "Did ever man, brother Toby, [...] receive so many lashes"?[8] This
last word subverts his therapist's neutrality. Taking the question literally,
Toby rings the bell for Trim, who can bear witness to the lashes received by
a grenadier in Flanders. As if shot at point-blank range, Walter falls down
again with his nose upon the quilt.

"Bless me! said my uncle Toby. Was it MacKay's regiment [...] where
the poor grenadier was so unmercifully whipp'd at Bruges about the

ducats? —O Christ! He was innocent! cried Trim with a deep sigh". And he could not hold back tears at the memory of grenadier Dick Johnson whose torment reminds him of his brother Tom—the three of them having been schoolfellows.

"... The children of honest people, going forth with gallant spirits to seek their fortunes in the world—and fall into such evils! [...]—O!—these are misfortunes [...] worth lying down and crying over". Trim pulls out his handkerchief. Walter blushes and Toby adds: "Tears are no proof of coward-ice, Trim.—I drop them oft-times myself".

In the next century, Herman Melville will tell a similar story in his *Billy Bud Sailor*,[9] about a young seaman hanged from the yardarm on account of a few gold coins hidden in his bag by a rascal envious of his kindness and beauty. The captain of the ship carries out the sentence, knowing the accusation is false. To the contrary, Toby takes the corporal's defence:

> —'Twould be a pity, Trim, [...] thou shouldst ever feel sorrow of thy own, —thou feelest it so tenderly for others —Alack-a-day, replied the corporal [...].—Your Honour knows I have neither wife or child;—I can have no sorrows in this world.—My father could not help smiling.

Such a "sentimental" dialogue, which contributed to Sterne's reputation, would probably be sneered at by postmodern critics. "—Please Your Honour, never fear, replied Trim cheerily. —But I would have thee never fear, Trim, replied my uncle; and therefore [...], whilst thy master is worth a shilling, —thou shalt never ask elsewhere, Trim, for a penny". Toby sud-denly sees fit to bequeath all his worldly goods to Trim. The corporal leaves the room in tears. "I have left Trim my bowling green", Toby confesses to his brother. Walter, who attaches no value to this bit of land, smiles again, before asking himself, his face still buried in the quilt: "Is this a fit time [...] to talk of PENSIONS and GRENADIERS"? Especially when the family money might pass into the hands of an outsider. This brief exchange is a lesson for analysts convinced that there can be no transference with a cata-tonic person.

The magic of the name[10]

Summoned by Toby and Trim, Walter is drawn out of his stupor. "Playing the same jig over again", more quickly this time, he rose to his feet, cir-cled the room three times and stopped before Toby to deliver a lesson on transmission:

> When I reflect, brother Toby, upon MAN, and consider [...] how oft we eat the bread of affliction, and that we are born to it as to the por-tion of our inheritance —I was born to nothing, [interrupted] my uncle

Toby, —but my commission.—Zooks said my father, did not my uncle leave you a hundred twenty pounds a year? —What could I have done without it?

Toby replied. In order to "lead him a little deeper into that mystery", Walter takes up Socrates's posture in Raphael's painting "The School of Athens". Holding "the forefinger of his left hand between the forefinger and the thumb of his right", he teaches Toby Socratic maieutics: "You *grant* me this—and this: and this and this, I don't ask of you:—they follow of themselves in course".

From this little performance, "the magic bias" of a Christian name emerges, able to "counteract and undo" the disastrous blow of the baby's crushed nose. In such a case, Levi Strauss would speak of "symbolic efficiency". Walter will not christen his son George or Edward, but Trismegistus, after the famous Egyptian initiate. "I wish it may answer", Toby hopes, getting up. The conversation continues on the first landing, where Walter savours this epiphany: "What a chapter of chances! [...] Take pen and ink in hand, brother Toby, and calculate it fairly".

The use of statistics dates back to 18th-century Germany and to British insurers of the maritime trade, Walter's occupation before retirement. Intended to repair the wreck of Tristram's nose, the name Trismegistus, meaning three times the greatest, should improve the child's odds.

My rule is not to have any[11]

After the brothers have gone down two steps, Sterne pauses for a moment and heaves a sigh of relief, since Walter has spared him the trouble of writing a chapter on chance. But given the fifteen steps that remain, he worries about having to write "as many chapters as steps". Fortunately, his hero comes to his aid:

> —Drop the curtain, *Shandy*. —I drop it. — Strike a line here across the paper, *Tristram*. —I strike it;—and hey for a new chapter! The deuce of any other rule have I to govern myself by in this affair. [...] Is a man to follow rules, —or rules to follow him?

Once the crisis is over, Sterne is glad he wrote his "chapter upon chapters—the best chapter in my whole work, [without] a sententious parade of wisdom". To convince us, he recommends that we read and reread Longinus's *On the Sublime*,[12] even if "we are not a jot the wiser by reading him". Here, Sterne is poking fun at high-potential children who dazzle their parents with their superior qualities. Walter's son will surpass other children thanks to his hyper-symbolic Christian name. "This Trismegistus [...] was the greatest of all earthly beings;—he was the greatest king, —the greatest lawgiver, —the greatest philosopher—and the greatest priest. And engineer, —said my uncle Toby. —In course, said my father".

But such superlatives will fail to propel the baby towards the sublime.

Mayday![13]

We are now back at the top of the staircase, where the two brothers are still pacing back and forth when Susannah walks by, out of breath, carrying a huge cushion. "And how does your mistress"? Walter asks. She ignores his question. "—And how is the child, pray"? he insists "—As well [...] as can be expected". Annoyed, Walter makes a phallocrat remark that his brother is prompt to contradict:

> ... from the very moment the mistress of the house is brought to bed, every female in it [...] becomes an inch taller for it, and give themselves more airs upon that single inch than all their other inches put together. —I think rather, replied my uncle Toby, that 'tis we who sink an inch lower.—'Tis a heavy tax upon that half of our fellow creatures. [...] —Yes, yes, 'tis a painful thing, —said my father, shaking his head too.

Sterne elucidates this head shake for future historians of sensibility:

> ...certainly since shaking of heads came into fashion, never did two heads shake together, in concert, from two such different springs. -- God bless 'em all, and deuce take 'em all—said my uncle Toby and my father, each to himself.

Once this historical fact is established, Sterne runs dry again.

Initially, his solution is to put them to sleep, since they have not shut their eyes for nine hours. He calls: "Holla!—you chairman"—to bring him a critic able "to get my father and my uncle Toby off the stairs, and to put them to bed". But now his priority is to overcome his problem with time by focusing on transference:

> Was every day of my life to be as busy a day as this, —[...], —truce!—I will not finish that sentence till I have made an observation upon the strange state of affairs between the reader and myself, just as things stand at present.

Sterne had warned us in Volume 1[14] that although we were "perfect strangers" to start with, we would "grow in familiarity and terminate in friendship".

Indeed, now we are asked to figure out the temporality of his narrative, as he is tangled up in the chronology and needs some help:

> I am [...] almost into the middle of my fourth volume—and no far-
> ther than to my first day's life [...] at this rate, I should just live 364
> times faster than I should write. [...] was it not that my OPINIONS
> will be the death of me, I perceive I shall lead a fine life out of this
> selfsame life of mine; or, in other words, shall lead a couple of fine
> lives together.

In *A Memoir of the Future*,[15] Wilfred Bion—who started to write "his" war after his exile in Los Angeles when he was past seventy—follows in Sterne's tracks and meets the same problem. His solution is to create a dialogue between the different ages of his life, from the germ cells called "somites" to PA, the psychoanalyst, including the 8-year-old child who left his native India to be schooled in England—as alone as the young Laurence sent away from Ireland for the same purpose—"18 years", who enlisted in the British army, and captain Bion who "died" at Cambrai in 1917 when his tank crew was killed, like captain Toby when he was wounded at Namur. in 1695.

Thankfully, the transference produces its effects and we move on speedily towards the next catastrophe.

Slip of the tongue[16]

The "chairman" has been paid a crown for his trouble. But the two men had barely closed their eyes when Susannah came rushing in again, and refused to hand "my father" his breeches:

> There's not a moment's time to dress you, sir, [...]—the child is as black
> in the face as my — [...]; —And where's Mr Yorick? —Never where he
> should be, said Susannah, but his curate's in the dressing room, with the
> child upon his arm, waiting for the name.

Susannah is frantic. Walter pronounces the illustrious name and is at once seized by doubt, shouting:

> But stay;—thou art a leaky vessel, Susannah, [...]; canst thou carry
> Trismegistus in thy head the length of the gallery without scattering?
> —Can I? cried Susannah, shutting the door in a huff. —If she can, I'll
> be shot, said my father, bouncing out of bed [...] and groping for his
> breeches.

As the child is struggling for breath, the tool with the name is going to fail. Panic can be heard in Walter's panting as he rushes to deliver the name himself. But:

> Susannah got the start and kept it.—'Tis Tris—something, cried Susannah. —There is no Christian name in the world [...] beginning with Tris—but Tristram. Then 'tis Tristram-*gistus*, quoth Susannah. — There is no *gistus* to it, noodle! —'Tis my own name, replied the curate, dipping his hand [...] into the basin. —Tristram! Said he, *etc. etc. etc. etc.....*, so Tristram was I called, and Tristram shall I be to the day of my death.

Thus, the title of the novel is the result of a misnomer which Walter ignores as he bursts in with a button on his breeches half fastened, when the christening is over. Hence, Sterne's promise of a chapter on buttonholes, which have a lot to do with the messing up of names:

> —She has not forgot the name, cried my father [...]. —No, no, said the curate, with a tone of intelligence. —And the child is better, cried Susannah. —And how does your mistress?—As well [...] as can be expected.

As the button slips out of its hole, Walter lets out a "Pish" providing a soundtrack for Hogarth's engraving showing him wearing a nightcap, holding up his breeches while facing the curate who holds Tristram in his arms and Susannah in the background wearing a sly little smile.

As I look more closely at Hogarth's picture, I ask myself why Walter did not take the baby in his own arms.

Chapter on sleep[17]

After all this commotion, the author-musician composes an intermezzo to help us relax. Tristram has been born, he survived suffocation and has been baptised:

> I wish I could write a chapter upon sleep. It is a fine subject! A fitter occasion could never have presented itself than [...] this moment [...], when all the curtains of the family are drawn, —the candles put out.

Sterne's chapter will not be a praise of sleep, such as Sancho Panza[18] addressed to his master, who was an insomniac like him: "... 'tis the refuge of the unfortunate, — the enfranchisement of the prisoner, — the downy lap of the hopeless [...]". Instead, Sterne admits: "I know pleasures worth ten of [this one]". Here, he quotes the chapter *Of Experience* in the Essays,[19] where Montaigne asks to be awakened from sleep in order to explore it.

In a further passage, I recognise Uncle Toby's hobby horse, and am not surprised at Sterne's love for him when I read:

> There is no occupation so pleasant as the military. The company of so many noble, young, and active men delights you; [...] the freedom of the conversation, without art, an unceremonious way of living; [...] the honour of this occupation, nay, even its hardships and difficulties [...]. Death is more abject, more languishing and troublesome, in bed than in a fight.

Both writers had military fathers. Pierre Eyquem de Montaigne fought in the Italian Wars, where Cervantes served as an elite soldier. Both of them dealt with their fathers' traumas. And the early death of their children. Léonore was Montaigne's only surviving daughter, like Sterne's Lydia. Both travelled across Europe. Sterne's journey through France and Italy, and his encounter with Maria, a maiden who lost her wits, is described in Volume 7. Montaigne's journey included Ferrara, where he visited Torquato Tasso in his prison asylum after the poet was driven mad by envious friends who attacked his masterpiece "Jerusalem Delivered".

When the tool with the name is broken[20]

Walter does not expect another shock when he sits down to breakfast with Toby and asks that Trismegistus be dressed and brought down to be presented to them formally. When he learns from Obadiah that Susannah is "sobbing, crying, and wringing her hands as if her heart would break", he looks at his brother wistfully and says, shaking his head again: "We shall have a devilish month of it, [...] fire, water, women, and wind [...], to have so many jarring elements breaking loose [...] in every corner of a gentleman's house".

The brothers remain "silent and unmoved" while the storm "is whistling" above them, until the maid arrives. "—And what's the matter, Susannah"? Walter asks. The matter strikes them like a thunderclap:

> They have called the child Tristram, —and my mistress is just got out of an hysteric fit about it. —No!—'tis not my fault, said Susannah.—I told him it was Tristram-*gistus*. —Make tea for yourself, brother Toby, [Walter] said, taking down his hat.

His eerily calm demeanour prompts Toby to send Obadiah to fetch Trim on the bowling green.

Each of us responds differently to a catastrophe. Sterne confesses that his own reaction is rage:

> It is not a half an hour ago when [...] I threw a fair sheet, which I had just finished and carefully wrote out, slap into the fire instead of the foul one. Instantly I snatch'd off my wig and threw it [...], with all imaginable violence, up to the top of the room, —indeed I caught it as it fell [...]. Nature [...] by an instantaneous impulse [...] determines us to a sally of this or that member, [...], or posture of body, we know not why.

Sterne is prone to self-analysis, as he did in a sermon entitled "Self Knowledge" published in 1560 and signed Pastor Yorick. He tells us—feminine readers— that an unconscious reaction to the unexpected is the best possible response:

> But mark, madam, [...] this, like a thousand other things, falls out for us in a way which [...] we cannot reason upon [...]—yet we find the good of it [...] and that's enough for us..... Now, my father could not lie down with this affliction [...], —nor could he carry it upstairs [...].—He walked composedly out with it to the fish pond.

In order to survive, Walter obeys the animal part of his brain and returns to the amniotic origins, the source of life. "Had my father reasoned an hour which way to have gone, —reason [...] could not have directed him [better]: there is something, sir, in fish ponds [...], under the first disorderly transport of the humours, [...] unaccountably becalming..."

The warrior's path[21]

In the meanwhile, Trim comes running and blurts out at once: "...it was not in the least owing to me". A misunderstanding is unavoidable. Toby looks at him kindly: "—To thee—Trim! [...]—'twas Susannah's and the curate's folly betwixt them. —What business could they have together, an' please you honor, in the garden? —In the gallery, thou meanest, replied my uncle Toby". Sensing that Toby was on the wrong track, the corporal finds it best not to speak of two misfortunes at once. "Trim's casuistry and address, under the cover of his low bow, prevented all suspicion in my uncle Toby", who then informed Trim of what happened.

Toby does not give a hoot about the name Tristram:

> But my brother, whom there is no arguing with in this case [...], says there never was a great or heroic action performed [...] by one called Tristram. —Tis all a fancy [...]. I fought just as well, replied the corporal, when the regiment called me Trim as when they called me James Butler.

Cervantes used the name Saavedra when he was a slave in Algiers, and when Don Quixote set out on his adventures, he forgot his real name. Wartime names testify to a new identity which instantly brings to mind the battles fought by the warrior:

—Does a man think of his Christian name when he goes upon the attack? Cried Trim.—Or when he stands in the trench? Cried my uncle Toby, looking firm.—Or when he enters a breach? Said Trim, pushing in between two chairs.—Or forces the lines? Cried my uncle, rising up and pushing his crutch like a pike.—Or when he marches up the glacis, [he] cried, looking warm and setting his foot upon his stool.

In the heat of action, they don't hear Walter enter the room. "Never was my uncle Toby caught riding [his hobby-horse] at such a desperate rate in his life"! Any other time, "my father" would have used all his eloquence to insult his brother's hobby horse. But now he simply hung up his hat as calmly as he had taken it down, and paying no attention to the disorder in the room, he placed a chair next to Toby's breach, "sat down in it, and […] broke out in a lamentation […], in the most querulous monotone imaginable".

The combat enacted in the room provides the words he needs. Like in an analysis of trauma, where causality is inoperant, words spring up unexpectedly from an interference between catastrophic zones of which both parties are unaware.

My father's lamentation[22]

Walter compares himself to a defeated warrior who no longer has the heart to fight:

It is in vain longer […] to struggle as I have done […]. Heaven has thought fit to draw forth the heaviest of its artillery against me […] for my own sins […] or the sins and follies of the Shandy family; and the prosperity of my child is the point upon which the whole force of it is directed.

"My father" does, in fact, acknowledge the flaws in his lineage and blames his age as well: Tristram is the son of an old man, the child of divine wrath. *Dies irae!* But he quickly transfers those "indignities" to the newborn. He calls his son a "mistake!, a child of decrepitude". And he adds:

'Tis pitiful, —brother Toby […] how were we defeated!—[…], —when the few animal spirits I was worth in the world, and with which memory and fancy should have been convey'd, —were all dispersed, confounded, scattered and sent to the devil.

The embryo was right to worry from the start.[23] Walter turns now against his wife's womb, accusing her of physical and psychic negligence. "Unhappy Tritram, [...] She could have paid [...] attention to her evacuations and repletions..." The mother-child relationship is nothing new, and neither is its role in the therapy of war trauma. At Craiglockardt in Scotland, where traumatised officers were treated by analyst William Rivers in 1917, his patients[24] described him as a "male-mother".

This is the role played by uncle Toby when he protects his nephew by shielding his mother from paternal wrath, suggesting to summon Mr. Yorick at once to provide Walter with psychological support.

Fantastic ride on Sterne's hobby horse[25]

At the same time, Sterne summons the reader again as a witness to his own difficulties. In the spring of 1760, he was appointed to a new parish in Coxwold, where he would write Volumes 3 and 4 after the first two volumes of *Tristram Shandy* were given a formidable reception in London. After critics attacked his novel when it was known that the author was a parson, Sterne pretends to plead his case: "What a rate have I gone on at, curvetting and frisking it away, two up and two down for four volumes together without looking once behind, or even on one side of me, to see whom I trod upon"!

Still, he could not help treading upon some medical and clerical eminences, since "he wrote for his life" as the "arch-jockey of jockeys" was chasing him. His frantic energy is described in the style of a sports journalist watching a cross-country horse race through binoculars:

> He has [...] galloped full amongst the scaffolding of the undertaking critics! [...] He's flung, —he's off, —he's lost his seat, —he's down, —he'll break his neck, —see! [...] —Don't fear [...], —I'll not hurt the poorest jackass upon the king's highway.—But [...] you've splash'd a bishop,

voices cry out in his wake.

The bishop in question is William Warburton, Bishop of Gloucester, who, after praising the first two volumes, vilifies the novel when he recognises himself in Tristram's tutor. In spite of Sterne's denial, the rumour persists and his mind is racing so fast that he is already in the middle of his next chapter starring King Francis I of France. So he dismounts and stands ready to tell that tale, worthy of the king's sister, Marguerite de Navarre, author of *The Heptameron*,[26] who shall open the first chapter of Volume 6.

One winter evening, Francis I was warming himself over a wood fire and "talking with his Premier of sundry things for the good of the state". The minister wished to reinforce the "good understanding" between France and Switzerland. "Poo! Poo! answered the king, —there are more ways [...] of bribing states besides that of giving money.—I'll pay Switzerland the honour of standing godfather for my next child". The minister corrects him, since Switzerland is a feminine *res publica.*

The Swiss answer that they want to choose the name of the child. The king expects to hear a name like Francis or Henry or Louis, but the Protestant republic proposes those of Daniel's companions thrown into the furnace with him: Shadrach, Mesech and Abed-nego. Francis I swears "by St Peter's girdle" that he will have nothing more to do with the Swiss, and pulling up his breeches, just like Walter, he is about to leave the room when his minister objects that he cannot back out of his promise:

> We'll pay them in money, —said the king. —Sire [...], the treasury [is nearly empty]. —I'll pawn the best jewel in my crown [...]. —[It is] pawn'd already. [...] Then, [...] said the king, —*Monsieur le Premier,* we'll go to war with 'em.

In case the "gentle reader" might be offended, Sterne swears that "in the affair of my father and his christen-names, I had no thought of treading upon Francis the First, (...) nor in the character of my uncle Toby, — of characterising militiating spirits of my country". To avert any future trouble from threatening inquisitors, he proclaims: "... my book is [not] wrote against predestination or free will or taxes.—If 'tis wrote against anything, —'tis wrote [...] against the spleen".

As Rabelais who wrote "It's better to write of laughter than of tears", Sterne will use the *Vis Comica,* comical power, to reveal the source of Yorick's death, whose epitaph is inscribed next to the black page in Volume 1.

Writing a book is like humming a song[27]

We are back in the parlour transformed into a battlefield—a setting which inspires Walter to fight for changing the name Tristram. Hence his question: "— But can the thing be undone Yorick"? Being no expert canonist, the pastor suggests bringing up the subject at a dinner in honour of Bishop Didius's visit, to which he has been invited. Although he hates these gatherings, Walter agrees to go to accompany the parson with his brother. Delighted, Toby asks Trim to air out his old wig and to hang his musty officer's uniform by the fire overnight.

The departure of the little troop is marked by a series of blunders. Sterne has inadvertently torn up the chapter describing their "setting out and journey", and he apologises to the reader: "No doubt, sir—there is a whole chapter wanting here, —and a chasm of ten pages made in the book by it;—but the book [...] is [not] a jot more imperfect..." Another blunder surfaces as they prepare to take the coach. When it was repainted after Walter's marriage, "to add my mother's arms", the painter drew a bar turned to the left— the symbol of bastardy—on the Shandy family coat of arms. Such an inauspicious omen—*bend sinister*—renders the coach unsuitable for the occasion.

Walter never stopped complaining about this "vile mark of illegitimacy", and the mention of a "coach", or "coachman" or "coach horse" was enough to set him off. Yet he never had it removed, any more than he had the hinges oiled. Now, he refuses to mount in the coach, although Yorick assures him that the clergy knows nothing of heraldry.

So it is decided that Yorick, who has a sermon to preach, "had better make the best of [his] way before". Trim and Obadiah will lead the way on two coach horses, followed by Walter and the captain in his regimental uniform perched on Mrs. Shandy's mare. No matter that we miss their quixotic discussions "on arms and letters",[28] for Sterne justifies this absence as "a necessary [...] balance betwixt chapter and chapter", and addresses his famous injunction that I take personally: "In my opinion, to write a book is for all the world like humming a song:—be but in tune with yourself, madam, tis no matter how high or how low you take it".

Yorick's death sentence[29]

The reasons for the pastor's death, announced in Volume 1,[30] come to light during the "visitation dinner". We arrive in the thick of things. Yorick has torn up the sermon he had prepared, transforming it into slips for lighting the pipes. Bishop Didius and doctor Kysarcius—from the Netherlands indicates and index finger—are outraged:

> Methinks, said Didius, [...]: if the sermon is of no better worth than to light pipes with, —'twas [...] not good enough to be preached [...]; and if 'twas good enough to be preached [...], —'twas [...] too good to light [...] pipes.

Yorick solves this aporia by pointing to a third option:

> I have undergone such unspeakable torment in bringing forth this sermon [...]—that [...] I would suffer martyrdom [...] before I would sit down and make such another: [...]—it came from my head instead of my heart [...].—To preach to shew the extent of our reading or the subtleties of our wit [...]—is a dishonest use of the poor single half-hour in a week which is put into our hands.—'Tis not preaching the Gospel, —but ourselves.—For my own part, [...], I had rather direct five words point-blank to the heart.

Toby was about to comment on projectiles:

> —when a single word [...], —a word of all others in the dictionary the
> last in that place to be expected, [...] uttered from the opposite side of
> the table, [...]—a word I am ashamed to write [...];—illegal, —uncanonical
> [...].—In short, I'll tell it in the next chapter. ZOUNDS! _____

The word is uttered, and followed by two lines of dashes to indicate the stupor of the learned company. Pronounced partly *in petto* but clearly enough
for everyone to hear, the sacrilegious cry God's Wounds, it seems to convey
bodily pain—worse still, to originate from the private parts of Phutatorius
(whose name means "screwer" in Greek). In fact, he accidentally received
a piping hot chestnut in that region through the aperture in his breeches.
Now, the carnival of a topsy-turvy world begins.

"How finely we argue upon mistaken facts! [Some] imagined that Phutatorius, who was somewhat of a choleric spirit, was just going to snatch the
cudgels out of Didius's hands in order to bemaul Yorick..." Faced with the
unknowable, the group quickly designates a scapegoat, based on a mere
look of suspicion cast upon Yorick.

The captain had already detected Phutatorius's hatred of the pastor: "My
uncle Toby's good nature felt a pang for what Yorick was about to undergo".
His fate is sealed—he is the undisputed author of the prank that sent the
burning chestnut into the saintly man's aperture. The proof is in Phutatorius's looks, first at Didius and then back at Yorick:

> But the truth was that Phutatorius knew not one word or one syllable of
> what was passing. [...] Still, all the while he looked at Yorick with sus-
> picion, and the learned company interpreted his look as an accusation.
> His opinion at once became the general one.

Although nothing is actually said, murder has been set in motion. Sterne
describes the mechanism of this manhunt "with all imaginable decency":
Gastripheres had ordered about two hundred roasted chestnuts, wrapped
up hot in a damask napkin, to be brought in to the company and placed
before Phutatorius, who was particularly fond of them. By chance, this char-
itable act intersected with his colleague's posture, as he sat astride his chair:

> Now, [...] one chestnut [...] was actually sent rolling off the table; and
> [...] it fell perpendicularly into that particular aperture of Phutatorius's
> breeches for which [...] there is no chaste word throughout all Johnson's
> *Dictionary*;—let it suffice to say [...] that particular aperture which, [...]
> like the temple of Janus (in peace at least), [is] universally shut up. The
> neglect of this punctilio [...] had opened the door to this accident.

And to the triumph of historical determinism. For the parson's enemies, it cannot be an accident:

> When great or unexpected events fall out upon the stage of this sublunar world, the mind of man which is [...] inquisitive [...], takes a flight behind the scenes to see what is the cause. [...] The search was not long in this instance.

Thus, the open aperture signals war.

Sterne remembers Swift's *Digression on Madness*[31]: "the triumph of slight incidents over the mind" may have huge political consequences.

A political subject[32]

Is it indeed by chance that the chestnut landed on that particular place, considering that twenty years earlier, Phutatorius had published a work entitled *On Keeping Concubines*, of which that very week he was "going to give the world a second edition (...)?" Yorick considered it as obscene. Without participating in the controversy, Sterne presents the facts:

> [...] the hiatus in Phutatorius's breeches was sufficiently wide to receive the chestnut; and [...] the chestnut [...] did fall perpendicularly and piping hot into it, [...] the heat gradually [...] getting [...] into the regions of pain. [...] A thought instantly darted into his mind that [...] it might [...] be a bite as well as a burn; and, if so, that possibly a Newt or an Asker, [...] some detested reptile had crept up and was fastening his teeth;— the horrid idea [...] seized [him] with a sudden panic [...];—the effect of which was [...] that he leapt incontinently up, uttering [...] that interjection Z—ds...

Phutatorius no longer thinks. Sterne notes the speed with which the blow leads to the search for a cause of the event: the rebellious pastor whose thoughtless gesture of picking up the chestnut designates him as the obvious target. Here is Sterne's description of the manhunt:

> This incident, trifling as it was, wrought in Phutatorius's head: he considered this act of Yorick's as a plain acknowledgement [...] that the chestnut was originally his, —and, in course, that it must have been [he], and no one else, who could have played him such a prank [...]: and consequently [...] his opinion at once became the general one.

Yorick's days are numbered, but he doesn't know it yet. Sterne's portrayal of his character brings to mind his own father, whose portrait he already quoted from his "Memoir" for his daughter Lydia.[33] "He was [...] void of all design, and so innocent in his own intentions, that he suspected no one". But this absence of suspicion leaves him defenceless in front of the public eye:

> It was well known that Yorick had never a good opinion of the treatise which Phutatorius had wrote, as a thing which he feared had done hurt in the world, —and 'twas easily found [...] a meaning in Yorick's prank, —and that his chucking the chestnut hot into Phutatorius's**** was a sarcastical fling at his book.

At first, the learned company is titillated by the sexually tinged jest. Somnolentus awakens, the impassive Agelastes smiles, Gastripheres tries to understand. Most of them believe they have witnessed a master stroke of arch-wit. But the pleasantry is short-lived, since they all support accusations "as groundless as the dreams of philosophy".[34] What makes his case worse:

> Yorick [...] *was a man of jest*, but it was temper'd with something which withheld him from [...] ungracious pranks. [...] All I blame and alternately like him for—was a singularity of his temper which would never suffer to set a story right with the world. [...] He could not stoop to tell his story to them, —and so trusted to time and truth to do it for him.

Forty years after his death, the ghost of Sterne's father also demands justice and, like Hamlet, his son portrays a "smiling villain". "Phutatorius [...] rose up from his chair a second time [...] with a smile [...] to let him know [...] that he would [...] not forget the obligation. [...]—The smile was for the company.—The threat was for Yorick".

After this sinister omen, Sterne stages a *Sottie judgement*[35] in which the smiling villain is stripped of his official garments.

Kinship structures in the theatre of fools[36]

We are witnessing the climactic moment when the Fools drag the important personage up on the stage and tear off his garb, revealing the fool's costume underneath. While Phutatorius lifts up his leg to ease the injured part, the most far-fetched remedies are proposed. According to the antique principle of *Similia similibus curantur*, "a soft sheet of paper just come off the press, strongly impregnated with oil and lamp-black" should be twisted around the tender part. In other words, he is told to take his *De concubinis* and shove it. Yorick insists that the page in question should not contain anything bawdy, so as not to worsen the already inflamed part.

Writing having reached "degree zero", as Roland Barthes would say, Yorick asks Eugenius to introduce the matter of Tristram's debaptisation.

This thorny question sets off a specious argument that fascinates Walter at once.

Didius longs for the time before the Reformation when, thanks to errors made in Latin recitation, a baptism could be annulled. Kysarcius starts to split hairs: "[If] the roots of the words continue untouch'd [...], the same sense continues in the words". When the authority invoked is Pope Leo the III, Toby objects:

> — But my brother's child [...] has nothing to do with the Pope:—'tis the plain child of a Protestant gentleman, christen'd Tristram against the wills [...] both of its father and mother, and all those who are akin to it.

A discussion on a precedent-setting case follows. Kysarcius casts doubt on the structure of parenthood and questions "whether the mother be of kin to her child". Ready to whistle *Lillibullero*, Toby puts down his pipe, but when Walter claps his hand over his mouth and whispers something in his ear, he nods, takes up his pipe again and whistles *Lillibullero* inwardly.

When the company breaks up, Toby asks Yorick how the affair of Tristram's name was settled by these learned men:

> Very satisfactorily, replied Yorick; no mortal, sir, has any concern with it, —for Mrs Shandy the mother is nothing at all akin to him, —and as the mother's is the surest side, —Mr Shandy, in course, is still less than nothing. [...] —That may well be, said my father, shaking his head. — Let the learned say what they will, there must certainly, quoth my uncle Toby, have been some sort of consanguinity betwixt the mother and her son. —The vulgar are of the same opinion, quoth Yorick, to this hour.

In Sterne's words, "'twas still but like the anointing of a broken bone".

Back to the starting point[37]

Walter's afflictions weigh him down even more, as happens, Sterne says, "when the staff we lean on slips from under us". He becomes pensive and walks to the pond more and more often, sighs frequently and no longer has his hasty sparks of temper. "He had certainly fallen ill with the extinction of them, had not [...] his health been rescued by a fresh train of disquietudes".

"One worry chases the other", ancient wisdom tells us. Walter's new worry is a legacy of £1,000 left by aunt Dinah, which reawakens desires he had drowned in the pond. Manic euphoria takes hold of him:

> —He would go to Rome, —he would go to law, —[...] —he would new fore-front his house and add a new wing [...].—he would build a new

windmill [...]. But above all, [...] he would enclose the great Ox Moor
and send out [his eldest son] Bobby immediately upon his travels across
France and Italy.

We met Bobby briefly at the end of Volume 2, when Walter discovered why
his eldest son was a blockhead. His second entrance into the story, as a
rival to the Ox Moor, is no more glorious. "But the sum was finite" and
both options contributed to the family's image: the feather in the cap of
the youngster when he returned from his travels would cost as much as
the clearing of the gorse-covered tract of land, to say nothing of fencing in
the Ox Moor—whose boundaries had already constituted the object of an
expensive lawsuit.

Walter was divided, especially since the prices of South Sea company
shares fell after the Mississippi Bubble burst. He had counted on a return
on his investment in these shares to send his son off on his travels. The
Grand Tour would give Bobby "free ingress, egress, and regress into foreign
parts before marriage". Why should he be "the first Shandy unwhirl'd about
Europe in a post-chaise, and only because he was a heavy lad"?

The argument in favour of the Ox Moor seemed more convincing. The
moor lay in full view before the mansion, bounded by the watermill on one
side and the projected windmill on the other. Obadiah, who rode over it
often, said that it was shameful how it had been neglected.

Walter starts to study books on farming to become the good gentleman
farmer Sterne failed to become in his Sutton-on-the-Forest parish:

> My father took pen and ink in hand and set about calculating the
> expense of the rotation recommended by Physiocrats at that time: [...]
> he should reap a hundred lasts of rape [...] the very first year, —besides
> an excellent crop of wheat the year following, —and the year after that
> [...] peas and beans, —besides potatoes without end.

Once again, Sterne takes a jab at those who, as Figaro would soon say,
"put themselves to the trouble of being born—nothing more".[38] He settles
accounts with firstborns by making Bobby die:

> My father, — who was torn by txo projects of equal strength, — had cer-
> tainly sunk under this evil, (...) had he not been rescued by a fresh evil
> — the misfortune of my brother Bobby's death. What is the life of man!

Sterne exclaims: "Is it not to button up one cause of vexation! – and unbutton another"?! Bobby's brother contents himself with the matter of fact
comment: "From this moment I am to be considered as heir apparent to
the Shandy family, —and it is from this point properly that the story of my
LIFE and my OPINIONS sets out, with [...] precipitation".

Four volumes were needed to clear the ground and "raise the building […], —and such a building […] as never was planned […] since Adam", which will immortalise the Sterne name thanks to a lineage of younger sons.

What remains to be done[39]

Sterne quickly concludes this fourth volume, before throwing his pen into the fire, with the last drop of ink left in his inkhorn. And too bad if he is unable to get to half of his projects, which he enumerates in the style of Jacques Prévert's "Inventory".[40] He still has:

> a thing to name, —a thing to lament […], —a thing to promise […], —a thing to declare […] and a thing to threaten. A thing to hope […], a thing to conceal. […] A thing to choose, —a thing to pray for […]—that God would give my subjects grace to be as WISE as they were MERRY; and then should I be the happiest monarch and they the happiest people under heaven.

Volume 4 ends on a manifesto, proclaiming true Shandeism as fighting "the influence of bilious and saturnine passions (…) upon the body politick as body natural", and Sterne takes leave of us for twelve months. "Unless this vile cough kills me in the meantime, I'll have another pluck at your beards and lay open a story to the world you little dream of". Volumes 5 and 6, promised for 1761, were to be published by Thomas Becker, who took over from R. & J. Dodsley.

Notes

1 Sterne, L., *Tristam Shandy,* op. cit., Vol. 4, ch. 1.
2 Lacan, Écrits, op. cit.
3 Sterne, L., *Tristam Shandy*, op. cit., Vol. 9, ch. XX.
4 Freud, S., *Group Psychology and the Analysis of the Ego*, S.E, 1: 103–104, London: Hogarth; Lacan, J, Subversion of the Subject and the Dialectic of Desire in the Freudian Unconscious, in *Écrits: A Selection,* Sheridan, A. (trans.), London: Tavistock/Routledge, 1997.
5 Sterne, L., *Tristam Shandy,* op. cit., Vol. 4, ch. I.
6 Sterne, L., *Tristram Shandy*, op. cit., Vol. 4, chs. I–IV.
7 Grossman, D., *On Combat*, op. cit.
8 Grossman, D., *On Combat,* op. cit.
9 Melville, H. (1891). *Billy Bud Sailor and Other Stories*, Penguin Books UK, 1985.
10 Sterne, L., *Tristram Shandy*, op. cit., Vol 4, chs. VI–VIII.
11 Sterne, L., *Tristram Shandy*, op. cit., Vol 4, chs. IX–XI.
12 Longinus, D., *On the Sublime,* Jowett, B. (trans.), CA: CreateSpace Publishing, 2014.
13 Sterne, L., *Tristram Shady*, op. cit., Vol. 4, chs. XII, XIII.
14 Sterne, L., *Tristram Shandy*, op. cit., Vol 1, ch. VI.
15 Bion, W., *A Memoir of the Future*, London and New York: Routledge, 2018.

16 Sterne, L., *Tristram Shady*, op. cit., Vol. 4, ch. XIV.
17 Sterne, L., *Tristram Shandy*, op. cit., Vol. 4, ch. XV.
18 Cervantes, M., *Don Quixote II*, op. cit., ch. 70.
19 De Montaigne, M., *The Complete Essays*, London: Penguin Classics, 1993, Book 3, ch. 13.
20 Sterne, L., *Tristram Shandy*, op. cit., Vol. 4, ch. XVI.
21 Sterne, L., *Tristram Shandy*, op. cit., Vol. 4, ch. XVIII.
22 Sterne, L., *Tristram Shandy*, Vol. 4, ch. XIX.
23 Sterne, L., *Tristram Shandy*, op. cit., Vol. 1, ch. I.
24 Barker, P., *Regeneration Trilogy*, op. cit.
25 Sterne, L., *Tristram Shandy*, op. cit., Vol. 4, chs. XX–XXIII.
26 De Navarre, Marguerite, *The Heptameron*, Penguin Classics, 1984.
27 Sterne, L., *Tristram Shandy*, op. cit., Vol. 4, ch. XXV.
28 Cervantes, M., *Don Quixote I*, op. cit., ch. 38.
29 Sterne, L., *Tristram Shandy*, op. cit., Vol. 4, ch. XXVI.
30 Sterne, L., *Tristram Shandy*, op. cit., Vol. 1., ch. XII.
31 Swift, J., Digression on Madness, in *A Tale of a Tub*, New York: Serenity Publishers, 2011.
32 Sterne, L., *Tristram Shandy*, op. cit., Vol. 4, ch. XXVII.
33 Ross, I.C., *Laurence Sterne, A Life*, op. cit., p. 31.
34 Shakespeare, W., Hamlet, op. cit., Act V, v. 192.
35 Davoine, F., *Mother Folly,* op. cit.; Aubailly, J. C., *Le Monologue, le dialogue et la sottie*, op. cit.
36 Sterne, L., *Tristram Shandy*, op. cit., Vol. 4, chs. XXVIII to XXIX.
37 Sterne, L., *Tristram Shandy*, op. cit., Vol. 4, ch. XXXI.
38 Beaumarchais, P., *The Marriage of Figaro*, op. cit.
39 Sterne, L., *Tristram Shandy*, op. cit., Vol. 4, ch. XXXII.
40 Prévert, J., "Inventaire", in *Paroles,* Paris: Gallimard, 1976.

5

Confinement[1]

During the first period of confinement imposed by COVID, I conversed with Sterne, who confined himself voluntarily at the beginning of this volume. But first, he chose as an epigraph a verse from Horace's *Satires*, asking the readers' indulgence should they find it "too facetious or sharp", and like Erasmus,[2] he invokes Democritus's protection. The latter was considered mad by his compatriots, who called upon Hippocrates to cure him of his unmotivated fits of laughter. La Fontaine recounts their meeting in the fable "Democritis and the People of Abdera"[3]:

> How I have always hated the opinions of the mob! [...]
> His countrymen thought him mad. Little minds!
> But then, no one is a prophet in his own country!
> The people themselves were mad, of course,
> And Democritus was the wise man.

Like Democritus, Sterne needs a refuge in which to write. His life depends on it since bleeding from his tuberculosis started again after his return from London—in a post-chaise driven by a "madcap of a postilion" wearing the fool's cap:

> He flew like lightning [...]—the motion was most rapid, —most impetuous;—'twas communicated to my brain;—my heart partook of it. [...] I made my vow: 'I will lock up my study door the moment I get home and throw the key of it ninety feet below the surface of the earth'.

During the confinement, I discovered that patients who had been hospitalised in psychiatric institutions displayed a surprising ability to deal with our topsy-turvy world and with the solitude which others complain about. Their so-called "psychotic structure" had become a source of wisdom, thanks to the interferences of the transference specific to extreme experiences described by Bion and others, which Lacan chose to ignore. As for

DOI: 10.4324/9781003224907-5

the reverential attitude of disciples towards their masters, Sterne does not mince words:

> Shall we for ever make new books, as apothecaries make new mixtures, by pouring only out of one vessel into another? Are we for ever to be twisting and untwisting the same rope? for ever in the same track, — for ever at the same pace? [...]—without working one [...] single miracle with them?

But he remains hopeful: "In every human era, MAN's powers 'dart him from earth to heaven'"; and he lists those who did more than "go sneaking on at this pitiful, —pimping, —pettifogging rate".

These powers, "Ye Powers"! whom he invoked earlier to awaken his inspiration, contradict the "relics of learning", such as the accepted dogma asserting that psychosis is unreachable by transference—except if the analyst recognises cut-out zones in his story, activated in the session by surviving images stemming from an unrepressed unconsciousness and voices them. "Trauma speaks to trauma and only to trauma", Jean-Max Gaudillière used to say, and despite my protests, adding that with each patient he was an analyst "once or twice a year — and those are the good years".

Bion asserted that *transference is transient*, and Martin Cooperman, analyst of psychosis at the Austen Riggs Center and veteran of the Battle of Guadalcanal, was no less provocative when he stated:

> The analysis of psychosis lasts eight days, but it takes five years to get to the point where the two people involved come out of hiding: the analyst from behind his theories and the patient from behind his symptoms, so that they can meet.

In his chapter "Upon Whiskers", Sterne describes such a meeting after showing us the production of a hallucinatory image and its subsequent inscription. Anticipating that "prudes and Tartufs" will be offended, he wishes "that there was a good farcical house large enough to hold [...] them, shag-rag and bob-tail, male and female, all together". I would not dare use such language today, in this era free of prejudices on the one hand, but full of restrictions about the use of words on the other. I am happy to let Sterne speak for me: "A chapter upon whiskers! alas! the world will not bear it. [...] 'twas as inconsiderate a promise as ever entered a man's head. I'm sorry I made it".

The next chapter, entitled "The Fragment", consists of two lines of asterisks the reader can interpret as he wishes.

Upon whiskers

In 1759, Sterne's first version of his novel, entitled *Fragment in the Style of Rabelais*, was refused by Dodsley, who advised him to make no reference to local events. The *Fragment* reappears here, transposed to Rabelais's era and to the Court of Marguerite de Navarre, King Francis the First's sister, who inherited her literary talent from her father, the poet Charles d'Orleans, and her political genius from her mother, Louise de Savoie. Since she welcomed supporters of the Reform, Sterne finds refuge at her court, where he can give free reign to his spirit of dissent. The story is introduced by a dialogue between two elderly persons who speak softly:

> — You are half asleep, my good lady, said the old gentleman, taking hold of the old lady's hand and giving it a gentle squeeze as he pronounced the word *whiskers*;—shall we change the subject? By no means, replied the old lady, —I like your account of these matters.

She leaned back in her chair, saying: "I desire you will go on". The old gentleman starts by uttering the word "whiskers", which he feared would shock his old friend. The story follows in the tradition of Boccacio's *Decameron* written in 1349, the year after the plague in Florence where he lived. It inspired Chaucer's *Canterbury Tales* and Marguerite de Navarre's *Heptameron*.[4]

The queen is surrounded by a bevy of lovely maidens, contrasting with the pot-bellied clerics in the previous volume. Their names bring to mind Couperin's, Rameau's and Scarlatti's pieces for harpsichord: La Fosseuse, La Batterelle, La Guyol, La Maronette, La Sabatiere, La Rebours, Lady Carnavallette and Lady Baussiere. As her name suggests, La Rebours— meaning "in reverse"—will turn the court upside down with the help of her best friend La Fosseuse, who takes the lead.

The word "whiskers" will run through the court, excited by its own sibilant sound, so greatly that it produces a collective trance, since it refers to the quivering pilosity of Suspense! Readers may fantasize about a handsome swain, like in a painting by François Clouet. La Fosseuse has barely finished pronouncing "whiskers" when the queen cries out:

> Whiskers! [...] dropping her knitting ball [...]. —Whiskers, madam, said La Fosseuse, pinning the ball to the queen's apron [...]. —Whiskers! Cried the queen, laying a greater stress upon the word and as if she had still distrusted her ears. —Whiskers, replied La Fosseuse, repeating the word a third time. —There is not a cavalier, madam, of his age in Navarre [...] that has so gallant a pair. —Of what? cried Margaret smiling.

Accompanied by the baroque tones of Sterne's bass viol, the word resonates a fourth time, casting its spell on a certain page sporting an elegant pair of:

> Of whiskers, said La Fosseuse, with infinite modesty [...]. The word *whiskers* still stood its ground [...] throughout the little kingdom of Navarre [...]. La Fosseuse had pronounced the word [...] upon sundry other occasions at court, with an accent which always implied something of a mystery.

The analyst, happy to see all these beauties heeding the signifier of their desire, will soon be disappointed to see them go mad.

The game of madness

Aby Warburg's *nymphae* have entered the scene in the kingdom of Navarre, to create havoc with the word "whiskers". "And as the court of Margaret [...] was at that time a mixture of gallantry and devotion, [...] the clergy were for it, —the laity were against it—and, for the women, —they were divided". The opposite might seem more plausible, but the signifier *whiskers* is related to *Whit* (Pentecost) or *wit*, *witness* and *wisdom*.

Yet, on this occasion, wisdom was absent and all the maidens turned their attention to the guards mounted at the palace gate, especially the Sieur de Croix. "It was the finest weather for [love] that ever was remembered in Navarre", and all the queen's maids fell in love with him, except La Fosseuse and La Rebours, who "knew better". In truth, "De Croix has failed in an attempt to recommend himself to La Rebours, and [she] and La Fosseuse were inseparable".

After this fiasco, La Fosseuse launches the word "whiskers" with an accent of mystery regarding the page's attributes. The damsels assess him from their bay window, from head to foot: "He is handsome, said the Lady Baussiere. —He has a good mien, said La Battarelle. —He is finely shaped, said La Guyol". La Maronette is more daring: "I never saw an officer of the Horse Guards [...] with two such legs. —Or who stood so well upon them, said La Sabatiere". La Fosseuse puts an end to the litany of praise: "But he has no whiskers". "— Not a pile", confirms La Rebours.

This is enough to incite revelry around the young man as whiskerless as Dionysus, and whose groupies become as wild as Maenads. Suddenly deprived of a metonymy to name their desire, they are left to hallucinate, according to Lacan's principle: "What is foreclosed in the Symbolic, returns in the Real".[5] Aby Warburg[6] would say that the word comes back as a "surviving image", surviving the maiden's disillusionment, and giving birth to as many whiskers as there were noses in Strasburg without exhausting its energy.

This is what happens when the object of desire is not lost, but intentionally destroyed. The two young vixens have introduced the signifier "whiskers" to make the other maidens dream, and then killed their fantasy. The proffered word is untrustworthy. Betrayed by her friends, each maiden is left to face on her own the word transformed into a thing, after it had circulated through the symbolic chain of unconscious desires revolving around the queen. Once launched, this word-thing sets everyone spinning, inducing experimental collective madness. Marguerite could have saved the day, but she too had fallen prey to the trickery: "The queen [mused] upon the subject, turning it this way and that in her fancy". She crossed herself several times. "What can La Fosseuse mean? said she".

The two damsels refuse to speak. What they want is to pursue the game to its climax, beyond all reason. Whiskers would later make their appearance again in *The Great Dictator*,[7] where Chaplin drives the crowds mad with it. But Sterne's third contribution to *Massen Psychologie* doesn't stop there. After displaying the dynamics of a social movement in Strasburg and of a witch-hunt among Church dignitaries, he gives us the tools to heal the psychic disturbances at the Court of Navarre after demonstrating how madness may be considered a form of resistance against perverse control.

Such an event is not new. At the time of Toby's wars in 1692, women were condemned to the gallows for witchcraft in Salem, New England, upon the accusation of young girls manipulated by clergy seeking to acquire the property of the accused. In contrast, the instigators of the wave of folly in Navarre were not acting in the service of any interest. Still, they drove their friends completely berserk.

The danger of words

The quartet composed of La Guyot, La Batterelle, La Maronette and La Sabatiere went to their respective chambers and bolted their doors, saying "Whiskers! *Vade retro*, hairy one! The Lady Carnavalette was counting her beads with both hands [...]—not a saint passed through her fingers without whiskers", not even Saint Ursula and Saint Bridget. At the height of the frenzy, Lady Baussiere on her horse is blind to everything around her except a pair of whiskers dancing in her field of vision. As she dismounts, she hands her page the bridle asking him to take care of her whiskers.

In an era when wars of religion are breaking out, the two damsels wreaking havoc in the kingdom of Navarre do not defend any cause. After driving the others crazy—as Harold Searle[8] was to say—they stop the game. Very soon, the maids form a circle around the queen again, looking at each other in amazement. But re-entering the circle is not enough to break the spell, until La Fosseuse dispels the enchantment. She pulls a pin out of the knot of her hair and traces the outline of a moustache over her upper lip, restoring the place of the word *whiskers* in the symbolic chain of speech.

Wittgenstein had the same idea in his *Investigations*[9]: "'Excalibur has a sharp blade' makes sense when the sword is whole or is broken up". And he adds that it is enough to agree on a gesture giving the name "a place in the language game, even when the tool no longer exists".

After the surviving image is filtered through the symbolic chain, everyone calms down. La Guyot smiles. "Fie, said Lady Baussiere"—an interjection my grandmother would utter with a smile. "Grammercy—cried La Carnavallette", relieved not "to be-whisker" Saint Bridget. The social link, which had been threatened by a deliberate "attack on linking", as Bion would say, is restored. Touching her eye with her forefinger, Marguerite indicates that now "she understands them all".

Sterne concludes this chapter with a discussion on the danger of words— the title of a book by Maurice O'Drury, Wittgenstein's disciple, in which he presents cases where a diagnosis of psychosis would be made today on the basis of words that were spoken. The author then reveals that the cases involved were Joan of Arc and other political visionaries—who would be given shock treatment or chemical therapies today instead of being burnt at the stake.

A century later, the word "whiskers", deemed "indecent and unfit for use", was finally banished from the kingdom of Navarre. This gives Sterne the occasion to address bigots condemning his language as "bawdy": "The best word, in the best language of the best world"—he has read *Candide*,[10] recently published—"must have suffered under such combinations. [...] Chastity, by nature the gentlest of all affections, —give it but its head—'tis like a ramping and a roaring lion". In 1947, Victor Klemperer's book *Lingua Rerii Imperii*[11] described the destruction of language in the Third Reich—in preparation for the extermination of European Jews—by introducing what Hannah Arendt[12] called "an experimental madness".

The regeneration process with Marguerite at its centre does not erase the triumph of bigotry at the court of Navarre. Likewise, at the end of Volume 4, the praise of true Shandeism which "opens the heart and the lungs" is no denial of the deadly threat posed by the author's "vile cough". Now, after this tale showing that hallucinations can be healed, Shandean psychoanalysis may be useful in facing Bobby's death.

Intersigns[13]

Death interrupts daily life in the Shandy household unexpectedly, foretold by intersigns, as Britons call them.[14] Walter is busy calculating the cost of his eldest son's travels abroad, measuring the stages with a compass on a map showing the post roads to be travelled, unaware that Bobby has taken his last journey. Yet the signs of a loss of vitality manifest themselves in the household through a shortage of yeast. Other disasters follow. Obadiah asks for the great coach horse to go and fetch it, Walter is happy to consent, but the horse needs a shoe. The stable has nothing else to offer. Obadiah will have to go on foot. "— I had much rather walk than ride", he says shutting the door. Just as Walter cries: "What plagues"! Obadiah comes back saying that the roads are flooded.

This is when a letter arrives—so unthinkable that Walter ignores it, "asking his brother to read it while he return to Nevers, where he hesitates to let Bobby stay more than one night in 'so lousy a town'". "What think'st thou, Toby"? Walter asks in a sprightly tone. "Unless it be a garrison town", his brother answers just as gaily, continuing to read the letter aloud. Four lines of long hyphens follow, after which Toby announces gravely: "He's gone"! Taking the understatement literally, Walter cries out:

"Where—who?"—My nephew said to my uncle Toby. "—What, — without leave, —without money, —without governor? [...] No:—he is dead [...]. —Without being ill? cried my father again. —I dare say not, said my uncle Toby in a low voice and fetching a deep sigh from the bottom of his heart; he has been ill enough, poor lad! I'll answer for him, —for he is dead". Walter stuck his compass into Nevers even deeper. "How he endured this misfortune deserves a chapter to itself", says Sterne, who proceeds to give us "a devil of a chapter".

Sterne analyses the different reactions of his characters to death, to which he has been confronted in his own life and that of his parishioners.

Rhetoric[15]

Pastor Sterne begins by asking that we look to ourselves. He then refers to a multitude of authors from Plato to St. Bernard, not forgetting Seneca—all of whom must have helped him prepare his sermons: "Seneca (I'm positive) tells us somewhere that such griefs evacuate themselves best by [weeping] for the loss of our friends or children", and he draws up a list of famous mourners.

But this method of evacuating grief is not suited to Walter:

> My father managed his affliction otherwise [...]; for he neither wept it away as the Hebrews and the Romans—or slept it off as the Laplanders, —or hang'd it as the English or drowned it as the Germans, —nor did he cure it or excommunicate it or rhyme it or lillibullero it. —He got rid of it, however.

He chose to follow Cicero's example. "When Tully was bereft of his dear daughter Tullia, at first [...] he listened to the voice of nature and modulated his own unto it. —O my Tullia! my daughter! my child!—still, still, still, —'twas O my Tullia! [...]" Walter was as proud of his eloquence as MARCUS TULLIUS CICERO. "It was indeed his strength, —and his weakness too [...]—for he was hourly a dupe to it".

Sterne probably met parishioners who on such occasions could switch from utter distress to fits of laughter. So he turns to a funny story illustrating the psychopathology of everyday life in the Shandy household, where "the neglects and blunders of servants or other mishaps unavoidable in a family", could diffuse Walter's anger and put everyone in a jolly mood.

The story sounds familiar to me, for I heard a very similar one set in the Savoy province between the two world wars. A friend of my grandfather's, who had been in the same cavalry regiment during the Great War, had a magnificent mare that he showed off to one and all. One day, he asked his children to take her to a farm to be mounted by a splendid stallion. But when the time came, she gave birth to a mule. Out of spite, the friend sold his beloved mare. "It caused quite a hubbub"! my father exclaimed, still laughing at the joke almost a hundred years later.

One day, Walter suddenly made the same decision, for "he was sanguine in all his projects". He had his favourite mare consigned to a beautiful Arabian horse and talked about the colt she would give him, "as if it had been reared, broke—and bridled and saddled at his door ready for mounting". But through some apparent neglect on the part of Obadiah, this mare also produced a mule—the ugliest ever seen. When Obadiah was summoned, "My mother and my uncle Toby expected my father would be the death of [him]:—See here! you rascal, cried my father, pointing to the mule, what you have done! —It was not me, said Obadiah. —How do I know that? Replied my father", delighted with his repartee.

How better to illustrate psychotherapy by storytelling than with this tale of Obadiah transformed into a centaur, which acted as a powerful anti-depressant? After this cathartic interlude, "let us go back to my brother's death".

Five *topoi*

A host of ready-made phrases "taken from the stores of philosophy" rush into Walter's head, such as:

> All must die. 'Tis [...] the first statute in Magna Carte [...]. If my son could not have died, it had been matter of wonder.. [...] To die is the great debt and tribute due onto nature [...]; the proudest pyramid of them all which wealth and science have erected has lost its apex and stands obtruncated in the traveller's horizon.

Walter orders Toby not to interrupt him, unaware that a slip of the tongue is about to bring down his rhetorical pyramid.

"Kingdoms and provinces, and towns and cities, have they not had their periods? And when those principles [...] which at first cemented them [...] have performed their several evolutions, they fall back". Seeing Toby put down his pipe, he quickly corrects himself: "Revolutions, I meant". But all is well. The captain congratulates his brother for his unconscious slip, saying that "evolutions" is no nonsense. Again, Walter screams at Toby not to interrupt him.

As the captain puts his pipe back in his mouth, Walter launches into a third *topos*, regarding civilisations which "have learned that they are mortal", as the French poet Paul Valery was to say. Walter carries on:

> ... When I sailed from Aegina towards Megara [...], I began to [think]: What flourishing towns now prostrate upon the earth! Alas! Alas! said I to myself, that man should disturb his soul for the loss of a child when so much as this lies awfully buried in his presence.— Remember [...], thou art a man.

This was an extract from Servius Sulpicius's letter to his friend Cicero after Tullia's death. But Toby assumes the "I" who travelled between Aegina and Megara to be his brother, pursuing his trade in that region: "[What] year of our Lord was this?] the captain asked. —'Twas no year of our Lord, replied my father", sailing the Mediterranean "forty years before Christ was born. —That's impossible! ", cried the captain.

With tears in his eyes, he prays for his brother, taking him for the "Wandering Jew", unless "his misfortunes had disordered his brain". His suspicions are confirmed when Walter goes on to his fourth *topos*:

> My son is dead!—so much the better;—'tis a shame in such a tempest to have but one anchor. But he is gone for ever from us!—be it so. He is got from under the hands of his barber before he was bald; he is but risen from a feast before he was surfeited, —from a banquet before he had got drunken. The Thracians wept when a child was born.

Walter's fifth *topos* brings to mind Baudelaire's verse: "O Death, old captain, let us set sail"![16] His exaltation mounts:

> Death opens the gate of fame and shuts the gate of envy after it. [...] There is no terror [...] in its looks but what it borrows from groans and convulsions [...] in a dying man's room. [...], when we are, —death is not;—and when death is, —we are not.

The question concerns Sterne directly. In Volume 7,[17] Tristram wishes that the moment might come not in his own house but "in some decent inn", where his soul will not be "crucified by the quivering affection" of his friends and where for a few guineas he will purchase an "undisturbed, but punctual attention". Laurence's wish was fulfilled in London on 18 March 1768.

As he strives to keep up with Walter's eloquence, Toby lays down his pipe again to absorb a gaggle of stories about sudden death, from Vespasian upon his close stool telling a joke to Augustus while proffering a compliment:

> I hope 'twas a sincere one, —quoth my uncle Toby. [...]—And lastly, [...] this anecdote of Cornelius Gallus, [...] which I dare say, brother Toby,

you have read. —I dare say I have not, replied my uncle. —He died, said my father, as ******.

Sixteen asterisks cover the death of the emperor who passed away while making love. Toby tries to dedramatise: "And if it was with his wife, [...] there could be no hurt in it. —That's more than I know, —replied my father".

The word "wife" puts an end to the funeral oration, allowing "my mother" to enter the scene. The reader realises that since the letter arrived, nobody thought of informing her of her son's death.

Eavesdropping[18]

Chapter 5 begins with "My mother was going in the dark along the passage which led to the parlour as my uncle Toby pronounced the word 'wife'", which produced "a shrill the subject of the penetrating sound" through the door left ajar by Obadiah, so that "she imagined herself the subject of the conversation". Sterne portrays her "laying her fingers across her two lips—holding in her breath, her head bent downwards and her neck twisted towards the door"—in the posture of the crouching slave engraved on an intaglio, listening to the goddess of Silence at his back. This goddess is responsible for the silences, passed down in lineages, heard by "those who listen at the door of History"—Toni Morrison's expression in her book *Beloved*.[19]

"I am determined to let her stand for five minutes, till I bring up the affairs of the kitchen to the same period", says Sterne, ignoring Mrs. Shandy's cramps, while providing the reader with a description of the well-oiled machine that constitutes the Shandy household.

We are in the era of Jacques de Vaucanson's invention of an automatic loom that was to be improved by Joseph Marie Jacquard in the next generation. This machine provides Sterne with his metaphor:

Though [...] our family was certainly a simple machine, as it consisted of a few wheels; yet [...] these wheels were set in motion by so many different springs [...]—that though it was a simple machine, it had all the honour and advantages of a complex one, —and [...] whatever motion [...] was going forwards in the parlour, there was generally another [...] upon the same subject, running parallel along with it in the kitchen. [...] Now, to bring this about, whenever an extraordinary message or letter was delivered in the parlour, [...] or the lines of discontent were observed to hang upon the brows of my father or mother —'twas the rule to leave the door [...] somewhat ajar [...].Obadiah did the same thing as soon as he had left the letter upon the table which brought the news of my brother's death, so that before my father had [...] entered upon his harangue, —had Trim got upon his legs to speak his sentiment upon the subject.

The intergenerational transmission of trauma also occurs through a door left ajar.

Comparative analysis[20]

We will now be given a panoptic view, as Michel Foucault would say, of the Shandy household. Sterne asks "curious observers of nature —though bye the bye [they] are seldom worth a groat"—to make a comparative analysis of "two orators so contrasted by nature and education, haranguing over the same bier":

> My father—a man of deep reading, —prompt memory, —with Cato and Seneca and Epictetus at his finger's ends.—The corporal—with nothing—to remember, —of no deeper reading than his muster roll [...]. The one proceeding from period to period by metaphor and allusion, striking the fancy [...]. The other [...] going straight forwards as nature could lead him to the heart. O Trim! would to Heaven thou hadst a better historian!—would -- thy historian had a better pair of breeches!

Sterne is afraid of not doing justice to the corporal's eloquence, and he projects his anxiety on us. After being placed in the role of objective observers, we are blamed for not reacting. "—O ye critics! will nothing melt you"? We run down the stairs to the kitchen where Obadiah just announced to Susannah, Jonathan the coachman and the fat scullion:

> My young master in London is dead!—A green satin night-gown of my mother's [...] was the first idea which [his] exclamation brought into Suzannah's head. [...] Then, quoth she, we must all go into mourning— But the word 'mourning' [...] excited not one single idea, tinged either with grey or black:—all was green.—[...] O! 'twill be the death of my poor mistress, cried Susannah.—My mother's whole wardrobe followed.—What a procession!—Not a rag was left behind.

A rainbow of colours passes in front of our eyes.

Sterne gives us a Freudian interpretation. Used as a metonymy, the green dress conjures up the grass-stained clothes of amorous girls who have frolicked in the prairies. But also the Green Man, the Spirit of regeneration, who impels the scullion to cry out: "He is certainly dead! — So am not I". As Trim enters the kitchen, Susannah announces with tears in her eyes:

> —Here is sad news, Trim! [...], —master Bobby is dead and *buried*;— the funeral was an interpolation of Susannah's;—[...] I lament for him from my heart and soul, said Trim, fetching a sigh.—Poor creature!— poor boy! poor gentleman! —He was alive at Whitsuntide, said the

coachman. —Alas! Cried Trim; [...] what is Whitsuntide [...] or any time or time past [...] to this?

The corporal confronts others with the arrested time of trauma by making a gesture more eloquent than any discourse:

> Extending his right arm, he strikes the floor with his stick perpendicularly (to indicate health and stability) and proclaims: 'Are we not here now [...], —and are we not—[dropping his hat upon the ground] gone in a moment!—'Twas infinitely striking!

And the corporal goes on: "We are not stocks and stones.—Jonathan, Obadiah, the cook maid all melted.—The foolish fat scallion herself who was scouring a fish-kettle was roused with it.—The whole kitchen crowded about the corporal".

Contrary to Walter's oration, Trim's "image-thinking", as Mieke Bal would say, awakens our sensitivity. I can't help contrasting this episode with the impassive expression of psychoanalysts, adopted to favour the emergence of third dimension of the Other—the treasure of signifiers—from the dual mirror of relationships called "imaginary" by Lacan. Is this a reason to show a sinister mien to those who come to see us?

Ostensive definition[21]

Shandean analysis requires that we pay particular attention to this close-up, since the corporal's gesture has political implications:

> Now, [...] I perceive plainly that the preservation of our constitution in Church and State, —and possibly the preservation of the whole world [...], may in time to come depend greatly upon the right understanding of this stroke of the corporal's eloquence.

The condemnation of the jesters' gestures by the Church in medieval times[22] was no doubt an attempt to avert such political implications.

In France, the absence of analysts to treat soldiers traumatised in the Great War[23] was probably due to the condemnation by the orthodoxy of the necessary first move allowing the analyst to engage with silent, petrified patients and create a first mirror if all others have been shattered. Jonathan Shay, psychiatrist at the Veteran Hospital in Boston, is emphatic: "When we refuse to hear the voice of trauma, we have blood on our hands". Trim's eloquence stems from this knowledge, as Sterne confirms:

> I said 'we were not stocks and stones', —'tis very well. [...] but men clothed with bodies and governed by our imagination. [...] Let it suffice to affirm that [...] the eye [...] has the quickest commerce with the soul,

—[...] and leaves something more inexpressible upon the fancy than words can either convey—or sometimes get rid of.

Wittgenstein, a veteran of the Great War and a great admirer of Trim's character, speaks of an "ostensive definition", in this scene replayed by the author in slow motion. When Trim says: "Are we not here now", he drops his hat suddenly, before adding, after a pause:

and are we not gone! in a moment? [...] There was nothing in the sentence:—'twas one of your self-evident truths we [hear] every day; and if Trim had not trusted more to his hat than to his head, —he had made nothing at all of it. [...] Nothing could have expressed the sentiment of mortality [...] like it;—his hand seemed to vanish from under it; it fell dead, —the corporal's eye fix'd upon it as upon a corpse, —and Susannah burst into a flood of tears.

The scene is viewed a third time, with the hat falling like "a heavy clod of earth". Does this mean that emotion should have priority over reason? Here, Sterne deepens "the understanding of the corporal's stroke of eloquence" by discussing the political consequences of discourses which trigger emotions that destroy the capacity to think. He speaks from experience, referring to the persecution he suffered when he stopped promoting his uncle Jaques's militant fanaticism:

Ye who govern this mighty world [...]—Ye who wing and turn the passions with this great windlass [...]—Ye, lastly, who drive—and, why not, ye also who are driven, like turkeys to market, with a stick and a red clout, —meditate, —mediate, I beseech you, upon Trim's hat.

To meditate on the risk of such transference, Sterne asks us to "STAY" and witness how Trim toys with Susannah's emotions.

Traumatic transference[24]

Prior to enacting this perilous transference, the corporal makes a distinction between two temporalities, contrasting the flow of time with its stoppage in the presence of death:

—To us, Jonathan, who know not what want or care is, —who live here in the service of two of the best masters—[...], I own it that from Whitsuntide to within three weeks of Christmas —'tis not long;—'tis like nothing;—but to those, Jonathan, who know what death is [the] havoc and destruction he can make [...], —'tis like a whole age. [...] 'Twould make a good-natured man's heart bleed to consider [...] how low many a brave and upright fellow has been laid since that time!

The dropping of Trim's hat enacts in the present the imminent fall of young men—"mowed down like wheat stalks", as my paternal grandfather used to say of the men he had seen gassed, from astride his horse—before he himself died years later from the same cause. The powerful surviving image fills Susannah with an irrepressible emotion, which Trim amplifies by conjuring up other horrifying pictures:

> —And trust me, Susy [...]—before that time comes round again, — many a bright eye will be dim.—Susannah, whose eyes were swimming in water, [...] curtsied [and] wept, —no tongue could have described [her] affliction. [...]—Are we not, continued Trim, looking still at Susannah, —are we not like a flower of the field?

Susannah is this flower for Trim: "A tear of pride stole betwixt every two tears of humiliation"; but Trim shatters her illusion: "—Is not all flesh grass?—'Tis clay, —'tis dirt.—They all looked directly at the scullion;—[she] had just been scouring a fish kettle.—It was not fair".

Like La Rebours and La Fosseuse, the corporal enjoys his power to arouse desire, only to crash it when he asks: "What is the finest face that ever man looked at! —I could hear Trim talk so for ever, [she] cried ([and] laid her hand upon Trim's shoulder) —but corruption"? At these words, Susannah draws back her hand as if she had touched rotting flesh.

To distance himself from this game, Sterne asserts his love of women, like an analyst fascinated by our hysteria. He adores us for "this delicious mixture" of attraction and repulsion, he calls us "dear creatures" and cannot chastise severely enough anyone who hates our whims: "he has either a pumpkin for his head — or a pippin for his heart, — and whenever he is dissected, 'twill be found so". However, Trim carries this little game no further. His discourse suddenly changes course in a perplexing manner, even to Sterne:

> Whether Susannah, by taking her hand too suddenly from off the corporal's shoulder [...]—broke a little the chain of his reflections)—Or whether the corporal began to be suspicious he [...] was talking more like the chaplain than himself—[...], 'tis certain, at least, the corporal went on thus with his harangue.

Pastor Sterne is well aware of the ambiguous effects his sermons could produce on an audience.

Forward psychotherapy[25]

Now, Trim's discourse changes direction:

> For my own part, I declare it that out of doors I value not death at all:—not this... added the corporal, snapping his fingers [...].—In battle,

I value death not this... and let him not take me cowardly, like poor Joe Gibbins in scouring for his gun.

We are transported to the front. The corporal's about-face precedes an appeal to the dead—uttered by Cervantes in the first *Don Quixote*[26] and by Bion in *The Long Week-End*. Death, a masculine agency, is addressed in a revival of the chaos of battle:

> What is he? A pull of the trigger, —a push of a bayonet an inch this way or that, —makes the difference.—Look along the line, —to the right, —see! Jack's down! [...] No, —'tis Dick. [...]—Never mind which, —we pass on, —in hot pursuit the wound itself which brings him is not felt, —the best way is to stand up to him, —the man who flies is in ten times more danger than the man who marches up into his jaws.

The corporal would be among the firemen described by military psychologist David Grossman,[27] who overcame the visceral fear of death to go into the burning towers of the World Trade Center. Trim may also bring to mind Socrates[28]—whose biography Walter is writing—when he served as a hoplite in the Peloponnesian Wars. At the end of the *Symposium*, Alcibiade, his commander, testifies to having seen him, from atop his horse, preventing his companions from fleeing after an Athenian defeat.

Like them, the corporal stared death in the face hundreds of times: "[I] know what he is.—He's nothing, Obadiah, at all in the field. —But he's very frightful in a house, quoth Obadiah". All those present express their view of death: the coachman would not mind it upon a coach box, Susannah finds it most natural in bed. Trim can finally confess his fear: "—And could I escape him by creeping into the worst calf's skin that ever was made into a knapsack, I would do it [...]—but that is nature". Faulkner uses a similar image in *Absalom, Absalom*,[29] which takes place during the Civil War, of "mindless old meat that don't even care if it was defeat or victory, [...] that will be out in the woods and fields, grubbing up roots and woods".

When the coachman concludes, "—Nature is nature", Susannah recovers her composure and laments the fate of her mistress. The dissociation born of the fear of death, which impelled Trim to play with her sensitivity, is no longer needed. Now he can think of his master's mourning, one storey above:

> Madam will get ease of heart in weeping, —and the squire in talking about it, —but my poor master will keep it all in silence to himself.—I shall hear him sigh in his bed for a whole month together as he did for Lieutenant Le Fever [...]. I cannot help it, my master would say, — it is so melancholy an accident, —I cannot get it off my heart.—Well, he would add, I will take care of Le Fever's boy.—And with that, like a quieting draught, [he] would fall asleep.

The choir of voices gathered in the kitchen sings Toby's praises, which could just as well be addressed to Roger Sterne by his son. The qualities of Uncle Toby as Sterne's *therapôn* are laid out in the kitchen:

> I like to hear Trim's stories about the captain, said Susannah, —He is a kindly-hearted gentleman, said Obadiah, as ever lived.—Aye, —and as brave a one too, said the corporal [...].— There never was a better officer in the king's army [...]; for he would march up to the mouth of the cannon [...], —and yet, for all that, he has a heart as soft as a child for other people.—He would not hurt a chicken. [...]—I would serve him to the day of my death out of love. He is a friend and a brother to me, —and could I be sure my poor brother Tom was dead, —continued the corporal, taking out his handkerchief, —was I worth ten thousand pounds, I would leave every shilling of it to the captain.

After Trim's testamentary proof of *philia*—the love between brothers in arms—they all form a circle around the fire to hear the story of Le Fever, told in the next volume. When the scullion left and shut the door, the space of storytelling was created. "The corporal begun". We are reminded of Karen Blixen's phrase, later quoted by Hannah Arendt[30]: "All sorrows can be borne if you put them into a story or tell a story about them".

Sterne'self-analysis

The only person in the household excluded from the circle is "my mother", who is still unaware of her son's death. Sterne delays Trim's narration, as he suddenly remembers that he left her in an untenable situation: "I am Turk if I had not as much forgot my mother, as if Nature had [...] set me down [...] without one". His cry reminds us that he could have died when he was far away in Yorkshire while she made no contact with him. Now, surrounded by his characters, he may dare to address his abandonment: "Set down naked upon the banks of the river Nile [...], madam [Nature]—I've cost you a great deal of trouble [...]—but you have left a crack in my back, —and here's a great piece fallen off".

The wound he cannot see forged his character:

> For my own part, I never wonder at anything—and so often has my judgement deceived me in my life that I always suspect it [...], I hate disputes, —and therefore [...] I would almost subscribe to anything which does not choke me [...] rather than be drawn into one.—But I cannot bear suffocation [...].—For which reasons, I resolved [...] that if ever the army of martyrs was to be augmented [...] I would have no hand in it.

Still, when he tosses his wig up in the air or when inspiration is deflated, he is compelled to look for what is cut out in the crack on his back, which he cannot explore alone:

> For all this, I reverence truth as much as anybody; and when it has slipped us, if a man will but take me by the hand and go quietly and search for it as for a thing we have both lost and can neither of us do well without, —I'll go to the world's end with him.

In this man, we recognise Uncle Toby, who appeared in March 1759 when Sterne was at the end of his rope, just as Don Quichotte appeared to Cervantes in his Sevillan prison cell. But now Sterne makes an about-face again.

Transference of ideas[31]

First, he has to take care of Mrs. Shandy: "—But to return to my mother", abandoned behind the door and driven mad by the word "wife", which she thinks is about herself. For once, Sterne comes to her defence: "Pray, madam, in what street does the lady live who would not have done the same"?

Mrs. Shandy's paranoid fancy is awoken when she hears her husband declaim a passage from Socrates's argument before his judges: "We and our children were born to die, —but neither of us born to be slaves". Still, she will have to wait a little longer in the corridor since Sterne, uncertain about his reference, launches into a digression on the traceability of quotes:

> No, —there I mistake; that was part of Eleazar's oration as recorded by Josephus [...]; [...] it was carried [...] into Greece;—from Greece it got to Rome, —from Rome to France, —and from France to England: [...]— Bless me! What a trade was driven by the learned in those days!

The trade of ideas did not help Walter face the death of his son—on the contrary:

> —Now, my father had a way, a little like that of Job's [...], when things went extremely wrong with him, [...] of wondering why he was begot [...]—every word would breathe the sentiment of a soul disdaining life [...], —sir, you scarce could have distinguished him from Socrates himself.

When Walter quotes another passage, in which Socrates alludes to his three desolate children to arouse his judges' pity, Mrs. Shandy enters the room and cries: "Then [...] you have one more, Mr Shandy, than I know of". But she is dismissed bluntly. "—By heavens! I have one less, said my father, getting up and walking out of the room".

His "I" disregards that she too has one child less. This heartbreaking subtraction impels Toby to enlighten his sister-in-law:

> They are Socrates's children [...];—not caring to advance a step but upon safe ground, he laid down his pipe [...] and, rising up and taking my mother most kindly by the hand, without saying another word [...], he led her out after my father, that he might finish the *éclaircissement* himself.

And discreetly leaves.

Intermission! We now learn that Act I, which started with the birth of the hero, is coming to an end. It took place between two deaths: Yorick's and Bobby's, allowing Sterne to speak of the wound on his back. The curtain falls on Laurence's mourning of his little siblings.

Act II. Music![32]

When the curtain rises again on Act II, we are watching a Theatre of Fools performance again:

> Had this volume been a farce, which [...] I see no reason to suppose, unless everyone's life and opinions are to be looked upon as a farce as well as mine [...], —the last chapter had finished the first act of it, and then this chapter must have set off thus.

Sterne tunes his viola da gamba: "Prr...r...r...ing—twing—twang—prut—trut [...].—Do you know whether my fiddle's in tune or no—trut... prut... Tis not so bad a tone.—Diddle, diddle, diddle, diddle, diddle, diddle, dum [...]". But the swing doesn't last: "but there's a man there—no—not him with the bundle under his arm —the grave man in black.—'Sdeath"!

He has been keeping it at bay since childhood, and he plays unabated in the face of a total "lack of empathy"—Dori Laub's[33] expression. Co-founder of the Fortunoff Video Archive for Holocaust Testimonies at Yale, he draws attention to the destruction of the "thou" by a ruthless agency Sterne knows well:

> —Sir, I had rather play a cappriccio to Calliope herself than draw my bow across my fiddle before that very man; and yet [...] I will this moment stop three hundred and fifty leagues out of tune upon my fiddle without punishing one single nerve that belongs to him.—Twaddle, diddle, [...]— prut-trut—krish— krash—krush.—I've undone you, sir, —but you see he is no worse.

Yet the sinister presence is retreating. *"Diddle diddle diddle diddle diddle diddle—hum—duù—drum"*. Thanks to his beat, Sterne feels no more alone:

> O! there is—whom I could sit and hear whole days, —whose talents lie in making what he fiddles to be felt, —who inspires me with his joys and hopes, and puts the most hidden springs of my heart into motion.—If you would borrow five guineas of me, sir, —which is generally ten guineas more than I have to spare, [...]—that's your time.

Seeing Sterne spend money he cannot spare, modern doctors would diagnose the manic phase of a bipolar disorder. In the background, I can hear Jean-Max accompanying him on his harpsichord.

Tristrapaedia[34]

The power of music has made it possible to turn the page after Bobby's death. Susannah has acquired the coveted green gown and "my father" continues to theorise. He "[sat] down coolly, after the example of Xenophon, [to] write a TRISTRAPAEDIA, [...] so as to form an INSTITUTE for the government of my childhood and adolescence".

Some people can't help founding institutions. As an experienced businessman, Walter's calculation is as follows, in Tristram's view:

> I was my father's last stake—he had lost my brother Bobby entirely;—he had lost, by his own computation, full three fourths of me, —that is, he had been unfortunate in his three first great casts for me:—my geniture, nose, and name;—there was but this one left, and accordingly my father gave himself up to it with as much devotion as ever my uncle Toby had done to his doctrine of projectiles.

Meanwhile, the child is developing faster than the teaching programmes— an unfortunate fact that ministers of education have had to acknowledge. Walter's reform draws its inspiration from a 16th-century clergyman, John de la Casse, archbishop of Benevento, who equated writing with a state of warfare and the writer with a fighter who uses his "WIT" to oppose an enemy whose identity changes with the times. In the archbishop's era, it was the temptations of the Devil. In the Age of Enlightenment, Walter says: "Prejudice of education [...] *is the devil*, —and the multitude of them which we suck in with our mother's milk—*are the devil and all*.—We are haunted with them, brother Toby".

Sterne goes on to summarise the educator's bane: "I was all that time totally neglected and abandoned to my mother; [...] the work upon which my father had spent the most of his pains was rendered entirely useless".

Fortunately, a "crossaccident" puts a stop to the race between theory and practice. Sterne promises to reveal it to the reader at once, "if it can be told with decency". It begins with a denial: "'Twas nothing:—I did not lose two drops of blood by it;—'twas not worth calling in a surgeon [...];—thousands suffer by choice what I did by accident".

Once more, the event was occasioned by a Freudian slip: Susannah forgot to place the ******** *** under Tristram's bed. When nature called, she had an idea:

> Cannot you contrive, master, quoth Susannah, lifting up the sash with one hand as she spoke and helping me up into the window seat with the other, —cannot you manage, my dear, for a single time to *******************? I was five years old.—Susannah did not consider that nothing was well hung in our family, —so slap came the sash down like lightning upon us.—Nothing is left, —cried Susannah, —nothing is left—for me, but to run my country.—My uncle Toby's house was a much kinder sanctuary; and so Susannah fled to it.

The threat of castration enters the Shandy household again. "Neither reason or instinct, separate or together, could possibly have guided Susannah's steps to so proper an asylum". Without thinking, she knows that a safe space has been created out of the madness of wars, but she doesn't know what to expect. And neither does the person who carries a burden of guilt and looks for a safe asylum in a psychoanalyst's office.

Taking responsibility[35]

She will not be disappointed:

> When Susannah told the corporal the misadventure of the sash, with all the circumstances which attended the *murder* of me—(as she called it), the blood forsook his cheeks; —all accessories in murder being principals, —Trim's conscience told him he was as much to blame as Susannah.

Who is at fault? Contrary to postmodern novels, the author steps in to help us understand, just as the corporal does. Both assume responsibility by providing a flashback to enlighten us: "It is in vain to leave this to the reader's imagination. [...] Why should I put them either to trial or to torture? 'Tis my own affair: I'll explain it myself". Here is the explanation:

> -'Tis a pity, Trim, said my uncle Toby, [...]—that we have not a couple of field pieces to mount in the gorge of that new redoubt; —'twould secure the lines all along there and make the attack on that side quite

complete:—get me a couple cast, Trim. —Your Honour shall have them, replied Trim, before tomorrow morning.

No sooner said than done, lead is taken from the gutters and melted in a shaving basin. To this, Trim adds two leaden weights from the nursery window, and there it is! Now, not only were the pulleys of no use, but once removed, they also served to make wheels for a cannon carriage. This explains the sudden fall of the sash window, called *fenêtre à guillotine* in French. Trim's surrealism does not stop there. He has already dismantled all the windows of Toby's house, "though not always in the same order; for sometimes the pulleys had been wanted, and not the lead". Sterne comments that "a great MORAL might be picked handsomely out of this, but I have no time". We are reminded of Buster Keaton movies, which dismantled the order of things in the aftermath of the Great War.

Of course, the corporal could have chosen to stay silent:

He might have kept [...] this stroke of artilleryship [...] entirely to himself and left Susannah to have sustained the whole weight of the attack as she could;—true courage is not content with coming off so. [...]—How would your honours have behaved?

Based on my experience, I answer that indeed silent neutrality may cover cowardice. "The corporal was determined at once not to take shelter behind Susannah and with this resolution upon his mind, he marched upright into the parlour to lay the whole manœuvre before my uncle Toby". The captain is in deep discussion with Yorick, who has not been mentioned since the disastrous chestnut incident, in which—contrary to Susanna—he had been betrayed by his hierarchy.

Jonathan Shay[36] defines trauma as betrayal by one's own command in wartime. Trim tests his captain. After telling his story "so that priests and virgins might have listened to it", he exclaims:

I would be picked to death, —a military punishment where one must stand on sharpened stakes—, [...] before I would suffer the woman to come to any harm;—'twas my fault, an' please Your Honour, — not hers. [...]—If anything can be said to be at fault, replied my uncle Toby, —'tis I certainly who deserve the blame;—you obeyed your orders.

The captain dons his hat as a sign of authority and assumes his responsibility in the chain of command. Yorick offers support by telling the story of Count Solmes. Had he acted like Trim at the Steenkerque defeat in 1692—where the corporal was run over by a cavalryman during his regiment's retreat— he would not have led the cavalry onto rough terrain, disobeying William of Orange's orders to send in the infantry. Toby tries to curtail the account of the massacre: "—They'll go to heaven for it". But too late. Trim has launched into an account of that battle, won by the Duke of Luxembourg:

> —'Twas owing [...] entirely to Count Solmes, —had we drubb'd them soundly at Steenkerque, they would not have fought us at Landen. [...] The [French] are a nation which will pop and pop forever at you.— There is no way but to march coolly up to them [...] and fall in upon them pell-mell.

The two warriors are caught up in the revival of the battle, reliving its violence to the iambic rhythm of fifes and drums: "Dong dong...Horse and Foot... Helter skeleter... Right and left..." Yorick has to draw back his chair for safety. Churchill, Malborough's descendant, would add: "Blood and tears"! The pastor is afraid that the squire will tear Trim apart for his attack on his lineage or imitate the King of England, who has forbidden Solmes to appear before him for months.

The thought of being disavowed by his brother drives Toby berserk: "I would spring a mine and blow up my fortifications and my house with them and we would perish under their ruins". The corporal approves his master's decision: "Trim directed a slight—but a grateful bow towards his master, —and so the chapter ends".

This situation closely reflects the critical moments when a patient threatens to destroy everything, including himself, unless the analyst recognises the role he played by unwittingly betraying the given word.

Debriefing[37]

In the next chapter, we observe the little procession on its way to Shandy Hall, dreading what awaits them: "... without either drums beating or colours flying, they marched slowly from my uncle Toby's house", with Yorick and Toby leading the way abreast, the corporal a few paces behind and Susannah in the rear, at Trim's request. Despite the solemn occasion, they talk in the ranks. Regretfully, Trim laments: "I wish [...]—instead of the sash weights I had cut off the church spout". Yorick interrupts him dryly: "You have cut off spouts enow".

When they arrive, Walter's wise reaction stuns them all. "—There was that infinitude of oddities in him, —it baffled, sir, all calculations. [...] every object before him presented a face [...] altogether different from the plan [...] seen by the rest of mankind". Sterne applies this singularity to himself, as an excuse to digress and gain time, since the window episode has faded from view behind Susannah's flight and he cannot bring it back. Having reached this impasse, the way out is to let the five-year-old speak for himself:

> Fifty thousand pannier-loads of devils [...] with their tails chopped off by their rumps could not have made so diabolical a scream of it as I

did—when the accident befell me: it summoned up my mother instantly into the nursery, —so that Susannah had but just time to make her escape down the back stairs as my mother came up the fore. Now, though I was old enough to have told the story myself—and young enough, I hope, to have done it without malignity; yet Susannah, in passing by the kitchen, had left it [...] with the cook;—the cook had told it with a commentary to Jonathan, and Jonathan to Obadiah; so that [...] Obadiah [was] enabled to give [my father] a particular account of it just as it had happened.

Contrary to his habit, Walter gives the briefest of answers as he tucks up his nightgown: "—I thought as much". Sterne wonders how he could have foreseen such an event: "One would imagine from this [...] that my father, [...] had actually wrote [...] in the *Tristrapaedia* [...] the chapter upon sash windows, with a bitter Philipic at the end of it upon the forgetfulness of chambermaids". But this supposition is clearly contrived, since Sterne admits having written that chapter himself.

In any case, Walter runs into the nursery behind "my mother", puts on his spectacles, examines the problem, takes off the glasses and goes back downstairs. His wife thinks he went to fetch basil and lint, but he returns with two large books under his arm, which she presumes to be herbals. Far from it! In fact, they are books about circumcision as practised by different nations, and include Maimonides as the primary reference. Offering no explanation, Walter sends his wife to summon Dr. Slop for emergency treatment.

After perusing the panorama of circumcised peoples in the 18th century, Walter concludes: "—if Solon and Pythagoras submitted, —what is Tristram?—Who am I, that I should fret or fume one moment about the matter"? This explains his calm reaction when the little group enters the parlour.

Circumcision[38]

While they expect the worst, Walter offers up a perspective that leaves them speechless:

> —Dear Yorick, this Tristram of ours, I find, comes very hardly by all his religious rites.—Never was the son of Jew, Christian, Turk or infidel initiated into them in so oblique and slovenly a manner. [...]—There has been certainly [...] the deuce and all to do in some part or other of the ecliptic when this offspring of mine was formed.

The pastor tries to play down the accident: "But he is no worse, I trust". As always, Toby is concerned about his nephew: "—But is the child, cried my uncle Toby, the worse?—The Troglodytes say not, replied my father.— [...] Now every word of this, quoth my uncle Toby, is Arabic to me".

Leaving the practice of circumcision in the Middle East, Walter cites to his brother the example of a general who had his entire army circumcised.

The captain objects: "I know not by what article of war he could justify it". The discussion reaches the political sphere, going from the baptism of Frank soldiers by Clovis and that of indigenous peoples by missionaries to the Picrocholine wars ignited by "polemic divines", as Walter calls them. Yorick is upset by his remark: "—I wish there was not a polemic divine [...] in the kingdom. [...] — Pray, Mr Yorick, quoth my uncle Toby, —do tell me what a polemic divine is".

The pastor takes his Rabelais from his pocket so they may hear, in Chapter 35 of Gargantua, "the best description I have ever read". Indeed, Rabelais stages, at his own risk, the Wars of Religion triggered by "polemic divines" under the cover of the Pichrocoline wars. The corporal is invited into the parlour to listen to Gymnast's victory over captain Tripet, one of Pichrocole's officers—Gargantua's father's enemy, whose name in Greek means "bitter bile". The juggler, disguised as a devil, carries out an acrobatic performance on his saddle with such virtuosity that a thrust of his sword "at once cut Tripet's stomach, [...] and the half of his liver".

While expressing reservations about this battle in which "the French come on capering", the two soldiers feel supported in their victory over the venomous claims propagated by fake news about Tristram's castration. "My uncle Toby never felt the consciousness of his existence with more complacency than what the corporal's and his own reflections made him do at that moment".

Cervantes is also at their side when they make their Quixotic sally to defend the honour of Susannah and Tristram.

The origin of the world[39]

Still in control of the situation, Toby lights his pipe, Yorick draws his chair nearer to the table, while Walter stirs the fire and opens his Tristrapaedia to read them the first chapters on the origin of the world. The picture is that of a conjugal society, where a man, a woman and a bull all labour under the same yoke. Yorick points out a fact Walter must have repressed: that the animal is, in fact, a castrated ox. A heated discussion rendered by two lines of asterisks ensues about the respective powers of man and wife, ending, once again, with a scene from the Theatre of Fools featuring Trim as the jester:

> I own, added my father, that the offspring [...] is not under the power and jurisdiction of the *mother* [...]—and besides, [...] *she is not the principal agent*, Yorick. —In what? quoth my uncle Toby, stopping his pipe. — Though by all means, added my father (not attending to my uncle Toby), '*the son ought to pay her respect*', as you may read, Yorick, [...] in the first book of the Institutes of Justinian [...]. —I can read it as well, replied Yorick, in the Cathechism. —Trim can repeat every word of it by heart, quoth my uncle Toby. [...].—Ask him, Mr Yorick.

The captain brings in the corporal, who is asked to recite the Ten Commandments. Trim performs a sketch of their recitation like a wound-up mechanical toy soldier. Shouldering his stick like a musket, his right hand on the firelock, he recites THE FIRST, THE SECOND and all through to the fifth about respecting one's parents—while Toby shouts the orders, in British style: "Poise your firelock! Rest firelock"! Finally, the corporal makes a low bow and goes back to the side of the room, within reach of my father's sarcasm: "Here is the *scaffold* work of INSTRUCTION, its true point of folly, without the BUILDING behind it". His maxim is spelled out in capital letters: "—SCIENCES MAY BE LEARNED BY ROTE, BUT WISDOM NOT".

In contrast, Yorick addresses the corporal to ask how he interprets, in practice, the meaning of the fifth commandment: "Honour thy father and mother". The corporal's answer illustrates Wittgenstein's assertion[40]: "In most cases, the meaning of a word is its use". "Allowing them [...] three half-pence a day out of my pay when they grew old.—And didst thou do that, Trim? [...]—He did indeed, replied my uncle Toby". The pastor rises from his chair to shake the corporal's hand and calls him "the best commentator upon that part of the Decalogue". All the more reason for the philosopher's love for the corporal.

On the subject of health[41]

The *Tristrapaedia* goes on to discuss medicine based on the equilibrium between humours, from Antiquity and the Middle Ages to today:

> O blessed health! Cried my father, [...].—He that has thee has little more to wish for; [...]. Now, could the man in the moon be told that a man in the earth had wrote a chapter sufficiently demonstrating that the secret of all health depended upon the due contention for mastery betwist the *radical heat* and the *radical moisture*, [...] '—He would cry, [...]—what have we MOONITES done?

Sterne probably chose his vantage point from the moon, as Voltaire did from Sirius in *Micromegas*, enabling him to foresee mood regulators for those who fluctuate between radical exaltation and deep depression. Walter invokes Hippocrates and Lord Verulam alias Francis Bacon. The former for "his sorrowful complaint of the *ars longa* — and *vita brevis*", which, because therapies take too long, encourages all sorts of quacks to deceive their patients through flattery and "loads of chymical nostrums". The latter, whom he calls "the principal of nostrum-mongers", encourages the trade of opium, saltpetre, grease unctions, purges and clysters, a list not unfamiliar to us—in short, opiates to put us to sleep at night and saltpetre to awaken us in the morning. But the result is the same: "to make man sad and apathetic, as he is after intercourse", according to Aristotle's *post coitum animal est triste.*

My father dismissed all this rubbish to build his own theory, which for once captured Toby: "The description of the Siege of Jerico itself could not have engaged the attention of my uncle Toby more powerfully than this last chapter;—his eyes were fixed upon my father throughout it". Then he removed the pipe from his mouth, beckoned to the corporal to come near and whispered something in his ear—rendered by a line of asterisks. The corporal answered out loud: "It was at the Siege of Limerick, an' please Your Honour", making a bow. Once again, traumatic memory is awakened

We are taken back to the year 1690 in Ireland during another siege: "The poor fellow and I, quoth my uncle Toby, [...] were scarce able to crawl out of our tents [...] upon the very account you mention". The humoral theory applies perfectly to this situation. As a theoretician interrupted by trivial anecdotes, Walter rejects this testimony inwardly: "Now, what can have got into that precious noodle of thine, my dear brother Toby? Cried my father mentally—By Heaven! [...], it would puzzle an Oedipus".

The Freudian reader asks himself what Oedipus has to do with this. Nothing, in fact, since Toby and Trim are crawling in the radical moisture of mud, like infantry men in the clay of Flanders, discovering radical heat thanks to:

> the quantity of brandy we set fire to every night and the claret and cinnamon with which I plied Your Honour off—quoth the corporal. — And the genever, Trim, added my uncle Toby, which did us more good than all —I verily believe, continued the corporal, we had both [...] left our lives in the trenches and been buried in them too. —The noblest grave, corporal! Cried my uncle Toby, his eyes sparkling as he spoke [...]. —But a pitiful death for [a soldier]! replied the corporal.

We see a zoom shot of the Great War, in which hooch fired up many a soldier crawling in the cold mud. Life in the trenches is as much Arabic to Walter as that of Troglodytes is to Toby. Seeing his brother waver between tears and laughter, the captain turns to Yorick to describe the siege of Limerick—a perfect clinical illustration. It starts with a dysentery epidemic caused by radical heat, which provoked "a most raging thirst" accompanied by a burning fever. Exasperated by the goings-on in soldier's guts, Walter takes a deep breath—but can't chase away the olfactory hallucination—as my uncle Toby continues:

> —It was Heaven's mercy to us which put it into the corporal's head to maintain that due contention betwixt the radical heat and the radical moisture by reinforcing the fever, as he did all along, with hot wine and spices.

Foreseeing Walter's "sentence that was likely to end with no sort of mercy", intended to silence veterans and erase their frontline experience, the pastor asked the corporal for his opinion.

Psychoanalysis of a battle[42]

We are transported to the siege of Limerick the year after Trim's recruitment into the army:

> With humble submission to His Honour's better judgement, quoth the corporal, making a bow to my uncle Toby. —Speak thy opinion freely, corporal, said my uncle Toby.—The poor fellow is my servant—not my slave, —added my uncle Toby, turning to my father.

So:

> with his hat under his left arm, with his stick hanging upon the wrist of it [...], [Trim] marched up to the ground where he had performed his catechism; then, touching his under-jaw with the thumb and fingers of his right hand [...], —he delivered his notions thus.

Like the ancient bard, he searches for the music of his account, which he hums before beginning to speak. In contrast, doctor Slop waddles in, allowing Walter to savour a diversion: "The corporal made a bow to his old friend, Dr Slop, and then delivered his opinion concerning radical heat and radical moisture in the following words". First, the topography: "a devilish swampy country. – 'Tis since surrounded, said my uncle Toby, by the Shannon and is by its situation, one of the strongest fortified places in Ireland".

A heated exchange arises between traumatic memory which does not forget any details and pseudo-scientific discourse which overlooks them. Slop protests against this new mode of introducing "a medical lecture", which Trim resists quixotically: "—'Tis all true". And Yorick suggests that the faculty adopt this new style of presentation.

The truth of Trim's memory, cut off from the past and unfolding in the present tense, is expressed by the use of the word "cut", repeated several times:

> 'Tis all cut through, an' please Your Reverence, said the corporal, with drains and bogs; and besides, there was such a quantity of rain fall during the siege, the whole country was like a puddle;—'twas that and nothing else which brought on the flux, and which had like to have killed both His Honour and myself; now, there was no such thing, after the first ten days [...], for a soldier to lie dry in his tent without cutting a ditch round it to draw off the water [and] without setting fire every night

to a pewter dish full of brandy, which [...] made the inside of the tent as warm as a stove.

Irritated by all these details, Walter urges him to come to a conclusion, and to everyone's surprise, Trim sums up what he has said with academic concision:

> I infer [...] that the radical moisture is nothing in the world but ditch-water—and that the radical heat, of those who can go to the expense of it, is burnt brandy—the radical heat and moisture of private man [...] is nothing but ditchwater—and a dram of genever. [...] —I am at a loss, Captain Shandy, quoth Doctor Slop, to determine in which branch of learning your servant shines most, whether in physiology or divinity. (...) The poor fellow has had the misfortune to have heard some superficial empiric discourse upon this point.

And he leaves to look at the cataplasm on Tristram's injury.

Any resemblance to the disdain of past, present or future Dr. Slops for the particularities of Shandean analysis applied to madness and war trauma is purely coincidental. Lacan himself dismissed the question of transference in such cases by asserting that "to use the technique established by Freud outside the experience to which it was applied, is as stupid as to toil at the oars when the ship is on sand".[43] Two centuries earlier, Sterne had already weighed anchor and set sail on the open sea.

Auxiliary verbs[44]

Sterne also uses a maritime metaphor to end Volume 5: "Come! Cheer up, my lads; I'll shew you land;—for when we have tugged through that chapter, the book shall not be opened again this twelve month.—Huzza"! He has two more chapters to write: one to summarise the pedagogical programme of the *Tristrapaedia*, the other to suggest a shortcut:

> Five years with a bib under his chin. [...]. A year and a half in learning to write his own name., seven long years and more [reciting] Greek and Latin, four years at his *probations* and his *negations*, —the fine statue still lying in the middle of the marble block—and nothing done, but his tools sharpened to hew it out!—'Tis a piteous delay!

Walter quickly consoles himself with the thought of learned men who acquired erudition late in life. A list is comprised in Rabelaisian style: in the 16th century, Scaliger was forty-four when he was proficient in Greek; in the 11th century, Peter Damianus, Bishop of Ostia, could not read when he reached adulthood; in the 14th century, "Baldus entered the law so late that it was said he intended to practice in the other world..." This is why a shortcut is needed—like the North-West Passage sailed in 1728 by Behring, a Danish explorer in the service of Peter the Great.

Walter is proud of his idea:

> —every child, Yorick! has not a parent to point out [this shortcut].—The whole entirely depends, added my father in a low voice, upon the auxiliary verbs. [...] I reckon it was one of the greatest calamities which ever befell the republic of letters that those who have been entrusted with the education of our children, [...] have made so little use of [this passage].

Would this secret passage raise our children's standing on an international scale? Yorick is befuddled and Toby even more. Walter goes on to enumerate the auxiliary verbs in the present, past and future tenses, in the affirmative, interrogative and hypothetical modes, using an example that was sure to awaken his brother's interest: "If the French should beat the English"?

This question is followed by a maieutic exercise, addressed to Trim, delivered in Socrates's style when he questioned Meno[45]:

> Didst thou ever see a white bear? [...]—No, an' please Your Honour, replied the corporal.—But thou couldst discourse about one [...] in case of need?—How is it possible, brother, quoth my uncle Toby, if the corporal never saw one?—'Tis the fact I want, replied my father, —and the possibility of it is as follows.

As he lists everything that can be said about A WHITE BEAR with no need ever to have seen one, Walter uses auxiliary verbs:

> Would I had seen a white bear? [...]If I should see a white bear, what should I say? [...] How would the white bear have behaved? Is he wild? Tame? Terrible? Rough? Smooth? [...] Is it better than a BLACK ONE?

Volume 5 ends with the colour BLACK at a time when slavery is at its height, as we shall read in Volume 9.

But first, Sterne will guide us through uncharted territory.

Notes

1 Sterne, L., *Tristram Shandy*, op. cit., Vol. 5, ch. I.
2 Erasmus, *The Praise of Folly*, London: Aeterna, 2010.
3 De Lafontaine, J., *The Original Fables of Lafontaine*, Madrid: HardPress Publishing, 2010.
4 Boccacio, G., *The Decameron*, London: Penguin Classics, 2003; Chaucer, G., *The Canterbury Tales*, New York: Bantam Classics, 1982; De Navarre, M., *The Heptameron*, op. cit.

5 Lacan, J., *Écrits*, op. cit.
6 Warburg, A., "A Lecture on Serpet Ritual", op. cit.
7 Chaplin, C., *The Great Dictator* (film), 1940.
8 Searles, H. The Effort to Drive the Other Person Crazy, *British Journal of Medical Psychology*, vol. 32, 1959.
9 Wittgenstein, L., *Philisphical Investigations*, op. cit., §39, 41.
10 Voltaire, *Candide*, New York: Simon & Schuster, 2005.
11 Klemperer, V., *Language of the Third Reich: LTI: Lingua Tertii Imperii: A Philologist's Notebook*, London, Oxford, New York, New Delhi, Sydney: Bloomsbury Publishing, 2002.
12 Arendt, H., *The Origins of Totalitarianism*, op. cit.
13 Sterne, L, *Tristram Shandy*, op. cit., Vol. 5, ch. II.
14 Le Braz, A., *Celtic Legends of the Beyond: A Celtic Book of the Dead*, Newburyport, MA: Red Wheel/Weiser, 1999.
15 Sterne, L., *Tristram Shandy*, op. cit., Vol. 5, ch. III.
16 Baudelaire, C., The Voyage, in *Invitation to the Voyage*, Brahic, B. B. (Trans.), London and Calcutta: Seagull Books, 2019.
17 Sterne, L., *Tristram Shandy*, op. cit., Vol. 7, ch. XII.
18 Sterne, L., *Tristram Shandy*, op. cit., Vol. 5, chs. IV–VI.
19 Morrison, T., *Beloved*, New York: Penguin Books, 1991.
20 Sterne, L., *Tristram Shandy*, op. cit., Vol.5, ch. VII.
21 Sterne, L., *Tristram Shandy*, op. cit., Vol 5, chs. VIII–IX.
22 Schmitt, J.-C., The Rationale of Gestures in the West, University of Groningen, 1991.
23 Guillemain, H., and Tison, S., *Du front à l'asile*, Paris: Alma, 2013.
24 Sterne, L., *Tristram Shandy*, op. cit., Vol. 5, ch. IX.
25 Sterne, L., *Tristram Shandy*, op. cit., Vol. 5, chs. X–XII.
26 De Cervantes, M., *Don Quixote I*, op. cit., ch. XL.
27 Grossman, D., *On Combat,* op. cit.
28 Plato, *Symposium*, Edinburgh, Scotts Valley, CA: CreateSpace, 2013.
29 Faulkner, W., *Absalom, Absalom*, New York: Vintage International, 1990, p. 283.
30 Arendt, H., *The Human Condition*, University of Chicago Press, 1998.
31 Sterne, L., *Tristram Shandy*, op. cit., Vol. 5, chs. XIII–XIV.
32 Sterne, L., *Tristram Shandy*, op. cit., Vol. 5, ch. XV.
33 Laub, D., and Auerhahn, N., Failed Empathy, *Psychoanalytic Psychology,* vol. 6, no. 4, Jan1989, pp. 377–400.
34 Sterne, L., *Tristram Shandy*, op. cit., Vol. 5, chs. XVI–XVII.
35 Sterne, L., *Tristram Shandy*, op. cit., Vol. 5, chs. XVIII–XXII.
36 Shay, J., *Achilles in Vietnam*, op. cit.
37 Sterne, L., *Tristram Shandy*, op. cit., chs. XXIII–XXVII.
38 Sterne, L., *Tristram Shandy*, op. cit., chs. XXVII–XXX.
39 Sterne, L., *Tristram Shandy*, op. cit., chs. XXXI–XXXII.
40 Wittgenstein, L., *Philosophical Investigations*, op. cit.
41 Sterne, L., *Tristram Shandy*, op. cit., Vol. 5, chs. XXXII–XXXIII.
42 Sterne, L., *Tristram Shandy*, op. cit., Vol. 5, chs. XXXIX–XL.
43 Lacan, J., On a Question Preliminary to Any Possible Treatment of Psychosis, in *Écrits: A Selection*, London: Tavistock/Routledge.
44 Sterne, L., *Tristram Shandy*, op. cit., Vol. 5, chs. XLI–XLII.
45 Plato, *Meno*, Victoria, BC: Empire Books, 2012.

6

Epitaph

Respite for the reader[1]

On Medieval maps, *Terrae incognitae* were indicated by drawings of monsters. In literature, the "space of the marvel" was the unknown territory inhabited by "the madman", or "Wildman", carrying a club and often a truckle of cheese to illustrate the fermentation of the brain. In this space, he met fay creatures outside the scope of language and time.

Like the hero of the *Folies Tristan*[2] written at the end of the 12th century—who returned to Ysolde disguised as a fool in order to escape King Mark's wrath—Sterne dons a fool's cap and defies the shadow hanging over him since childhood:

> We'll not stop two moments, my dear sir, —only, as we have got thro' these five volumes [...], let us just look back upon the country we have pass'd through.—What wilderness has it been! and what a mercy that we have not both of us been lost or devoured by wild beasts in it!

The trajectory of the author's wanderings will be drawn at the end of this volume.

I believe we have explored the Jamaican territory where his father's tomb was as out of reach to the eighteen-year-old Laurence as a white bear to Trim. In Volume 1, Sterne has already provided his father with an epitaph next to the double black page honouring Yorick's death.[3] Now he will honour his father through the story of Lieutenant Le Fever's death—a rank to which Roger Sterne was only promoted in extremis. But, Le Fever does not die alone; his son is there with him.

We are in December 1761. Sterne has a new publisher, but he worries that Volumes 5 and 6 will not sell as well as the previous ones. It's time to review the situation. The beasts in the wilderness are the reviewers who disparaged the author. He calls them "jackasses", braying donkeys on the model of the "braying contest" in the second *Don Quixote*,[4] which derides Cervantes's

DOI: 10.4324/9781003224907-6

colleagues, so jealous of his first novel's success that they paid a forger to write an infamous sequel:

> —How they view'd and review'd us as we passed over the rivulet at the bottom of that little valley!—and when we climbed over that hill and were just getting out of sight—good God! what a braying did they all set up together! [...]—Bray, bray [...] Was I a jackass, I would bray in G-sol-re-ut...

Animals take part in the novel—we will meet an actual ass in Volume 7:

> Now my father had danced his bear backward and forward through a dozen of pages, he closed the book for good an'all" and announced tiumphally; 'Tristram shall be made to conjugate every word in the dictionary, backwards and forwards the same way. [...] The force of this engine is incredible in opening a child's head. —'Tis enough, brother Shandy, cried my uncle Toby, to burst it into a thousand splinters.

Walter is still intending to place his son ahead of all other children.

The list of child prodigies has grown since his attempt to name the boy Trismegistus, and includes names such as the great Pascal and Lipsius, who composed a work the day he was born. "They should have wiped it up, said my uncle Toby, and said no more about it"; in other words, it should be used as a *torchecul*, baby Pantagruel's favourite game.

Class struggle[5]

Now, the focus shifts from babies' bottoms to Tristram's foreskin, which Susannah and Dr. Slop are tending to. The scene is worthy of the *comedia dell'arte* since the child, who had already caused his parents' quarrel before being born, becomes the focus of class struggle. Asked to hold the candle while Slop tends to Tristram, Suzannah considers the task too demeaning. Today, he would have given her tranquilizers, but he chose to attack her instead: "Oh! oh!— [...] then, I think I know you, madam.—You know me, sir! cried Susannah [...] with a toss of her head". Slop pinches his nose between his finger and his thumb, calling her an "impudent whore". A fine example of "splenetic cordiality"! Sterne comments.

In the meantime, Walter continues to develop his Tristrapedia, dwelling now on the choice of a private governor to take the boy "out of these women's hands". We are not spared a long list of governors since ancient times, from the best to the worst, like Emperor Commodus's tutors who turned their pupil into a monster with the help of his mother, who had a gladiator

for a lover when the child was conceived. To avoid such disaster, the appli-
cant's qualifications will be submitted to close scrutiny:

> [He] shall neither lisp or squint or wink or talk loud or look fierce or
> foolish, —or bite his lips, or grind his teeth, or speak through his nose
> [...].—He shall neither walk fast—or slow, or fold his arms, —for that is
> laziness;—or hang them down, —for that is folly.

Psychological tests are also requested to predict the child's character, in the
way Democritus predicted that the young Protagoras—Socrates's future
sophist opponent—would be an intellectual by the ingenious fashion in
which he bound a bundle of brushwood. "Now, this is all nonsense again,
quoth my uncle Toby to himself". Walter wants a modern tutor: "cheerful,
[...], prudent, attentive to business, [...], acute, [...], inventive, [...] wise and
judicious, and learned". Yorick is more traditional: "And why not humble
and moderate and gentle-tempered and good"? To which Toby adds: "And
why not [...] free and generous and bountiful and brave"? They shake hands
and the captain seizes the opportunity to promote his protégé, "poor Le
Fever's son", whose story was left in suspense in the kitchen.[6]
Here, Sterne has a memory lapse! He can't remember at what point he
interrupted the narration of the story. In fact, he abandoned "my mother"
in the corridor to analyse the dissociated part of himself, fallen off his back:

> —Fool that I was! nor can I recollect [...], without turning back to the
> place, what it was that hindered me from letting the corporal tell it in
> his own words;—but the occasion is lost, —I must tell it now in my own.

The lost occasion allows him to find his own words, unspoken since his
father died alone so far away. Has Roger's unrestful soul joined Hellequin's
Riders,[7] the army of dead warriors led by King Herla? Although I don't
believe in ghosts, I see them arriving in my office with their clamorous
symptoms, demanding that we inscribe their untold stories.

The story of Le Fever[8]

The story starts on the evening of a summer day in 1706—the year when the
British took Dendermonde—"seven years [...] after [...] my uncle Toby and Trim
had [...] decamped [...] in order to lay some of the finest sieges to the finest fortified cities in Europe". Toby would be delighted to learn that today the Vauban
fortifications, considered world heritage sites, are protected by UNESCO:

> The captain was getting his dinner with Trim sitting behind him.—I
> say sitting—for in consideration of the corporal's lame knee (which

sometimes gave him exquisite pain), —my uncle Toby [...] would never suffer the corporal to stand.

"It was practically the only thing they squabbled about", Sterne interjects: "—Why do I mention it?—Ask my pen:—it governs me;—I govern not it".

His pen takes him to the land where his father died in 1731. Laurence was eighteen and had not seen him since he was ten. In the Memoir he wrote for his daughter Lydia when she was ten, Sterne recorded the only details he knew about her grandfather's final days: that tropical fever had made him regress to a childlike state until the day when, without a complaint, he sat down in his armchair to draw his last breath. Laurence's pain will be inscribed in history through the story of Le Fever's last days in the company of his eleven-year-old son—the deadly fever becoming a family name. The story will be told by the author in five episodes.

The first episode revolves around a glass of sherry. The innkeeper of the neighbouring inn has just burst into Toby's house in the middle of his supper, holding an empty phial:

> 'Tis for a poor gentleman, —I think, of the army [...], who has taken ill at my house four days ago and has never held up his head since or had a desire to taste anything till just now, that he has a fancy for a glass of sack and a thin toast.

Toby gives him two bottles and offers a dozen more, expressing the wish to meet this soldier: "I cannot help entertaining a high opinion of [this] guest too, [who] in so short a time should win so much upon the affections of his host".

The innkeeper doesn't remember the soldier's name and promises to ask the man's son. Toby is stunned: "Has he a son with him then? —A boy [...] of about eleven or twelve years of age". Young Laurence has entered the scene from which he has been excluded, and Sterne makes us witness the boy's pain through the innkeeper's voice: "he does nothing but mourn and lament for him night and day: —he has not stirred from the bedside these two days". "Proximity", Salmon's first principle of forward psychotherapy during World War I,[9] is restored with young Laurence's long-lost father, abolishing transatlantic distance.

Toby asks for his pipe and tobacco and meditates while he smokes. When he finishes his pipe, he tells Trim: "I have a project in my head". Salmon's second principle, Immediacy, is expressed by the leitmotiv of the novel: "I wish". The captain wishes to put on his coat at once and go to the inn to visit the poor gentleman. The third principle, Expectancy, a reason to hope, is at work. Trim objects:

> Your Honour's roquelaure [...] has not once been had on since the night before Your Honour received your wound [...];—and besides, it is so

cold and rainy a night that [...] 'twill be enough to give Your Honour your death and bring on Your Honour's torment in your groin. —I fear so, replied my uncle Toby, but I am not at rest in my mind, Trim.

Faced with this dilemma, the corporal assumes the role of *therapon* for both his master and the soldier in the no man's land of his final battle. First, he will go on a reconnaissance mission with a shilling from Toby to drink with the soldier's servant and "get it all out of him".

Once he leaves, Toby lights a second pipe to muse at his leisure on this father and son.

Bridge to the beyond[10]

A passage has opened to the beyond, through which, in some sessions, lost souls are ushered in by those who come to see us. This passage is materialised in Japanese Noh theatre[11] by a bridge connecting the small stage with the world of disquieted souls. A Noh performance is punctuated by *kyogens* (comic interludes) and by percussion music. The scenario usually starts with a meeting between a tired traveller, *waki*, and a humble figure, *shite*—driving the action—whom the traveller asks where he is. The *shite* informs him about a historical event which took place there, and then disappears. The traveller falls asleep.

Now the *shite* appears, at the "crossroad of dreams", advancing slowly on the bridge, wearing a white mask and a ceremonial kimono, to show the public an event cut out of History: the betrayal of a fallen warrior; that of a child tormented by a cruel stepmother; or that of an exiled without shelter. Translator René Sieffert remarks: "This process is psychoanalytic, literally".

The meeting with the innkeeper takes place at the crossroads of Sterne's dreams and those of a dying soldier who enters the stage slowly with his son. The time it takes to cross the bridge from the beyond is measured in pipes smoked by Toby, who shakes out the ashes of the third when Trim returns to give his report.

The second episode presents the corporal's debriefing. At first, he had little hope of finding anything out because the lieutenant had no servant. Having learned the soldier's rank, Toby can't wait to know the name of his regiment, but Trim wants to tell him "everything straight forwards, as [he] learnt it", from the child, in fact. "I'll fill another pipe [...] and not interrupt thee", Toby says.

But he is no more able to keep his promise than Don Quixote[12] was able to keep his with Cardenio, the madman of Sierra Morena. Roaming in the wild space of the mountain, Cardenio meets the knight, who asks him to tell his story. He agrees and lies down on the grass, asking not to be interrupted. Don Quixote can't help commenting and the meeting ends in a fight. Still, the analysis bears its fruit twelve chapters later when, thanks to the knight, the young man is reunited with his fiancée, who had been kidnapped by his best friend.

The corporal begins his account by making his old bow, "which generally spoke, as plain as a bow could speak". He says that he limited himself
to "everything which was proper to be asked", and Toby approves. Trim
started by questioning the landlady, who had heard the "death watch", an
insect announcing death. Then the child came down, asking for a toast for
his father and refusing to be pitied when Trim offered to make it for him.
But when the corporal introduced himself as an old soldier, the boy burst
into tears. "Poor youth"!, exclaimed Toby:

> —he has been bred up from an infant in the army, and the name of a
> soldier, Trim, sounds in his ear like the name of a friend—I wish I had
> him here. [...] —I thought; continued the corporal, it was proper to tell
> him I was Captain Shandy's servant, and that Your Honour [...] was
> extremely concerned for his father;— and that if there was anything in
> your house or cellar—(And thou mightst have added my purse too, said
> my uncle Toby), —he was heartily welcome to it.

When the boy makes a very low bow without answering, Trim understands
that "his heart is too full" to speak, and tells him that his father will recover.
He does not leave him alone in his silence. In contrast, Sterne depicts the
cynical neutrality of Yorick's curate who smokes his pipe by the fire without uttering a comforting word to the child. "I thought it wrong, added the
corporal.—I think so too, said my uncle Toby".

Somewhat revived by the sherry and the toast, the lieutenant sends word
asking Trim to come up to see him in about ten minutes, during which the
corporal and the curate have a heated exchange. The curate proclaims his
scorn of the military. Trim's response echoes Don Quixote's "Discourse
on arms and letters"[13] delivered in *basso continuo*: "standing twelve hours
in the trenches up to his knees in cold water, [...] harassed [...] today;—
harassing others tomorrow;—detached here, —countermanded there, —
resting this night out upon his arms; [...]—benumbed in his joints ..." But
when Trim concludes: "I believe [...] that when a soldier gets time to pray, —
he prays as heartily as a parson, —though not with all his fuss and hypoc-
risy", Toby finds that he has gone too far: "Thou shouldst not have said that,
Trim, said my uncle Toby;—for God only knows who is a hypocrite and who
is not".

Action[14]

Ten minutes have gone by. Trim goes up to see the lieutenant, who is expecting him. There is a clean Cambrai handkerchief beside him and a cushion,
with a prayer book on it. The child wants to take it away, but his father
says: "—Let it remain there, my dear". Sterne writes these words as if they
were addressed to him.

The third episode stages a tragedy revealed by the lieutenant after introducing himself:

> I served three campaigns with [the captain] in Flanders, and remember him, —but 'tis most likely [...] that he knows nothing of me.—You will tell him, however, that the person [...] under obligation to him is one Le Fever, a lieutenant in Angus's; [...]—possibly he may know my story [...], —pray tell the captain I was the ensign at Breda, whose wife was [...] killed with a musket shot as she lay in my arms in my tent.

Trim remembers the story. The lieutenant shows him a small ring on a black ribbon around his neck, which he raises to his lips with tears in his eyes, calling the boy, who kisses it too, then kisses his father, sits down on the bed and weeps. "—I wish, said my uncle Toby, with a deep sigh—I wish, *Trim,* I was asleep. [...]—But finish the story thou art upon".

Sighing again, Toby remembers that the lieutenant and his wife "were universally pitied by the whole regiment, a circumstance the lieutenant had modestly omitted". When the boy accompanies him down the stairs, he explains how they were on their way from Ireland to Flanders when his father took ill—on the road so often travelled by ensign Roger Sterne. "—Then what is to become of his poor boy? cried my uncle Toby", deciding at once to go to the inn. Great captains know how to make quick decisions.

In the fourth episode, Toby visits the dying man. The siege of Dendermonde on the bowling green can wait. Now, Toby "bent his whole thoughts towards the private distresses at the inn". Sterne is grateful to uncle Toby, who has comforted him in his own distress: "The king BEING who is 'a friend to the friendless' shall recompense thee for this". In Volume 9, he will use the same expression in favour of those taken into slavery.

For the moment, Toby rebukes the corporal for not having offered him his purse, given the soldier's modest pay. Trim replies that he had no such orders:

> —True [...], thou didst very right, Trim, as a soldier, —but certainly very wrong as a man. [...]—thou shouldst have offered him my house too:—a sick brother officer should have the best quarters [...], and what with thy care of him and the old woman's and his boy's and mine together we might recruit him again at once and set him upon his legs.

Sterne understands palliative care. The refusal to accept imminent death is the first stage described in Elizabeth Kubler Ross's pioneering book.[15] "In [...] three weeks, added my uncle Toby, smiling, —he might march.—He will never march [...], —said the corporal.—He will march, said my uncle Toby, rising up from the side of the bed, with one shoe off". In Renaissance paintings, monosandalism is a sign of an agitated mind.

The captain denies death:

> An' please Your Honour [...], he will never march but to his grave.
> [...] —He shall march to his regiment. (...) —Ah, well-o'-day, —do what
> we can for him, said Trim [...], the poor soul will die. — He shall not die,
> by G—, cried my uncle Toby.

The revolt of the living bursts into blasphemy. This is where Sterne writes
one of the most beautiful sentences of his book:

> —The ACCUSING SPIRIT which flew up to heaven's chancery with
> the oath blush'd as he gave it in, —and the RECORDING ANGEL,
> as he wrote it down, dropp'd a tear upon the word and blotted it out for
> ever.

The fifth scene is that of the lieutenant's final moments. The angel has in no
way lessened Toby's determination:

> —My uncle Toby went to his bureau, —put his purse into his breeches
> pocket and, having ordered the corporal to go early in the morning for
> a physician, —he went to bed and fell asleep. The sun looked bright in
> the morning after to every eye in the village but [...] the hand of death
> press'd heavy upon [Le Fever's] eyelids.

Toby was at his bedside an hour earlier than he had intended. He spoke to
the lieutenant in the straightforward manner characteristic of frontline psychotherapy, intended to reach men who could not bear falsehoods:

> There was a frankness in my uncle Toby, —not the effect of familiarity,
> —but the cause of it. [...] Without preface or apology, [he] sat himself
> down upon the chair by the bedside, [...] opened the curtain in the man-
> ner of an old friend [...] and asked him how he did.

Then, without letting him answer, he added:

> —You shall go home directly, Le Fever [...], to my house, —and
> we'll send for a doctor to see what's the matter;—and we'll have an
> apothecary, —and the corporal shall be your nurse;— and I'll be your
> servant, Le Fever.

Billy senses that despite Toby's fervent desire, his father has already sev-
ered all ties with life: "[...] The son insensibly pressed up close to his knees
and had taken hold of the breast of his coat and was pulling it towards
him". Le Fever will not die alone, abandoning his son. His peaceful

passing is described by pastor Sterne, who was often called to the bedside
of the dying:

> The blood and spirits of Le Fever [...] were waxing cold and slow [...];—
> the film forsook his eyes for a moment;—he looked up wistfully in my
> uncle Toby's face, —then cast a look upon his boy, —and that *ligament*,
> fine as it was, —was never broken.

The betrayal suffered by Roger Sterne when he entrusted his son to his
brother Richard's care has been avenged: "—the film returned to its
place, —the pulse fluttered, —stopp'd, —went on, —throbb'd, —stopp'd
again, —moved, —stopp'd, —shall I go on?—No". Laurence, the child, has
closed his father's eyes, but Sterne, his *therapon*, returns from his funeral
duties unsure of his own image.

Sermons given by Yorick alias Sterne[16]

The painter Magritte,[17] whose mother drowned herself in the Sambre River
after her husband made her sons spit on her crucifix, confesses:

> I'm nauseous when I see my paints and pallet and know I have to mess
> around with them. In my paintings, I show objects located where we
> never expect them to be. It is about a new vision where the viewer redis-
> covers his isolation and hears the silence of the world. Without modesty
> or pride, I did what I thought I had to do.

Sterne wrote his sermons in the same state of mind.

Tristram, an adult once again, consults the family archives where Yorick's
sermons have been stored. He finds the homily given at Le Fever's funeral,
and learns that Toby paid for the service and attended the funeral, holding
Billy by the hand during the ceremony in Yorick's church. The pastor has
carefully "chronicled down the date and the place and the occasion" of the
preaching of his sermons, inscribed on the first page, with:

> short comments upon the sermon itself, for instance:—I don't like it at
> all [...]—'tis all tritical. [...]—This is a flimsy kind of a composition, what
> was in my head when I made it?—For this sermon I shall be hanged, —
> for I have stolen it.

In the text, we see the drawing of a hand pointing an accusatory index: "Set
a thief to catch a thief". We are aware of Sterne's obsession with plagiarism
since Walter's discourse on the journey of ideas.

Yorick's sermons "take their originality from the way they are tied
together—with the lash of a whip—and from the comments they bear, like

pieces of music". On about a dozen sermons, Yorick has written "so-so"!
Two of them bear the mention "moderato", others "lentamente" and sometimes "adagio". Tristram is puzzled to read "a l'octava alta", and on the back
of another, "con strepito", "con l'arco" (with the bow) on one and "senza
l'arco" (without the bow) on another: "—All I know is that [...] he was a
musical man".

The enigmatic reference to the lash of the whip goes back to the lashes
Laurence received at his school in Halifax, as I mentioned in the first volume.
They are now setting the various tempos recorded by Yorick. His biogra-
pher[18] tells us of the drawings of soldiers, the initials LS and the inscription:
"This is Laurence Sterne" are drawn in the margins of his school notebook.
In his complete loneliness, his identity has to be proclaimed.

The sermons are chanted on a rhythm transforming whiplashes into musical scansion rendered by Shandean dashes. Le Fever's eulogy is the sermon
Yorick liked best. Unlike the others, it is "tied [...] with a yarn thrum, and
then rolled up [...] with a half sheet of dirty blue paper [...], which to this day
smells horribly of horse drugs". In the right upper corner of the last page,
"which, you know, is generally covered with your thumb", he had written:

> Bravo!: it was wrote besides with a crow's quill so faintly in a small Ital-
> ian hand as scarce to solicit the eye [...], —so that from the manner of
> it, it stands half-excused; and being wrote moreover with very pale ink,
> diluted almost to nothing, —'tis more like a *ritratto* of the shadow of
> vanity than of VANITY herself—[...] resembling rather a faint thought
> of transient applause.

Such is the simplicity of the creative mind, which Erwin Schrodinger,[19]
inventor of quantum mechanics equations, sees in Renaissance paintings:

> The portrait of the artist himself, as a humble side-figure [...] might as
> well be missing. [...] On the one hand mind is the artist who has produced
> the whole; in the accomplished work, however, it is but an insignificant
> accessory that might be absent without detracting from the total effect.

On the sermon, this humility is illustrated typographically: "[...] the word
was struck through sometime afterwards [...] with a line quite across it in
this manner: BRAVO as if he had retracted or was ashamed of the opinion
he had once entertained of it".

Toby keeps his word[20]

After the funeral, the captain appoints himself executor of Le Fever's modest worldly goods. He gives Trim the lieutenant's military coat and keeps
his sword in case Billy would have "a heart to fight [his] way with it in the

world". In the meantime, he teaches him to inscribe a regular polygon in a circle—as seen on the plans of the Vauban fortifications—and enrols him in a public school, from which he comes home for the Christmas and Easter holidays.

At 17, Billy stops studying Greek and Latin and asks for his father's sword, intending to join Marlborough's army allied with Emperor Charles XI of Germany against the Turks. Toby gives him the sword, polished to a shine, telling him: "If Fortune [fails thee], come back again to me, Le Fever, and we will shape thee another course". Four years later, the youth comes back after a series of misfortunes. He had written from Marseille six weeks before the accident with the window, and was expected at any moment. The year is 1623; Billy is twenty-one. Toby recommends him to his brother as the perfect preceptor for his nephew, saying: "He has a good heart".

Now, Sterne's praise of the captain's loyalty is abruptly cut short by Slop's gossip, claiming that the Shandy family heir's genital apparatus has been permanently damaged. Eight lines of asterisks synthesize the abhorrent habit of using patients as material for shocking stories. Sterne is revolted:

> What a jovial and merry world would this be [...], but for that inextricable labyrinth of debts, [...] melancholy, large jointures and lies! Doctor Slop, like a son of a w—, as my father called him for it—to exalt himself, —debased me to death—and made ten thousand times more of Susannah's accident then there was any grounds for; so that in a week's time, or less, it was in everybody's mouth, that poor Master Shandy ********* entirely.

Six lines of asterisks spread the rumour, just as Internet would do today.

Walter fell prey to the pity of those who mentioned the affair, and knew that his denials or his silence would only provoke jubilant certainty. Toby proposed an evidence-based solution: "I would show him publicly, at the market cross. —'Twill have no effect, said my father". Instead, Walter decides to support the boy's virility by putting him in breeches: "let the world say what it will". The theme of psychic and physical impotence could provide material for many seminars, but Sterne prefers to settle the matter on his own couch in two sessions.

More praise of manic depression[21]

Like Cervantes,[22] who published his second *Don Quixote* in 1616, the year of his death, Sterne writes with his back to the wall, under the pressure of tuberculosis and hostile rivals. He stands up to them with an obstinate "I wish", repeated throughout the novel. But let it be clear: his "I wish" rarely means "I desire", but rather "I would have liked", as the subjunctive indicates, right from the initial cry of Tristram's embryo. This is how Walter speaks of the window incident: "I wish it had never happened". But too late! How to transform what cannot be undone?—a question we are frequently asked in critical sessions. Sterne's solution is to use the bipolar energy of madness to write.

In a manic burst of "defiance of all mankind", Walter resolves to put his son into breeches, but beforehand, he decides to talk it over "judicially" with his wife in several "beds of justice". The expression refers to the custom of French kings to preside over sessions of parliament in person on a couch and impose their decisions. In this instance, the Latin *litis*—"bed"—also means "trial". Walter uses the word literally. To engage in free association about his decision, he lies down on the marital bed when such matters may be "examined on all sides with [...] coolness".

Once again, Shandy's bed is not "The Sofa" portrayed in Crébillon's novel.[23] The two writers met during Sterne's stay in France and planned to publish a humorous fictional correspondence about the controversy sparked by *Tristram Shandy*. But Walter is in no mood for a hoax; instead, he lists the different modes of decision-making throughout history, which relied on bipolarity.

For instance, the Goths and Vandals debated important questions in two stages: first in a drunken state, so their arguments would not lack vigour, and a second time sober, so they would not lack discernment. As for Walter:

> when any difficulty [...] [was] to be settled in the family which required great sobriety and great spirit too in its determination, —he fixed and set apart the first Sunday night in the month and the Saturday night which immediately preceded it to argue it over in bed with my mother. [...] From two different counsels taken in these two different humours, a middle one was generally found.

The idea is offered to the reader, who can try it out, as suggested under cover of four lines of asterisks.

According to the Medieval formula, "madness is more intelligence — *ingenium* — than destiny". Sterne makes use of his mood swings:

> My way is this:—In all nice and ticklish discussions—(of which Heaven knows, there are but too many in my book) [...], —I write one *half-full*, — and t'other *fasting*—and correct it full, for they all come to the same thing.[...]—in fasting 'tis a different story—I pay the world all possible attention and respect.—So that betwixt both, I write a careless kind of a civil, nonsensical, good-humoured Shandean book, which will do all your hearts good.—And all your heads too, —provided you understand it.

Indeed, the ups and downs of his Shandean analysis are good for my heart and my head, especially in this volume where he renders justice to children.

Bed of justice[24]

All things considered, an analyst's office is the place of a bed of justice where the analyst is called upon to witness "events without a witness", Dori Laub says, specifying: "a passionate witness" able to answer the question: "Who are you, for me to talk to you?" Born in Czernowitz, Ukraine, Dori was deported to a concentration camp in Romania when he was 6, and became an analyst of extreme traumas.

But Walter's attempt to bring justice to his son does not encounter a passionate witness, since "my mother" stays neutral instead of taking a stand. Let us enter Shandy's bedroom again on one of those Sundays. Walter half turns in bed and brings his pillow closer to his wife's to start the discussion: "—We should begin to think, Mrs Shandy, of putting this boy into breeches". The dialogue takes place in three parts, separated by her silences. Like a Lacanian analyst, she repeats her husband's words, avoiding any suggestions. Walter goes on:

> Not but the child looks extremely well [...] in his vests and tunics. —He does look very well in them, —replied my mother. [...] —But indeed he is growing a very tall lad [...]. —He is very tall for his age, indeed, —said my mother. —I cannot [...] imagine [...] who the deuce he takes after. —I cannot conceive, for my life [...] —Humph! [...] I am very short myself [...]. You are very short, Mr Shandy [...] Humph! quoth my father to himself a second time.

Walter's anxiety is projected onto the child:

> —When he gets these breeches made, cried my father in a higher tone, he'll look like a beast in 'em. —He will be very awkward in them at first, replied my mother. [...] They should be of leather, said my father, [...]. They will last him [...] the longest.

The question of the lining, more or less warm, follows: "—One must not give him his death however [...]. —By no means, said my mother—[...] and so the dialogue stood still again".

The silence that follows conjures up the shadow of Tristram's dead brother. Walter goes on to discuss the usefulness of pockets:

> There is no occasion for any, said my mother. [...] —Though if he gets a gig or a top—poor souls! [...] —Order it as you please, Mr Shandy. [...] —There's for you! Cried my father [...].—You never will distinguish, Mrs Shandy, [...], betwixt a point of pleasure and a point of convenience.

Sterne might have addressed this reproach to his mother or his wife. He stops there: "This was on the Sunday night;—and further this chapter saith not".

This chapter has said enough about stereotypes that deepen the absence of otherness. When castration was no longer symbolic but a real threat to Tristram, the bed of justice became denial of justice. As for Walter, who has "lost the horse, but not the saddle", he finds a more reliable other in Albertus Rubenius, the painter's son, author of a treatise about ancient dress: "— My father [...] ordered my breeches to be made with hooks and eyes". The first part of Volume 6, where Toby and Trim play the role of *therapons* for the dying lieutenant and his son, ends with fierce criticism of mainstream psychotherapies.

The second part is dedicated to the great game of war. "We are now going to enter upon a new scene of events" where, as Winnicott says, "The analyst must be able to play and display imagination" in order to reach a time out of time.

The art of war[25]

The previous scenes are summed up in a cumulative song style:

> Leave we then the breeches in the tailor's hands, with my father standing over him [...] reading him [...] a lecture upon the *latus clavus* [...]. Leave we my mother [...]—indifferent whether [the work] was done this way or that [...].—Leave we Slop likewise to the full profits of all my dishonours.—Leave we poor Le Fever to recover and get home from Marseilles as he can.—And last of all, —because the hardest of all—Let us leave, if possible, myself.—But 'tis impossible:—I must go along with you to the end of the work.

At first, we are enlisted to work on the bowling green, like "engineers of lost time", to use Marcel Duchamp's expression.[26] Sterne does not care whether we are fit for the job:

> If the reader has not a clear conception of the rood and a half of ground which lay at the bottom of my uncle Toby's kitchen garden [...], the fault is not in me, —but in his imagination—for I am sure I gave him so minute a description, I was almost ashamed of it.

The next scene opens a transitional space in which "the intertwining of images outside of reason, *aloga*", says Socrates in the Theatetus,[27] "produces the *logos*, speech and reason". Sterne calls this intertwining "the ceremony of the name".

The ceremony of the name

Toby's method was "the simplest one in the world". All he needed was the daily papers informing him of the ongoing military campaign. When a town was invested, he took the map of it and enlarged it in scale to the exact size of his bowling green. Next, "with the help of a large rope and a number of small piquets, he transferred the lines from the paper to the ground", determining the profile of the talus, the glacis and the exact height of parapets. He then set the corporal to work:

> The nature of the soil, —the nature of the work itself—and, above all, the good nature of my uncle Toby sitting by from morning to night and chatting kindly with the corporal upon past-done deeds, —left LABOUR little else but the ceremony of the name.

This expression brings to mind Wittgenstein's assertion[28]: "One could almost say that man is a ceremonial animal". After World War I, he returned to Cambridge in 1929 to create the bowling green of his "second philosophy", after spending ten years in Vienna plagued by traumatic revivals. No wonder he loved Sterne's novel.

"Labour" also refers to giving birth to speech emerging from "that which cannot be said" but is shown through "surviving images"—Aby Warburg's expression. The art historian used his library as a bowling green until he became delusional at the start of the Great War. He was haunted by the Franco Prussian War of 1870 which took place in his childhood and by the subsequent rise of mass anti-Semitism which he witnessed as an adolescent against his family in Hamburg. Like Toby, he took himself to be the commander-in-chief of the German military in World War I, and spread out maps of the war zones, asking his wife and children to bring him newspaper clippings to pin on the map the movements of troops on different fronts.

But unlike the captain, he had no one to assist him until his disciple Fritz Saxl returned from fighting in the Austrian army and visited him regularly at Binswanger's clinic where he was confined. Acting as *therapon* for his master, he assured him that his research was just as intelligent when conducted in a delusional mode. Since he kept shouting that he wanted to get out of this hell, Binswanger challenged him to give a one-hour lecture. With Saxl's help, Warburg prepared a *Lecture on Serpent Ritual* among the Hopis,[29] presented in April 1923 before the medical staff and the patients. It was a "ceremony of the name" that eventually allowed him to emerge from delusion, as he states in his conclusion: "What we have seen in this [...] summary of the snake cult is intended to show the change from real and substantial symbolism which appropriates the actual gestures to that symbolism which exists in thought alone".

This formulation applies to Trim and Toby's work as well. Building fortifications on the bowling green translates into actual gestures the symbolism which exists in thought. While Trim is working with his hands, Toby talks to him. This "talking cure" transforms them into subjects on the site of the battles where they once lay wounded, without speech and reason. When Toby takes command, he first identifies with Vauban by "[running] his first and second parallels betwixt two rows of cabbages and cauliflowers". Now, time is set in motion and he can emulate the Duke of Marlborough's attacks or defensive movements—terms encountered in the psychoanalytic vocabulary. "When the Duke [...] made a lodgement, —my uncle Toby made a lodgement too.—And when the face of a bastion was battered down or a defence ruined, —the corporal took his mattock and did as much".

I can imagine this "flimsy performance", as Sterne calls it. In my native Savoy, at the Little St. Bernard Pass, the road taken by Sardinian cannons goes over the mountains as far as the *Fort de la Redoute Ruinée*, and the Essaillon Forts built by Vauban still stand in the neighbouring valley. Recently, I caught a glimpse of the captain's fervour on the Italian side just beyond the pass, in a place called *Terre Noire*, where the names of hostages were called out in a ceremony of the name. They had been arrested in the valley in July 1944 and shot after they dug the pit into which they fell. I was a one-year-old and my father would have been among them had he not escaped once again.

The Franco-English wars[30]

Dates and places are of paramount importance to veterans. Sterne wishes us to remember those of the wars fought by Toby—that of the League of Augsburg between 1689 and 1697, in which the battle of Landen and the siege of Namur took place, the War of the Spanish Succession in 1697, brought to an end by the Treaty of Utrecht in 1713, leading to the demolition of the Dunkirk fortifications the year Sterne was born. "I have loved war too much", Louis XIV confessed on his deathbed in 1715.

Dr. Slop, who confused the transitional space of play with the horrors of war, will no doubt misunderstand the following passage:

> What an honest triumph in my uncle Toby's looks as he marched up to the ramparts! What intense pleasure swimming in his eye as he stood over the corporal, reading the paragraph ten times over to him as he was at work, lest, peradventure, he should make the breach an inch too wide—or leave it an inch too narrow. [...] [With what] spirit [...] my uncle Toby, with Trim behind him, sallied forth; — the one with the *Gazette* in his hand, —the other with a spade on his shoulder to execute the contents. [...] But when the *chamade* was beat and the corporal helped my uncle up it and followed with the colours in his hand to fix them upon the ramparts—Heaven! Earth! Sea!

Their war games on the bowling green are by no means virtual. Sterne chronicles the historical sequence of their achievements: in 1693, the Battle of Landen; 1695, the Siege of Namur; 1699, the decamping from Shandy Hall; 1701, the discovery of the bowling green therapy; 1702, the construction of a drawbridge after the sieges of Liège and Ruremond; 1703, the addition of two gates with portcullises; and at Christmas "a handsome sentry box painted white three times, to stand at the corner of the bowling green [...].—The sentry box was in case of rain".

Indifferent to this practical detail, Walter sees its phallic structure as worthy of Louis XIV's style of carrying out his campaigns. "But let us go on". After the sentry box, towns still needed to be added, for "there was no town at that time within the polygon". Since many towns fell in 1703, it occurred to the corporal that "to talk of taking so many towns without one TOWN to show for it—was very nonsensical..." The verb is important, since it is a matter of showing in order to be able to speak. "[He] proposed a little model of a town built for them [...], and clapped within the interior polygon to serve for all. My uncle Toby felt the good of the project instantly". Its style would be representative of cities in Brabant and Flaunders, "with every house standing on its own, so that they could reshape the town as they pleased". And the list of sieges continues:

From 1704 to 1706, "the perfect Proteus was, in turn", one of a dozen towns whose names are enumerated:

> In the fourth year, my uncle Toby, thinking a town looked foolishly without a church, added [...] one with a steeple.—Trim was for having bells in it;—my uncle Toby said the mettle had better be cast into [...] half a dozen brass [cannons], —planted three and three on each side of [the] sentry box.

This is what eventually led to "the hobby-horsical affair" of tearing up Walter's jackboots and the damage to the window sash of Tristram's nursery.

Apollinaire, the "starry head" poet hit by shrapnel through his helmet in 1916, invented the word "surrealism" in 1917[31] for situations as hobby-horsical as Toby's. But in Sterne's novel, the most surrealistic event is yet to come. In 1708, the year when the English took Lille, Ghent and Bruges, Toby, whose imagination was inflamed by newspaper accounts, regretted not having gunpowder; "and 'twas well for the Shandy family", Sterne comments, since he would have blown away the entire property. "SOMETHING therefore was wanting, as *succedaneum* [...], —without which this had been objected to by military critics to the end of the world".

Trim, "whose principal strength lay in invention" thinks of three objects that he can use for this purpose. Three "found objects"—dear to Surrealists—trifling, worthless things which become talismans when the future merges with the past.

Memory of the future[32]

Trim's found objects are gifts that "poor Tom", his brother, gave him before being arrested by the Inquisition: a military Montero cap, "scarlet, of a superfine Spanish cloth [...] mounted all around with fur", and "two Turkish tobacco pipes with flexible tubes of Morocco leather and gold wire", tipped at their ends, one with ivory and the other with ebony. Transformed into artillery, they would set off tremendous firing. The following day was when "the most memorable attack in the whole war" would take place—against Lille—"the most gallant and obstinate on both sides—and [...] the most bloody too". Toby prepared himself for it with unaccustomed solemnity, asking Trim the night before to bring him his Ramillies wig lying in the corner of an old campaign trunk by his bedside.

The morning of D-day is described in mock-heroic style. Trim is already gone. Toby, usually very punctual, wrestles to put on his regimental coat without his help. He finally sallies out at ten o'clock, a half hour later than usual. Astounded, he sees that the corporal has started the attack without him, disobeying orders: "The corporal..." But Sterne can't go on. A powerful emotion overwhelms him once again.[33] His father's memory resurfaces—as he describes another facet of the corporal—and no doubt of ensign Sterne. It is for him that the funeral eulogy addressed to the corporal is intended:

> Tread lightly on his ashes, ye men of genius, —for he was your kinsman. Weed his grave clean, ye men of goodness, —for he was your brother.— Oh corporal! had I thee but now, —now that I am able to give thee a dinner and protection, —how would I cherish thee! [...]—But alas! alas! alas! [...] thou art gone;—thy genius fled up to the stars from whence it came;—and that warm heart of thine, with all its generous and open vessels, compressed into a clod of the valley!

This poignant lyricism transports Sterne to Toby's future military funeral:

> — But what—what is this to that future and dreaded page where I look towards the velvet pall, decorated with the military ensigns of thy master, —the first, —the foremost of created beings;—where I shall see thee, faithful servant! Laying his sword and scabbard with a trembling hand across his coffin and then returning pale as ashes to the door to take his mourning horse by the bridle to follow his hearse...

Walter attends his brother's funeral, in contrast with Roger Sterne's brothers who did not mourn him:

> All my father's systems shall be baffled by his sorrows; and, in spite of his philosophy, I shall behold him, as he inspects the lacquered plate, twice taking his spectacles from off his nose to wipe away the dew which nature has shed upon them [...]—O Toby! In what corner of the world shall I seek thy fellow?—Gracious powers! which erst have opened the lips of the dumb in his distress and made the tongue of the stammerer

speak plain, —when I shall arrive at this dreaded page, deal not with me, then, with a stinted hand.

The powers that opened Sterne's lips in his distress, so that he might tell Le Fever's story, also open the way to a "memory of the future". This expression, coined by Kurt Vonnegut in his novel *Slaughterhouse-Five*[34] was probably borrowed by Bion[35] and became *A Memoir of the Future* about his war.

Earlier, another captain, William Rivers, a neurologist, anthropologist and psychoanalyst for traumatised officers at Craiglockardt in Scotland, heard the poet Siegried Sassoon tell him when he returned wounded from the front:

> Sometimes, when you're alone in the trenches at night you get the sense of something ancient. One trench we held, it had skulls in the side, embedded [...]. It was actually easier to believe they were men from Marlborough's army, than to think they'd been alive a year ago. It was as if all the other wars had distilled themselves into this war. A hundred years from now they'll still be ploughing up skulls. And I seemed to be in that time and looking back. I think I saw our ghosts.[36]

After a similar prophetic vision, Sterne comes back to the present of his narrative. The artillery attack on the bowling green can begin. The plan the corporal devised the night before was sure to succeed:

> [...] by means of his two Turkish tobacco pipes, with [...] three smaller tubes of wash leather at each of their lower ends to be tagg'd by the same number of tin pipes fitted to the touch holes and sealed with clay next the cannon [...]—he should be able to fire the six field pieces all together and with the same ease as to fire one.

His ingenuity leads Sterne to make an observation. The advancement of knowledge is not the result of abstract speculation, but is created, like his novel, "from hints [of] tags and jags":

> Heaven! Thou knowest how I love them, —[the crazy inventors]. I would give the shirt off my back [to them].—Thou art a fool, Shandy, says Eugenius, —for thou hast but a dozen in the world, —and 'twill break up thy set.—No matter for that, Eugenius. I would give [my] shirt to be burnt into tinder, were it only to satisfy one feverish inquirer.

The corporal spent the night perfecting his project, and "having [charged] his cannon [...] to the top with tobacco, —he went with contentment to bed". The next morning, wearing his Montero cap, "he slipped out ten minutes before Toby, to give the enemy a shot or two", but he got carried away. When his master saw him "furiously playing off his two cross batteries at the same time against the counterguard which faced the counterscarp where the attack was to be made that morning", the two puffs he had planned had lead "from puff to puff" to a proper attack. Learning about this feat later, Walter reflected that "it was well his brother had not to make his will that day".

For once, Toby is enraged; an explosion is imminent. Suspecting nothing, Trim hands the ivory pipe to his master, who takes it, looks at it for half a minute and returns it. This sequence is repeated again, with minor variations. The second time, the captain raises the pipe halfway to his mouth, then gives it back. Completely absorbed in what he is doing, Trim redoubles the attack, oblivious to his master's state of mind. At last, Toby is disarmed:

> —my uncle Toby smiled, —then looked grave, —then smiled for a moment, —then looked serious for a long time.—Give me hold of [it], Trim, said my uncle Toby;—[he] put it to his lips, —drew it back directly, —gave a peep over the hornbeam hedge;—never did my uncle Toby's mouth water so much for a pipe in his life.—[He] retired into the sentry box with the pipe in his hand.

But his safe retreat is short-lived, for "the serpent in Genesis—which is what the ingenious tube turned into—is about to draw into the garden the Eve in the house next door. Pastor Sterne tries to warn Toby: "Dear uncle Toby! don't go into the sentry box with the pipe, —there's no trusting a man's self with such a thing in such a corner".

Freud couldn't have said it better. In fact, the novel soon drifts towards the psychoanalysis of repressed sexual desire after an event that puts an end to war games. Toby's courtship, recounted in the last two volumes, starts here with a sudden disruption that empties the bowling green.

Tabula rasa[37]

Sterne prepares the reader for an about-face as abrupt as that made by Freud[38] when he announced to Fliess in September 1897 that he was abandoning the psychoanalysis of trauma—refusing to believe that cases of child sexual abuse were so frequent and preferring to see them as fantasies. As for Sterne, he enlists us without warning:

> I beg the reader will assist me here to wheel off my uncle Toby's ordnance behind the scenes— to remove his sentry box and clear the theatre, if possible [...];—that done [...], we'll sweep the stage with a new broom, —draw up the curtain and exhibit my uncle Toby dressed in a new character, throughout which the world can have no idea how he will act: and yet, if pity be akin to love—and bravery no alien to it, you have seen enough of my uncle Toby in these to trace these 'family likenesses' betwixt the two passions.

Wittgenstein will speak of "family resemblances".

The reader remains perplexed. Sterne enlightens him no further, for he himself is puzzled. The question is not new, since Socrates discussed it in the *Symposium*[39] when, through the prophetess Diotima, he proposed a definition of Eros radically different from those offered by the other guests. At the end of the dialogue, Alcibiades informs us that Socrates may have conceived this definition on the battlefield. As I often point out, these two forms of Eros depend on whether we are dealing with repressed desire or with revivals of the cut-out unconscious.

Sterne seems to have heard my reflection, for he turns to me to emphasize the captain's *modesty*, which leaves him defenceless in the face of strategies of desire:

> There was, madam, in my uncle Toby, a singleness of heart which misled him so far out of the little serpentine tracks in which things of this nature usually go on.]—With all this, madam [...] my uncle Toby had that unparalleled modesty of nature I once told you of, and which [...] stood eternal sentry upon his feelings.

Here, Sterne turns a watchful eye on himself: "But where am I going? These reflections crowd in upon me ten pages at least too soon, and take up that time which I ought to bestow upon facts".

This is what happens when we hasten to untangle the intricacies of repression and neglect the catastrophes of History.

Return to history[40]

History makes its entrance through the enumeration of heroes of ancient and modern times who "never felt what the sting of love was". Sterne explains: "The truth is, they had all of them something else to do, —and so had my uncle Toby—till Fate [...] basely patched up the Peace of Utrecht.—Believe me, sirs, 'twas the worst deed she did that year". But why does he say "sirs", won't he talk to me anymore? The year is 1713, when the Peace of Utrecht was signed, soldiers returned home and Laurence was conceived—and that was not Fate's worst deed that year!

But for the captain, the consequences were quite contrary. He almost lost his appetite for sieges, and "to the end of his life, he never could hear Utrecht mentioned [...] without fetching a sigh as if his heart would break in twain. My father [...] would always console my uncle Toby upon these occasions", though sarcastically:

> —Never mind, brother Toby, [...]—by God's blessing we shall have another war break out again some of these days; and when it goes, —the belligerent powers [...] cannot keep us out of play—I defy 'em, my dear Toby, [...] to take countries without taking towns, —or towns without sieges.

Walter's scorn is not aimed at Toby's military career, gladly left to younger brothers, but at his transitional space, which he attacks mercilessly:

> My uncle Toby never took this backstroke of my father's at his hobby-horse kindly.—He thought the stroke ungenerous; and the more so because in striking the horse he hit the rider too, and in the most dishonourable part a blow could fall; so that, upon these occasions, he always laid down his pipe upon the table with more fire to defend himself than common.

One evening, before going to bed, Walter set aside his disdain in order to write down Toby's "apologetical oration".

The reader is informed by the adult Tristram:

> I have had the good fortune to meet with my uncle Toby's 'Justification of His Own Principles and Conduct in Wishing to Continue the War' amongst my father's papers, with here and there an insertion of his own, betwixt two crooks [...]. I have read over this apologetical oration [...] a hundred times and think it so fine a model of defence, —[showing] so sweet a temperament of gallantry and good principles in him, that I give it to the world word for word.

Toby's discourse on arms and letters

Toby begins by saying "I"—the letter standing for the subject is in bold print:

> I am not insensible, brother Shandy, that when a man whose profession is arms wishes [...] for war, —it has an ill aspect to the world. [...] For this cause, if a soldier is a prudent man [...], he will be cautious of doing it even to a friend, —lest he may suffer in his esteem.—But if his heart is overcharged and a secret sigh for arms must have its vent, he will reserve it for the ear of a brother who knows his character to the bottom and what his true notions, dispositions and principles of honour are.

Toby goes on to explore the transference between them:

> But such as I am, you, my dear brother Shandy, who have sucked the same breast with me—and with whom I have been brought up from my cradle, —and from whose knowledge [...] I have concealed no one action of my life and scarce a thought in it;—such as I am, brother, you must by this time know me.

A soldier is not a perpetrator:

> Tell me then, [...] upon which of [my deeds] it is that when I condemned the Peace of Utrecht and grieved the war was not carried on with vigour a little longer, you should think [I] did it upon unworthy views; [...]. Tell me, brother Shandy, upon what one deed of mine do you ground it?

When, as a schoolboy, the sound of drums made his heart start racing, was it his fault? "Because [...] my heart panted for war, —was it a proof it could not ache for the distress of war too? O brother! 'tis one thing for a soldier to gather laurels, —and 'tis another to scatter cypress".
Toby continues in this Quixotic vein:

> —'Tis one thing, brother Shandy, for a soldier to hazard his own life, — to leap first down into a trench where he is sure to be cut in pieces, [...]—and 'tis another thing to reflect on the miseries of war;—to view the desolations of whole countries.

The oration advances the notion of "just war", waged by NECESSITY, in the name of liberty and honour, by peaceful and harmless people getting together with their swords in their hands "to keep the ambitious and the turbulent within bounds". Toby ends his speech with the "infinite delight" he and the corporal have taken in carrying out the sieges on the bowling green.
Returning to his narrative, Sterne feels distressed by the *tabula rasa* performed on the bowling green. I feel the same way when time stops during the sessions.

Downturn[41]

> When a man is telling a story in the strange way I do mine, he is obliged continually to be going backwards and forwards to keep all tight together in the reader's fancy;—[...] there is so much unfixed and equivocal matter starting up, with so many breaks and gaps in it [...], I hang up in some of the darkest passages, knowing that the world is apt to lose its way, [...]—and now, you see, I am lost myself.

In such circumstances, one may turn to genetics. Sterne blames his failure on a congenital cerebral defect. "But 'tis my father's fault. [...] As you will perceive] whenever my brains come to be dissected". He does not yet know that, in fact, dissection of his stolen corpse would take place, although it was forbidden at the time, and that a medical student would recognise his face. His remains, not found until 1969, were buried near his Coxwold rectory, familiarly called "Shandy Hall" by pilgrims. As early as 1761, Sterne describes his own autopsy: "You will perceive, without spectacles, that [my father] has left a large uneven thread, as you sometimes see in an unsaleable piece of cambric".

What must he do now to take up the thread of his story? First, get rid of the paragraph on neuronal causality since, he says: "'tis morally impracticable"; then start the chapter again, with a new metaphor on the discord between Toby's hobby horse and its rider: "— his horse [...] flung him, —and somewhat viciously".

The new trope has a dynamic quality that connects the captain's singular story with History—particularly with Queen Mary's objection to the destruction of the Port of Dunkirk, requested by the Treaty of Utrecht. The queen of England, "who was but a woman", heeded the pleas of the town's people not to demolish the wharf. The process took nine months, from March to November 1713. "A fatal interval of inactivity"! Sterne exclaims, since "the peace of Utrecht was within an ace of creating the same shyness betwixt Toby and his hobby horse as it did between the queen and the rest of the confederating powers". On the next page, five lines of asterisks convey the feeling of another imminent catastrophe.

This period of inactivity was devastating for both veterans. "The corporal was for beginning the demolition by making a breech in the ramparts", but Toby was afraid that "because the French are treacherous as devils, [although] they don't want personal bravery, they will attack the English garrison". Finally, the captain ordered that fort Louis be demolished first, then the wharf, followed by the citadel, "which will be blown up into the air, and, having done that, corporal, we'll embark for England".

A memory of the future takes us to 1940, when British troops sailed from the French beaches through the English Channel. Trim brings his master back to earth: "We are there, quoth the corporal.—Very true, said my uncle Toby—looking at the church". But his heart is no longer in it. Speaking from experience, Sterne comments: "the magic left the mind the weaker;— STILLNESS, with SILENCE at her back, entered the solitary parlour and drew their gauzy mantle over my uncle Toby's head".

The Treaty of Utrecht separated the hobby horse from his rider, just as a psychotropic drug might have done. Heart-wrenching "no longer" accumulates, like the "Nevermore" in Poe's "Raven"[42]:

No longer Amberg and Rheinberg and [...] Dendermond [...] hurried on the blood:—no longer did saps and mines and blinds and gabions and palisades, keep out this fair enemy of man's repose: —no more could my uncle Toby, after passing the French lines as he ate his egg at supper, from thence break into the heart of France [...] and fix the royal standard upon the tower of the *Bastile*...

Instead, blood is being shed on the manuscript, since Sterne is bedridden with tuberculosis again and feels his dreams abandoning him. He comes up with the idea that he might ride his own hobby horse and "invade" France, where he plans to write about Toby's amours.

Toby's courtship[43]

Certain innuendos warn us that the captain will have to withstand the siege of a tougher enemy than the French—that of his formidable neighbour Mrs. Wadman. For the moment, we are not yet in the know, but we can imagine that his psyche—like those in the myth Socrates depicts in *Phaedrus*[44]—will no longer follow the god Mars, but rather Apollo and his sister Aphrodite. "Softer visions, —gentler vibrations stole sweetly in upon his slumbers;—the trumpet of war fell out of his hands;—he took up the lute, sweet instrument! of all others the most delicate! The most difficult"!

Toby's amours are lying in wait in Sterne's "writing box", but he has no idea how to begin. Starting with a definition of love proves to be a daunting task. He could focus, like Walter, on questions like "whether love is a disease [...], whether the seat of it is in the brain or liver..." But no, like his author, he hates dissertations! Walter's "theories of love [...] crucified my uncle Toby's mind almost as much as his amours themselves". The story:

> will come out of itself by and by.—All I contend for is that I am not obliged to set out with a definition of what love is. [...] Let love therefore be what it will, —my uncle Toby fell into it.

But this advice is not so easy to follow. As a student, I used to hand in blank dissertations, terrified by the required three-stage writing plan. So imagine my surprise when I saw a real blank page used by Sterne as a typographical illustration at the end of this volume.

The blank page[45]

Our help is requested once again, this time to draw the portrait of the fair lady who stole Toby's heart:

> Call for pen and ink—here's paper ready to your hand.—Sit down, sir, paint her to your own mind—as like your mistress as you can, —as unlike your wife as your conscience will let you—'tis all one to me;—please but your own fancy in it.

Cervantes taught us that the Lady of One's Thoughts, invented in the 12th century by the warrior poets of courtly love, is a vacant place. Dulcinea is merely an address which makes thinking possible when everything has fallen apart. Sterne, who always has "a Dulcinea in mind", knows that the blank page must remain so. He congratulates his book for the "virginal page" actually inserted into the novel. "Thrice happy book! Thou wilt have one page at least, within thy covers, which MALICE will not blacken and IGNORANCE cannot misrepresent".

The author's Dulcinea, like Cervantes's, is literature. She is the "Far away Lady" who guides the pen and protects the writer from imbeciles. Just when Sterne has run out of ideas, she whispers that he should introduce Toby's courtship through the voice of gossip: "Susannah was informed by an express from Mrs Bridget of my uncle Toby's falling in love with her mistress fifteen days before it happened". We are given the news when we enter Shandy's bedroom for the third time.

For once, Mrs. Shandy initiates the dialogue to inform her husband:

> Now, my father [...] was musing within himself about the hardships of matrimony as my mother broke silence. '—My brother Toby is going to be married to Mrs. Wadman.—Then he will never be able to lie diagonally in his bed again as long as he lives,

Walter answers. After staying silent as usual, she insists:

> If he marries, 'twill be the worse for us. [...] —Not a cherry stone, said my father; —he may as well batter away his means upon that as anything else. —To be sure, said my mother. [...] —It will be some amusement to him, too, —said my father. —A very great one, answered my mother.

And she let fly her Parthian arrow: "...if he should have children. —Lord have mercy upon me, —said my father to himself".

Four lines of asterisks give us ample time to imagine the ripples caused by this stone thrown into the pond. A prohibition to procreate has just been pronounced loud and clear. Sterne is relieved to have imparted the truth to posterity:

> I am now beginning to get fairly into my work; and by the help of a vegetable diet, with a few of the cold seeds, I make no doubt but I shall be able to go on with my uncle Toby's story and my own in a tolerably straight line.

But alas, when he looks back at the path he has travelled, he notices that the line has curves and indentations, ins and outs, highs and lows, corresponding to moments of enthusiasm and periods of dejection. It is not the "tolerably straight line" expected by critics. Still, instead of sinking into melancholia, he draws winding lines in a gesture of defiance to illustrate his meanders. I will show them to those who denigrate Shandean psychoanalysis, for his path is neither the "right line" of causalist certainties nor "the best line! of cabbage planters".

"What a journey"! Sterne exclaims, as he is about to sail to France without a passport in the middle of the Seven Years' War.

Notes

1 Sterne, L., *Tristram Shandy,* op. cit., Vol. 6, chs. I–II; Vol. 9, ch.VI; Vol. 1, ch.XII.
2 *La Folie Tristan d'Oxford* and *La Folie Tristran de Berne* (late 12th century), Hoepffner, Publications de la faculté des lettres de l'Université de Strasbourg, 1943, 1949.
3 Sterne, L., *Tristram Shandy*, op. cit., Vol. 1, ch. XII.
4 De Cervantes, M., *Don Quixote II*, op. cit., ch. 25.
5 Sterne, L., *Tristram Shandy*, op. cit., Vol. 6, ch. III.
6 Sterne, L., *Tristram Shandy*, op. cit., Vol. 5, chs. X–XI.
7 Schmitt, J.-C., *Ghost in the Middle Ages: The Living and the Dead in Medieval Society*, University of Chicago Press, 1999.
8 Sterne, L., *Tristram Shandy*, op. cit., Vol. 6, ch. VI.
9 Davoine, F., Gaudillière, J.-M., *History Beyond Trauma*, New York: Other Press, 2004.
10 Sterne, L. *Tristram Shandy*, op. cit., Vol. 6, ch. VII.
11 Pinnington, N. J., *A New History of Medieval Japanese Theatre: Noh and Kyogen from 1300 to 1600*, Cham, Switzerland: Palgrave Macmillan, 2019.
12 De Cervantes, M., *Don Quixote I*, op. cit., chs. 24 and 36.
13 De Cervantes, M., *Don Quixote I*, op. cit., ch. 38.
14 Sterne, L., *Tristram Shandy*, op. cit., Vol. 6, chs. VIII–X.
15 Kubler-Ross, E., *On Death and Dying*, New York: Scribner, 1993.
16 Sterne, L., *Tristram Shandy*, op. cit., Vol. 6, ch. XI.
17 Magritte, R., *Selected Writings*, Minneapolis, MN: University of Minnesota Press, 2016; Roisin, J., *René Magritte. La première vie de l'homme au chapeau melon* (The First Life of the Man with the Bowler Hat), Bruxelles: Impressions Nouvelles, 2014.
18 Ross, I. C., *Laurence Sterne: A Life*, Oxford University Press, 2001, p. 35.
19 Schröedinger, E., *What Is Life? Mind and Matter*, Cambridge, UK: Cambridge University Press, 1958.
20 Sterne, L., *Tristram Shandy*, op. cit., Vol. 6, chs. XII–XIV.
21 Sterne, L., *Tristram Shandy*, op. cit., Vol. 6, chs. XV–XVI.
22 De Cervantes, M., *Don Quixote II*, op. cit.
23 Grébillon, C. P. J. de, *The Soda: A Moral Tale*, Folio Society, 1951.
24 Sterne, L., *Tristram Shandy*, op. cit., Vol. 6, chs. XVIII–XIX.
25 Sterne, L., *Tristram Shandy*, op. cit., Vol. 6, chs. XX–XXI.
26 Duchamp, M., *The Engineer of the Lost Time*, Agras Publications (Greece), 1989.
27 Plato, *Theatetus*, New York: The Liberal Arts Press, 1955.
28 Wittgenstein, L., *Remarks on Frazer's Golden Bough*, op. cit.
29 Warburg, A., *A Lecture on Serpent Ritual*, op. cit.
30 Sterne, L., *Tristram Shandy*, op. cit., Vol. 6, chs. XXI–XXII.
31 Letter to Paul Dermée, March 1917, in Becker, A., *Une biographie de guerre 1914–1918*, Paris: Tallandier, 2009.
32 Sterne, L., *Tristram Shandy*, op. cit., Vol. 6, chs. XXIV–XXV.

33 Sterne, L., *Tristram Shandy*, op. cit., Vol. 3, ch. XXXIV.
34 Vonnegut, K., *Slaughterhouse-Five,* op. cit.
35 Bion, W., *The Long Week-End, All My Sins Remembered, A Memoir of the Future,* op. cit.
36 Pat Barker, *Regeneration Trilogy,* London: Penguin Books 1995.
37 Sterne, L., *Tristram Shandy*, op. cit., Vol. 6, ch. XXIX.
38 Freud, S., letter to Fliess, October 1897, in *The Complete Letters of Sigmund Freud to Wilhelm Fliess, 1887–1904,* Cambridge, MA: Harvard University Press, 1986.
39 Plato, *Symposium,* op. cit.
40 Sterne, L., *Tristram Shandy*, op. cit., Vol. 6, chs. XXX–XXXI.
41 Sterne, L., *Tristram Shandy,* Vol. 6, chs. XXXIII–XXXV.
42 Poe, E.A., *The Complete Poetry of Edgar Allan Poe,* Kolkata: Signet Classics, 2008; "The Raven", p. 92.
43 Sterne, L., *Tristram Shandy*, op. cit. chs. XXXVI–XXXVII.
44 Plato, *Phaedrus,* Newburyport, MA: Focus Publishing/R. Pullins Co., 2003.
45 Sterne, L., *Tristam Shandy,* op. cit, Vol. 6, ch. XXXVIII.

7

Journey to France

This volume relates Sterne's journey through France between January 1762 and May 1764. He is 48 and this is his first trip abroad. He will spend six months in Paris, where he is lionized in the salons of d'Holbach and de La Poupelinière, and receive a passport from the Duke of Choiseul, foreign minister under Louis XV. There, he declares: "I shandy it more than ever", but seeing his tuberculosis worsen, he heads for Occitania, the land of troubadours, staying near Toulouse until March 1764. Sterne's account is not a travel diary, but the record of a race across France against death, "the man in black", whom he outwits with laughter, as his master Rabelais taught him.

Reanimation[1]

A resounding "No" starts the volume—no to "the vile cough which then tormented me and which to this hour I dread worse than the Devil". If it gives him some respite, he plans to write two volumes a year. Though he only sleeps five hours a night, Sterne writes: "Now, as for my spirits, little have I to lay to their charge [...] (unless the mounting me upon a long stick and playing the fool with me nineteen hours out of twenty-four)". He thanks them, in terms that remind me of the Sioux medicine man Joe Eagle Elk during a ceremony on the Rosebud Reservation in South Dakota:

> In no one moment [...] have ye once deserted me [...]; in dangers ye gilded my horizon with hope, and when DEATH himself knocked at my door, —ye had him come again, and in so gay a tone of careless indifference [...] that he doubted of his commission.

Still, the Black Man is after him again:

> This son of a whore, Eugenius, has found out my lodgings, [when] I have forty volumes to write, and forty thousand things to say and do which

DOI: 10.4324/9781003224907-7

nobody in the world will say and do for me except thyself; and so thou seest he has got me by the throat.

Indeed, his friend could hardly hear him across the table. He plans to "fly to France for his life", gather "the few scatter'd spirits" he has left and if:

> these two spider legs of mine [...] are able to support me [...] I will lead him a dance he little thinks of, —for I will gallop [...] without looking once behind me to the banks of the Garonne, and if I hear him clattering at my heels, —I'll scamper away to the world's end, where, if he follows me, I pray God he may break his neck.—He runs more risk there, said Eugenius, than thou.

Volume 7 would have to wait to be written, two years later, in 1764, when Sterne returned to foggy Yorkshire. But now he is about to leave: "Eugenius [...] led me to my chaise.—*Allons*! Said I; the post boy gave a crack with his whip;—off I went like a cannon, and in half a dozen bounds got into Dover".

Seasickness[2]

When the British introduced the Grand Tour tradition across Europe, they invented tourism. Sterne invented anti-tourism:

> —A man should know something of his own country too before he goes abroad, —and I never gave a peep into Rochester church, or took notice of the dock of Chatham, or visited St Thomas at Canterbury, though they all three laid in my way.

Too late! "Without arguing the matter with Thomas Becket, I skipped into the boat under sail".

Asked if Death has not come on board as well, the captain, "a cursed liar", assures Sterne that he will not have time to be sick, although he is already:

> sick as a horse. [...]—When shall we get to land, captain?—They have hearts like stones.—O I am deadly sick!—Reach me that thing, boy;—I wish I was at the bottom.— Madam! How is it with you?—Undone! undone! un—O! undone! sir.

Indeed, the lady is driven round the bend:

> — What the first time?—No, 'tis the second, third, sixth, tenth time, sir, —hey-day—what a trampling overheard!—Hollo! Cabin boy! what's the matter—The wind chopp'd about! 'Tis Death!—Then I shall meet him

full in the face. What luck!—'Tis chopp'd about again, master.—O the devil chop it— Captain, quoth she, for Heaven's sake, let us get ashore.

Tempestuous seas, a recurrent theme in the writing of Sterne's favourite authors, offer him the chance to toss into the Channel his fear of death as well as the occasion to meet a lady who shares his distress. At the start of *A Sentimental Journey*, he portrays her landing with him in Calais in 1765, where their fingers touch in steamy sensuality when he leads her to this post-chaise. But on his first landing, he gives priority to his itinerary, described with the precision of a Baedeker guidebook. After hesitating for half a day between three routes leading to Paris, he will choose the second through Amiens, which we shall follow stage by stage.

First stage: Calais[3]

Sterne's attitude would discourage the most talented tour operator:

> Now I think it very much amiss—that a man cannot go quietly through a town and let it alone when it does not meddle with him, but that he must be turning about and drawing his pen at every kennel he crosses over.

He knows no more about Calais—*Calatium, Calesium*—than he does about Cairo, but he is willing to bet that he could "write a chapter upon Calais as long as [his] arm" and could even serve as a guide to the city:

> a small village belonging to one of the first Counts de Guines, — its fourteen thousand inhabitants, [...] its convents, great square [...], town house [...], district quarter inhabited solely by sailors and fishermen [...]. A traveller [...] must not omit [...] La Tour de Guet [...].

We might add the Six Burghers of Calais (who offered their lives to the king of England to save the city in 1346), sculpted by Rodin in 1895 and exhibited around the world. Sterne foresees the enticing posters serving the aims of mass tourism: "But courage! gentle reader!—I scorn it;—'tis enough to have thee in my power;—but to make use of the advantage which the fortune of the pen has now gained over thee".

Let us gallop after him.

Second stage: Boulogne[4]

Sterne arrives at an inn at BOULOGNE: "hah!—so we are all got together— debtors and sinners before heaven; a jolly set of us, —but I can't stay and quaff it off with you:—I am pursued like a hundred devils". His guarded attitude raises suspicion:

> —Tis for high treason, quoth a very little man, whispering [...] to a very tall man [...].—Or else for murder, quoth the tall man [...] No, quoth a third, the gentleman has been committing—[...]. No; it can't be that, quoth a fourth (watching him woo the host's daughter). — 'Tis certainly for debt, quoth a fifth...

And so on. This is what happens when one refuses to drink with the locals.

His paranoia is projected onto the reader: "Do stop that death-looking, long-striding scoundrel of a scare-sinner [...];—he never would have followed me but for you; [...] I beseech you, madam;—do, dear lady". The agency of the Lady is more essential than ever when all trust seems lost; it does its work well, for now he "hurries on his ideas ninety-times faster than the vehicle" taking him to Montreuil. Sterne curses the postillon, but this time with reason: "Something is always wrong in a French post-chaise [...]. What's wrong now?—*Diable!*—a rope's broke!—a knot has slipped!—a staple's drawn! [...]—a tag, a rag, a jag, a strap, a buckle [...] want altering". His writing has regained its rhythm to punctuate the tricks used to extract money from the English tourist. When the coach stops, Sterne holds up "a four-and-twenty *sous* piece": "the dog grinn'd [...] from his right ear to his left, [showing] such a pearly row of teeth that Sovereinty would have pawn'd her jewels for them. Just Heaven! What masticators!—What bread"!

Still, the famous baguette will have to await Napoleon's era to be invented.

Third stage: Montreuil, Abbeville[5]

Aside from French bread, Sterne does not find much to admire at the next stage either. In his opinion, no French city looks so good on the map and so pitiful in reality as MONTREUIL, except for the innkeeper's daughter who has been eighteen months in Amiens and six in Paris, learning to knit, to sew, to dance, "and does the little coquetries very well". Indeed, he adds: "within the five minutes that I have stood looking at her, she has let fall at least a dozen loops in a white thread stocking". This is enough to prompt him to image *Janatone* (pronounced with an English accent) posing for a drawing by Reynolds. But "Your Worships choose rather that I give you the length and [...] height of the great parish church, or a drawing of the fascade of the Abbey of St Austrebert [...];—everything is just as the masons and carpenters left them— and if the belief in Christ continues so long, will be so these fifty years to come, your worships [...] may all measure them at your leisure".

Is his visionary brain foreseeing the French Revolution? In fact, his mind is meandering in the 16th century when Ronsard[6] sang the praises of his

Helen, anticipating the loss of her charms. But his style resembles that of Hogarth in the *Harlot's Progress*: "[...] he who measures thee, Jeanneton, must do it now [...], thou mayest grow out like a pumpkin and lose thy shapes, —[...] nay, thou mayest go off like a hussy—and lose thyself". I was ready to object, but he sped off, seizing the occasion to keep ahead of Death, which "might be much nearer me than I imagined". He hastens to ABBEV-ILLE where he hopes to see how they card and spin, but "the carders and spinners were all gone to bed". This sets him thinking about his final sleep.

It is here in chapter XII that Sterne writes the premonitory passage already quoted, spelling out his last wishes for the day of "this great catastrophe". He wishes:

> that it happen not [...] in my own house, — but rather in some decent inn;—at home, I know it, —the concern of my friends and the last ser-vices of wiping my brows and smoothing my pillow which the quivering hand of pale affection shall pay me, will so crucify my soul that I shall die of a distemper which my physician is not aware of.

His final wish will be realised in a rented apartment, where he died on 18 March 1768 in London.

Fourth stage: Amiens[7]

Now that Death may be nearer than he imagines, Sterne objects to inter-preting his "rolling about" as "unquietness"—or hyperactivity, as we would say today. "I think differently, that so much of motion is so much of life and so much of joy—and that to stand still or get on slowly is death and the devil". Hence his early departure from the inn:

> Let the horses be in the chaise exactly by four in the the morning.—Yes, by four, Sir, —or by *Genevieve!* I'll raise a clatter in the house, shall wake the dead. [...] Hollo! Ho!—the whole world's asleep— [...] I'll not lose a moment.

I can only agree. Psychodynamic Shandean analysis stimulates life, contrary to static approaches which immobilise the psyche in a psychotic structure.

Sterne goes on to prophesize about the fate of the small souls of his con-temporaries, referring to Lessius, a "cooler man" of the Renaissance era, whose calculations showed that the souls of his time would shrink and soon come to almost nothing. Sterne agrees: "[...] in half a century [...] we shall have no souls at all".

Indeed, "shrinks" are psychoanalysts who have replaced the word "soul" with "Psyche", although for Apuleius she was, in fact, the soul welcomed to Olympus by Jupiter. Sterne has read the myth of Eros and Psyche in *The*

Golden Ass,[8] and exclaims: "Blessed Jupiter! And blessed every other heathen god and goddess!—What jovial times"! Unfortunately, he has to come back to earth:

> But where am I? [...] I who must be cut short in the midst of my days and taste no more of 'em than what I borrow from my imagination;—peace to thee, generous fool! and let me go on.

Imagination was named *la folle du logis*, "Folly in the house", by philosopher Nicolas Malebranche, Toby's contemporary.

Here, Folly is also that of Erasmus,[9] who speaks as a woman in *Praise of Folly*, composed on horseback when Erasmus was returning from Italy across the Alps. The rhythm of the wheels has enlivened Sterne's soul. "Crack your whip"! His mood suddenly brightens: "We danced it all along to Ailly-le-Haut-Clochers, famed in days of yore for the finest chimes in the world, [...]—greatly out of order [today]—(as in truth they were through all France)". Finally, he arrives in AMIENS, not deigning to write a single word about the Cathedral. Could his uncle Jaques's anti-Papism have left its mark?

Sixth stage: Chantilly, Saint Denis, Paris[10]

Sterne cannot sleep in the post-chaise since it stops every eight miles. New horses must be paid for, "sous by sous", because the currency changes from one place to the other. "Then Monsieur le Curé offers you a pinch of snuff, — or a poor soldier shews you his leg, [...], —or the priestess of the cistern will water your wheels [which] do not want it". He finally dozes off, until the postillon starts a quarrel about a two-*sous* piece. So he jumps out of the post-chaise, visits Chantilly where nothing holds his interest and in this dark mood, continues through St. Denis, ignoring its Abbey. "—Richness of their treasury! stuff and nonsense! Batting their jewels, which are all false".

The wheel turns together with his "bipolar" mood: "Crack, crack, — crack, crack" goes the whip that punctuates his grumpiness until his arrival in Paris, which he finds sinister. His depiction resembles Hogarth's prints of misery on London streets:

> [...] so this is Paris! quoth I [...]—and this is Paris!—humph!—Paris! cried I, repeating the name the third time—The first, the finest, the most brilliant—The streets however are nasty. But it looks, I suppose, better than it smells—crack, crack [...]—What a fuss thou makest! [...]—Ha!— and no one gives the wall!—but in the SCHOOL of URBANITY herself, if the walls are besh-t, —how can you do otherwise? [...] the streets are so villainously narrow that there is not room in all Paris to turn a wheelbarrow. [...] And prithee, when do they light the lamps? [...]—Ten

cook's shops! And twice the number of barber's [...]: the French love good eating. [...]—Ho! 'tis the time of salads [...]—soup and salad, — salad and soup, *encore*.

Then, his perspective becomes anthropological. The abundance of food shops and barbers means that the French "are all *gourmands*, [...] their god is their belly, — [...] and the periwig maketh the man". Sterne admits:

> The French are certainly misunderstood:—but [...] the fault is theirs in not sufficiently explaining themselves [...]—or the fault may be altogether on our side in not understanding their language [...], — when they affirm that they who have seen Paris have seen everything, they must mean to speak of those who have seen it by daylight. [...] As for candlelight, I give it up.

The City of Lights would have to await the invention of street lamps in 1820 to deserve its name. In the meantime, Sterne strolls across our bridges and squares, giving an account of our streets and avenues, district by district, until he reads upon the portico of the Louvre: "EARTH NO SUCH FOLKS!—NO FOLKS E'ER SUCH A TOWN AS PARIS IS!— SING, DERRY, DERRY, DOWN. The French have a gay way of treating everything that is great; and that is all can be said upon it". Apparently, we were a merry people in those days.

Spleen

Such gaiety brings to Sterne's mind the word SPLEEN, and he reflects on the "ground of alliance" between the two words. His analysis of bipolarity is not psychopathological, but political. "'Tis an undercraft of authors to keep up a good understanding amongst words as politicians do amongst men". The word SPLEEN, written in capital letters, is associated with the name of its remedy: "decampment", which helped Toby to recovery. Disagreeing with today's psychiatry which speaks of "pathological travels", Sterne does see a problem with it—not so much the departure, which is most often euphoric, but its precipitation.

On second thought, Sterne's self-analysis attributes his criticism of Paris to the speed of his journey, which put him in a foul mood, bringing on psychosomatic symptoms: "It has [...] brought on a bilious diarrhea, which has brought me back again to my first principle on which I set out". Hence his decision to decamp to the banks of the Garonne after spending three days and nights in Paris. In fact, he stayed in Saint-Germain-des-Prés for six months, starting in January 1762, and then for a month in 1764 before going back to England. He enjoyed the capital—"foutreland", as he called it in a letter—where he was celebrated and had his portrait painted by Carmontelle.

Sterne resumes his race against death: "Still I must away;—the roads are paved, —the posts are short, —the days are long;—'tis no more than noon;—I shall be at Fontainebleau before the king—Was he going there? not that I know". The fact is that in July 1762, when his wife and daughter arrived in Paris, Sterne suffered another lung haemorrhage. In his narrative, he identifies with "the most unchristian sufferings" of the skinny horse loaded with a mountain of baggage, unable to get on but for the coachman's trashy talk, especially the two words ***** and *****. "I long [...] to tell the reader what they are, but [...] their reverences may laugh at [them] in the bed-chamber [...], and abuse [them] in the parlour".

These words serve to move the novel along:

> My ink burns my fingers to try—and, when I have, —'twill have a worse consequence:—it will burn (I fear) my paper.—No, —I dare not. —But if you wish to know how the abbess of Andouillets and a novice of her convent got over the difficulty, —I'll tell you without the least scruple.

The art of storytelling slows down his desperate race to escape the Black Hunter—still roaming through Fontainebleau Forest—while he looks for words that trigger laughter, like the French word *andouillette*,—a savoury tripe sausage—whose sexual connotation is explained in a note for the English reader.

The abbess of Andouillets[11]

The story, told in Rabelaisian style, takes place on the border between Burgundy and Savoy in a convent where the abbess suffers from "a stiff joint" in her knee, which prevents her from kneeling during services. Everything possible has been tried: "[...] prayers [...] invoking to every saint who had ever had a stiff leg [...], —then touching it with all the relics of the convent [...], —then ointing it with oils and hot fat of animals", treating it with secular herbs and wood smoke, "holding her scapulary across her lap" and so on.

Since nothing helped, the abbess was persuaded to try "the hot baths of Bourbon"—in Bourbonne-les-Bains. She could have taken with her an old nun suffering from sciatic troubles, but chose instead the company of Margarita, a seventeen-year-old novice "with whitlow in her middle finger from sticking it constantly into the abbess's poultrices".

The carpenter and the smith made the abbess' calesh ready for the voyage and the nuns lined up in two rows to say their solemn farewells. The abbess walked slowly to the coach, leaning on Margarita's arm—both of them dressed in white, black rosaries hanging from their necks, veils floating in the air, their hands joined on their breasts, their eyes lifted to heaven. A connoisseur of Cervantes will recognise this scene as a remake of the bearded dueñas' musical in the second *Don Quixote*.[12]

The gardener of the convent—turned muleteer for the occasion—is about to take the plot in another direction. Sterne is elated. "I wish I had been there", just as Cid Hamete Benengeli "would have given his best tunic" to be present at the secret meeting between Don Quixote and dueña Rodriguez. Here, the plot thickens. "The muleteer was a son of Adam" with more earthly appetites than the knight. He had hidden a cask of wine at the rear of the carriage and made frequent trips to it, so that by the time half the journey was over, "all his wine had leak'd out of the legal vent of the borachio".

In the meanwhile, Sterne has time to draw his portrait:

> [He] troubled his head very little with the hows and whens of life [...].
> Man is a creature born to habitudes. The day had been sultry, —the
> evening was delicious, —the wine was generous, —the Burgundian hill
> on which it grew was steep.

A bough over the door of an inn seemed to say: "Come—come, thirsty muleteer—come in". Glancing at the two women, he gave his mules another crack, spurring them on, and entered the inn furtively through the back door to join the travellers who had stopped there:

> —A little, joyous, chirping fellow, who thought not of tomorrow, nor
> of what had gone before or what was to follow it, provided he got but
> his scantling of Burgundy and a little chit-chat along with it, [...] he so
> contrived his story as absolutely to forget the heroine of it.

As a result, the heroines are left to deal with the mules: the older and craftier one sees an opportunity to take advantage of the situation. "[...] inasmuch as their parents took [advantage] of them, —they [were not] in a condition to return the obligation downwards". The Shandean analysis of the barren animals explains their acting out: they started to climb the hill prompted by the whip, but at a bend in the road, the older one, a "shrewd old devil", looked back and saw no muleteer behind them. "By my fig! said she [...], I'll go no farther.—And if I do, replied the other, —they shall make a drum of my hide".

They stopped, by common accord, no matter what the nuns did: "— Wh - - - - ysh cried Margarita. Sh - - - a—shu - - u—sh - - aw—shaw— shaw'd the abbess, —Whu—v—w—whew—whuv'd Margarita"; the mules did not budge. "Thump-thump-thump—obstreperated the abbess [...] with the end of her gold-headed cane against the bottom of the calesh—the old mule let a f—". Her lack of empathy makes the two women panic: "We shall be plunder'd, we shall be ravish'd"—which was not so improbable after all. "Santa Maria! Cried the abbess (forgetting the O!), why was I govern'd by this wicked stiff joint? why did I leave the convent [...]? and why didst thou not suffer thy servant to go unpolluted to her tomb"?

Margarita cries "O my finger"! wishing she had placed it anywhere rather than "in this strait". It's time to analyse her wish in proper psychoanalytic fashion. The abbess does so, repeating the word "strait" that the terrified novice echoes. "The one knew not what she said, —the other what she answer'd. O my virginity! virginity! Cried the abbess—inity!—inity! said the novice, sobbing". Sterne enjoys echoing repressed signifiers as a means of lifting their repression:

> My dear mother, quoth the novice, coming a little to herself, —there are two certain words which [...] will force any horse or ass or mule to go up a hill whether he will or no [...]. There are words magic! cried the abbess [...].—No, [...]—but they are words sinful.— [...] But you may pronounce them to me,

says the abbess, encouraging free association. "They will make all the blood in one's body fly up into one's face.—But you may whisper them in my ear, quoth the abbess".

Pastor Sterne implores heaven to rescue the innocent women by sending a "generous spirit unemploy'd" to jolt the muleteer out of his wine, and he shouts: "Rouse! Rouse"! The double entendre is obvious. "But 'tis too late: — the horrid words are pronounced this moment". The abbess, who in her distress has become casuist, has solved their problem:

> All sins [...] are either mortal or venial: there is no further division. Now, a venial sin [...], —being halved—in course becomes diluted into no sin at all.—Now I see no sin in saying *bou, bou, bou,* [...] a hundred times together; nor is there any turpitude in pronouncing the syllable *ger, ger, ger* [...], were it from our matins to our vespers.

As shrewd as the old mule, the abbess has guessed the word that the novice cannot say, and both sing *a capella* to the tune of "fa, sol, la, re, mi, do: Abbess: Bou – bou – bou—Margarita: —ger, - - ger, - - ger—Margarita: Fou – fou – fou --Abbess: —tre, - - tre, - - tre". The two mules applaud the performance by a mutual lash of their tails, encouraging the artists to speed the rhythm. "—They do not understand us, cried Margarita.—But the Devil does, said the Abbess". End of story.

This story gave Sterne the words and the rhythm to keep the Black Man at bay, at least for a time.

Eighth stage: Auxerre[13]

Back on the road, Sterne muses on all the memories he is collecting:

> What a tract of country have I run! [...] how many fair and goodly cities have I seen during the time you have been reading and reflecting,

Madam, upon this story...but as I never blot anything out, —let us use some honest means to get it out of our heads directly.

Today, we might have advised him to "delete" it, but the 18th-century lady has another retort: "Why, it's a strange story, Tristram".

But he is not absolved of his guilt: "Alas Madam, had it been some melancholy lecture [...] on the pure abstraction of the soul [...] you would have come to a better appetite for it". When I answer that boring abstractions about the psyche do not whet my appetite, he calls Folly for help:

—Pray, reach me my fool's cap.—I fear you sit upon it, madam;—'tis under the cushion;—I'll put it on. —Bless me! (the madam answers) You have had it upon your head this half hour.—There then let it stay.

Singing "fa-ra diddle di and fa-ra diddle dum", Sterne leaps back over the years to join Tristram on the "grand tour" Bobby never had a chance to complete. "And now, madam, we may venture, I hope, a little to go on". True to his reputation of having invented the modern novel, he takes us back to Fontainebleau, famous for its royal hunts, dubbed "carnivals"; then Sens cathedral—left unvisited, Joigny, of which "the less one says [...], the better", until we stop in Auxerre where we meet Tristram, his father, his uncle, the corporal and Obadiah—"except my mother, who, being taken up with [...] knitting my father a pair of breeches [...] stayed at home". A guided tour shows us the Abbey of Saint-Germain l'Auxerrois and the tomb of St. Heribald, "a renowned prince" under the reigns of Charlemagne and his sons:

I dare say he has been a gallant soldier, said my uncle.—He was a monk, — said the sacristan. [...] My father clapp'd both his hands upon his codpiece, which was a way he had when anything hugely tickled him.

Toby and Trim escape "to mount the rampart" while I no longer know what year I am in. Sterne himself gets confused: "Now, this is the most puzzled skein of all, —for [...] I have been getting forwards in two different journeys together and with the same dash of the pen..." In such a "timequake",[14] Shandeism reaches "a certain degree of perfection [that] no traveller ever [attained] before me", Sterne brags.

Ninth stage: Lyon[15]

The verb to shandy means to mix together—as it happens when the arrow of time deviates from a straight course:

I am this moment walking across the marketplace of Auxerre with my father and my uncle Toby in our way back to dinner, —and I am this moment also entering Lyon with my post-chaise broke into a thousand pieces [...]—all higgedly-piggedly, with my baggage in a cart which was moving slowly before me [...]—and I am moreover this moment in a handsome pavilion [...] built upon the banks of the Garonne, [...] and where I now sit rhapsodizing all these affairs.—Let me collect myself and pursue my journey.

After mixing temporalities, Sterne looks at his purse and decides to continue by water towards Avignon, "which will not cost me seven *livres*;—from thence [...] I can hire a couple of mules and cross the plains of Languedoc for almost nothing". We must keep in mind that he has little strength left and seeks renewed energy:

What a flame will it rekindle in the lamp to snatch a blushing grape from the Hermitage and Côte Rôtie [...]! And what a fresh spring in the blood to behold upon the banks [...] the castles of romance whence courteous knights have whilome rescued the distress'd, —and see [...] all the hurry which Nature is in with all her great works about her!

A precursor of romanticism, he soon has to deal with more mundane matters when a sly chaise-undertaker offers to buy his broken one for a trifling. Yet, as his Jenny can testify:

this is my usual method of bookkeeping, at least with the disasters of life:—making a penny of every one of 'em [...].—Do, my dear Jenny, tell the world for me how I behaved under one, the most oppressive of its kind which could befall me as a man, proud, as he ought to be, of his manhood [...] as I stood with my garters in my hand, reflecting upon what had *not* pass'd.—'Tis enough, Tristram, and I am satisfied, said'st thou, whispering [...] in my ear, *** ***** —any other man would have sunk down to the centre. —Everything is good for something, quoth I.

His Jenny is marvellous, of course. And so is the famous phrase that follows:

I think myself inexcusable for blaming Fortune so often as I have done, for pelting me all my life long like an ungracious duchess, [...] with so many small evils [...]: surely if I have any cause to be angry with her, 'tis that she has not sent me greater ones;—a score of good, cursed, bouncing losses would have been as good as a pension to me.

This oxymoron says more than hours of a seminar on the loss of the object/cause of desire, as his stay in Lyon—where losses multiply—will illustrate:

To be a day in Lyon, the most opulent city in France, enriched with the most fragments of antiquity, —and not be able to see it [...] must be a

vexation; but to be withheld by a vexation—must certainly be [...] VEX-
ATION upon VEXATION.

Sterne starts the day full of expectations. He has just drunk two bowls of
café au lait, recommended against tuberculosis. Realising that his boat
would not leave before noon, he decides to visit the cathedral and the great
clock built by Lippius of Basel as well as the Jesuits' library which houses
a history of China in thirty volumes written in Chinese. But above all, he
wants to see the tomb of the lovers Amandus and Amanda, who lived in the
period of Cervantes's slavery. He has read their story:

Amandus, HE, and Amanda, SHE, are captured by the Turks and taken
captive to the court of the Emperor of Morocco. The emperor's daughter
falls in love with Amandus, but since he remains true to Amanda, he spends
twenty years in prison, while SHE wanders barefoot and dishevelled over
rocks and mountains, as mad as Cervantes's Cardenio in the Sierra Morena.
She cries out his name—Amandus, Amandus—and sits forlorn at the gate
of every city until, "after going round and round", chance brings them
together at the gate of Lyon. There, they fly into each other's arms and drop
down dead for joy. This is why "to this hour lovers called upon [their tomb]
to attest their truths".

Now, Sterne presents a piece of self-analysis once again:

Such a story affords more *pabulum* to the brain than all the *frusts* and
crusts and *rusts* of antiquity which travellers can cook up for it.—'Twas
all that stuck on the right side of the colander in my [brain].

This cerebral location of images anticipates a recent article entitled "The
Right Brain. Implicit Self Lies at the Core of Psychoanalysis".[16]

In fact, madness has been long represented by donkey ears on a fool's cap
as an emblem of "Follysophy".

Dialogue with the ass[17]

Just as Sterne comes into the yard, heading towards the tomb of the lovers,
"a poor ass" blocks his way on the threshold. Despite his disdain for the
rusty scraps of Antiquity, I must mention that asses inspired major writers
as far back as Lucian, Apuleius, Machiavelli, Giordano Bruno and others
up to the last century, when donkeys disappeared from our landscape:

Now, says Sterne, 'tis an animal [...] I cannot bear to strike;—there is
a patient endurance of sufferings [....] that [...] always disarms me; [...]
meet him where I will [...]—I have always something civil to say to him
on my part; and surely never is my imagination as busy as in framing his
responses from the etchings of his countenance [...], —in flying from my

own heart into his and seeing what is natural for an ass to think, — as well as a man, upon the occasion.[18]

He analyses his transference to the only animal with whom he never tires of communicating—unlike parrots, his dog and his cat, whom he values, but who do not "possess the same talents for conversation". When he meets the donkey's doubtful gaze towards the street, he tells it: "Come, Honesty! [...] art thou for coming in or going out? [...] Well, —replied I, —we'll wait a minute for thy driver. [...]—if thou takest a wrong step in this affair, he will cudgel thee to death". An anti-slavery advocate, Sterne speaks of "a bitter day's labour" as he watches the ass chew on the stem of an artichoke, dropping it out of his mouth over and over: "—God help thee, Jack! And now thine mouth [...] is as bitter, I dare say, as soot— and thou hast not a friend perhaps in all this world that will give thee a macaroon". He gives the ass one of the macaroons he just bought, feeling guilty for wanting to observe how he would eat it.

While the ass enjoys the treat, Sterne pulls on his halter to bring him into the courtyard. His legs trembling, the ass resists. The halter breaks. The animal's pleading gaze seems to say:

> Don't thrash me with it—but if you will, you may.—If I do, said I, I'll be d—d. The word was but one half of it pronounced, like the abbess of Andouillet's— (so there was no sin in it)—, when a person, coming in, let fall a thundering bastinado upon the poor devil's crupper, which put an end to the ceremony.

The ceremony ends with Sterne's cry when his breeche's pocket is torn by an osier sticking out of the donkey's basket; the pocket is rent "in the most disastrous direction you can imagine. [...] This I leave to be settled by The REVIEWERS of MY BREECHES".

Police![19]

Now, an intruder enters the scene, a commissary sent to collect money from the traveller as "the part of the king". This ludicrous request destabilises Sterne's very identity:

> — My good friend, quoth I, —as sure as I am I—and you are you—And who are you? said he. —Don't puzzle me, said I.—But it is an indubitable verity, continued I, [...]—that I owe the King of France nothing but my goodwill [...]. *Pardonnez-moi*, —replied the commissary, you are indebted to him six *livres* four *sous*.

Thus, Sterne discovers the intricacies of the French administration. Tempted to call the commissary by the animal's name, he asks why he should pay for the transport he takes and for that which he does not. *"C'est tout égal"*, replies the official. This lack of HUMOUR makes him send the man to the devil, even if he "will go to ten thousand Bastilles, and regret his homeland: "O England! England! Thou land of liberty and climate of good sense, thou tenderest of mothers—and gentlest of nurses..."

A priest who happens by takes him for an illegal immigrant and offers humanitarian aid, which Sterne refuses, protesting against discrimination:

> —And pray, Mr Commissary, by what law of courtesy is a defenceless stranger to be sued just to reverse from what you use a Frenchman in this matter? —By no means, said he. —Excuse me, said I, [...]—had you first taken my pocket, as you do with your own people, —[...] I had been a beast to have complain'd.

Deaf to his arguments, the tax collector hands him a paper bearing the heading *"PAR LE ROY"*. Followed by five lines of hyphens implying that "if a man sets out in a post-chaise from Paris—he must go on travelling in one all the days of his life—or pay for it". The commissary confirms:

> Excuse me, [...] if you set out with an intention of running post [...], the REVENUES are not to fall short through your fickleness.—O by Heavens! cried I; if fickleness is taxable in France, —we have nothing to do but to make the best peace with you we can.—
> AND SO THE PEACE WAS MADE
> —And if it is a bad one, —as Tristram Shandy laid the cornerstone of it, —nobody but Tristram Shandy ought to be hanged.

Carried away by a megalomaniac impulse, Sterne lays claim to having inspired the Treaty of Paris—signed in 1763 while he was in Toulouse. Tristram does not risk any blame here, since the English gained Canada, India and Louisiana.

Maypoles[20]

But the joke is short-lived. Searching in his pocket for his travel notebook to write down the clever things he just said, he cannot find it: "Heaven! earth! sea! fire! cried I [...].—My remarks are stolen!—what shall I do?—My Commissary! pray, did I drop any remarks as I stood besides you?—You dropp'd a good many very singular ones, replied he". His complaints are borrowed from Cervantes[21]:

> — they were the best remarks [...], —the wisest, —the wittiest. [...] Sancho Panza, when he lost his ass's FURNITURE, did not exclaim more bitterly. —It then occurr'd to me [...] that, in selling my chaise, I had sold my remarks along with it to the chaise-vamper.

Cursing under cover of a dozen asterisks, he returns quickly to the chaise-vamper's shop and finds it closed, since it is the 8th of September, the Feast of the Nativity, a holiday—of which there are so many in France, as La Fontaine pointed out in his fable "The Cobbler and the Financier".[22] So, everywhere, people are dancing around maypoles, "— tantarra-ra-tan-tivy [...], —frisking here, —copering there;—nobody cared a button for me or my remarks". There is nothing for it but to wait on a bench in front of the shop, "philosophating upon my condition". Soon, the mistress of the house arrives, to take the *papillotes* from her hair before going dancing. Sterne notes that "French women [...] love maypoles *à la folie*".

The sexual innuendo applies to English women as well, when they danced with hobby horses around maypoles on the May Day festival in Merry England[23] before the Reformation brought these festivities to an end. Hence Sterne's political statement:

—give 'em but a maypole, whether in May, June, July or September, — they never count the times, —down it goes, —'tis meat, drink, washing and lodging to 'em, —and had we but the policy [...] to send them but plenty of maypoles—The women would set them up, and [...] they would dance round them (and the men for company) till they were all blind.

While he is dreaming of conquering France, Sterne recognises his handwriting on the curl papers falling out of the chaise-vamper's wife's hair. Once again, the tone is that of the theatre of fools, where metaphors are acted out literally:

— *O Seigneur!* cried I, —you have got all my remarks upon your head, madam!—*J'en suis bien mortifiée*, said she. —*Tenez!* so [...] she took them from her curls and put them gravely one by one into my hat;— one was twisted this way, —another twisted that;—ay! by my faith; and when they are published, quoth I, —They will be worse-twisted still.

Before he embarks on the Rhône, Sterne cancels his visit to Lyon's cathedral and to the library of the Jesuits, "who have all got cholic"—with good reason, since they would soon be ousted from the kingdom (in 1764)—and he sets out for Amandus and Amanda's burial place, to:

pay the homage [...] without a witness of my weakness [...]—with all imaginable joy [...];—when I saw the gate [...] I cried:—Tender and faithful spirits! [...] —long—long have I tarried to drop this tear upon your tomb.—I come—I come—When I came, —there was no tomb to drop it upon. What would I have given for my uncle Toby to have whistled *Lillibullero!*

Another coitus interruptus!

Tenth stage: Avignon[24]

In Avignon, the only thing worth seeing, according to Sterne, is the Duke of Ormond's house—not the famous *Pont d'Avignon où l'on danse tout en rond* as the song says—nor the Palace of the Popes or the inhabitants who take themselves to be "all Dukes, Marquises and Counts". Even the reputation of the cold wind called "Mistral" is overblown: "[...] merely because a man's hat has been blown off his head [...] he should [not] say: 'Avignon is more [windy] than any town in all France'". Soon, we see Sterne crossing the Rhône on a mule, followed by his valet, François, on horseback, carrying his portmanteau. The mule's owner rides ahead of them with a long gun on his shoulder and a sword under his arm, "least peradventure we should run away with his cattle".

At last, Sterne can say:

> I ride at my leisure—for I have left Death [...] far behind me. He thumbs his nose at Him. Still he followed, —and still I fled him, —But I fled him cheerfully;—still he pursued, —but like one who pursued his prey without hope [...];—why should I fly him at this rate? So, I changed the mode of my travelling once more, and after so precipitate [...] a course as I had run, I flattered my fancy with thinking of my mule, and that I should traverse the rich plains of Languedoc upon his back as slowly as foot could fall.

Slowing down has therapeutic effects. Sterne's only problem now is of a literary nature, and he rises to the occasion:

> There is nothing [...] more terrible to travel writers than a large [...] plain they have upon their hands which they know not what to do with [...] [It] is of little use to them but to carry them to some town, [...] a new place to start from to the next plain, —and so on.—This is most terrible work; judge if I don't manage my plains better.

Sterne solves the problem by means of a play on words, specifically on the signifier "plain", which means "simple" when used as an adjective. His travel tales will be entitled PLAIN STORIES.

The man with the gun may check on his property from time to time— Sterne doesn't care. He loiters at his ease, stops and talks to everyone he meets, offers a pinch of snuff, waits for those who are behind, hailing others—and does not pass "a woman in a mulberry tree without commending her legs". From another, he buys a basket of ripe figs, discovering "two dozen eggs cover'd with vine-leaves at the bottom of it". Chance plays its part, as it does in the transference with madness and trauma:

> [...]—in short, by seizing every handle, of what size or shape soever, which chance held out to me in my journey, —I turned my plain into

a city.—I was always in company; [...] and as my mule loved society as much as myself [...]—I am confident we could have passed through Pall Mall or St James's Street for a month together with fewer adventures—and seen less of human nature.

In Rousseae's manner, he praises "the simplicity which poets sang in better days" and "deludes his fancy" to dispel his solitude. Sterne's arrival in Montpellier resembles the apotheosis experienced by Don Quixote[25] when he saw the sea for the first time in Barcelona at dawn on the day of solstice, not far from there.

Eleventh stage: Montpellier

Volume 7 ends at sunset with a pastoral scene between Nîmes and Lunel. Here, Sterne adopts the style of the eclogue:

> [...] the nymphs had tied up their hair afresh, —and the swains were repairing for a carousal.—My mule made a dead point.—'Tis the pipe and tabourin, said I.—I'm frighten'd to death(...) —By St Boogar [...], said she [...], I'll not go a step further.—'Tis very well, sir, said I, —I never will argue a point with one of your family as long as I live; [...]—I'll take a dance, said I, —so stay you here.

Warrior writers like Miguel de Cervantes in Spain, Honoréd'Urfé in France and Luis de Camoëns in Portugal wrote pastoral poems to celebrate their return to life after having stared death in the face. "Galatea", the heroin[26] of Cervantes' pastoral, comes to meet Sterne:

> A sunburnt daughter of Labour rose up from the group to meet me as I advanced towards them; (...) 'We want a cavalier', said she, holding out both of her hands, [...].—And a cavalier ye shall have, said I, taking hold of both of them. Hadst thou, Nannette, been array'd like a duchesse!—But that cursed slit in thy petticoat! [...] We could not have done without you, said she [...] with self-taught politeness.

Like "the duchess in wooden clogs, whom the three captains called *vilaine*" in a popular French song, Nannette is not concerned with the slit in her petticoat, nor the fantasies it might trigger. The villagers begin to dance to the sound of the tabourin and the pipe, played by "a lame youth whom Apollo had recompensed" in this fashion. As for Nannette's cavalier, he celebrates their encounter poetically: "[I learned] to forget that I was a stranger—We had been seven years acquainted".

In a few more years, Nannette might perhaps dance the *Carmagnole* during the French Revolution. As for Sterne, his reverie takes him back a quarter of a century, to *Lascia la spina, cogli la rosa* (Leave the thorn, gather the rose) composed by Handel in Toby's era[27]:

> The youth struck the note upon the tabourin;—his pipe followed, and off we bounded. The sister of the youth, who had stolen her voice from heaven, sung alternately with her brother [...] a Gascon roundelay.
> VIVA LA JOIA!
> FI DONC LA TRISTESSA!
> The nymphs join'd in unison, and their swains an octave below them.

Viva la joia shone in the young girl's eyes:

> A transient spark of amity shot across the space betwixt us. [...] Why could I not live and end my days thus? [...] cried I, why could not a man sit down in the lap of content here—and dance and sing and say his prayers and go to heaven with this nut-brown maid?

"Oh, Time, stop your flight"![28] Lamartine would write in 1820. Sterne will dance his way to his little house near Toulouse, where we find him now, taking "a paper of black lines, that [he] might go on straight forwards, without digression or parenthesis in [his] uncle Toby's amours".

But the suspension of time has stopped his inspiration as well.

Notes

1 Sterne, L., *Tristram Shandy*, op. cit., Vol. 7, ch. I.
2 Sterne, L., *Tristram Shandy*, op. cit., Vol. 7, chs. II–III.
3 Sterne, L., *Tristram Shandy*, op. cit., Vol 7, chs. IV–VI.
4 Sterne, L., *Tristram Shandy*, op. cit., Vol. 7, chs. VII–VIII.
5 Sterne, L., *Tristram Shandy*, op. cit., Vol. 7, chs. IX–XI.
6 Ronsard, P. (1568), *Sonnets for Helen*, Wolfe, H. (Trans.), London: Unwin Books, 1972.
7 Sterne, L., *Tristram Shandy*, op. cit., Vol 7, chs. XIII–XV.
8 Apuleius,*The Golden Ass, or Metamorphoses,* London: Penguin Classics, 1999.
9 Erasmus, D., The Praise of Folly, op. cit.
10 Sterne, L., *Tristram Shandy*, op. cit., Vol. 7, chs. XVI–XX.
11 Sterne, L., *Tristram Shandy*, op. cit., Vol. 7, ch. XXI.
12 De Cervantes, M. *Don Quixote II*, op. cit., chs. 38 and 48.
13 Sterne, L., *Tristram Shandy*, op. cit., Vol. 7, chs. XXVI–XXVII.
14 Vonnegut K. *Timequake*, New York: Berkeley Books, 1997.
15 Sterne, L., *Tristram Shandy*, Vol. 7, chs. XXVIII–XXXI.
16 Schore, A.N., The Right Brain. Implicit Self Lies at the Core of Psychoanalysis, *Psychoanalytic Dialogues, The International Journal of Social Sciences Perspectives*, No. 21, 2011: 75–100.
17 Sterne, L., *Tristram Shandy*, op. cit., Vol. 7, ch. XXXII.
18 Lucian of Samosata, *Loukios or the Ass*, in *The Works of Lucian of Samosata*, London: Forgotten Books, 2007; Apuleius, *The Golden Ass*, London: Penguin

Classics, 1999; Segur, Comtesse de, *The Story of a Donkey*, Yateley, UK: Abela Publishing, 2017.

19 Sterne, L., *Tristram Shandy*, op. cit., Vol. 7, chs. XXXV–XXXVI.
20 Sterne, L., *Tristram Shandy*, op. cit., Vol. 7, chs. XXXVII–XL.
21 De Cervantes, M., *Don Quixote I*, op. cit.
22 La Fontaine, Jean de, The Cobbler and the Financier, Book 8, Fable 2. *The Complete Fables of Jean de la Fontaine*, Chicago: University of Illinois Press, 2007.
23 Laroque, F., *Shakespeare's Festive World*, Cambridge, UK: Cambridge University Press, 1991.
24 Sterne, L., *Tristram Shandy*, op. cit., Vol. 7, chs. XLI–XLIII.
25 De Cervantes, M., *Don Quixote II*, op. cit., ch. 61.
26 De Cervantes, M., *Galatea: A Pastoral Romance*, Whitefish: Kessinger Publishing, 2008.
27 Handel, G.F. (1705). *Almira* (opera), Act III.
28 De Lamartine, A., The Lake, in *The Meditations Poetiques*, Hillery, D. (Ed.), Durham: University of Durham Press, 1993.

8

The politics of love and slavery

The art of storytelling is one of the oldest psychotherapies in the world. During sessions, I tell stories that come to my mind, when words stop or when I want to give an illustration. A young woman I met at the psychiatric hospital long ago told me: "It was not your theories, but the little stories you told me, sometimes about yourself, which helped me get out of madness".

In Volume 8, Laurence Sterne tells the story of Toby's amours, his "choicest morsel", announced early on and postponed until the last two volumes. We will also hear Trim tell the story of his own amours, hitherto unknown to the captain. Better than any abstract discourse, such storytelling untangles "the confusion of tongues"—Ferenczi's expression—often present in the psychoanalysis of trauma and madness.

It is with love as with cuckoldom[1]

When Sterne arrived in Toulouse in 1762, his haemorrhages returned, and the Franco-English war was not yet over. Sterne wrote to a friend: "I ran a risk of being taken up for a Spy, I [...] jogg'd myself out of all other dangers".[2] Although he resides "in this clear climate of fantasy and perspiration [...], — in this fertile land of chivalry and romance", Volumes 7 and 8 will be written and published only after his return in 1764 to Yorkshire, "Freezeland [and] Fogland", before going back to Italy for a year in 1766.

Sterne has a knack for *incipits*. The first sentence does not exactly evoke courtly love: "It is with LOVE as with CUCKOLDOM". The rest should follow from there:

> But now I am talking of beginning a book, and have long had a thing upon my mind to be imparted to the reader, which, if not imparted now, can never be imparted [...]. I am confident my own way [...] is the best [...], —for I begin with writing the first sentence—and trusting to Almighty God for the second.

DOI: 10.4324/9781003224907-8

The verb "to impart", repeated three times, insists on the transference between the author and the reader. Sterne's method is intended to be therapeutic:

> 'Twould cure an author for ever of the fuss and folly of opening his street door and calling in his neighbours [...]. I wish you saw me, half-starting out of my chair, with what confidence, as I grasp the elbow of it, I look up—catching the idea, even sometimes before it halfway reaches me—I believe in my conscience I intercept many a thought which Heaven intended for another man.

Wilfred Bion[3] probably intercepted this thought when he read *Tristram Shandy*, and wrote about "thoughts without a thinker searching for a thinker to be thought". But Sterne is also aware of propaganda floating in the air that exempts one from thinking. So, he turns to Molière for support: "I have no Zeal or Anger—or Anger or Zeal (printed in the middle of the page). [...], —the errantest TARTUFFE in science, in politics—or in religion shall never kindle a spark within me". Neither will charlatans like Doctor Diafoirus, mocked in *The Imaginary Invalid*. At this point, Sterne inserts a conversational scene, still familiar to us today: "*Bonjour*—good morrow! [...]—And how goes it with thy concubine— thy wife—and thy little ones o' both sides? [...]. I hope they have got better of their colds, coughs [...], toothaches, fevers [...], sciaticas..."

Sterne, like Molière, suffered from tuberculosis, and rails against blood-letting, purges and drugs: "—What a devil of an apothecary! To take so much blood [...].—And why so many grains of calomel? Santa Maria! and such a dose of opium! Pereclitating, *pardi*! the whole family of ye, from head to tail". He has a score to settle with doctors and apothecaries in Toulouse and Montpellier, whose drugs almost killed him and may have transgenerational effects: "This is the reason [...] that in all our numerous family, for these four generations, we count no more than one archbishop, a Welsh judge, and a single mountebank",—plus "a dozen of alchemists in the sixteenth century".

His incipit is explained at long last:

> —the suffering party is at least the third, but generally the last in the house, who knows anything about the matter; this comes, as all the world knows, from having half a dozen words for one thing; and so long as what in this vessel of the human frame is love—may be hatred in that, —sentiment half a yard higher—and nonsense—no, madam, —not there, —I mean at the part I am now pointing with my forefinger, —how can we help ourselves?

Is his forefinger pointing at the place widow Wadman will be obsessed with?

In any case:

> Of all mortal, and immortal men too, [...], who ever soliloquized upon
> this mystic subject, my uncle Toby was the worst fitted to have push'd
> his researches thro' such a contention of feelings; and he had infalli-
> bly let them run on, [...] had not Bridget's pre-notification of them to
> Susannah, and Susannah's repeated manifestations thereupon to all the
> world, made it necessary for my uncle Toby to look into the affair.

Is this the confusion Shandean psychoanalysis intends to untangle?

Phallus, when you hold us in your spell...[4]

Sterne answers this question with another question:

> Why weavers, gardeners and gladiators, —or a man with a pinned leg
> [...]—should ever have had some tender nymph breaking her heart in
> secret for them, are points, well and duly settled and accounted for by
> ancient and modern physiologists.

And by psychoanalysts too. Then comes another question: "how is it that
such a nymph may be infatuated with a water-drinker? —it seems to run
opposite to the natural work of causes and effects", for instance, when "a
rill of cold water dribbling through my inward parts [lights] up a torch in
my Jenny's —".
   A modern analyst might answer in a flash that the nymph is a hysteric
"whose desire is to have an unsatisfied desire".[5] Sterne has already shown
that the logic of desire is nothing new to him. The gentleman's glass of water
causing a tsunami in the lady proves that lack is at the root of desire, Lacan
argued. Sterne's argument is staged like in a Medieval morality play:

> The moment thou presses against the flood-gates of the brain, —see
> how they give way!—In swims CURIOSITY, beckoning to her dam-
> sels to follow;—they drive into the centre of the current.—FANCY sits
> musing upon the bank, and [...] turns straws and bulrushes into masts
> and bowsprits.—And DESIRE, with vest held to the knee in one hand,
> snatches at them as they swim by her.

However, like in a Sottie, his analysis turns into an attack on perversion:

> O ye water-drinkers! Is it then by this delusive fountain that ye have so
> often governed and turn'd this world about like a millwheel, —grinding
> the faces of the impotent, —bepowdering their ribs, —bepeppering their
> noses and changing sometimes even the very frame and face of nature?

This diatribe occasions a discussion between Sterne's friends. I wish I could summarise it, but the task seems too daunting. Here is a short example.

Mysteries of feminine sexuality[6]

The year is 1764; Sterne is at Crazy Castle and reads these pages to his friends. "If I was you, quoth Yorick, (alias Sterne) I would drink more water, Eugenius.—And if I was you, Yorick, [...] so would I. Which shews they had both read Longinus's *On the Sublime*",[7] in which, when a Councillor suggests to Alexander the Great that in his place he would make peace on the enemy's terms, the emperor answers: "But I am not you".

Hence his declaration to the world:

> For my own part, I am resolved never to read any books but my own, as long as I live.—I wish my uncle Toby had been a water-drinker, for then the thing had been accounted for. That the first moment widow Wadman saw him, she felt *something* stirring within her in his favour.

The word is repeated four times. "Something!—something.—Something perhaps more than friendship, —less than love— something—no matter what—no matter where..."

Sterne may have borrowed the art of speaking of "the thing" without speaking of it from his French friend Crébillon fils, who wrote *The night and the moment*.[8] Soon, we will know the night and the moment when widow Wadman "felt something stirring", although "my uncle Toby was neither a weaver, a gardener or a gladiator [...]". His leg "was a little stiff and awkward [...], but it was plump and muscular, and [...] as good and promising a leg as the other".

Now, Sterne's life "as an author and a man" is threatened again. His tuberculosis has gotten worse, but like Billy Le Fever, he wants no pity: "Is it but two months ago that in a fit of laughter, on seeing a cardinal make water like a chorister (with both hands), thou brakest a vessel in thy lungs"? In fact, he lost a lot of blood in a few hours. Like at critical moments in an analysis when a destructive agency threatens, his "thou" is transferred to us.

Toby's amours: second try[9]

Sterne blames us: "—But for Heaven's sake, let us not talk of quarts or gallons [...] somehow or other, you have got me thrust almost into the middle of [the story].—I beg we may take more care". Appeased by the transference, he now begins the tale of Toby's amours. It all started in 1700, the year when the captain "decamped" from London with the corporal: "[They] posted down with so much heat and precipitations [...] that they had forgot one of the most necessary articles of the whole affair; [...]. It was a bed to lie on".

At the time, Shandy Hall was not furnished, since Walter had not yet moved back to the country. Even the inn where Le Fever died had not yet been built. As a result, Toby was forced to accept hospitality at his neighbour's house for a night or two, while Trim was building a bed in Toby's own house. This is how the neighbour enters the scene: "... such was widow Wadman, and 'tis all the character I intend to give of her —'*that she was a perfect woman*'". Sterne explains:

> There is nothing in it out of doors and in broad daylight where a woman has a power, physically speaking, of viewing a man in more lights than one;—but here, (in her house) she can see him in no light [...] and [...] he gets foisted into her inventory.—And then good night.

Sterne is referencing Don Quixote,[10] who was captured in this manner at the ducal castle, where he was immediately foisted into the Duchess's inventory. Should this passage be toned down? Sterne foresaw the request:

> But this is not matter of SYSTEM, for I have delivered that above;—nor is it matter of BREVIARY, —for I make no man's creed but my own;— nor matter of FACT, —but 'tis matter copulative and introductory to what follows.

We are invited to witness the lady's ritual upon retiring for the night, which has not varied in the seven years of her widowhood. Her night garb follows the common vogue in King William's and Queen Anne's era, and a pin— yes, a pin again—is an essential part of it. Each night, Bridget uses it to pin the hem of the widow's night shift, "with all suitable decorum", to prevent her feet from getting cold "in the many bleak and Decemberly nights". But the presence of the captain in the next room disturbs this well-established "ordinance of the bedchamber". Sterne has no doubt drawn on Chaucer's *Canterbury Tales*,[11] with the widow Wadman in the role of Bath's wife, who lost five husbands.

"The subversion of the subject and the dialectic of desire",[12] to quote Lacan, are described in two stages, from the emergence of repression to acting out.

Repression versus suppression[13]

The first night, the widow thinks, with her cheek resting on her hand—in the classical posture of melancholia. The second night, she takes out her marriage settlement and reads it with great devotion. The third night, the last Toby was spending under her roof, when Bridget tried to pin her night shift, she kicked the pin out of her fingers with both heels. This kick was "the most natural kick that could be kick'd in her situation [...], it was a north-east kick, for supposing********** to be the sun in its meridian". The ten asterisks censure the name of the place hot as the sun, while the *etiquette* drops to the ground. "From all which it was plain that widow Wadman was in love with my uncle Toby".

The Freudian interpretation is obvious. But not for the captain, who lies in the next room, unaware of the kick. "My uncle Toby's head at that time was full of other matters, so that it was not till the demolition of Dunkirk, when all the other civilities of Europe were settled, that he found leisure to this". That's a long time: from 1700 to the Treaty of Utrecht in 1713. Sterne considers this period an armistice for Toby, and a period of vacancy for Mrs. Wadman's passion, until she decides to launch her campaign. "But in all cases of this nature, as it is the second blow [...] which makes the fray, —I choose [...] to call these the amours of my uncle Toby with Mrs Wadman".

The second blow will be described in chapter XXVIII, when Toby realises that he is in love. But from the start, Sterne makes sure to point out the difference between their respective loves. Toby's Eros, as I already mentioned, is the Eros Socrates speaks of in the *Symposium*[14] through Diotima—the foreigner who kept at bay for a time the plague in Athens—associated with traumatic times. Its analysis will take place on a couch in the next volume. Her Eros is more in keeping with traditional psychoanalysis:

> Now, as widow Wadman did love my uncle Toby—and my uncle Toby did not love widow Wadman, there was nothing for [her] to do but to go on and love my uncle Toby—or let it alone. [She] would do neither the one or the other.

The mystery of feminine desire, expressed in this "neither... or," is presented as an ordeal in the tale of Chaucer's "Wife of Bath"[15] to a young knight who raped a young girl: "What do women desire the most"? If he can answer this question, his life will be spared, but he can neither answer the question nor let it go. Chaucer solves the dilemma, in the manner of the 14th century, through the voice of an old woman who whispers the answer to the knight provided he marries her. The young man accepts: "A woman wants [...] sovereignty/Over her husband as over her lover/And master him; [...] That is your greatest wish, whether you kill/Or spare me; please yourself". This is when the old woman changes into a lovely young girl.

Widow Wadman has an entirely different solution in mind; she reconciles her "neither...or" by invading Toby's sacred space.

Cunt[16]

Sterne identifies with the widow and "understands" her:

> Gracious heaven!—but I forget I am a little of her temper myself; for whenever it so falls out [...] that an earthly goddess is so much this and that and t'other that I cannot eat my breakfast for her, —and that she careth not three halfpence that I cannot eat my breakfast for her— Curse on her! And so I send her [...] to the devil [...]. But as the heart is tender and the passions in these tides ebb and flow ten times in a minute, I place her in the very centre of the Milky Way.

The Milky Way then sends him spinning to the Origin of the World, painted by Gustave Courbet, about which he phantasises while playing with his fur cap:

> By all that is hirsute and gashly! I cry, taking off my furr'd cap and twisting it round my finger, —I would not give sixpence for a dozen such!—But [...] (putting it upon my head and pressing it close to my ears), 'tis warm, —and soft; especially if your stroke it the right way.

Rabelais called it the *"con-ment s'appelle"* ("what's it called")—playing on the first syllable of *comment*, pronounced *con*—for cunt—in the 16th century. The difficulty of naming it contrasts with the countless words for the male organ, and with the list of adjectives qualifying love, which Sterne enumerates in alphabetical order. Whatever it's called, "Widow Wadman [...] stood, however, ready harnessed and caparisoned at all points to watch accidents". Sterne calls her attitude "love militancy", using the captain's vocabulary. Indeed, her actions will be portrayed in the style of his sieges, when "Fate" provoked her acting out.

Touché[17]

The Fates, who had foreseen the amours of widow Wadman and my uncle Toby, had established "such a chain of causes and effects" so as to render the meeting inevitable, thanks to the hedgerow between their gardens:

> [From there] she could observe my uncle Toby's motions and was mistress likewise of his councils of war; and as his unsuspecting heart had given leave to the corporal, [...] to make her a wicker gate [...] to enlarge her walks, it enabled her to carry on her approaches to the very door of the sentry box, [...] and endeavour to blow my uncle Toby up in the very sentry box itself.

Her invasion follows a precise course: "'tis certain from every day's observation of man, that he may be set on fire like a candle at either end, —
provided there is a sufficient wick standing out; [...] and—by lighting it at
the bottom". Mrs. Wadman decided to light the captain at both ends. Using
all available means, she resorted to the pins—yes, pins again—that held the
maps fastened in the sentry box. A scene of hand-to-hand combat grants her
success in no time:

> Mrs Wadman had nothing more to do [...] but to extend her right hand
> and, edging in her left foot at the same movement, to take hold of the
> map [...], with outstretched neck [...], —to advance it towards her, on
> which my uncle Toby's passions were sure to catch fire, —for he would
> instantly take hold of the other corner of the map in his left hand and,
> with the end of his pipe in the other, begin an explanation.

The phallic object becomes a war trophy, thanks to a "stroke of generalship":

> which was to take [his] tobacco pipe out of his hand [...] under the pre-
> tence [...] of pointing more distinctly at some redoubt or breastwork in
> the map, [...] before my uncle Toby (poor soul!) had well march'd above
> half a dozen toises with it.—It obliged [him] to make use of his fore-
> finger. [...] Whereas, in following my uncle Toby's forefinger with hers,
> [...]—pressing sometimes against the side of it, —then treading upon
> its nail, [...], —then touching it here, —then there and so on, — it set
> something at least in motion.

The widow's next action is to attack "the main body". When the map falls:

> [...] my uncle Toby, in the simplicity of his soul, would lay his hand flat
> upon [the map] in order to go on with his explanation, and Mrs Wad-
> man, by a manoeuvre as quick as thought, would [...] place hers close
> beside it;—Thine [hand], dear uncle Toby! was never now in its right
> place.—How could she forget to make him sensible that it was her leg
> (and no one else's) slightly press'd against the calf of his?—So that [he]
> being thus attacked [...] on both his wings, — was it a wonder if [...] it
> put his centre into disorder? —The deuce take it! said my uncle Toby.

The erotic influence of Parisian salons is visible.

Proof of the attack is offered by the document found by Tristram, after his
father's death, in the family archives:

> These attacks [...], you will readily conceive to be of different kinds, [...]
> like the attacks which history is full of [...]. A general looker-on would
> scarcely allow them to be attacks at all [....];—but I write not to them.

He writes for those of us who value the writings of veterans, in moleskin notebooks forgotten at the back of drawers, which I ask their descendants to bring me. Stéphane Audoin-Rouzeau, historian of World War I, based his book *Quelle histoire*[18] on three and a half pages written by his grandfather during a terrifying night between the 24th and the 25th of August 1915, which left deep psychological scars.

Bion[19] reproduced the sketches and maps he drew at the front in Northern France in his *War Memoirs*, written to replace the lost diary he had kept in lieu of letters to his parents. These sketches are so precise that Jean-Max Gaudillière, who spent his youth in Picardie, was able to recognise landscapes, villages and canals. The map found by Tristram "in perfect preservation" was that of Bouchain:

> [...] there is still remaining the marks of a snuffy finger and thumb, which there is all the reason [...] to imagine were Mrs Wadman's; for the opposite side of the margin, which I suppose to have been my uncle Toby's, the pipe smoker-- is absolutely clean.

The novel delimits two psychic spaces mapped out by pipe tobacco or snuff. Topologically, they inscribe Toby's traumatic memory on the map of Namur and his sexual desire on the map of Bouchain:

> By all that is priestly! I value this precious relic [...] more than all the relics of the Roman Church, — excepting [...] the pricks which enter'd the flesh of St Radegunda in the desert, which in your road from FESSE (buttock) to CLUNY the nuns of that name will shew you for love.

Clearly, the nuns of Burgundy are a rich source of puns—but not for long. Suddenly, Sterne changes course, going from the play on signifiers of desire to the erasure of traces on the bowling green in 1713, when the Peace of Utrecht was signed.

Arrested time

When peacetime discourse erases the traces of war experience, traumatic revivals keep occurring, striving for their inscription. Captain Bion's *Long Week-End*,[20] written during his late exile in Los Angeles, ends with the sentence: "I was 21 and had not yet experienced what it was to be a relic. Though we did not realize it, we were men who had grown from insignificance to irrelevance in the passage of a few short years". His second book, *All My Sins Remembered*, begins with:

> Nevertheless, I did not see; I did not see that peacetime was *no time* for me. I didn't know, however many pretty ribbons I put on my wartime uniform, that wartime also was *no time* for me. I was twenty-four

[...]; — no good for war, no good for peace, and too old to change. It was truly terrifying. Sometimes, it burst out in sleep. Terrified. What about? Nothing, nothing.

Bion studied medicine and became a psychoanalyst after having tried the couch of an analyst he nicknamed "FIP, Feel-It-in-the-Past", who ignored "his" war, which went on in the present. In 1937, he met his second analyst, John Rickman,[21] who was a Quaker and had worked during the war with traumatised civilians and soldiers. Rickman's mentor was William Rivers, who treated traumatised officers at Craiglochardt in Scotland during World War I, and asserted that in such cases, the unconscious was not "repressed" but "suppressed".[22]

Returning to the novel, we are now introduced to Toby's Shandean analysis with corporal Trim.

Frontline psychotherapy[23]

In the aftermath of the Treaty of Utrecht in April 1713,[24] stipulating the demolition of the port of Dunkirk, Trim arrives on the bowling green to rid it of "military little stores, [...] with an air the most expressive of disconsolation that can be imagined [...]—when a heigh-ho! from the sentry box forbad him". Not having the heart to continue, he decides to do the job during the night and pretends to go on as if nothing had happened. All the while, he comes closer to uncle Toby, until he sits down at his feet and begins a psychotherapy, whose stages we recognise.

First, a careful assessment:

> It was a thousand pities then, said the corporal, [...] to destroy these works, —and a thousand pities to have let them stood. —Thou art right, Trim, in both cases, said my uncle Toby. —This, continued the corporal, is the reason that from the beginning of their demolition to the end, —I have never once whistled or sung or laugh'd or cri'd, or talk'd of pass'd done deeds.

Another instance of "neither...nor", which leaves one speechless.

Such a dilemma is called a "catch twenty-two", after the title of Joseph Heller's novel[25] in which a pilot on a US Air Force base during World War II, exhausted by constant air raids, pretends he has gone mad in order to be grounded. But considering the general madness around him, his argument shows that his mind is sound and his request is denied.

The second stage of the psychotherapy is the art of storytelling:

> Thou hast many excellencies, Trim, said my uncle Toby, and I hold it not the least of them, as thou happenest to be a storyteller, that of the

number thou hast told me either to amuse me in my painful hours or divert me in my grave ones—thou hast seldom told me a bad one. — Because, an' please Your Honour, except one of a *King of Bohemia and his seven castles*, —they are all true, for they are about myself.

To get out of a zone of death during a session, I too tell stories, as I said, sometimes about myself, risking the disapproval of my colleagues. The seven castles of the King of Bohemia intrigue the captain:

But prithee, what is that story? Thou hast excited my curiosity. [...]— Provided [...] it is not a merry one [...]. —Nor would I have it altogether a grave one [...]. —It is neither the one nor the other, replied the corporal, but will suit Your Honour exactly.

The corporal makes an uneasy bow and pulls off his Montero cap with some difficulty, since he is squatting on the ground. The tale emerges from "the ashes of history"—the title of Cathy Caruth's book[26]—from the imminent destruction of Dunkirk on the bowling green. Trim tries to find "in what key his story would best suit his master's humour, —hemming once or twice. He exchanged a single look of kindness with him and set off thus".

The Story of the King of Bohemia and His Seven Castles

The title of the tale has a deep resonance for Sterne. In 1759, the year he "turned author", his wife was raving that she was the Queen of Bohemia. Moreover, the king has as many castles as Roger Sterne had children—four of them having died when Laurence was a child. This title is repeated five times before the story actually starts, since Toby keeps interrupting. Finally, the corporal will tell a story about himself that he had never told before. Shandean analysis, like that of madness and traumas, consists of repeated attempts to tell an untold story.

1 **First attempt: the erasure of traces**

The role of *therapon* vacillates between Trim and Toby throughout the novel. The corporal has barely reached the land of Bohemia, under the reign of "a certain king of Bo - - he —", when Toby suggests that he put his cap on to avoid catching cold. Seeing Trim glance at his frayed cap, he adds encouragingly: "Nothing in this world, Trim, is made to last for ever". The captain's well-meaning comment brings back the disappearance of Trim's brother: "But when tokens, dear Tom, of thy love and remembrance wear out, [...] what shall we say?—The corporal [...] put it on [...] passing his hand across his forehead to rub out a pensive wrinkle". This is precisely when there is more to say.

2　Second attempt: a stoppage of time

Trim loses track of chronology and sets the tale in the age of giants. Toby interrupts him again: "Tis thy own [story], Trim, so ornament it after thy own fashion; and take any date [...] thou art heartily welcome". The corporal chooses:

> the *very worst* year of the whole bunch [...]—It was the year next him, —which being the Year of Our Lord Seventeen Hundred and Twelve, when the Duke of Ormonde was playing the devil in Flanders, —the corporal took it and set out with it afresh on his expedition to Bohemia.

By alluding to current events, Trim breaks the rule of Greek tragedies: to invoke far-off mythical eras, in order to avoid traumatic revivals triggered in the audience by recent wars.

3　Third attempt: the time-space of a battle

The expected effect is indeed produced, since 1712 was a year of defeat for the English. Toby interrupts Trim for the third time:

> To tell thee truly, Trim [...], any other date would have pleased me much better, not only on account of the sad stain upon our history that year [...], —but likewise on the score [...] of thy own story; because if there are [...] giants in it [...]—thou shouldst have carried [them] back some seven or eight hundred years out of harm's way [...] of critics.

Upset, Trim swears never to tell the story again "either to man, woman or child". This is how an analysis stops, when confronted with the impossibility of inscribing in the past that constantly returns in the present. Toby sweeps away the difficulty with a "poo — poo"! uttered "with accents of such sweet encouragement [...] that the corporal went on [...] with more alacrity than ever". But the recent date has revived the battles in Flanders for him as well.

The fourth stage of Toby's psychotherapy depicts the critical moment when roles are reversed. "Trauma speaks to trauma", as Jean-Max Gaudillière said, reactivating in the analyst's history a cut-out unconscious tied to events out of time.

4　Fourth attempt: war revivals

The corporal took up the story again "in a louder voice, rubbing his hands together cheerily", not at all expecting what was to come. "There was [...] a certain King of Bohemia —Leave out the date entirely, Trim, quoth my uncle Toby, [...]; a story passes very well without these niceties, unless one is pretty sure of 'em". Trim agrees, with a nod, not suspecting that leaving out the date will bring war into the present. Toby himself sends chronology flying:

> —It is not easy, Trim, for one bred up as thou and I have been to arms, who seldom looks farther forward than to the end of his

musket or backwards beyond his knapsack, to know much about this matter. —God bless Your Honour! said the corporal, won by the manner of my uncle's Toby's reasoning.

Such a manner of reasoning sends him off to battle at his captain's side, listing the attributes that earned him his war name "Trim", meaning one who takes good care of everything—and he concludes triumphantly: "What business [...] has a soldier [...] to know anything at all of *geography*? —Thou wouldst have said *chronology*, Trim, said my uncle Toby". We are reminded of Don Quixote's corrections of Sancho's vocabulary.[27] In the sentry box, Toby rises up, followed by Trim, to cross all of Europe under Marlborough's command—an advance not possible without the aid of geography, Sterne notes.

As they advance, the two men argue about who invented gunpowder first, whether it was the Moors, the Christians or the Chinese, called by Trim "a pack of liars". Toby considers the Great Wall a "miserable" example of military architecture, since it lacks flanks. "Like one of my seven castles", says Trim, trying to bring his master back from the Far East, since he still had "half a dozen [castles] in Bohemia which he knew not how to get off his hands".

5 Fifth attempt: the reality of fiction

Trim tries to start again: "This *unfortunate* King of Bohemia...—Was he unfortunate then"? Toby interrupts. The corporal sent the epithet with all its synonyms to the devil and "after a hem and a hew, he went on: —The King of Bohemia [...]—taking great pleasure [...] in navigation [...] was *unfortunate* [as] throughout the whole Kingdom of Bohemia [there was] no seaport town whatever". Toby objects that the King's dream meant the overflowing of a great part of Germany and the destruction of millions of its inhabitants. "Scandalous! cried Trim. [...] He made a bow of unfeigned conviction and went on".

Now, verbs are conjugated in the present tense of the indicative, showing the reader that the two soldiers have entered the tale. Trim uses the verb *happen*, unaware that it would lead to a debate on chance and necessity:

> Now, the King of Bohemia with his queen and courtiers *happening* one fine summer's evening to walk out —Aye! there the word happening is right, Trim, cried my uncle Toby, for [...]—'twas a matter of contingency, which might happen or not, just as chance ordered it.

One of the stock phrases used in our psychoanalytic school was: "It's no coincidence that..." But, in fact, when the times are out of joint and causality no longer applies, chance becomes crucial. Trim would agree with such analysts, since he reminds Toby that king William of Orange often said that "every ball had its billet". Diderot[28] remembered this debate when he began *Jacques the Fatalist and His Master* in 1765 after

Sterne's stay in Paris—a novel he went on writing until his death in 1783. It begins:

> How had they met? By chance like everyone else. What were their names? What's it to you? Where were they going? Does anyone really know where they're going? What were they saying? The Master wasn't saying anything, and Jacques was saying that his Captain used to say that everything that happens to us here below, for good and for ill, was written up there, on high.

Trim subscribes to Jacques's captain's theory:

> I believe [...] to this day that the shot which disabled me at the Battle of Landen was pointed at my knee for no other purpose but to take me out of his service and place me in Your Honour's, where I should be taken so much better care of in my old age.—[...] Besides, said the corporal [...], —if it had not been for that single shot, I had never [...] been in love.

Thunderbolt! The captain is stunned. His therapy enters a sixth stage, in which the analyst may disclose a piece of his own history.

6   **The Battle of Landen and Trim's amours**

Unwittingly, Toby has triggered the corporal's trauma, suffered when he was left for dead on the battlefield. The captain inquires with a smile:

> So thou wast once in love, Trim! —Souse! replied the corporal, — over head and ears! [...] Prithee, when? where?—and how came it to pass? —I never heard one word of it before, quoth my uncle Toby. [...] It's high time I should.

The 1693 Battle of Landen unfolds before our eyes. Toby has not forgotten the total rout of the English camp, during which Maréchal de Luxembourg encircled William of Orange:

> I see him with the knot of his scarf just shot off, infusing fresh spirits into poor Galway's regiment (...) —Brave! brave, by Heaven! cried my uncle Toby;—he deserves a crown. —As richly as a thief a halter, shouted Trim.

Trim's reply makes the glory of battle drop to the ground, where the corporal relives the solitude of imminent death among the men lying around him. "Remembrance of hell, the hell of remembrance" was the phrase used by Claude Barrois,[29] head psychiatrist and psychoanalyst at the Val de Grâce military hospital in Paris. But Trim is no longer alone, for Toby is there to witness the carnage: "As the number of wounded was prodigious and no one had time to think of anything but his own safety [...] I was left upon the field, said the corporal. —Thou was so, poor fellow! replied my uncle Toby".

The corporal lay on the field all night, until noon the next day, when he was put into a cart to be taken to a hospital. Two and a half centuries later, the daughter-in-law of an English soldier left wounded in no man's land brought me a similar story, neatly written out by the soldier for his fiancée after the Great War. The letter described the timeless time during which he pretended to be dead, under sniper fire, until he could crawl slowly towards his own lines.

Trim and Toby's haunting memories turn into a contest of injuries:

> There is no part of the body, an' please Your Honour, where a wound occasions more intolerable anguish than upon the knee — Except the groin, said my uncle Toby. [...] —In my opinion, replied the corporal, the knee must certainly be the most acute, there being so many tendons and what-d'ye-call-'ems all about it. -- It is for that reason, quoth my uncle Toby, that the groin is infinitely more sensible, —there being not only as many tendons [...]—, —but more over ***—.

Sterne's dashes are additional lungs, amplifying the breath he lacks when he lies in the same distress on his bed. In the meantime, Mrs. Wadman, hidden behind the hedge, is hit full in the face by the volley of dashes and asterisks in their conversation. "Instantly [she] stopp'd her breath, unpinn'd her mob at the chin and stood up upon one leg". The *pin* is back, unbeknownst to the two men: "The dispute was maintained with amicable and equal force [...] for some time; till Trim [...], —at length, recollected that he had often cried at his master's suffering, but never shed a tear at his own".

Thanks to Toby's attentive presence, Trim is able to express the pain buried in the desolate battlefield of Landen:

> The anguish of my knee [...] was excessive in itself; and [...] the roughness of the roads [...] making bad still worse, —every step was death to me [...] —(Poor soul! said my uncle Toby), —an' please Your Honour, was more than I could sustain.

The corporal recounts his torment to a "passionate witness", a term we owe to Dori Laub, who was only able to talk about his deportation at the age of six to a concentration camp in Romania after his analyst acted as a witness to the liberation of the Terezin camp. Then, "a curtain lifted" on the horrors of the camp, which had been cut out for the sake of survival.

The lady of Trim's thoughts[30]

The curtain rises for Trim on the scene which had remained dissociated for the same purpose. The cart carrying him halts by chance before a peasant's house, where he is helped in. "I had much rather lie down [...] and die than go on". A young woman gives him a cordial, poured over some sugar, and takes him to a bed in a corner. As he remembers that moment when he fainted in her arms, Trim wipes away a tear: "She was a good soul! as Your Honour, said the corporal [...], will hear. —I thought love had been a joyous thing, quote my uncle Toby. — 'Tis the most serious thing [...] that is in the world".

The story begins not unlike that of Le Fever. The young woman persuades the coachman to leave. When Trim comes to, she is rubbing his temples and he takes her for the peasant's daughter:

> ... so [I] offer'd her a little purse with eighteen florins which my poor brother Tom (here Trim wip'd his eyes) had sent me as a token, by a recruit, just before he set out for Lisbon —I never told Your Honour that piteous story, —here he wiped his eyes a third time.

Traumatic memory which confuses time periods addresses itself to two therapists at the same time: Toby in the present of the narrative and the young woman in "the past presented" of Tom's arrest by the Inquisition—and Bion's title for the second part of his *Memoir of the Future*.[31] She tells Trim: "I'll be your banker;—but as that office alone will not keep me employ'd, I'll be your nurse too".

Reassured, he looks more attentively at her long black dress and the cambric-trimmed cape that hides her hair, concluding that she is one of the nuns often seen in Flanders. Toby knows about them:

> By thy description, Trim [...], I dare say she was a young Beguine, of which there are none to be found anywhere but in the Spanish Nether-lands [...];—they differ from nuns in this: that they can quit their cloister if they choose to marry; they visit and take care of the sick by profession. [...] —She often told me, quoth Trim, she did it for the love of Christ; —I did not like it.

Beguinages, which can still be seen in Bruges and Ghent, were also places of refuge for women without protection.

The Beguine's talent for psychotherapy[32]

Trim's Beguine starts by inventing the four principles: Proximity, Immediacy, Expectancy and Simplicity, which Thomas Salmon was to formulate in 1917. Once real *proximity* is established between Trim and the Beguine, she hurries away—*immediacy*—to the kitchen and comes back quickly with flannels. For the better of two hours, she massages his knee, gives him a bowl of gruel and wishes him a restful night, promising—*expectancy*—to return early in the morning. Running a high fever, he spends the night "cutting the world in two, —to give her half of it… I was so accustomed to receive life from her hands that I lost colour and my heart sickened when she left the room".

Here, Sterne writes that:

> the corporal made one of the strangest reflexion in the world: '*It was not love.*—for during the three weeks she was almost constantly with me, fomenting my knee with her hand, night and day, —I can honestly say […] that ******** *once*.

Two long rows of asterisks express what failed to happen. "That was very odd, Trim, quoth my uncle Toby. —I think so too, said Mrs Wadman (behind the hedge). —It never did, said the corporal".

The simplicity of Trim's sentence marks the physical difference between an intense relationship aimed at survival—called *philia* in ancient Greek—and sexual desire. The corporal has his own theory:

> But 'tis no marvel […], —for love […] is exactly like war in this: that a soldier, though he has escaped three weeks complete o' Saturday night, — may nevertheless be shot through his heart on Sunday morning. —It happened so here […], with this difference only:—that it was on Sunday in the afternoon when I fell in love all at once […];—it burst upon me […] like a bomb, —scarce giving me time to say 'God bless me'.

The war metaphor, for once, stupefies Toby: "I thought a man never fell in love so very suddenly. —Yes, an' please your Honour, if he is in the way of it". At his master's request, Trim describes this path with military precision. That Sunday afternoon, the peasant and his wife were absent. "Everything was still and hush as midnight about the house—There was not so much as a duck or a duckling about the yard—When the fair Beguine came in to see me". The adjective "fair" insists; the wound is "in a fair way" of healing. The inflammation has subsided, but a terrible itch above and below his knee has kept Trim awake all night. Now that his wound is closing, Trim emerges from symbiosis with his guardian angel while she unknowingly foments desire.

To "foment" also means to massage, an art in which the Beguine is an expert. She kneels down to rub below the knee with the index of her right hand, back and forth around the edge of the wound. Then he feels her second finger rubbing around the wound for a long time:

> —I blush'd when I saw how white a hand she had;—I shall never […] behold another hand so white whilst I live —Not in that place, said my uncle Toby. […] The corporal […] could not forbear smiling. —Then she proceeded to rub at length with three [finger], —till she brought down the fourth, and then rubb'd with her whole hand. […], —it was softer than satin.

Worried that she would tire of the effort, he hears her reply, much to his chagrin: "I would do a thousand times more [...] for the love of Christ". Still, repressed desire manifests itself in a transgressive gesture when her hand moves above the flannel to rub the part above the knee:

> She continued rub-rub-rubbing, [...], I perceived, then, I was beginning to be in love —[...]—I felt it spread [...] to every part my frame—[...] the longer strokes she took, —the more the fire kindled in my veins, —till at length, by two or three strokes longer than the rest, —my passion rose to the highest pitch; —I seiz'd her hand —And then thou clapp'd it to thy lips, Trim, said my uncle Toby, —and madest a speech.

Sterne leaves the lovers to their romance. Voyeurs have no place here. Now, he can tackle Toby's amours, which triggered his decision to "turn author" in 1759, when he was at his wits end. The word author comes from the Latin verb *augeo*, "I augment", hence the noun *auctoritas*—that we hear in "authorship". The tale of Tim's love puts Toby in mind of the Lady of Thoughts of courtly love, a Dulcinea, the *Dame lointaine* (far-off Lady) of warriors poets, not so out of reach when she is embodied by a fair beguine who smiles and takes care of a wounded soldier.

The story of the eye[33]

Trim's psychotherapy proves effective, for Toby has accepted the destruction of Dunkirk on the bowling green and asked the corporal to take away the wheelbarrow with all his tools. Seeing this, the widow "silently sallied forth from her arbour" and conceived of a new offensive. As soon as the corporal finished telling the story of his amours, she replaced the pin that held her mob and went through the wicker gate.

The occasion was too good to miss. She cried out:

> holding up her cambric handkerchief to her left eye as she approach'd, and squeezing herself down upon the corner of his bench: —I am half-distracted, Captain Shandy, [...];—a mote—or sand—or something, —I know not what, has got into this eye of mine.

The mysterious "something" is back, since nothing is visible, though Toby looks into it "with innocency of heart".

Here, the Story of the Eye—Georges Bataille's title—is told by Sterne in a merry style:

> I see him yonder with his pipe pendulous in his hand and the ashes falling out of it, —looking— and looking [...], with twice the good nature

that ever Galileo look'd for a spot in the sun.—In vain! [...]—widow
Wadman's left eye shines this moment as lucid as her right;—[...] there
is nothing, my dear paternal uncle! but one lambent delicious fire, furtively shooting out from every part of it, [...] into thine—If thou lookest
[...] in search of this mote one moment longer, —thou art undone.

The warning comes too late, for Mrs. Wadman has launched the second
stage of her campaign. I am asked not to witness her strategy:

> Now, of all the eyes which ever were created, —from your own, madam,
> up to those of Venus herself [...]—there never was an eye of them all so
> fitted to rob my uncle Toby of his repose as the very eye at which he was
> looking;—it was not, madam, a rolling eye [...], —petulant or imperi-
> ous [...], —but 'twas an eye full of gentle salutations, —[...] whispering
> soft—like the last low accents of an expiring saint.

Sterne describes Toby as a man devoid of worldly sophistication, a man with
a child's soul, who has lived through war experiences that shatter the mirror
of appearances. Now that his safe space has been destroyed by the Treaty of
Utrecht, he longs for the eye that whispers:

> How can you live comfortless, Captain Shandy, and alone, without a
> bosom to lean your head on? [...]— It was an eye —But I shall be in love
> with it myself if I say another word about it. — It did my uncle Toby's
> business.

In the background, we can see the silhouette of the Duchess who lured Don
Quixote with the same simpering tone. Both "knights" are easily taken in,
contrary to Walter:

> My father [...] was very subject to this passion before he married, —but
> [had] a little subacid kind of drollish impatience in his nature. [...] He
> would never submit to it, but would pish and huff and bounce and kick
> and write the bitterrest Philippicks against the eye that ever man wrote.

His brother:

> sat still and let the poison work in his veins without resistance;—in the
> sharpest exacerbation of his wound (like that on his groin), he never
> dropped one fretful or discontented word [...];—he sat solitary and pen-
> sive with his pipe, looking at his lame leg, —then shifting out a senti-
> mental heigh-ho! which incommodated no one mortal. He took it like
> a lamb—I say.

Lovesickness, in Toby's case, will not lead to depression, but express itself as a blunder worthy of the "fool" he portrays in the novel.

Let us remember that in the Middle Ages, the Feast of Fools was celebrated in late December, at the same time as Innocents' Day, the Feast of Children. "In truth the captain had mistook his pain, at first, for having taken a ride with my father that very morning [...], — by trotting on too hastily [...] upon an uneasy saddle". The result is a blister in "the nethermost part of my uncle Toby", until the blister breaking and the pain remaining, he was "convinced that his wound [...] had gone to his heart". Blisters in the heart are invisible and take time to heal, especially after lengthy submission. When they break open in my office, the long-ago child, man or woman wonders how they could have borne them for so long.

This slow process will go on until the end of the novel.

In Love[34]

The captain is familiar with zones of catastrophe, but like Don Quixote, he is estranged from normal life:

> The world is ashamed of being virtuous.—My uncle Toby knew little of the world; and therefore, when he felt he was in love with widow Wadman, he had no conception that the thing was [...] to be made a mystery of.

He informs the corporal, his "humble friend", in a matter-of-fact tone: "I am in love, corporal".

Trim is as stunned as Toby was when he learned of Trim's love:

> Your Honour was very well the day before yesterday when I was telling [...] the story of the King of Bohemia [...] —What became of that story, Trim? —We lost it [...] somehow betwixt us, —but Your Honour was as free from love then as I am. —'Twas just whilst thou went'st off with the wheelbarrow;—with Mrs Wadman, quoth my uncle Toby. —She has left a ball here, —[he] added, pointing to his breast.

The corporal senses the danger and proposes "to begin with making a good thundering attack upon her in return".

On the other side of the hedge, the fake ingénue is holding a war council with her servant Bridget. The Devil, "who never sleeps", although he pretends to "lie dead in a ditch", is prompting the widow to assess "the monstrous wound upon the poor captain's groin". The adjective underscores the gap between her repulsion and the care provided by the Beguine. Not persuaded, Bridget argues: "It may not, madam, be so very large". She believes besides "that 'tis dried up". But she has to obey her mistress' orders:

> I could like to know, —merely for his sake, said Mrs Wadman —We'll know the long and the broad of it in ten days, —answered Mrs Bridget, for whilst the captain is paying his addresses to you, —I'm confident Mr Trim will be for making love to me, —and I'll let him as much as he will [...], —to get it all out of him.

On the other side of the frontline, Trim plans the counterattack, as Toby promotes him to the rank of aide-de-camp, giving him a crown to celebrate the occasion. The corporal has much to do: repair Toby's laced uniform, "put [his] white Ramillies wig into pipes", wipe his sword with chalk and have the tailor turn his scarlet breeches. Toby would prefer the plush ones, but Trim finds them "too clumsy". As for him, he will be wearing his Montero cap and poor Le Fever's uniform. The contrast is obvious between the plot hatched in secret and their flamboyance displayed for all to see. "I'll answer for it, said the corporal, snapping his fingers over his head—that the day is our own".

Toby is not so bold:

> I wish I may but manage it right, said my uncle Toby, —but I declare, corporal, I had rather march up to the very edge of a trench —A woman is quite a different thing, —said the corporal. —I suppose so, quoth my uncle Toby.

The captain feels the anguish common on the eve of battle.

Return of the hobby horse[35]

The captain will need time to trust the subliminal messages he has recorded. In the meanwhile, Walter makes fun of his younger brother's love story:

> If anything in this world [...] could have provoked my uncle Toby during the time he was in love, it was the perverse use my father was always making of an expression of Hilarion the Hermit; who, in speaking of his abstinence, —would say [...] that they were the means he used to make his *ass* leave off kicking. [...] 'twas his constant mode of expression:—he never used the word *passions* once, —but *ass* always.

Sterne points out the difference between Walter's animal and Toby's hobby horse. Our talismans against danger, like the books I carried around before I knew how to read during the war, are not objects of desire. I imagine one could write a dissertation on their respective functions, but I prefer Sterne's personal comparison:

> My hobby-horse [...] is no way a vicious beast; [...]—'Tis the sporting little filly-folly which carries you out for the present hour—a maggot, a butterfly, a picture, a fiddlestick—an uncle Toby's siege. [...]—But for my father's ass—oh! mount him—[...]mount him not:—'tis a beast concupiscent.

"Ass" and "filly-folly" may embody the kicking of repressed sexual desire and the galloping away from death zones. But despite his passion for theory, Walter confuses the two paradigms, as mainstream analysts often do. When he learns about Toby's amours, he taunts him glibly: "Well! dear brother Toby [...], —and how goes it with your ASS"? Toby takes the question literally and informs Walter about the blister on his bottom, using his brother's words: "My A—, quoth my uncle Toby, is much better, —brother Shandy".

Despite his apparent candour, the captain understands the sexual allusion and prefers to look like a fool:

> When a man, writes Sterne, is hemm'd in by two indecorums and must commit one of 'em—I always observe—let him choose which he will, the world will blame him;—so I should not be astonished if it blames my uncle Toby.

Shandean analysis, like some of our sessions, mixes—*shandies*—the two types of unconscious: repressed and suppressed, but do not confuse them.

On the edge of catastrophes, the jester shows the break in the social link and makes us laugh, at the risk of being reduced to nothing—like the famous vagrant in *The Tramp* embodied by Charlie Chaplin,[36] akin to "Ole Tristram" whose statue stood in front of the church in Halifax where Laurence went to school. Similarly, when the captain plays the fool, he triggers liberating laughter:

> Everybody, said my mother, says you are in love, brother Toby, —and we hope it is true. —I am as much in love, sister [...], as any man usually. — Humph! said my father. —And when did you know it? quoth my mother. —When the blister broke, replied my uncle Toby.

This reply having restored Walter's good humour, he renewed his offensive by drawing on Plato's *Symposium*,[37] to compare two kinds of love: "I think when a man is in love it behoves him a little to consider which of the two he has fallen into". We recognise the two Aphrodites mentioned in the dialogue: the "heavenly" Uranian and the "popular" Pandemian, but "my father" says nothing about the love involved in Toby's Eros that Socrates—a veteran of the Peloponnesian War—invokes by quoting Diotima.

Habeas phallus[38]

Still, unlike analysts who quote Platonic dialogues without checking the translation, Walter has Plato at his fingertips and is about to launch into a seminar on transference when Toby causes a commotion by asserting that he just wants to marry, love his wife and have a few children.

His brother is outraged: "A few children! Cried my father, rising out of his chair and looking full in my mother's face [...] as he walk'd to and fro. [...]—not that I should be sorry hadst thou a score", he added, recovering himself. Then he sits down again to think of a new way of destroying Toby's offspring, and delivers another treacherous blow:

> On the contrary, I should rejoice, —and be as kind, Toby, to every one of them as a father. Nay, moreover, [...], —so much dost thou possess, my dear Toby, of the milk of human nature, —'tis piteous the world is not peopled by creatures which resemble thee; and was I an Asiatic monarch [...], —I would [...] procure thee the most beautiful women in my empire, and I would oblige thee, *nolens volens*, to beget for me one subject every month. [At this], my mother took a pinch of snuff.

An old hand at the game of war, Toby senses the ploy and brings Walter back from Asia by invoking the principle of *habeas corpus*. "Now, I would not, quoth my uncle Toby, get a child *nolens volens*, that is, whether I would or no, to please to greatest prince upon —". At this objection, Walter strikes at the very core of Toby's wound:

> And 'twould be cruel of me, brother Toby, to compel thee, said my father, —but 'tis a case put to shew thee that it is not thy begetting a child —'in case thou shouldst be able'—but the system of Love and marriage thou goest upon which I would set thee right in.

The suspicion of impotence recruits into its service two characters as diverse as the widow and Walter to undermine Toby as much as they please.

In contrast, we recall the words of Diotima when she endows Eros with a filiation: his father is *Poros*, meaning "the passage"—hence the word "porosity"—and his mother is *Penia*, meaning "poverty"—penury. Acting as a psychotherapist during the plague in Athens in 430 BC, Diotima draws attention to the transferential porosity needed to counteract the penury of speech when one is attacked by a ruthless agency.

The parson comes to Toby's rescue and opens a passage when he lacks words: "There is at least, said Yorick, a great deal of reason [...] in Captain Shandy's opinion of love...." But he is cut short by Walter's condescendence: "I wish, Yorick, said my father, you had read Plato..." At the height of the dispute, Slop tries to leave the pagan realm by invoking the Immaculate Conception: "Well push'd, nun! quoth my father".

War! [39]

After insulting Slop, treating Yorick like a dunce and calling his brother impotent, Walter is about to attack all convents in Christendom, when Trim arrives to inform Toby that the scarlet breeches had already been turned before by the tailor. "Then turn them again, brother, said my father rapidly. [...]. —They are as rotten as dirt, said the corporal. —Then by all means [...], bespeak a new pair, brother".

Since the dispute is now as worn out as the breeches, Walter is impelled to spill the beans, revealing to all those present a plan Toby knows nothing about: "Widow Wadman has been deeply in love with my brother Toby for many years and has used every art and circumvention of woman to outwit him into the same passion". We realise then that at Shandy Hall—like in psychiatric staff meetings about patients—what is true of cuckolding applies perfectly: the person concerned is the last to be informed. Now, Toby also learns his brother's diagnosis concerning the widow's "hysterical structure": "[...] now that she has caught him, — her fever will be pass'd its height". And he goes on theorising:

> In this case [...], which Plato, I am persuaded, never thought of, —love, you see, is not so much a SENTIMENT as a SITUATION into which a man enters as my brother Toby would do into a *corps*, —no matter whether he loves the service or no;—being once in it, —he acts as if he did, and takes every step to shew himself a man of prowess. [...] For this reason, [...] not withstanding all the world knows that Mrs Wadman *affects* my brother Toby—and my brother Toby [...] *affects* Mrs Wadman [...], yet I will answer for it that this selfsame tune will not be play'd this twelvemonth. [...] The hypothesis [...] was plausible enough, and my uncle Toby had but a single word to object to it, —in which Trim stood ready to second him.

This word is reflected in the questioning look Toby gives the corporal: "We have taken our measures badly". When everything falls apart, they both follow William of Orange's motto: "I will maintain". Trim bets a shilling on his precious Montero cap that the attack will be carried out that very night. Such high stakes are unsettling for Walter:

> —Now, what dost thou believe? —That widow Wadman [...] cannot hold it out ten days, answers the corporal.. —And whence, cried Slop jeeringly, hast thou all this knowledge of woman, friend? —By falling in love with a popish clergy woman, said Trim. —'Twas a Beguine, said my uncle Toby.

Doctor Slop is too enraged to grasp the distinction, which also escapes Walter as he proceeds to "fall in helter-shelter upon the whole order of nuns".

When Toby goes off to have measures taken by the tailor and Yorick to prepare his sermon, "my father", with half an hour to fill before bedtime, "called
for pen, ink and paper, and wrote my uncle Toby [a] letter of instructions".

Sterne has already drawn inspiration from the letter of instructions written by Don Quixote[40] to Sancho Panza before he set off to play the fool by
governing the fictional island of Baratria. But the letter proves useful once
again.

Walter's instructions to Toby on the eve of marriage

The list of instructions follows closely those given by his role model. First,
the recommendation to God's protection; next, advice about grooming, in
an era when baldness was associated with syphilis:

> 'Twere better to keep ideas of baldness out of her fancy. Always carry it
> in thy mind, Toby [...]—women are timid. Let not thy breeches be too
> tight or hang too loose [...] like the trunk-hose of our ancestors. —A just
> medium prevents all conclusions.

Psychological counselling follows:

> Whatever thou hast to say, [...] forget not to utter it in a low soft tone
> of voice. Silence weaves dreams of midnight secrecy into the brain. [...]
> Avoid all kinds of pleasantry and facetiousness and [...] keep from her
> all books and writings [except] devotional tracts [...]; but suffer her not
> to look into Rabelais or Scarron or *Don Quixote* —They are all books
> which excite laughter; and thou knewst, dear Toby, that there is no pas-
> sion as serious as lust.

Sterne is mocking fundamentalism of all kinds, including on matters of
wooing.

Walter recommends a medical approach if all else fails:

> If thou art permitted to sit upon the same sofa with her and she gives
> you occasion to lay thy hands upon hers, —beware of taking it:—[...]
> and if she is not conquer'd by that, and thy ASS continues still kicking,
> which there is great reason to suppose, —thou must begin with first
> losing a few ounces of blood below the ears, [...]., after that, is for [eat-
> ing] little or no [animal] flesh [...] —As for thy drink, [...] it must be the
> infusion of VERVAIN...

After this diet, Walter had nothing else to wish his brother, "unless the
breaking out of a fresh war".

The amorous offensive is to take place the next day, at exactly eleven o'clock. Volume 8 ends with a sudden wish Walter reveals to his wife: "Come, my dear, [...]—'twill be but like a brother and sister if you and I take a walk down to my brother Toby's—to countenance him in this attack of his". Sterne focuses his camera on the arrival of the Shandy couple just as the two men come out of the house to make their sally. "My father had no time but to put the letter of instructions into my uncle Toby's coat pocket— and [wish] his attack prosperous", before turning around to leave the scene. But his wife holds him back, seized with curiosity. "Call it by its right name, my dear [...]—And look through the keyhole as long as you will".

Are the readers invited to take a peek? This question is vitally important in Shandean psychoanalysis.

Notes

1 Sterne, L., *Tristram Shandy*, op. cit., Vol. 8, chs. I–IV.
2 Ross, I. C., *Laurence Sterne: A Life*, op. cit., p. 278.
3 Bion, W., *Second Thoughts*, op. cit., p. 165.
4 Sterne, L., *Tristram Shandy*, op. cit., Vol. 8, ch. V.
5 Lacan, J., Desire and Its Interpretation, in *The Seminar of Jacques Lacan*, Cambridge, UK: Polity, 2019.
6 Sterne, L., *Tristram Shandy*, op. cit., Vol. 8, ch. VI.
7 Longinus, *On the Sublime*, Scotts Valley, CA: CreateSpace, 2017.
8 De Crébillon, P. J. (1765), *The Night and the Moment*, Gale ECCO, 2010. Online.
9 Sterne, L., *Tristram Shandy*, op. cit., Vol. 8, chs. VIII, IX.
10 De Cervantes, M., *Don Quixote II*, op. cit., ch. 31.
11 Chaucer, G., *The Canterbury Tales*, London: Bantam Classics, 1982.
12 Lacan, J., The Subversion of the Subject and the Dialectic of Desire, in *Écrits*, op. cit.
13 Sterne, L., *Tristram Shandy*, op. cit., Vol. 8, chs. IX–XI.
14 Plato, *Symposium*, op. cit.
15 Chaucer, G., The Wife of Bath's Tale, in *The Canterbury Tales*, op. cit.
16 Sterne, L., *Tristram Shandy*, op. cit., Vol. 8, chs. XI–XIII.
17 Sterne, L., *Tristram Shandy*, op. cit., Vol. 8, chs. XIV–XVII.
18 Audoin-Rouzeau, S., *Quelle histoire. Un récit de filiation 1914–2014*, Paris: EHESS-Gallimard-Seuil, 2013.
19 Bion, W., *War Memoirs, June 1917 - January 1919*, London: Karnac, 1997.
20 Bion, W., *The Long Week-End; All My Sins Remembered*, op. cit.
21 Gaudillière, J.-M., *The Birth of a Political Subject*, Routledge, 2021.
22 Rivers, W. The Repression of War Experience, *The Lancet*, Feb. 1918.
23 Sterne, L., *Tristram Shandy*, op. cit., Vol. 8, chs. XVIII, XIX.
24 Sterne, L., *Tristram Shandy*, op. cit., Vol. 6, ch. XXXI.
25 Heller, J., *Catch 22*, New York: Simon & Schuster, 2001.
26 Caruth, C., *Literature in the Ashes of History*, Baltimore: Johns Hopkins University Press, 2013.
27 Davoine, F., *Fighting Melancholia*, Karnac, 2016; Davoine, F. and Gaudillière, J.-M., *A Word to the Wise*, London and New York: Routledge, 2018.
28 Diderot, D., *Jacques the Fatalist and His Master*, New York: Penguin, 2006.

29 Barrois, C., *La psychanalyse du guerrier* (Psychoanalysis of the Warrior), Paris: Hachette, 1993.
30 Sterne, L., Tristram Shandy, op. cit., ch. XX.
31 Bion, W., *A Memoir of the Future, London, Karnac 1995,* Third Part: «The Past Presented.»
32 Sterne, L., *Tristram Shandy*, op. cit., chs. XX–XXII.
33 Sterne, L., *Tristram Shandy*, op. cit., Vol. 8, chs. XXIII–XXVI.
34 Sterne, L., *Tristram Shandy*, op. cit., Vol. 8, chs. XXVII–XXX.
35 Sterne, L., *Tristram Shandy*, op. cit., Vol. 8, chs. XXXI–XXXII.
36 Chaplin, C., (Dir.) *The Tramp*, film, 1915.
37 Plato, *Symposium*, op. cit.
38 Sterne, L., *Tristram Shandy*, op. cit., Vol. 8, chs. XXXIII–XXXIV.
39 Sterne, L., *Tristram Shandy*, op. cit., Vol. 8, ch. XXXIV.
40 De Cervantes, M., *Don Quixote II*, op. cit., chs. 22–23.

9

No to perversion

At the end of the novel, Shandean psychoanalysis is political, as it is in the tradition of the Theatre of Fools which attacks the abuses of the times, like in the analysis of madness and trauma. When Jean-Max Gaudillière and I held our weekly seminars on "Madness and the Social Link"[1] at the EHESS (École des hautes études en sciences sociales), our research director and sociologist Alain Touraine asked us, regarding our work as analysts at the psychiatric hospital: "What are you getting yourselves into"? Since the word "trauma" was not yet in fashion, we answered that madness was an exploration of catastrophic ruptures in the social link. Later, Touraine understood our work and said: "Mad people are the subject of social sciences". In the 1920s, Harry Stack Sullivan, a pioneer of the psychoanalysis of psychosis in the US, had already said this.

Volume 9 concludes the story of Toby's amours, ending with his conquest of liberty in a context where slavery was being abolished.

The great man

The novel began with a dedication "to the Right Honourable Mr Pitt", preceding the first volume, published by Dodsley in 1760. The "DEDICATION TO A GREAT MAN" at the beginning of Volume 9, published in 1767 by Becket and Dehont, is addressed to the same statesman.

In his first Dedication, Sterne spoke of his thatched house, where he strives "to fence against the infirmities of ill health, and other evils of life, by mirth", saying: "[...] every time a man smiles, —but much more so, when he laughs, [...] it adds something to this fragment of life". After resigning in 1761, William Pitt returned in 1766 as Prime Minister, and was elevated to the rank of Earl Chatham. By 1767, Sterne's confidence is great enough to allow him to joke. He compares his1760 dedication, addressed *a priori* to the Right Honourable Mr. Pitt for his "amusement", with the second one addressed *a posteriori* to Lord *******, whose promotion is celebrated with a greater number of asterisks.

DOI: 10.4324/9781003224907-9

Foreseeing that we might not understand the pun, the author adds a literal explanation. In Latin, *a posteriori* refers to the part of the minister that the author, exposed to "the jealousy of Their Reverences", will be accused of kissing, in the vain hope of preferment. Diderot[2] will pick up the allusion in *Rameau's Nephew*, when the Nephew mocks the parasites who flock to "kiss the ass of the little Hus", their protector's mistress, "both literally and figuratively". Sterne first claims that the true purpose of his "amusement" is to offer the minister "a total change of ideas", then he changes his mind and dedicates his volume to the "gentle shepherd" praised by Alexander Pope[3] in *An Essay on Man: Epistle I*. And he signs "The AUTHOR" in capital letters.

The stage is set for Toby's amours, his "choicest morsel", which the reader is invited to follow from a perspective of pastoral simplicity.

Vertex[4]

At the end of Volume 8, when Toby sallies forth with Trim to conduct his amorous campaign, his sister-in-law wishes to take a peep at them. Walter repeats word for word what he told her then: "Call it, my dear, by its right name [...], and look [...] as long as you will". Mrs. Shandy refutes the innuendo of looking through a key hole by a slight tap of her fingers on his arm, causing a shift in his vertex: "As he turned his head, he met her eye.— Confusions again! He saw a thousand reasons to wipe out the reproach, and as many to reproach himself. A temperate current of blood ran orderly through her veins".

Presuming his readers too will be reluctant to take part in the peep show, Sterne/Tristram quixotically defends the honour of keyholes:

> And here I am sitting, this 12th day of August 1766, in a purple jerkin and yellow pair of slippers, without either wig or cap on, a most tragicomical completion of [my father's] prediction 'that I should neither think nor act like any other man's child. [...] Keyholes were made for other purposes; and [denying them]—it became a violation of nature, and was so far, you see, criminal. [...]—Which leads me to my uncle Toby's amours.

The opening of Volume 9, like the overture of an opera, announces the themes of Sterne's choice morsel: the voyeurism of the widow and the violation of Toby's amours—Toby playing the role of the fool.

The fool[5]

The first striking feature of those who "neither think nor act like any other man's child" is often their appearance. An illustration of Swift's definition of the fool, in his "serene state among knaves",[6] is given by Toby donning his old uniform, his ramallies wig that resists Trim's attempts at styling and his ridiculous hat:

> [Such a] sweet look of goodness sat upon my uncle Toby's brow [...] and NATURE had [...] wrote GENTLEMAN with so fair a hand [on] his countenance, that even his tarnish'd gold-laced hat and huge cockade of flimsy taffeta became him.

The same is true of the barber's shaving bowl donned by Don Quixote as a helmet. It is so much part of him that we can't image him without this headgear with its edge scooped out to fit around the client's neck. We are also reminded of the strange gear worn by soldiers in World War I trenches, which "became them" in that circumstance, as well as the objects they created—the "art of the trenches" says historian Annette Becker[7]—with the same ingenuity Trim displayed on the bowling green, revealing the knavery of those who ridiculed them.

Such objects decorate the shelves of my office, like talismans brought back by my grandfather, a stretcher-bearer on the frontlines: a lighter made from a bullet, an inkwell from a shell tip, tin rings, sewing kits, his tin mug—in which I placed a small doll of Freud's, his contemporary. From this perspective, a remark made by Wittgenstein,[8] himself a World War I veteran, sheds light on Swift's enigmatic phrase: "It is indeed important that I must also make my own the contempt that anyone may have for me, as an essential and significant part of the world as seen by me".

Gotten up in his outmoded military garb, Toby goes off to war, although his blue and gold uniform is now too tight for him, so that Trim tries pulling on the sleeves, which are, unfortunately, "laced [...] down the back [...] in the mode of King William's reign". He sallies forth, followed by the corporal, dressed in "poor Le Fever's" regimental coat, his hair tucked under the Montero cap, restored for the occasion.

Walter is impressed. His brother's garb:

> shone so bright against the sun [...] that had my uncle Toby thought of attacking in armour, nothing could have so well imposed upon his imagination. [...] The corporal [...] march'd three paces distant from his master: a whiff of military pride had puff'd out his shirt at the wrist, and upon that, in a black leather thong clipp'd into a tassel beyond the knee, hung [his] stick.—My uncle Toby carried his cane like a pike.—It looks well, at least, quoth my father to himself.

But the anguish felt on the eve of battle is there—familiar to me in critical sessions when I suddenly lose all my skills.

Before the battle[9]

Their gestures, observed from the Shandy couple's vantage point, contradict their bravado:

> My uncle Toby turn'd his head more than once [...] to see how he was supported by the corporal, [who] gave a slight flourish with his stick, and [...] bid His Honour 'never fear'. Now, my uncle Toby did fear. [...]: he knew not (as my father had reproach'd him) so much as the right end of a woman from the wrong, and therefore was never altogether at his ease near any one of them, —unless in sorrow or distress; then infinite was his pity.

Coming to the rescue of widows—and Mrs. Wadman qualified—should have been easy, theoretically. But in practice, Toby was seized with unreasoned terror.

Having been trained in close combat, did he sense that, through their physical contact in the sentry box, despite her simpering, the lady was a formidable opponent? As they near the widow's door, his fear stops him in his tracks:

> She cannot, quoth my uncle Toby, halting [...], —she cannot, corporal, take it amiss. —She will take it [...] just as the Jew's widow at Lisbon took it of my brother Tom. —And how was that? quoth my uncle Toby, facing quite about to the corporal. [...] —If Tom had not married the widow, the honest soul had never been taken out of his warm bed and dragg'd to the Inquisition.—'Tis a cursed place, — added the corporal [...] —'Tis very true, said my uncle Toby, looking gravely at Mrs Wadman's house.

Illustrating Wittgenstein's assertion "I don't choose the mouth which says 'I have toothache'",[10] Toby's fear is voiced through Trim's mouth, transforming the house next door into an Inquisition jail—a foreshadowing of the inquisitory welcome awaiting him. This brings to mind the ducal castle where Don Quixote and Sancho,[11] under cover of a generous reception, were, in fact, bullied cruelly, until they left without a word to regain their freedom.

Now, Trim expands on the subject:

> Nothing [...] can be so sad as confinement for life—or so sweet [...] as liberty. [...]—Whilst a man is free, —cried the corporal, giving a flourish with his stick thus—A thousand of my father's most subtle syllogisms could not have said more for celibacy. My uncle Toby look'd earnestly towards his cottage and the bowling green.

An emblem of freedom, the flourish of the stick is drawn across a quarter of a page. Sterne's typographical invention illustrating Trim's gesture to ward off Toby's panic is followed by storytelling:

> The corporal had unwarily conjured up the spirit of calculation with his wand, and he had nothing to do but to conjure him down again with his story, and in this form of exorcism most unecclesiastically did the corporal do it.

The exorcism consists of telling the story—promised since he read the sermon—of his brother Tom's singular courting and then his arrest in the presence of his two children. Now, the story of Tom's amours replaces Toby's, which Sterne finds so hard to tell. The difference between them is that in Tom's case, the enemy is unmistakable, while in Toby's it takes on a beguiling appearance. Nothing is more difficult than to escape double-talk obscuring the real danger.

Slavery[12]

Tom's romance could be entitled "Tom's Progress". Like Hogarth's paintings, it unfolds in three successive scenes: from courting to marriage and then to the tortures of the Inquisition, not unlike those of slavery.

The weather is warm in Lisbon and Tom is thinking of settling there. Just then, a Jew who owns a sausage shop on his street dies suddenly, leaving his widow with a flourishing business. Tom enters the shop, telling himself that "let the worst come of it that could, he should at worst get a pound of sausages for their worth; but if things went well, he should [...] get a wife—and a sausage shop [...] into the bargain".

He has set out dressed in his best. Trim speaks of him first in the present tense:

> I see him this morning, with a smile and a cheerful word for everybody he met.—But alas! Tom! Thou smilest no more, cried the corporal, looking [...] upon the ground, as if he apostrophized him in his dungeon. — Poor fellow! said my uncle Toby, feelingly. —He was an honest, lighthearted lad, as ever blood warm'd —Then he resembled thee, Trim, said my uncle Toby, rapidly. The corporal blush'd down to his fingers' ends;— Tear(s) ran sweetly down his cheek together [...]—Kindled as one lamp does at another; and taking hold of the breast of Trim's coat [...] as if to ease his lame leg [...], Toby stood silent for a minute and a half.

When Tom entered the shop, there was no one there "but a poor Negro girl" chasing flies with a bunch of feathers tied to a stick—"not killing them", Trim points out. "—'Tis a pretty picture, said my uncle Toby;—she had suffered persecution, Trim, and had learned mercy". Now, the 18th-century portrayal takes on political overtones:

> She was good an' please your honour, from nature as well as from hard-ships; and there are circumstances in the story of that poor friendless slut that would melt a heart of stone, said Trim; and some dismal winter's evening, when Your Honour is in the humour, they shall be told you with the rest of Tom's story.

Suddenly, Trim asks: "A Negro has a soul"? This question had been raised by the Valladolid Debate in 1559. Toby's answer is the one given by Bartolomé de Las Casas:

> I am not much versed [...] in things of that kind; but I suppose God would not leave him without one any more than thee or me. —It would be putting one sadly over the head of another, quoth the corporal. [...] Why then [...] is a black wench to be used worse than a white one? —I can give no reason, said my uncle Toby. —Only, cried the corporal [...], because she has no one to stand up for her. —'Tis that very thing, Trim, [...], — which recommends her to protection, —and her brethren with her.

Sterne has not forgotten that Cervantes too was a slave for five years in Algiers.

Ignatius Sancho[13]

But Cervantes could not have foreseen that two centuries later another Sancho would approve of his disciple. In the summer of 1766, when Sterne was writing this passage, he received a letter from a former slave named Ignatius Sancho, dated 26 July, and triggered by a sentence in Sterne's sermon published in 1760 under the pseudonym Mr. Yorick: "Consider slavery—what it is—how bitter a draught—and how many millions are made to drink it".

In his letter, Ignatius Sancho introduced himself as "one of those people whom the vulgar and liberal call 'Negurs'". Born on board a slave ship in 1729, he was bought by a family "who judged ignorance the best and only security for obedience", but was sold again to "one of the best families in the kingdom", where he had access to books—"his chief pleasure". Hence, his gratitude to Sterne: "How very much, good Sir, am I (amongst millions) indebted to you for the character of your amiable uncle Toby!—I declare, I would walk ten miles in the dog days, to shake hands with the honest corporal".

Ignatius Sancho was one of the 15,000 black slaves living in London at the time. Freed by the Duke of Montagu, he opened a chandler shop and devoted himself to music and literature. His portrait was painted by Thomas Gainsborough. In his letter to Sterne, he mentions the triangular slave trade and speaks of "the uplifted hands of thousands of my brothers" deported in the cargo holds of ships. Sterne answered the letter at once[14]:

> There is a strange coincidence, Sancho, in the little events [...] of this world: for I had been writing a tender tale of the sorrows of a friendless poor negro-girl [...], when your Letter of recommendation in behalf of so many of her brethren and sisters, came to me—but why *her* brethren?—or yours, Sancho! any more than mine? [...]—but 'tis no uncommon thing, my good Sancho, for one half of the world to use the other half of it like brutes, & then endeavour to make 'em so.

His position was far from common among the best minds of his century. During his second stay in Paris, Sterne met the philosopher David Hume, secretary to the Ambassador of England, nicknamed "the Great Infidel", who wrote that Negroes are inferior to whites.[15] Rumour has it that Voltaire, whose Candide "got acquainted" with the Negro of Surinam, invested in the slave trade. Yet, in the same period, Quaker farms bordering on one of the American Southern states helped slaves make their escape along the "Underground Railway".

In 1772, the Lord Chief of Justice published a decree making the slave trade illegal, but the trafficking went on unabated. Sterne's sermon quoted by Ignatius Sancho was published again in 1782 after his death under the title "Slavery". In 1773, a phrase in Sterne's letter "Am I not a man and a brother"? was engraved by ceramist Josiah Wedgwood on a medallion depicting a kneeling slave in chains.

After world history bursts into his novel, Sterne has trouble taking up the thread of his narrative. Trim has also lost his spirited tone, and tries to go on twice, finally giving "a stout hem"! In such cases, the best strategy is to try laughter—"only a small step away from tears", as our great jester Raymond Devos used to say. We are back in the sausage shop. Tom takes a chair and places it near the table where the widow is working. "There is nothing so awkward as courting a woman, an' please Your Honour, whilst she is making sausages".

As a matter of fact, condoms, called "capotes anglaises" in French, had been invented in England at the start of the 18th century. Now, Trim uses them as pedagogical devices to illustrate the progress of the captain's courtship.

Tom's amours[16]

Wasting no time in the pursuit of the lady, "he began a discourse" upon the sausages, "first gravely" about the ingredients:

> then a little gaily—with what skins, —and if they never burst, —whether the largest were not the best, [...]—taking care to season what he had to say upon sausages, [...]—that he might have room to act in.

Ignoring the sexual innuendo, Toby associates the remark with a failed offensive of the French army:

> It was owing to the neglect of that very precaution, said my uncle Toby, laying his hand upon Trim's shoulder, that Count de la Motte lost the Battle of Wijnendale: he pressed too speedily into the wood; which if he had not done, Lille had not fallen into our hands, nor Ghent and Bruges [...], and so terrible a season came on, that [...] our troops must have perished in the open field.

While the English victory unfolds in Toby's mind, Tom is gaining ground. He is now holding the ring of the sausages while the widow forces the meat down with her hand. Then he cuts the strings to the length needed, until, becoming bolder, he puts them across his mouth, for her to take as she needs them. Finally, he ventures to tie the sausage himself while she holds the snout. The widow's consent is certainly gained even before Tom makes his proposal, for "a widow [...] always chooses a second husband as unlike the first as she can". Tom snatches up another sausage at once"but seeing [his] had more gristle in it—She signed the capitulation, —and Tom sealed it; and there was an end of the matter".

Trim explains the metaphor to his master:

> All womankind [...] love jokes; the difficulty is to know how they choose to have them cut; and there is no knowing that but by trying, as we do with our artillery in the field [...]. —I like the comparison, said my uncle Toby, better than the thing itself. —Because Your Honour [...] loves glory more than pleasure.

Indeed, the captain keeps clinging to "the knowledge of arms —, and particularly that branch which we have practised together in our bowling green, [which] has no other object but to shorten the strides of AMBITION".

A dolly zoom shot takes us back to the spot where we left the Shandy couple: "Now, what can their two noodles be about? cried my father to my mother". Walter imagines that they are setting up the first Vauban lines of circumvallation around the widow's territory. But Mrs. Shandy has barely uttered "I dare say...", when Sterne silences her to address the reader his "ejaculation". After the *coitus interruptus* that almost prevented his conception, it's Tristram's turn to interrupt his parents' dialogue:

> But stop, dear sir, —for what my mother dared to say upon the occasion, —and what my father did say upon it [...], shall be read, [...]—or to say it all in a word, shall be thumb'd over by Posterity in a chapter apart.

Sterne is, in fact, tormented by his illness as well as by his wife, who is now in the Vaucluse region with their daughter and is constantly asking for money. He is also harassed by the consequences of the Enclosure Act which has provoked political unrest in his parish. More than ever, he thinks of Cervantes,[17] who wrote to the Count of Lemos on the eve of his death in April 1616—a year after Volume II of *Don Quixote* was published: "With one foot already in the stirrup [...], great lord, I write to you. [...] The time is short, my pains are increasing, my hopes are diminishing; and yet [...], the desire I have to live keeps me alive".

His disciple was filled with the same desire to live when he wrote the last volume of *Tristram Shandy*, published one year before his death. By interrupting Mrs. Shandy's "I dare say...", he brought time to a halt.

Timequake[18]

In this interval of arrested time, Sterne writes a prose poem addressed to his "dear Jenny": "Time wastes too fast; every letter I trace tells me with what rapidity life follows my pen. [...]—whilst thou are twisting that lock; — see! it grows grey..." And he adds: "—Heaven have mercy upon us both!"—a line borrowed from François Villon's "Testament". Then, he thumbs his nose at Posterity, before taking up his narrative:

> Now, for what the world thinks of that ejaculation, —I would not give a groat. My mother had gone with her left arm twisted in my father's right till they had got to the fatal angle of the old garden wall where Doctor Slop was overthrown by Obadiah on the coach-horse.

The use of the past tense startles the reader. We are now in 1713 and Slop's fall, alluded to in the past tense, will actually take place five years later in 1718, the day Tristram is born. Sterne admits that his narrative tangles up chronology—on the rhythm of Shandean analysis: "The story went on— and on:—it had episodes in it;—it came back and went on—and on again; there was no end of it;—the reader found it very long". Similarly, psychoanalysis goes on and on, then returns to the starting point, with no end in sight.

But Walter did not have an analyst's patience and "gave the corporal's stick, with all its flourishings [...], to as many devils as chose to accept of them", shouting again: "Now, what can their two noodles be about"? Mrs. Shandy's answer is now given in its entirety:

> I dare say, they are making fortifications. —Not on Mrs Wadman's premises! cried my father, stepping back. —I suppose not, quoth my mother. I wish, said my father, raising his voice, the whole science of fortification at the devil, with all its trumpery of saps, mines, blinds, gabions [...] and cuvettes.

Their squabble follows a well-rehearsed pattern, going from *piano* to *fortissimo*, punctuated with "Amens", until in her "Amen" Walter heard "a sighing cadence of personal pity" so unusual that he instantly took out his Almanach to verify the date of his conjugal duty. Indeed, it is the first Sunday of the month, confirmed by "Yorick's congregation coming out of church": "The first Lord of the Treasury, thinking of *ways and means*, could not have returned home with a more embarrassed look".

The gentleman's embarrassment transmits itself to the author, who cannot go on. Indeed, a "timequake" has taken place, to use the title of Kurt Vonnegut's last novel,[19] which ends with the recognition of Kilgore Trout as a science fiction author and not just a homeless World War II veteran who regularly throws his manuscripts into the trash.

Sterne shall soon throw two good chapters into the fire instead of their rough drafts.

The author's confession[20]

How to "reset" the writing process "and keep up that just balance betwixt wisdom and folly without which a book would not hold together a single year"? When faced with this dilemma, Sterne resorts first to self-analysis "by addressing myself directly to the soul herself and arguing the point over and over again with her upon the extent of her own faculties". But often, this recourse fails: "I never could make them an inch the wider", as happens time and again when the soul keeps elements dissociated from the discussion. So, he turns to physical therapies: "Then by changing my system and trying what could be made of it upon the body by temperance, soberness and chastity".

Modern diets prohibiting almost everything were already in fashion. Physicians in Montpellier practically starved Sterne, "poisoning me with what they call *bouillons rafraîchissants*", refreshing broths.[21] As for spiritual virtues, also preached nowadays, they were of no help either:

> These [methods], are good [...] in themselves [...], they are good for happiness in this world, [...] in the next.—In short, they were good for everything but the thing wanted;—[...] [They left] the soul just as Heaven made it.

Sterne then questions the logic of his symptom—yes, it is the word he uses:

> Certainly, if there is any dependence upon logic and that I am not blinded by self-love, there must be something of true genius about me merely upon this symptom of it: that I do not know what envy is: for never do I hit upon any invention or device which tendeth to the

furtherance of good writing but I instantly make it public that all man-kind should write as well as myself.—Which they certainly will, when they think as little.

We understand that his lack of envy is rooted in a fierce taste for independence.

This other "symptom" is analysed in the chapter entitled "Paris" of his last book, *A Sentimental Journey*:

> For three weeks together I was of every man's opinion I met—*Pardi! ce Monsieur Yorick [...] raisonnne bien [...]*. And at this price I could have eaten and drank and been merry all the days of my life at Paris; but it was a dishonest reckoning.—I grew ashamed of it.—It was the gain of a slave, —every sentiment of honour revolted against it;—the higher I got, the more I was forced upon my beggarly system, —the better the *coterie*, —the more children of Art;—I languished for those of Nature; and one night, after a most vile prostitution of myself to half a dozen different people, I grew sick.

This passage relates to his second journey to France and Italy in 1765–1766, preceding the writing of Volume 9 upon his return home, when he com-plained that "What I can find appetite to write, is so so".[22]

Transitory mirror stage

To resolve this impasse, he resorts to a transitory "mirror stage", as Lacan would say[23]:

> Now, [...] when [...] I am got, I know not how, into a cold, unmetaphor-ical vein of infamous writing, and cannot take a plumb-lift out of it for my soul, so must be obliged to go on writing like a Dutch commentator [...]. Unless something be done—I never stand conferring with pen and ink one moment...

For someone who is out of ideas, this sentence is of impressive length, and we are only halfway through it:

> ... for if a pinch of snuff or a stride or two across the room will not do the business for me, —I take a razor at once; and [...] without further ceremony, I shave off my beard [...]; this done, I change my shirt, —put on a better coat, —send for my last wig, —put my topaz ring upon my finger and, in a word, dress myself from one end to the other of me after my best fashion. Now, [...] consider, sir: as every man chooses to be pres-ent at the shaving of his own beard [...] and unavoidably sits over against

himself the whole time it is doing in case he has a hand in it, —the Situation, like all others, has notions of her own to put into the brain.

The Situation of being present allows Sterne to retrieve parts of himself left on the other side of the looking glass, which were reawakened by Toby's fear. "Notions" that had previously been dissociated are "put into his brain". Cervantes, the barber's son, has come to his rescue to enact a "bearding" ceremony allowing him to write down the events without a witness that have always haunted him.

Since my life as an embryo took place partly behind prison walls, I recognise my own transitory mirror stage in *Tristram Shandy*, having only to change the gender when the text says:

> [...] a man cannot dress but his ideas get cloth'd at the same time; and if he dresses like a gentleman, every one of them stands presented to his imagination genteelized along with him; —so that he has nothing to do but take his pen and write like himself. [...] How Homer could write with so long a beard, I don't know;—and as it makes against my hypothesis, I as little care.

"The style is the man himself", Count Buffon declared in his speech to the *Académie Française* in 1753. But ten years later, Sterne noted that "detestable men can have impeccable style", in which case "all the personal washings [...] do a sinking genius no sort of good—but just the contrary, [...] the dirtier the fellow is, the better generally he succeeds..."

After this digression has produced its cathartic effects, Sterne concludes: "'twere better to get all these things out of our heads and return to my uncle Toby".

The It[24]

Toby and Trim suddenly remember that their business lies the other way, and they march to Mrs. Wadman's door. The captain would prefer to go on talking with the corporal. But too late! Trim has already passed him, mounted the three steps to the door, hemmed twice and putting to flight his master's ideas, stood there with the rapper in his hand for a full minute.

On the other side of the door, Bridget holds her finger and thumb on the latch. Her mistress sits breathless behind the curtain of her bedchamber, watching them approach "with an eye ready to be defloured again". Toby calls Trim, but to no avail since he lets the rapper fall at that very instant. "All hopes of a conference were knock'd on the head by it". So Toby could only whistle *Lillibullero* and like him, Sterne goes blank again, especially as at that very moment he hears his tailor rapping at the door, for he owes him at least £25.

To vent his panic, he rails against smooth talkers in politics and mocks philosophers:

> For the six months I'm in the country, I'm upon so small a scale that [...] I outdo Rousseau a bar length, —for I keep neither man or boy, or horse or cow or dog or cat or anything that can eat or drink, except a thin poor piece of a Vestal (to keep my fire in), and who has generally as bad an appetite as myself, —but there is no treating the subject while my uncle is whistling *Lillibullero*.—Let us go into the house.

The next two pages, entitled Chapter XVIII and Chapter XIX, are entirely blank. Once again, the typographical invention is more eloquent than a seminar on the Real. The blank in Toby's mind persists into Chapter XX, indicated by six lines of asterisks, after which the captain is seated on the sofa next to Mrs. Wadman and answers a question we are able to guess: "You shall see the very place, madam, said my uncle Toby". Let us keep our eyes open.

The reader hears the widow's internal monologue and sees her turn red at the thought of the "it" she is dying to see. The Es^{25} in Freud's formula comes to mind: *Wo Es war, soll Ich werden* ("Where It was, shall I be"). But the "It" suggested by Sterne is, more modestly, uncle Toby's crotch with its wound, which makes the widow vibrate to the rhythm of a six-line stanza, ending with her acting out:

> L—d! I cannot look at it—What would the world say if I look'd at it?-- I should drop down if I look'd at it—I wish I could look at it—There can be no sin in looking at it.—I will look at it.

Skilled in the martial arts, Toby stands up right away to remove the strategic place from the firing line of her eyes—an image Sterne advised us to keep in mind—and walks to the door of the parlour to whisper an order in Trim's ear after another line and a half of asterisks. The corporal answers that he saw "it" that morning in the garret. Putting on his Montero cap, he goes out "as fast as his lame knee would let him", laughing to himself at the misunderstanding.

Toby is enlisting the help of the famous map that has already saved him from the visitors' curiosity at his brother's house. Things are heating up on the sofa: "You shall lay your finger upon the place, —said my uncle Toby. —I will not touch it, [...] quoth Mrs Wadman to herself".

Sterne then steps into the role of supervising analyst, suggesting that taking the widow's history would help, since we already know something about Toby's:

> This requires a second translation—it shews what little knowledge is got by mere words;—we must go up to the first springs. Now, in order to

clear up the mist which hangs upon these three pages, I must endeavour to be as clear as possible myself. Rub your hands thrice across your foreheads, —blow your noses, —[...] sneeze, my good people!—God bless you— Now give me all the help you can.

As a colleague, I should contribute some psychoanalytic concepts, but my mind has gone blank.

Sottie[26]

Fortunately, Sterne is ready to do the work himself and stages the widow's desire in the style of a Theatre of Fools. His perspective is not neutral, given his own marital troubles as well as his father's:

> As there are fifty different ends [...] for which a woman takes a hus-band, she first sets about and carefully weighs, then separates and dis-tinguishes in her mind which [...] is hers; then by discourse, inquiry, argumentation and inference she investigates and finds out whether she has got hold of the right one;—[...] then, by pulling it gently this way and that way, she further forms a judgement whether it will not break in the drawing.

Although anticipating our indignation, "the imagery [...] is so ludicrous that the honour I bear the sex will not suffer to quote it;—otherwise 'tis not des-titute of humour". What follows makes my hair stand on end. Sterne quotes his source to be Slawkenbergius's third Decad:

> She first [...] stops the ass and, holding his halter in her left hand (lest he should get away), she thrusts her right hand into the very bottom of his pannier to search for it —For what? —You'll not know the sooner, quoth Slawkenbergius, for interrupting me.—I have nothing, good Lady, but empty bottles, says the ass. I'm loaded with tripes, says the second.—And thou art no better, quoth she to the third, for nothing is there in thy panniers but trunk-hose and pantofles.

The "it" is presented in the style of Medieval Joyous Societies such as "Mother Folly" in Dijon, "The Fools of Paris" or "The Dunces of Rouen". Sterne has some inkling of the offense to our dignity, but can't help going on. After searching through the baskets of several donkeys, where the object of her desire is desperately absent, the lady finally finds the ass that carries the famous "it":

> [...] she turns the pannier upside down, looks at it, —considers it, — samples it, — measures it, —stretches it, —wets it, —dries it, —then takes her teeth both to the warp and weft of it —Of what? for the love of

> Christ! I am determined, answered Slawkenbergins, that all the powers
> upon earth shall never wring that secret from my breast.

The German analyst would have loved Lacan, who launched enigmatic for-
mulae such as:

Il n'y a pas de rapport sexuel ("There is no sexual relation") and *La femme
n'existe pas* ("Woman does not exist"). But Sterne does not go so far and
concludes:

> We live in a world beset on all sides with mysteries and riddles, [...]—it
> seems strange that Nature, who makes everything so well to answer its
> destination [...], should so eternally bungle it as she does in making so
> simple a thing as a married man. [...] With regard to my uncle Toby's
> fitness for the marriage state, [...] she had formed him of the best and
> kindliest clay, [...] she had disposed [...] [him for] the tenderest offices.

Three lines of asterisks allow us to imagine these tender offices, after which
it is made clear that this "DONATION was not defeated by my uncle Toby's
wound". Therefore, the widow should have no reason to worry. But:

> the Devil, who is the great disturber of our faiths in this world, had
> raised scruples in Mrs Wadman's [...] and, like a true devil as he was,
> had done his own work [...] by turning my uncle Toby's virtue [...] into
> nothing but empty bottles, tripes, trunk-hose and pantofles.

The man in black who pursues Sterne is akin to that ruthless agency. Each
day, Sterne endures disastrous loss of blood and fever that causes confusion
"in the subtle aura of the brain". As he is about to give up, saying: "anyone
is welcome to take my pen and go on with the story for me", he turns to
another Spirit: "I have been hastening towards this part of the choicest morsel of what I had to offer to the world, yet now that I am got to it [...]—an
invocation can do no hurt".

The ultimate remedy is a spiritual transfusion from the good genius Don
Quixote, uncle Toby's ancestor, through the medium written in bold letters
in the middle of the page, "THE INVOCATION":

> Gentle spirit of sweetest humour, who erst didst sit upon the easy pen of
> my beloved CERVANTES; thou who glided'st daily through his lattice
> and turned'st the twilight of his prison into noonday brightness by thy
> presence, —tinged'st his little urn of water with Heaven-sent nectar and
> [...] cast thy mystic mantle o'er his wither'd stump, and wide extended it
> to all the evils of his life—Turn in higher, I beseech thee!—Behold these
> breeches!—They are all I have in the world;—that piteous rent was given
> them at Lyons—.

The rent in the breeches illustrates the tear in the story, which Sterne tries to mend by recounting his adventures on the roads of France and Italy, where he returned, as I mentioned, for a second stay between October 1765 and June 1766, hoping that the air of Naples would do him some good. Don Quixote plays the role of resuscitator, rekindling Sterne's eloquence in castigating his contemporary, Tobias Smollett, translator of *Don Quixote* and author of *Travels through France and Italy*, published in 1766, whom he calls *Smelfungus* in his own *Sentimental Journey through France and Italy*,[27] since he complains endlessly about the poor condition of the roads and the greed of innkeepers.

Sterne's criticism prefigures contemporary tourists who argue over trifling prices:

> I do not think a journey through France and Italy [...] so bad a thing as some people would make you believe; [...]. We really expect too much, and for the *livre* or two above par for your suppers and bed—[...] who would embroil their philosophy for it? [...]—pay it with both hands open [...] [to] your fair hostess and her damsels [...];—and besides, my dear sir, you get a sisterly kiss of each of 'em worth a pound;—at least I did.

Another gift bestowed on Sterne by this journey was his encounter with Maria, a maiden who has gone mad and will appear again in *A Sentimental Journey*.

Maria, the mad maiden

When he returns from Italy, where the air did him good, Sterne can't wait to finish his novel:

> For my uncle Toby's amours running all the way in my head, they had the same effect upon me as if they had been my own.—[...] so that, whether the roads were rough or smooth, it made no difference: everything touch'd upon some secret spring either of sentiment or rapture.

Although he has entered the state of serenity of "the fool among knaves", Sterne knows that knaves may spring up just around the corner. He has read Cervantes's *Galatea*,[28] and will confirm that the *locus amoenus* is far from idyllic in the pastoral decor. Somewhere along the road, music strikes his ears:

> They were the sweetest notes I ever heard, and I instantly let down the fore-glass to hear them more distinctly. —'Tis Maria, said the postilion, observing I was listening.—Poor Maria, continued he [...], is sitting upon a bank playing her vespers upon her pipe, with her little goat

beside her. [...] —And who is poor Maria? said I. The love and pity of all the villages around us [...];—it is but three years ago that the sun did not shine upon so fair, so quick-witted and amiable a maid.

Maria has been prevented from marrying by the curate's intrigues.

Sterne wants to stop and listen to the maid's sweet music. She takes up her pipe and plays the same notes again, ten times sweeter:

It is the evening service to the Virgin, said the young man, —but who has taught her to play it—or how she came by her pipe no one knows; we think that Heaven has assisted her in both, for ever since she has been unsettled in her mind, it seems her only consolation—she [...] plays that service upon it almost night and day.

Sterne sees in the young man "much discretion and natural eloquence bespeaking something [...] above his condition, [...] and I should have sifted out his history, had not poor Maria's taken such full possession of me". His transference resonates with Toby's betrayed love, as we shall see.

The chaise draws near the bank where Maria is sitting, wearing a white jacket, "with her hair [...] drawn up into a silk net, with a few olive leaves twisted a little fantastically on one side". An enchanted fairy, she is so beautiful that he cries out, broken-hearted: "God help her! poor damsel"! The young man tells him that that God has not come to her aid:

Above a hundred masses [...] have been said [...] for her, —but without effect; we have still hopes, as she is sensible for short intervals, that the Virgin at last will restore her to herself; but her parents, who know her best, are hopeless upon that score, and think her senses are lost for ever.

Sterne does not agree with this gloomy prognosis and the maiden senses it. She has been listening to the conversation—despite appearances: "As the postilion spoke this, MARIA made a cadence so melancholy, so tender and querulous, that I sprung out of the chaise [...] and found myself sitting betwixt her and her goat before I relapsed from my enthusiasm".

Salmon's principles, formulated during World War I to heal young soldiers who had lost their wits, are clearly at play here. *Proximity* is enacted when Sterne sits by the maiden who has lost faith in others. Surprised, she looks at her goat, then alternately at each of them. "Well, Maria, said I softly, —what resemblance do you find"? *Immediacy*: he regrets at once having said too much. "I would not have let fallen an unseasonable pleasantry in the venerable presence of Misery [...];—and yet I own my heart smote me", so that "I swore [...] never attempt again to commit mirth with man, woman or child [...]. Adieu, Maria!—adieu, poor hapless damsel!—Some time, but not *now*, I may hear thy sorrows from thy own lips".

Their first meeting allows Sterne to hope—*Expectancy*—that he will see her again, —a hope fulfilled in his last novel when he finds her again. But for the moment he has trouble believing it, when he sees her take up her pipe to play such a woeful air that he is left defenceless. The chapter ends with a sigh of relief at leaving sorrow behind: "What an excellent inn at Moulins"! In *A Sentimental Journey*[29] written a year later, Maria will give back to Yorick the handkerchief embroidered with the initial S—Shandy and Sterne—that he had given her to wipe her tears.

Simplicity is the fourth Salmon principle, illustrated by simply respecting the given word, which bridges the abyss of time:

> I asked her if she remembered a pale thin person of a man, who had sat down betwixt her and her goat about two years before. She said, she was unsettled much at that time, but remember'd it upon two accounts— that ill as she was, she saw the person pitied her; and next, that her goat had stolen his handkerchief, and she had beat him for the theft—she had wash'd it [...] in the brook, and kept it ever since in her pocket to restore it to him in case she should ever see him again, which, she added, he had half promised her.

Time can take up its flow again, allowing her to "put her arm within mine" as they went together to Moulins.

This "digression on madness" heals the author's dissociation, marked by the blank of Chapters 18 and 19. As Trim did for Toby, Sterne told a story "his own way, about himself", as I do when unspeakable cut-out events emerge in a session.

Back to the chapters left blank

In Chapter XXV, Don Quixote responds to Sterne's appeal by placing a maiden as mad as himself on his path—which produces a haemostatic effect on the loss of his wits:

> When we have got to the end of this chapter (but not before), we must all turn back to the two blank chapters on the account of which my honour has lain bleeding this half-hour;—I stop it by pulling off one of my yellow slippers and throwing it with all my violence to the opposite side of my room, with a declaration at the heel of it—That [...] I look upon a chapter which has only nothing in it with respect.

To combat annihilation, Maria always plays the same music on her pipe, in different tones. Like her, Sterne cannot stop writing: "Live or write... in my case means the same thing". His choicest morsel resonates with the betrayed maiden's music. This kind of transference occurs at critical moments of arrested time and speech. The analyst may then tell a story about himself instead of following the course of free association, provoking his colleagues' indignation, which Sterne makes explicit: "I do not know any more than my heels how to answer". And he adds:

> I'll let them do it, as Bridget said, as much as they please; for how was it possible they should foresee the necessity I was under of writing the 25th chapter of my book before the 18th etc.—So I don't take it amiss:—all I wish is that it may be a lesson to the world, 'to let people tell their stories their own way'.

This is a crucible of Shandean analysis, to let the analyst tell his/her stories his/her own way and connect them to the chapters left blank in the analysand's story, since another was/is not there to confirm them. Sterne inscribes this strange temporality in bold gothic characters—another typographical invention marking the bursting through of the past into the present. Here, in a flashback, the chapters left in suspense behind the asterisks can enter the scene, lifting the curtain on the cut-out scene depicting Toby's entrance:

> My uncle Toby saluted [her] after the manner in which women were saluted by men in the Year of Our Lord God One Thousand Seven Hundred and Thirteen;—then facing about, he march'd up abreast with her to the sofa and, in three plain words [...] told her 'He was in love' [...]. [He] left the matter to work after its own way [while she] looked down upon a slit she had been darning up in her apron in expectation [...] that my uncle Toby would go on; but [he had] no talents for amplification, and LOVE moreover [...] being a subject of which he was the least a master.

Sterne suggests a Freudian interpretation of the metaphor alluded to earlier, when Toby was staring at a crevice in the chimney piece. As for the captain's silence, Lacanians may point to lack as the source of desire, and Walter agrees with them both:

> My father was always in raptures with this system of my uncle Toby's, as he falsely called it, and would often say that, could his brother Toby, to his [silent] process, have added but a pipe of tobacco, —he had wherewithal to have found his way [...] towards the heart of half the women upon the globe.

A discussion now unfolds on the sofa about the purpose of marriage. From our perspective, Toby appears quite old-fashioned, since he invokes the biblical injunction: "Be fruitful and multiply". The widow, however, being ahead of her time, differentiates sexual desire from procreation. The political standoff gets out of control when it comes to the question of children. Mrs. Wadman is not inclined to raise children. No more than Jean Jacques Rousseau who, between 1746 and 1752, abandoned his five infants in the *Hospice des Enfants Trouvés* to be adopted, forcing their mother, Thérèse Levasseur, to consent. In any case, Toby does not have this problem. Sterne depicts their showdown in the following terms:

> Let us go on [...] to almost the first pulsation of that minute wherein silence [...] generally becomes indecent; so, edging herself a little more towards him and [...] sub-blushing as she did it, —she took up the gauntlet [...] and communed with my uncle Toby thus. The cares and disquietudes of the marriage state [...] are very great. [...] And therefore, when a person [...] is so much at his ease as you are—so happy [...] in yourself, your friends, and your amusements, —I wonder what reasons can incline you to the state—They are written, quoth my uncle Toby, in the Common prayer Book. [...]. —As for children, —said Mrs Wadman [...]—do not we all find they are certain sorrows and very uncertain comforts? And [...] what compensation for the many tender and disquieting apprehensions of a suffering and defenceless mother [...]? I declare, said my uncle Toby, smit with pity, I know of none, unless it be the pleasure which it was pleased God —A fiddlestick! quoth she.

Toby's future love for his nephew, evidenced by his rejection of Walter's disastrous predictions about his son's fate, is already suggested when he resists the widow's vision of maternal sacrifice. On this subject, she reminds us of Cervantes's Dolorida,[30] who threw herself at the knight's feet in a fit of lamentation. Hurled like the lash of a whip in the captain's face, the word "Fiddlestick"! makes the blood rush into his cheeks and, his hand upon his heart, he offers to share her sufferings. In his disarray, he opens the Bible placed on the table intentionally, falling by chance on the passage about the Siege of Jericho, where he takes refuge, leaving his proposal "to work with her after its own way".

But things don't go as expected:

> Now, it wrought neither as an astringent or a loosener, nor like opium or bark or mercury or buckthorn, or any drug which nature had bestowed upon the world;—in short, it work'd not at all in her, and the cause of that was that there was something working there before. —Babbler that I am! I have anticipated what it was a dozen times; but there is fire still in the subject—*allons*.

The French verb takes us right to Chapter XXVII, after the two cut-out Chapters 18 and 19, focusing on the question of children, are inserted here.

The fire smouldering in the subject is, in fact, of a scientific nature. The identity of that "something" stirring in her has to be evidence-based, as we would say today. And yet, in the 1950s, Erwin Schrödinger,[31] inventor of the equations of quantum physics, launched an appeal to psychologists asking them to abandon the principle of objectivation, arguing that in the field of elementary particles the observer is part of the observed field. His argument contradicts Walter's diagnosis that his son is handicapped and his brother is "borderline", considering his bowling green nonsense. On the same basis, Sterne is clearly bipolar, since he admits fluctuating between mania and depression.

Mind control[32]

Mrs. Wadman would be the first to agree with this "scientific" approach. The cause of her torment is entirely biological. Her first husband had been "afflicted with a sciatica", very likely interfering with his performance, hence her eagerness to measure the distance between Toby's groin and that part which might be affected. She has conscientiously thumbed through anatomy books, has consulted a text on the brain "but could make nothing of it", tried to reflect by herself, considered certain hypotheses, but drew no conclusions.

She then sought medical advice, submitting the thorny question to Dr. Slop, whose answer was unequivocal. When asked if:

> poor Captain Shandy was ever likely to recover of his wound—[he] would say, —He is recovered. —What! Quite? — Quite, madam. —But what do you mean by a recovery? [...] Doctor Slop was the worst man alive at definitions, and so Mrs Wadman could get no knowledge; in short, there was no way to extract it but from my uncle Toby himself.

By the way, the meaning of "recovery" is still being debated when it refers to madness and trauma.

When the widow decides to grill the captain under the guise of compassion, her impersonal questionnaire is administered with the rigour of a sociological interview:

> There is an accent of humanity, Sterne writes, in an enquiry of this kind, which lulls SUSPICION to rest—and I am half persuaded the serpent got pretty near it in his discourse with Eve; for the propensity in the sex to be deceived could not be so great that she should have boldness to hold chat with the Devil without it.—But there is an accent of humanity [...] which [...] gives the enquirer a right to be as particular with it as your body surgeon.

I can see myself, as if it was yesterday, arriving at Alain Touraine's labo-ratory at the EHESS at the end of 1968 to be given the questionnaires of a survey sponsored by a Pension Fund and conducted among pensioners in Britanny. They answered willingly, but asked me other poignant questions that went far beyond the topic of the research. Toby met with questions in the same style:

> Was it without remission?
> — Was it more tolerable in bed?
> — Could he lie on both sides alike with it?
> — Was he able to remount a horse?
> — Was motion bad for it? et cetera...

All these questions were:

> so tenderly spoke to and so directed towards Toby's heart that every item of them sunk ten times deeper into it than the evils themselves — but when Mrs Wadman went round about by Namur to get at my uncle Toby's groin,

we remember Trim hurrying "cheerfully" to get the map, enjoying the trick his master unwittingly plays on the inquisitive widow.

Yet the reviviscence awakened by the traumatic event is as sharp as ever. Toby finds himself back with the Dutch in the topography of the counter-scarp, "to take the counterguard of St Roch sword in hand". Only this time, his Lady is there when he is pulled out of the trench bleeding. She is wiping away his tears as he is carried into his tent. His delusion is ecstatic: "Heaven! Earth! Sea! — [...] an angel of mercy sat beside him on the sofa, — his heart glow'd with fire; — and had he been worth a thousand, he had lost every heart of them to Mrs Wadman".

Like the Duchess in *Don Quixote*, the widow usurps the role of Dulcinea until her tone and her facial expression betray her scheme when she asks the captain "a little categorically" where he received the terrible blow, while throw-ing a slight glance towards the waistband of his red plush breeches, expecting him to put his forefinger on the exact place. But "it fell out otherwise".

For Toby, the "where" in question does not have to do with the place she is obsessed with, nor with ordinary time-space. Her objective survey does not take into account that the object of the questionnaire is trained "to smell danger", as psychoanalyst and World War I veteran Wilfred Bion described transference in extreme experiences. Toby uses the map of Namur to escape from voyeurism once again. For the second time, the act of planting a pin on the map in the spot where the stone struck his groin allows him to stand up instead of crawling before her, like in the mud of the trenches.

Sterne analyses the efficiency of his therapeutic action:

> [The blow] struck instantly upon my uncle Toby's sensorium—and, with it, struck his large map of the town and citadel of Namur and its environs, [...] purchased and pasted down upon a board by the corporal's aid during [Toby's] long illness.

A triangulation takes place, linking the actual blow, received in total solitude, with the pin stuck in the map for everyone to see, while Trim is standing at his side. Shandean analysis helps Toby to flee from the anatomical chart on which he was pinned.

After removing his groin from her line of vision, he takes the scissors with which she intended to evaluate the famous distance, and measures off thirty toises (unit of measure) from the salient angle between the demibastion of Saint-Roch and the gate of Saint-Nicolas, the place where he was wounded:

> My uncle Toby [...] with such a virgin modesty laid her finger upon the place that the goddess of Decency, if then in being [...], —shook her head and, with a finger wavering across her eyes, —forbid her to explain the mistake. Unhappy Mrs Wadman!—For nothing can make this chapter go off with spirit but an apostrophe to thee—but [...] in such a crisis an apostrophe is but an insult in disguise, and ere I would offer one to a woman in distress, —let the chapter go to the devil.

The following chapter states simply that "My uncle Toby's map is carried down into the kitchen". The reader expects a comical repetition of what took place above, in the masters' quarters. But not at all. We shall witness instead the overturning of the research protocol through the subversion of the objectivation principle. "Unhappy doctors"!, I tell myself when I declare, "You are not schizophrenic", to those who tell me about the abuses inflicted on them, hoping that the psychiatrists I am thinking of don't take this as a disguised insult.

What if I told them the story of Bessel Van der Kolk[33] who, as a young doctor discouraged by his failurers with Vietnam veterans, wanted to understand what was going on in their brain and turned to neurology when brain imaging had just been introduced. On the brain scans of a couple who had just escaped death in a car accident, he saw a disconnection between the "animal brain" of the limbic system and the prefrontal cortex involved in speech and time perception. He then developed an interpersonal approach to reach what Sterne would call "Toby's sensorium"—a survival mode we share with other species—in which an experience strives to be recognised and connected to a narrative.

In the captain's "sensorium", we also recognise Aby Warburg's "seismograph of the soul" which records "surviving images"—Bion's "beta elements" recorded on his Grid[34] and Socrates's[35] "primary *aloga* elements"—without reason, which can be linked up, thanks to another "to produce *logos*, words and reason" Bion's alpha function. Without this interconnection, diagnoses based on observation alone perpetuate arrested time. Bessel Van der Kolk writes: "I met countless patients who told me they are 'bipolar' or 'borderline', or that they have PTSD, — as if they had been sentenced to an underground prison for the rest of their lives, like the Count of Monte Christo".

This catastrophic fate hanging over the captain is eluded once again thanks to a Theatre of Fools performance given in the kitchen.

Psychological war[36]

The role of jester is played by Trim, who starts by showing on the map the confluence of the Sambre and the Meuse. Then, casually touching the taboo anatomical spot, he conducts his demonstration at the rhythm of gestural language that shows what cannot be said:

> And here is the Meuse [...], said the corporal, pointing with his right hand extended [...] and his left upon Mrs Bridget's shoulder [...], — and this is the town of Namur—and this is the citadel—and there lay the French—and here lay his Honour and myself—and in this cursed trench, Mrs Bridget, quoth the corporal, taking her by the hand, did he receive the wound which crush'd him so miserably *here.*—In pronouncing which, he slightly press'd the back of her hand towards the part he felt for, —and let it fall.

The widow's dearest wish was to touch the affected part, but since the maid's mind was not as twisted as that of her mistress, she gave away her secret mission by using the plural form of the first person: "We thought [...] it had been more in the middle, —said Mrs Bridget. That would have undone us for ever, —said the corporal, rallying his master in the same way. —And left my poor mistress undone too, —said Bridget". Trim makes no reply, gives her a kiss and keeps his opinion to himself.

But he speaks up to defend his master's honour when Bridget simulates unambiguously the rumoured loss of erection:

> Come – come – said Bridget holding the thumb of her left hand parallel to the plane of the horizon, and sliding the fingers of the other over it, in a way which could not have been done, had there been the least wart or protruberance. —'Tis every syllable of it false, cried the corporal, before she had half finished the sentence. —I know it to be a fact, said Bridget, from credible witnesses. —Upon my honour, said the corporal, laying his hand upon his heart and blushing [...], 'tis a story [...] as false as hell.

The deceitfulness of the questioning conducted on the upper storey is revealed on the storey below.

We are watching a *Sottie Jugement*, whose aim is to distinguish the truth from false testimony through wit and gestures. Summoned to appear before this court, Bridget reveals the stratagem:

> Not [...] that either I or my mistress care a halfpenny about it [...], — only that when one is married, one would choose to have such a thing by one at least. It was somewhat unfortunate for Mrs Bridget that she had begun the attack with her manual exercise, for the corporal instantly....

Four and a half lines of asterisks suggest the corporal's manual counterattack, proving that, *manu militari*, both soldiers have a pair each.

Now, poetry comes into its own again in a pantomime which sweeps away the budding spy's duplicity. Trim knows everything he wanted to know:

> It was like the momentary contest in the moist eyelids of an April morning 'whether Bridget should laugh or cry'. She snatch'd up a rolling pin;—'twas ten to one she had laugh'd. [...]— she cried; [...]; but the corporal understood the sex a quart major to a tierce, at least, better than my uncle Toby, and accordingly he assailed Bridget after this manner.

As I have already said, the second part of *Sottie* consists of unmasking the deceit of the powerful by dragging onto the stage an important personage and tearing off his official attire, to reveal publically the bipartite costume of the Fool underneath. Mrs. Wadmann has been stripped of her humanitarian mantle. As Don Quixote would do, Trim flies to the maid's aid to draw her out of submission to her mistress. A shrewd analyst, he starts by praising her honesty before divesting the widow of her power:

> I know, Mrs Bridget, said the corporal, giving her a most respectful kiss, that thou art good and modest by nature, and [...] thou wouldst not wound an insect, much less the honour of so gallant and worthy a soul as my master, wast thou sure to be made a countess of—; but thou hast been set on and deluded [...], as is often a woman's case, 'to please others more than themselves'.

Bridget confirmed his interpretation by shedding abundant tears.

In the 16th century, such submission was analysed by La Boétie[37] in his *Discourse on Voluntary Servitude*, which Sterne, an admirer of Montaigne, La Boétie's close friend, had certainly read. The *Discourse* throws light on voluntary submission on a larger scale, which impels a whole population to willingly give away their goods, their wives, their children and their souls to "a single little man; [...] the most cowardly [...] in the nation", who is supported by those he has corrupted.

Bridget's deconditioning is achieved by Trim:

Tell me [...], my dear Bridget, continued the corporal, taking hold of her hand [...] and giving a second kiss, —whose suspicion has misled thee? Bridget sobb'd [...], —then opened her eyes;—the corporal wiped 'em with the bottom of her apron;—she then open'd her heart and told him all.

The captain would need time to become aware of his servitude because the two men conduct their operations independently, without communicating, as if "separated [...] by the Meuse or the Sambre". We are reminded that in *Don Quixote*,[38] in order to weaken the inseparable heroes, the ducal couple put geographical distance between them, sending Sancho to the fictional island of Baratria and keeping the knight at the castle.

The "attack on linking",[39] Bion says, is a major weapon of perversion.

The end of Toby's amours[40]

The episode involving the map does not suffice to open Toby's eyes. He woos the widow every afternoon in his red and silver uniform or his blue and gold one. Trim says nothing to anyone, not wanting to let the "media" exploit his master's love life, as we so readily do today:

[The captain] sustained an infinity of attacks [...] without knowing them to be attacks, —and so had nothing to communicate.—The corporal, on his side, [...] had gain'd considerable advantages, —and consequently had much to communicate;—but [...] the corporal durst not venture upon it; and [...] he would have been contented to have gone [...] without laurels for ever than torture his master's modesty.

The right moment, *Kairos*, came one evening when Toby laid down his pipe to count on his fingers Mrs. Wadman's perfections, and losing track of the count, he decided to have Trim write them down. The corporal sat down beside him, pen in hand, before "a full sheet of paper":

She has a thousand virtues, Trim! said my uncle Toby. [...] But they must be taken in their ranks, [...] for of them all, Trim, that which wins me most [...], is the compassionate turn and singular humanity of her character.—I protest, added my uncle Toby, [...], —that was I her brother [...], she could not make more constant or more tender enquiries after my suffering—though now no more.

Interest in the prey's suffering usually ceases when the trap works. The corporal is not fooled and answers with a short cough while writing out HUMANITY in capital letters at the top of the page. Once the word is written out in bold, the captain wishes to compare their sweethearts' virtue.

Tartuffe[41] makes his entrance in the third Act of Molière's comedy reciting a humanitarian couplet: "I'm gone to share my alms among the prisoners", after two acts spent in vain, by everyone in the household, trying to rid Orgon of his blind faith in "The Impostor"—the subtitle of the play. The maid Dorine's lucid criticism describes the situation in which Toby finds himself as well: "But he's quite lost his senses since he fell/ Beneath Tartuffe's infatuating spell":

> Prithee, corporal, said my uncle Toby [...]—how often does Mrs Bridget enquire after the wound on the cap of thy knee [...]? She never, an' please Your Honour, enquires after it at all. [...] —That shews the difference in the character of the mistress and maid;—had the fortune of war allotted the same mischance to me, Mrs Wadman would have enquired into [...] it a hundred times. —She would have enquired [...] ten times as often about Your Honour's groin. —The pain, Trim, is equally excruciating, —and compassion has as much to do with the one as the other.

It takes a long time to become disillusioned. Elmire, Orgon's wife, catches Tartuffe in his own net at the end of Act IV, when she appears ready to yield to his desire after hiding her husband under the table. Trim succeeds in exposing the widow's strategy after a few months by means of a soldierly metaphor:

> [—what has a woman's compassion to do with a wound upon the cap of a man's knee? Had Your Honour been shot into ten thousand splinters at [...] Landen, Mrs Wadman would have troubled her head as little about it as Bridget; because, [he] added, lowering his voice and speaking very distinctly, [...]—the knee is such a distance from the main body, —whereas the groin, Your Honour knows, is upon the very curtain of the place.

The familiar words, spoken softly as if to elude the enemy, elicit a long but barely audible whistle from Toby, letting the air out of the pretty balloon of proclaimed humanity. "The corporal had advanced too far to retire;—in three words he told the rest—My uncle Toby laid down his pipe as gently [...] as if it had been spun from the unravellings of a spider's web".

The pipe holds the trace of the web patiently spun around him for over eleven years. The captain breaks out of his silence, saying: "Let us go to my brother Shandy's". This puts an end to Toby's amours.

The end of Sterne's novel is a revolution, literally and politically, since it ends five years before its beginning, forcing the reader to leap backwards to Tristram's embryo's cry of revolt, rooted in the captain's rebellion, signalling the birth of a political subject who makes the author's own revolt heard.

His novel is published in 1767, a year before his death and some twenty years before the advent of democracy in America and in France. As I already mentioned at the beginning of this book, Sterne's biographer declares in his Preface[42]: "Sterne's work speaks in a radically democratic style of the uniqueness and unique value of each individual's experience". As the novel draws to a close, this uniqueness acquires mythological dimensions.

The power of the powerless[43]

Time, a major actor in the novel, slows down while the two men walk to Shandy Hall at the slow pace of the rumours that had reached it long before Trim enlightened Toby:

> Mrs Wadman had, some moons before this, made a confident of my mother; and Mrs Bridget, who had the burden of her own as well as her mistress's secret to carry, had got happily delivered of both to Susannah behind the garden wall. [...] Susannah [...] instantly imparted it by signs to Jonathan, —and [he] by tokens to the cook [...]; [who] sold it with some kitchen fat to the postilion [...], who truck'd it with the dairymaid [...];—and [...] FAME caught the notes with her brazen trumpet [...].— In a word, there was not an old woman in the village or five miles round who did not understand the difficulties of my uncle Toby's siege and [...] the secret articles which had delay'd the surrender.

These secret articles reveal to one and all his alleged impotence. Presented under various aspects throughout the novel, it is transformed into the Powers—"Ye Powers"—of literature.

This chapter reveals the power of powerlessness—that of fools, children, slaves and all those who have to resist perversion. The word "resistance" was defined after World War II by Jean Cassou,[44] translator of *Don Quixote*, in his little book *La mémoire courte*[45] (*Short Memory*). Cassou, a Resistance fighter, was incarcerated for a year in the military prison of Toulouse in 1943. There, he composed without pencil or paper, his "33 Sonnets of the Resistance" (*Sonnets composés au secret*), published underground in 1944. Cassou's definition is as follows: "But what is this Resistance if not — in all cases — the first faltering stammer of conscience which said "no" to the obvious and sided with the improbable, the impossible"?

The first "I wish" in the novel expresses the improbable and impossible embryo's "no" to its annihilation. Toby's final NO to objectification finds the improbable support of an animal, the Shandy bull.

Before the two men arrive at Shandy Hall, Walter has already launched into an antifeminist diatribe into which he expects to draw his brother, presumed to be humiliated by the failure of his amours:

> My father [...] had but just heard of the report as my uncle Toby set out and, catching fire suddenly at the trespass done his brother by it, was demonstrating to Yorick [...]—not only 'that the Devil was in women

and that the whole of the affair was lust', but that every evil and disorder in the world [...] was owing [...] to the same unruly appetite. Yorick was just bringing my father's hypothesis to some temper, when my uncle Toby entering the room with marks of infinite benevolence and forgiveness in his looks, my father's eloquence rekindled again the passion.

Is Toby in shock? The reader remembers that five years later, as he is seated by the fire with Walter waiting for Tristram's birth, he was to speak—he spoke, he will speak—of "the shock I received [...] in my affair with widow Wadman".[45] So, just after the shock, his look of "infinite benevolence and forgiveness" may be due to denial, or worse, he may be behaving like the family idiot, smiling foolishly no matter what.

Walter is ready to believe this, and taking advantage of Toby's presumed vulnerability, he now focuses his attack on his brother's hobby horse:

> The act of killing and destroying a man, continued my father, raising his voice—and turning to my uncle Toby, —you see, is glorious, —and the weapons by which we do it are honourable.—We march with them upon our shoulders. [...]—We gild them.—We carve them. [...]— My uncle Toby laid down his pipe to intercede for a better epithet [...]—and Yorick was rising up to batter the whole hypothesis to pieces,

when "Obadiah broke into the [...] room with a complaint which cried out for an immediate hearing".

At the height of the recurrent confrontation between the power of the firstborn—heir to all worldly and intellectual property—and the powerlessness of the youngest son—heir to nothing except the bowling green and the memory of his wars—Sterne introduces a new catastrophe which will explain Toby's mysterious looks upon entering the room.

The totemic Shandy bull

An ancient custom obliges Walter to keep a bull for the service of the parish where he collects tithes. "Obadiah had had led his cow upon a pop visit to him" the day he married my father's housemaid, so that when she would give birth, he could expect to have a calf as well:

> When Obadiah's wife was brought to bed, —Obadiah thanked God— [...] [and] went daily to visit the cow. [...] The cow did not calve—no:— she'll not calve till next week;—the cow put it off terribly, —till at the end of the sixth week Obadiah's suspicions [...] fell upon the bull.

In the animal's defence, the parish being very large, the bull could not always be equal to the task; but "he went through the business with [...] a grave face" and Walter "had a great opinion of him". A lively discussion follows about the honour of the bull, who has given rise to rumours like those about Toby. Obadiah says that people believe it is the bull's fault. Walter asks Slop if a cow can be barren. The doctor can't help interpreting Obadiah's worry as castration anxiety and doubt about his paternity. Unimpressed, Obadiah swears that the child came into the world as hairy as himself, which was saying a lot. Walter blows "an exclamatory whistle": "wheu --u----u------" which will finally elevate the Shandy bull to the rank of a totemic animal:

> And so, brother Toby, this poor bull of mine, who is as good a bull as ever p-ss'd, and might have done for Europa herself in purer times— [...], might have been driven into Doctors' Commons (Doctors of civil law, the note specifies) and lost his character, —which to a town bull, brother Toby, is the very same thing as his life.

Toby does not comment, since the bull's story speaks for him. Not that he would have been afraid to lose his reputation by failing the stud test, but because he was at risk of "losing his character" by exposing himself to the widow's politics of love, which ignored his war experience. Like the bull, he said NO, and his relief is reflected in "the infinite benevolence in his looks". It is Yorick who has the last word: "L—d! said my mother, what is all this story about? —A COCK and BULL, said Yorick. —And one of the best of its kind I ever heard".

Thus, Shandean analysis, carried out by an author who dons the fool's cap, sides with an improbable cock and bull story to bring forth a political subject—Tristram's embryo's "I wish"—rooted in his Uncle Toby's resistance to the erasure of historical events throughout this "damned clever book".[46]

Notes

1   Gaudillière, J.-M., *Madness and the Social Link; The Birth of a Political Self,* seminars 1985–2014, London and New York: Routledge, 2021.
2   Diderot, D., *Rameau's Nephew*, Oxford: Benediction Classics, 2011.
3   Pope, A., *An Essay on Man*, Oxford University Press, 2006.
4   Sterne, L., *Tristram Shandy*, op. cit., Vol. 9, ch. I.
5   Sterne, L., *TristramShandy*, op. cit., Vol. 9, ch. II.
6   Swift, J., *Digression on Madness*, op. cit.
7   Becker, A., *L'immontrable: guerres et violences extremes dans l'art et le litérature,* Saint-Étienne: Créaphis éditions, 2021.
8   Wittgenstein, L., *Remarks on Frazer's Golden Bough*, op. cit.
9   Sterne, L., *Tristram Shandy*, op. cit., Vol. 9, chs. III, IV.
10 Wittgenstein, L., *Notes for lectures on "private experience" and "sense data"*, op. cit.
11 De Cervantes, M., *Don Quixote II*, op. cit., chs. 57–58.
12 Sterne, L., *Tristram Shandy*, op. cit., Vol. 9, chs. V–VI.

13 Ross, I. C., *Laurence Sterne: A Life*, op. cit., p. 351.
14 Sterne, L., *Selected Prose and Letters*, Moscow: Progress Publishers, 1981.
15 Ross, I. C., *Laurence Sterne: A Life*, op. cit.
16 Sterne, L., *Tristram Shandy*, op. cit., Vol. 9, chs. VII–VIII.
17 Carnavaggio, J., *Cervantes*, New York: W.W. Norton, 1991.
18 Sterne, L., *Tristram Shandy*, op. cit., Vol 9, chs. IX–X.
19 Vonnegut, K., *Timequake*, op. cit.
20 Sterne, L., *Tristram Shandy*, op. cit., Vol. 9, ch. XII.
21 Ross, I. C., *Laurence Sterne: A Life*, op. cit., p. 304.
22 Ross, I. C., *Laurence Sterne: A Life*, op. cit.
23 Lacan, J., The Mirror Stage as Formative of the Function of the I, in *Écrits*, op. cit.
24 Sterne, L., *Tristram Shandy*, op. cit., Vol. 9, chs. XIV–XX.
25 Freud, S., *New Introductory Lectures*, S.E., 22, London: Hogarth.
26 Sterne, L., Tristram Shandy, Vol. 9, chs. XXI–XXIV.
27 Sterne, L., "In the Street. Calais", in *A Sentimental Journey*, op. cit.
28 De Cervantes, M., *Galatea: A Pastoral Romance*, op. cit.
29 Sterne, L., *A Sentimental Journey*, op. cit., "Maria".
30 De Cervantes, M. *Don Quixote II*, ch. 38.
31 Schrödinger, E., *What is Life? With Mind and Matter*, Cambridge, UK: Cambridge University Press, 2012.
32 Sterne, L., *Tristram Shandy*, op. cit., Vol. 9, chs. XXVI–XXVII.
33 Van der Kolk, B., *The Body Keeps the Score*, op. cit.
34 Bion, W., *Elements of Psychoanalysis*, London: Karnac, 1989.
35 Plato, *Theaetetus*, op. cit.
36 Sterne, L., *Tristram Shandy*, op. cit., Vol. 9, chs. XXVII–XXVIII.
37 La Boétie, É., *Discourse on Voluntary Servitude*, Indianapolis, IN: Hackett, 2012.
38 Cervantes, M., *Don Quixote II*, op. cit.
39 Bion, Attacks on Linking, in *Second Toughts*, London: Karnac, 1967.
40 Sterne, L., *Tristram Shandy*, op. cit., Vol. 9, chs. XXX–XXXII.
41 Molière, *Tartuffe*, Act III, Sc. 2; Act I, Sc. 2; Act IV, Sc. 5, George G. Harrap, 1949.
42 Ross, I. C., *Laurence Sterne: A Life*, op. cit., Preface, p. X.
43 [4] Sterne, L., *Tristram Shandy*, op. cit., Vol. 9, chs. XXXII–XXXIII.
44 Ross, I. C., Laurence Sterne: A Life, op. cit., Preface, p. X.
45 Sterne, L., Tristram Shandy, op. cit., Vol. 2, ch.VII.
46 Boswell, J. (1760). "A Poetical Epistle to Doctor Sterne, Parson Yorick and Tristram Shandy", by a young Scotsman aged 20.

Index

For Product Safety Concerns and Information please contact our EU
representative GPSR@taylorandfrancis.com
Taylor & Francis Verlag GmbH, Kaufingerstraße 24, 80331 München, Germany

9 781032 125121